The Creation of Wing Chun

The Creation of Wing Chun

A Social History of the
Southern Chinese Martial Arts

Benjamin N. Judkins and Jon Nielson

The cover art shows a set of 19th century *hudiedao* similar to those used in Southern China during the Opium Wars and the Red Turban Revolt. Photo by Benjamin Judkins.

Published by State University of New York Press, Albany

© 2015 State University of New York

All rights reserved

No part of this book may be used or reproduced in any manner whatsoever without written permission. No part of this book may be stored in a retrieval system or transmitted in any form or by any means including electronic, electrostatic, magnetic tape, mechanical, photocopying, recording, or otherwise without the prior permission in writing of the publisher.

For information, contact State University of New York Press, Albany, NY
www.sunypress.edu

Production, Diane Ganeles
Marketing, Michael Campochiaro

Library of Congress Cataloging-in-Publication Data

Judkins, Benjamin N., and Jon Nielson.
 The creation of Wing Chun : a social history of the Southern Chinese martial arts / Benjamin N. Judkins and Jon Nielson.
      pages cm
 Includes bibliographical references and index.
 ISBN 978-1-4384-5693-5 (hc : alk. paper)—978-1-4384-5694-2 (pb : alk. paper)
 ISBN 978-1-4384-5695-9 (e-book : alk. paper)
 1. Kung fu—China. 2. Martial arts—China. I. Nielson, Jon. II. Title.

GV1114.7.J83 2015
796.815'9—dc23   2014030980

10 9 8 7 6 5 4 3 2 1

*For all he has taught the world about Wing Chun,
for his enthusiasm and never-ending curiosity,
this book is dedicated to the memory of Ron Heimberger.*

Contents

List of Maps and Figures — ix

Acknowledgments — xv

Introduction — 1

PART I: HAND COMBAT, IDENTITY, AND CIVIL SOCIETY IN GUANGDONG, 1800–1949

Chapter 1 Growth and Disorder: Paradoxes of the Qing Dynasty — 25

Chapter 2 Setting the Stage: The Evolution of Guangdong's Martial Arts, 1800–1911 — 67

Chapter 3 Northern Tigers versus Southern Heroes: Local Identity, National Reform, and the Golden Age of Guangdong's Martial Arts, 1911–1949 — 111

PART II: CONFLICT, IMPERIALISM AND MODERNIZATION: THE EVOLUTION OF WING CHUN KUNG FU, 1900–1972

Chapter 4 The Public Emergence of Wing Chun, 1900–1949 — 169

Chapter 5 Ip Man and the Making of a Modern Kung Fu Master — 211

Epilogue Wing Chun as a Global Art — 265

Notes	283
Glossary	313
Works Cited	327
Index	337

Maps and Figures

Maps

1. Southern China — x
2. Historic and Modern Guangdong Province — x
3. The Pearl River Delta — xi
4. Ip Man's Hong Kong, 1950–1972 — xii

Figure

3.1. Timeline of Foshan's Martial Arts Societies — 147

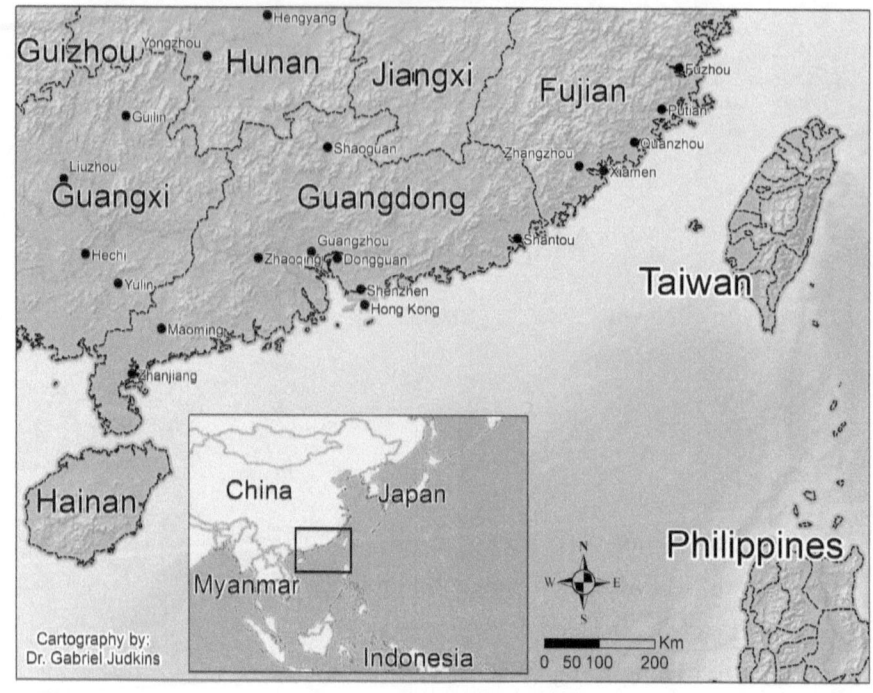

Map 1. Southern China

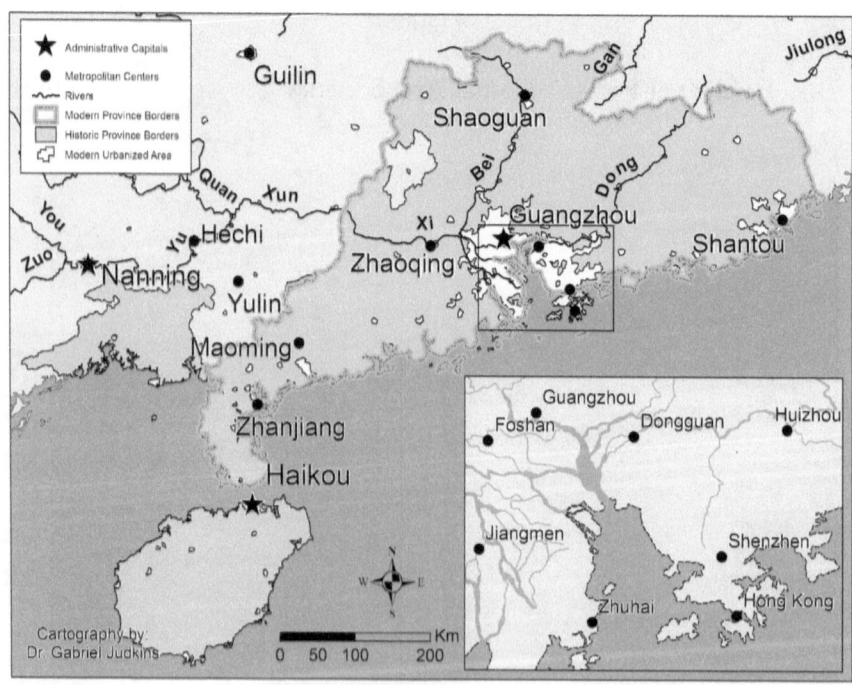

Map 2. Historic and Modern Guangdong Province

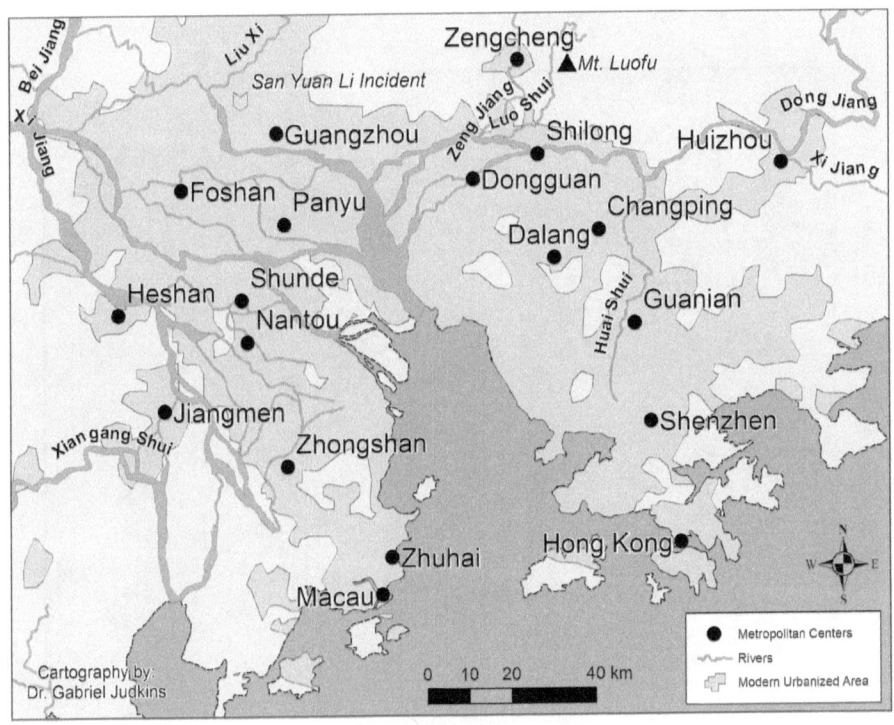

Map 3. The Pearl River Delta

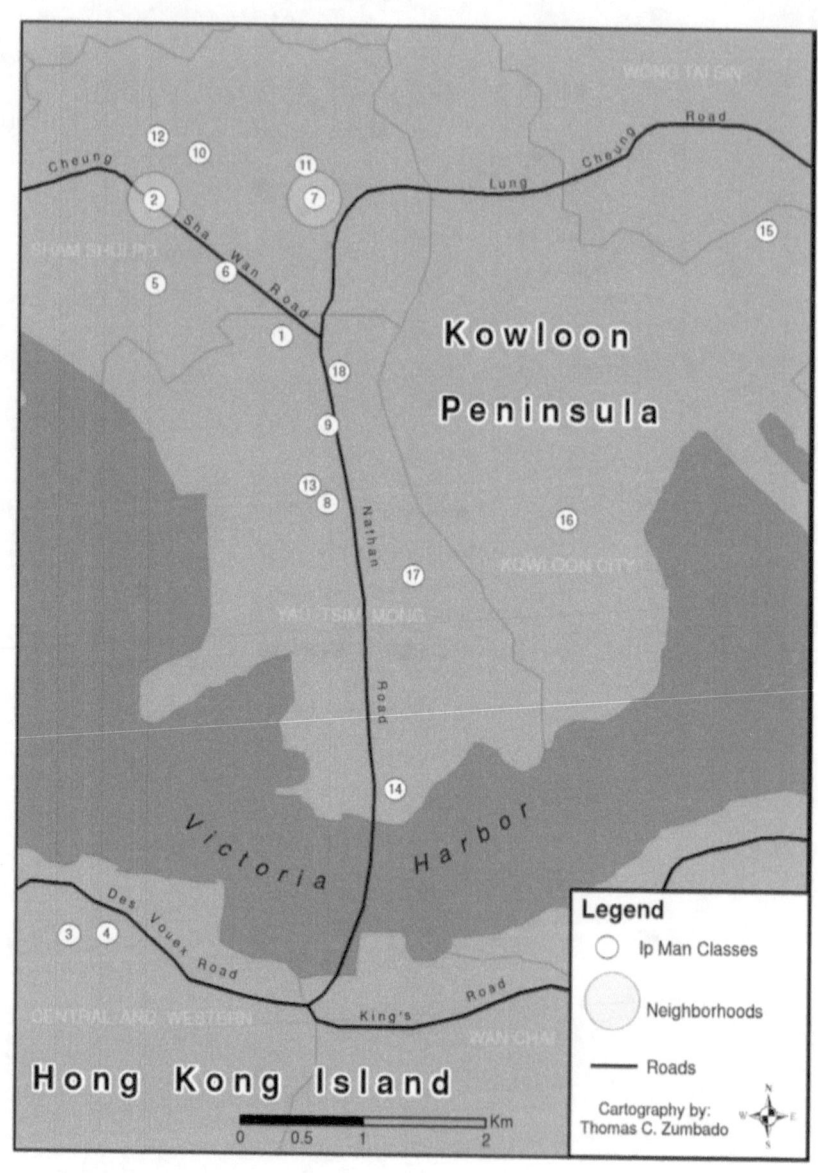

Map 4. Ip Man's Hong Kong, 1950–1972

Important Locations, including Schools and Classes, in Ip Man's Hong Kong, 1950–1972

1. 159 Tai Nan Street (Restaurant Workers Union), 1950.
2. Sham Shui Po district of Kowloon. Location of Master Chan Dau's Do Pai school.
3. Bridges Street. Roof top classes conducted here in 1951.
4. Wah Ying Restaurant, Stanley Street. Classes held here in 1951.
5. Hoi Tan Street School, 1953.
6. Sam Tai Tze Temple, advanced evening classes, 1953.
7. Shek Kip Mei neighborhood.
8. Lee Tat Street in Yau Ma Tei. Classes moved here in 1956.
9. Mun Tin Fang Restaurant in Mongkuk, Kowloon. Feast with White Crane clan, 1956.
10. Li Cheng UK Estate, 1957.
11. School moved to Shek Kip Mei, 1958.
12. Hing Ip Building on Castle Peak Road, 1961.
13. Tai Sang Restaurant on Fook Chuen Street in Tai Kok Tsui, 1961–1963.
14. Yee Wa's tailor shop in Tsim Sha Tsui. Private classes held here in the early 1960s.
15. Hong Kong police officers and detectives, San Po district. Early to mid-1960s.
16. Yee Fai Building on Tung Choi Street. Apartment bought by Ip Man in 1964.
17. Queen Elizabeth Hospital. Classes taught here in the late 1960s and early 1970s.
18. 3 Nullah Road, Headquarters of the Hong Kong Ving Tsun Athletic Association.

Acknowledgments

We would like to extend our thanks to a number of individuals who have assisted us in this project. Our gratitude goes to Grand Master Ip Ching for discussing his father's life and answering many of the questions that arose while researching this volume. Thomas Zumbado and Gabriel Judkins contributed their cartographic skills to help us better visualize the story of the southern Chinese martial arts. Our thanks also go to Shaohua Lei and Shuying Poon, who provided invaluable assistance with the translation of many sources that we used in our research; Dr. Matthew B. Christensen, the Academic Director at BYU, for his help and advice; and William Leung, who spent hours assembling this volume's glossary.

We appreciate the efforts of all those who read this manuscript in full or part. Our writing benefited from the highly informed recommendations that we received from the two anonymous reviewers provided by SUNY Press. Anne Routon offered critical advice that helped us to better navigate the publication process. Special thanks go to the editorial and production staff at SUNY Press for their support in bringing this project to fruition. We would also like to thank Ip Man for continuing to make Wing Chun relevant in an ever-changing environment and Bruce Lee for introducing it to a global audience.

Benjamin Judkins would like to express his gratitude to his many teachers: to Helen Milner and David Baldwin who helped him think about institutions, to Richard Bushman for introducing him to the discipline of history, and to Russell Judkins who showed him the many dimensions of culture. Lastly, he would like to thank his wife Tara whose belief and unwavering support made this book possible.

Jon Nielson would like to thank his children; Jerry Gardner for introducing him to Wing Chun; Malcolm Lee for accepting the challenge to teach a pushy, arrogant teenager; Eddie Chong for his inspiration to keep questioning, no matter what anyone says; Ron Heimberger for unlocking the mysteries of Wing Chun; Ip Ching for tying all of it together into one unified whole; Andrea Nielson for her patience with and support of this obsession; and Benjamin Judkins for helping to make this dream a reality.

Introduction

> A man should always think of the source of the water as he drinks it; it is this shared feeling that keeps our kung fu brothers together.
>
> —Ip Man, "History of Wing Chun," Undated[1]

In April of 2011 Hong Kong Airlines did something out of character for a commercial carrier. Most airlines seeking a share of the lucrative business-class market attempt to impress the public with photos of their genteel and sumptuous cabins. Some seem to be engaged in an arms race to find ever more attractive and demure flight attendants. Instead, Hong Kong Airlines announced that their flight crews would be taking mandatory training in a southern Chinese form of hand combat called Wing Chun. Having earned a reputation as a brutal street fighting art on the rooftops of Hong Kong in the 1950s, this move appears paradoxical.[2] It is one thing to quietly train cabin crews in rudimentary self-defense skills. It is quite another to offer press releases, give interviews, and post Internet videos of how an unruly customer might be restrained.[3]

It would be wrong to suggest that there is no glamour attached to Wing Chun. This was the only martial art that the iconic Bruce Lee ever studied. Nevertheless, when one juxtaposes the image of a bloody Lee (straight from the promotional material for *Enter the Dragon*) with a petite flight attendant from any competitor's television commercial, one must ask what the advertising executives of Hong Kong Airlines know about their regional markets that we do not.

It is also unclear what practical problem this move was designed to address. While air rage has been an issue in some parts of China, this airline does not have a greater percentage of drunken or unruly customers than any other regional carrier. Nor do the videos of flight attendants practicing their forms create much confidence in them as our last line of defense against "the terrorists." None of this was ever the real motivation behind the decision. Instead the airline was attempting to align itself more closely with Wing Chun because this art is one of the quickest growing and most widely recognized markers of Hong Kong identity.

Traditionally, Hong Kong was a city of immigrants, refugees, and traveling business persons. It refused to create much of a communal identity and was notoriously unsentimental about its own past. It ruthlessly discarded the old to make way for the new, and if the new came in the form of imposing glass and steel architecture, for instance, so much the better.

Slowly these attitudes have begun to change. The return of the territory to Chinese control in 1997, as well as more recent brushes with the mainland over questions of governance, catalyzed a growing appreciation for Hong Kong's unique identity. In many ways these debates intersect with, and grow out of, a prior history of southern Chinese frustrations with a northern culture that forever seeks political and social hegemony. Newly minted millionaires from cities like Shanghai and Beijing are pouring their fortunes into Hong Kong, and the Pearl River Delta region more generally, displacing local economic and social interests. As real estate prices soar, residents and local businesses find themselves pushed out of the city center. They are forced to move ever closer to the Chinese border and the throng of competing interests and firms that exists just on the other side.

Despite all of this, or perhaps because of it, residents of Hong Kong refuse to view themselves as simply "Chinese." In fact, popular political identification with mainland China has been slipping every year since its high point in 1997. Local government is viewed as often inept and ineffectual, unable to stand up for the interests of Hong Kong's citizens. All of this has led to a renewed sense of social tension and a strengthening discourse of local identity.[4]

A similar process is underway just on the other side of the Guangdong border, in gritty manufacturing centers like Guangzhou and Foshan. Residents of these areas have seen much of their own history plowed under to make way for an endless expanse of high-rise buildings and shopping malls. They are dependent on overseas demand for their products, and in return they receive large amounts of investment and a seemingly endless stream of migrant workers looking for a better life. While these "foreign" market forces sustain the economy of the Pearl River Delta, they also threaten the population with environmental pollution, social conflict, and a growing sense of alienation.

Given that their architecture and material culture is constantly recycled, it is only natural that the residents of southern China would turn to the shared realm of custom, language, and legend for a source of local identity and pride. This is where Wing Chun and the southern Chinese martial arts, more generally, enter our story.[5] Hong Kong Airlines chose to advertise the training of their attendants in this art not because it was a practical solution to a pressing problem, but because when their customers imagined the golden age of southern Chinese life, this is what they "remembered." Wing Chun kung fu has become a widely acknowledged touchstone of local tradition and lore.

The Imagined Past

On purely historical grounds, it is rather odd that anyone seeking the past should "remember" Wing Chun, or any other traditional martial art, at all. The blunt truth is that for most of China's history, the martial arts have not been very popular. While there has always been a subset of people who took up these pursuits, they were something that the better elements of society studiously avoided.[6] In the mid-1950s, when Bruce Lee was learning Wing Chun from his teacher Ip Man, there were probably less than a 1,000 practitioners of the art in all of Hong Kong. When Ip Man learned the style from his teacher (or Sifu) in Foshan at the turn of the twentieth century, it seems likely that there were less than two dozen students of the art in total. Studying the "traditional" Chinese martial arts is actually a quintessentially *modern* activity. Given this disconnect with mundane reality, how have these arts come to be such effective symbols of local identity and continuity with the past in southern China? There are two answers to this question. One focuses on very recent events, and the other on harder to perceive, but ultimately more substantial, long-term trends.

The brief answer has to do with the mania that swept Hong Kong after the December 2008 release of the quasi-biographical film *Ip Man*. This movie was directed by Wilson Ip and starred Donnie Yen. It was an immediate hit with both audiences and critics alike. This wildly positive reception was all the more notable as the public's interest in martial arts films, a genre increasingly dominated by turgid costume dramas featuring sweeping nationalist themes [*Red Cliff* (2008), *Curse of the Golden Flower* (2006), *House of the Flying Daggers* (2004)] had been waning.

Ip Man promised the public something different. Most obviously it turned away from grand nationalist dramas and focused instead on a local hero and his struggles with the occupying Japanese army during WWII. Yet also critical to the story were Ip Man's repeated conflicts with other "foreign" martial artists—from northern China. These individuals, boorish and violent in turn, were all intent on making their way to the south and setting up schools in Foshan's already crowded martial arts marketplace. Ultimately the movie purports to explain how Ip Man's Wing Chun kung fu came to Hong Kong on the heels of the Japanese defeat in WWII.[7]

As later chapters in this volume demonstrate, the basic historicity of this account leaves much to be desired. The Communist Party's conquest of Guangdong in 1949 had much more to do with Ip Man's decision to move to Hong Kong than the Japanese ever did. Still, a slavish dedication to history has never been a hallmark of the Hong Kong film industry.

What the film lacked in biographical realism it made up for in the martial arts department. The director cast Donnie Yen, a local film star and martial artist, in the lead. The fight scenes were gritty and brutal, keeping special effects to a minimum. Further, the fight directors made an effort to showcase real Wing Chun and other local styles in the final product. The production staff even consulted with Ip Man's two sons, Ip Chun and Ip Ching, both of whom still lived and taught in Hong Kong.

All of the hard work paid off, and the movie proved to be a hit. It spawned two successors, *Ip Man 2* (2010) and *The Legend is Born: Ip Man* (2010), along with countless newspaper articles and television spots profiling the master and his better known students. *Ip Man: The Final Fight* (2013) directed by Herman Yau and *The Grandmaster* (2013) by Wong Kar-wai further expanded the reach of these stories while at the same time striving to create a more sophisticated vision of what a martial arts film could be.

This spate of movies and the press that they generated might be enough to explain why Hong Kong Airlines adopted Wing Chun. Yet Wilson Ip made this movie precisely because there was already a ground swell of excitement around the figure of Ip Man, a seemingly frail martial arts instructor who had died in 1972. Throughout the 1990s and the early 2000s his profile had been quietly rising in the martial arts world. Wing Chun was becoming increasingly popular in Hong Kong, southern China, and the West. Many of his senior students came to be regarded as masters in their own right, and in 2002 Foshan (his birthplace) opened a museum in his honor built on the grounds of the city's central ancestral temple. It was Ip Man's growing reputation as a local martial arts hero that led to a rush by multiple studios and directors (including both Wilson Ip and Wong Kar-wai) to start simultaneous Wing Chun-themed projects.

The current volume attempts to explain this longer term trend of the identification of the southern Chinese martial arts with narratives of local identity and resistance in both Guangdong and Hong Kong. This project is divided into two sections. Part I advances a general survey of the development of civilian martial arts in Guangdong province from roughly the start of the nineteenth century until 1949.

Chapter 1 introduces the reader to the specific economic, social, and political institutions that shaped life in the Pearl River Delta region of Guangdong province in the final decades of the Qing dynasty. Of particular interest is the discussion of Guangzhou and Foshan in the nineteenth century. These two cities were the center of the region's economic and political development, as well as incubators for the creation and perfection of multiple hand combat systems. The political, social, and economic structures that arose in this period shaped the evolution of the local martial arts discussed in later chapters of this volume.

Chapter 2 begins by noting that a social stigma has traditionally followed the Chinese methods of hand combat. Unlike in Japan, where the martial arts were often the prerogative of social elites, good society in China usually shunned hand combat training. So who studied the martial arts? And how does the answer to this question vary geographically and temporally? These questions are addressed in some detail. We further explore what factors allowed Guangzhou and Foshan to develop a busy marketplace in hand combat training.

Chapter 3 examines the further development of these same trends in the Republican period. Special attention is paid to the growth of a number of important modern styles including Wing Chun, White Eyebrow, and Choy Li Fut. Throughout the 1920s and 1930s these arts found new audiences and managed to weave themselves into the fabric of local civil society as never before. At the same time diverse challenges began to emerge. Political factions sought to use the various kung fu clans to advance their own partisan agendas, often with disastrous results for the regional martial marketplace.

Further, reform movements from northern China, including both the Jingwu Association and the later Guomindang (GMD) backed Central Guoshu Institute, sought to modernize and purify the martial arts so that they could be used to strengthen the people and promote nationalism. This modernizing agenda, along with a cadre of northern teachers, was exported to southern China. These individuals and the institutions that they represented had little use for the heterodox forms of local boxing that they found in Guangdong. The ensuing disputes between southern and northern styles are a microcosm of the broader conflicts about the value of centralization versus local autonomy that were taking place throughout Chinese society.

Part II turns our attention to Wing Chun. Having discussed the general development of the southern boxing styles, we begin to explore the nature and history of this iconic fighting system. Chapter 4 examines the emergence and first flowering of Wing Chun as a publicly taught martial art in Foshan between 1900 and 1949. The discussion introduces a number of individuals who made important contributions to the Wing Chun clan, and who are often overlooked by students of the art today. We also explore the links between Foshan's various martial arts schools and the town's radicalized, sometimes unstable, class structure. While Choy Li Fut was a favorite among the town's working-class population, Wing Chun was dominated by the bourgeoisie. This left the art in a very weak position after 1949 and led to its near extermination in mainland China.

Chapter 5 reviews the story of Ip Man. Originally a wealthy landowner from Foshan, he had studied Wing Chun as a child. After working as a plainclothes detective for the police in Foshan he fled to Hong Kong ahead of the Communist Party's advance in 1949. It was here that Ip Man took up the mantle of Sifu, spreading his art to the angry, sometimes near delinquent, youth who came to his school. As a product of a dual conquest, first by the British and later by the communists, these youths were acutely aware of Hong Kong's limited economic and social horizons. They used Wing Chun as a means of crafting narratives of personal resistance and as a vehicle for self-creation in the midst of a society that did not value them. Ip Man was forced to carefully negotiate the relationship between his sometimes volatile students and Hong Kong society, which tended to be distrustful of the traditional martial arts.

Nevertheless, by the mid-1950s social attitudes about the martial arts were once again starting to shift. The images of heroic warriors created by the novelist Jin Yong and the Hong Kong's film industry helped to radically expand the pool of potential students. The elderly, quick-witted, and gentle Ip Man seemed to perfectly fill the role of the "little old Chinese man," a stock character in any good kung fu story. His skill and prior experience in Foshan allowed him to build an organization that would take Wing Chun into the future at exactly the time that many of southern China's hand combat methods began to fade from living memory.

In the Epilogue we examine Wing Chun's subsequent transformation into a global art. Bruce Lee is the critical figure in this revolution. Indeed, his appearances on television and in film helped to make the Asian fighting systems a fixture of modern popular culture. Our concluding discussion situates Wing Chun against a global backdrop to reveal some of the distinctive roles that the martial arts have come to play in a modern and interconnected world.

Ip Man remains a puzzling figure. He was an undeniably authentic martial arts master, and yet his life directly intersected with the creation of some of the twentieth-century's greatest kung fu legends. It is little wonder then that, when Hong Kong Airlines looks to the past, what they "remember" is Ip Man.

Shaolin Dreams: The Mythic Origins of Wing Chun

It should be noted that the southern Chinese schools of hand combat have their own legends which purport to explain their origins and history. In most cases these founding stories vary dramatically from the more historically grounded accounts that we offer here. While the frequently repeated assertion that the traditional Chinese martial arts left no written records is simply untrue, it is an inescapable fact that the southern Chinese boxing methods are transmitted from one generation to the next through a rich oral culture that has little time or need for formal history.

It is important not to dismiss these traditional legends out-of-hand as some students occasionally do. While almost all of these stories are late inventions, dating to the end of the nineteenth century or the start of the twentieth, the fact remains that they are meaningful to the communities that transmit them. In a sense, these myths convey much of the lived experience of the group that traditional history simply misses.

Unfortunately a complete survey of the mythology of the southern Chinese martial arts lies outside the scope of the present volume. Such an exercise would make for a lengthy book in its own right. Nevertheless, it is important that readers be familiar with the general shape and nature of these stories.

As such we would like to introduce a brief overview of the traditional Wing Chun creation myth. While a number of southern hand combat styles are discussed in this volume, the history of Wing Chun is the central case study for a variety of reasons. As a larger and well-established art it is relatively easy to study and more of its history has been preserved and recorded than is the case with some other regional styles.

While many of the unique combat methods of southern China have slipped into obscurity, Wing Chun has become closely linked with local identity. An examination of this style's history opens a valuable window onto the process of regional identity formation and the development of civil society in Guangdong in the late Qing and the Republic of China periods. It should also be noted that the story of the origins of this style shares a number of common features with other southern kung fu schools.

The narrative, as transmitted within the Ip Man Wing Chun clan, starts out by telling us that at some time during the early 1700s, the monks at the Shaolin Temple (on either Mt. Song in Henan, or at an unknown location somewhere in Fujian Province) became famous for their mastery of the fighting arts.[8] Fearing this potential power, the Qing Emperor decided to move against the monks; and with the help of corrupt officials and a traitor inside the temple, managed to burn the monastery to the ground and slaughter most of its inhabitants. Five masters, including the Abbot, escaped. One of the survivors was said to be the nun Ng Mui. Fleeing to the south, she took refuge at the White Crane Temple. There she encountered a local family by the name of Yim. Yim Yee was a tofu merchant who had both a daughter and a problem. His daughter, named Wing Chun, had become the object of a local ruffian's interest.

The nun agreed to train Yim Wing Chun in the Shaolin martial arts and took her to a mountain where she practiced diligently so that she could defeat the local bully and marry her fiancé, a salt merchant by the name of Leung Bok Chau. After vanquishing the bully in a challenge match, Wing Chun then went on to teach the art to her husband, who in turn taught it to Leung Lan Kwai. He passed it on to Wong Wah Bo, a member of a local Cantonese opera company (often referred to as the "Red Boat" opera). Wong became friends with another member of the troupe named Leung Yee Tai, who happened to have mastered a powerful pole form that he learned from the escaped Abbot of the Shaolin Temple, Jee Shim. Leung and Wong traded their knowledge of the pole form and the unarmed method, bringing together the complete Wing Chun system that exists today.

Leung Yee Tai and Wong Wah Bo passed their knowledge on to a well-known herbal doctor in Foshan by the name of Leung Jan.[9] Leung Jan taught his sons the art, and only accepted one outside student, a fellow merchant (actually a moneychanger) from the marketplace, named Chan Wah Shun.[10] Chan was only able to teach a small number of students in his lifetime (sixteen in total), the last of which was Ip Man. After fleeing to Hong Kong in the face of the communist advance in 1949, the previously well-off Ip Man found himself forced to seek employment. He began teaching martial arts classes at the local Restaurant Workers Union, and from there his students, including Bruce Lee, spread the fame of Wing Chun around the world.

Many southern Chinese arts have a creation myth that is quite similar to this one. The destruction of the Shaolin Temple is a common, almost universal, theme and helps to date the origin of these stories to the late nineteenth century when literary works containing these elements came into vogue.[11] These myths are often interpreted as a sort of social constitution which guides the performance of the art and the actions of the community. For instance, Wing Chun practitioners are often told to be relaxed and flexible as they are practicing an art created by a woman who by necessity had to overcome strength with relaxation. Of course, each creation myth has its own unique elements. Very few of these stories have female protagonists.[12]

Nor does there appear to be any kernel of truth behind these stories. The historical Shaolin Temple in the north was never destroyed by the Qing, and the so-called Southern Shaolin Temple most likely never existed. It was simply a product of nineteenth-century folklore and literary invention.[13] Likewise, the nun Ng Mui is not listed in any credible historical record. She first appears as a traitor in a late Qing martial arts novel published in the 1890s (where she helps to burn down the Shaolin Temple), and is not reimagined as a heroine until the 1930s.[14]

All of these creation stories are better thought of as myths than history. They evolved in direct dialogue with the popular fiction of the day. Given the names and stories referenced, the Wing Chun creation myth cannot have been composed prior to the first few decades of the twentieth century. All of the figures in this story prior to Leung Jan, who died at the turn of the century, are either clearly fictional or unverifiable.

In searching for the actual origins of these arts we cannot rely on their folklore alone.

While on the subject of historical continuity, it may be worth noting one other thing that this volume does not attempt to accomplish. Recent years have seen an explosion of interest in "newly discovered" Wing Chun lineages claiming a wide variety of origins and traditions of transmission. Often these lineages have their own, even more recently composed, creation myths. This volume deals only with the direct Ip Man lineage of Wing Chun. This tradition emerged in the city of Foshan sometime in the mid-nineteenth century, was transmitted through Chan Wah Shun to Ip Man and was then taken to Hong Kong. From there his students spread the art throughout the global system, making Wing Chun one of the most popular Chinese martial arts in the world today.

This project focuses only on the Ip Man lineage for three reasons. First, it is the largest of the Wing Chun lineages and there is quite a bit of primary and secondary source material available, making its history relatively more accessible and reliable. Second, it was Ip Man's student Bruce Lee who is responsible for introducing Wing Chun to a global audience. Since one of the goals of this study is to appreciate its place in the world today, understanding the history of this specific lineage is of central importance.

Lastly, this work presents a "social history" of Wing Chun. Most of the present volume is dedicated to a discussion of the specific cultural, economic, religious, political, and military factors that shaped southern China during the late Qing and the Republic of China periods. While these factors are critical to understanding the emergence of Ip Man's lineage, they have also shaped many other traditions and arts that emerged in the same geographic area. This volume attempts to provide a broad enough study that it will be valuable to any student of Guangdong's martial heritage.

A few notes on the Chinese language are also in order. While China shares a single written language, multiple spoken dialects exist, the largest being Mandarin (the national standard) and Cantonese (spoken most frequently in our southern research area). A single written word or name can sound quite different when read in these two dialects. For instance, in the Wing Chun myth we encountered the nun Ng Mui. "Ng Mui" is the Cantonese variant of her name. In Mandarin the same name is said "Wu Mei." Likewise, in Mandarin traditional martial arts teachers are usually referred to as "Shifu," but in Cantonese the same title is pronounced "Sifu."

Further complicating matters, there is no universally accepted standard for how Chinese characters should be transcribed into English. The two most commonly seen styles are Pinyin and Wade-Giles. These systems will Romanize the exact same word very differently, so some caution is in order. For instance, "Taijiquan" and "Tai Chi Chuan" both refer to the same art. The first name is rendered using Pinyin while the second is a product of the Wade-Giles system. Pinyin has increasingly become the global standard since the mid-1980s, but both are still commonly encountered.

We have attempted to use Mandarin and the Pinyin system when introducing general Chinese words or names. However, it should also be noted that Wing Chun and many of the other martial arts we are most interested in are products of the southern Cantonese linguistic area. As local identity is an important focus of the current volume, it is critical to tell the story of these individuals in their own language. When discussing people or events in the south we have used Cantonese names and words where possible and appropriate. A Chinese language glossary of names and terms has been provided at the end of this volume. Readers should be aware that in a few cases there are no universally agreed upon spellings or characters for names that have emerged from the oral traditions surrounding these arts.

There are also unresolved questions of terminology. The Chinese language has a large number of names for the "martial arts," and each one has a certain connotation. The use of one term rather than another is often a politicized choice. For instance, during the Qing period the government made a distinction between those arts practiced by the military and civilians. The fighting methods of the mostly Han citizenry were referred to as "Quanbang" (boxing and staff).[15] The term is rarely used today, and it still carries certain associations that are far from neutral. In the 1930s the GMD coined the name "Guoshu" (meaning the "national arts") because they liked the ring of centralism and nationalism that the term tended to evoke in listeners. After seizing power the Communist Party dropped this label and named their martial program "Wushu."

Some of these disputes have bled over into English language discussions. Occasionally, martial arts practitioners from northern China object to the Western use of the term "kung fu," rather than "Wushu." They see it as being improper or possibly even disrespectful. They point out that the term "kung fu" really just means "diligent practice" and could apply to any field of endeavor. Likewise, traditional martial arts practitioners outside of mainland China sometimes refuse to use the term "Wushu" because of its close links with a government-sponsored competitive sport (also known as Wushu) which, truth be told, has as much in common with modern gymnastics as it does the traditional fighting arts.

Kung fu, as a slang reference for hand combat, seems to be more popular in southern China. Since Guangdong has exported huge numbers of people to the West, the term traveled with them. Bruce Lee referred to the Chinese fighting systems as "gong fu" and he did more to popularize their practice in the West than any other single individual. His use of the term accurately reflected local Cantonese speech patterns, but it is not always accepted by individuals from other parts of China.[16]

There are other controversies as well. One traditional term for Chinese martial artists in the West was "boxers." This usage is still seen in the names of certain styles (e.g., Five Ancestors Boxing). Some authors worry that lingering baggage from the Boxer Uprising taints the term with a negative connotation.[17]

In his writings on Shaolin, Meir Shahar has advocated the phrase "hand combat." While a solidly neutral expression, it can be become awkward if used repetitively. Much the same can be said of the term "martial art," though that is not its only difficulty.[18]

The larger problem with this last label is that most people are already quite sure that they know what the "martial arts" are. Unfortunately, there is a lot of intellectual baggage packed into that term. When most Western students use the phrase they subconsciously assume that in any properly formed "martial art" there will be clearly demarcated masters, teachers, and students. Further, the students will be ranked based on their skills. We tend to assume that there are competing direct lineages that are stable and continuous over long periods of time. Often students assume that an art must have an ancient and well-documented history. It is now fashionable to expect that an art should also have all kinds of vaguely New Age spiritual benefits (especially if it is of Chinese origin). Anachronistic and impractical uniforms are always part of the mental image of the "traditional" martial artists. Lastly, we assume that it should be a franchise, like an Asian McDonald's, easily available anywhere in the world. People carry these beliefs with them because this is how Wing Chun and almost every other martial art, regardless of their place of origin, looks today.

We fail to realize that this vision of the "martial arts" is in fact a very modern phenomenon. More than that, it really reflects the types of sports organizations and professionalism that the various Japanese styles developed in the pre-World-War-Two period and subsequently exported to the West, creating a set of expectations to which we still seek to conform. American consumers have simply accepted and internalized these norms. Nevertheless, the elaborate systems of colored belts and advancement tests seen in modern Karate or Tae Kwon Do schools are not really all that compatible with the history and nature of most Chinese fighting systems.

In attempting to discuss history, we often find that our expectations about what the martial arts are, and *should* be, are inappropriately read backwards in time. This distorts and impedes our understanding of the development of southern Chinese hand combat. We want to see larger organizations, we want to see exotic competing lineages, we want to see a well-documented history and enlightened civilian sages (preferably Chan Buddhists; Daoist mystics will do in a pinch) because that is what we have come to expect. When readers do not see these things, they simply construct that sort of narrative out of the few facts that they do have. Often our preconceived notions of what the "martial arts" are determine what we find when examining the historical record. Students of Chinese martial studies must guard against this danger.

It does not appear that there is any single, perfect term for the civilian Chinese fighting arts of the nineteenth and twentieth centuries. In this text the preferred terms are "martial art" and "hand combat system," yet "boxing" and "kung fu" are also used to remind us that we are attempting to reconstruct distinctly southern Chinese traditions. These arts are quite different from their better known Japanese and Korean cousins.

A Critical Review of the Chinese Martial Arts Literature

This volume relies heavily on contributions from the most respected authors in both the Chinese and English language literatures. Given that Chinese martial studies is a relatively new research area, a brief review of the literature may be helpful. Traditionally, few scholars studied the history or social meaning of the Chinese martial arts, either in the East or the West. Much of the available information was incomplete and unreliable. Even well-respected Western researchers with extensive firsthand experience tended to pass on as many myths as facts.[19] Nor was the situation always much better in Taiwan or the People's Republic of China.

The first truly academic historian of Chinese hand combat was Tang Hao (1887–1959). A lawyer by training, Tang's true passion was the discovery and restoration of China's traditional fighting arts. He studied various systems in both China and Japan and worked briefly for the Central Guoshu Institute.[20] While his specific contributions are discussed in greater length elsewhere, Tang is rightly considered the father of Chinese martial arts history. Much of his research was first published in the 1930s, and his books on the history of Taijiquan and Shaolin Boxing exploded many myths and pointed future scholars in fruitful directions. Unfortunately, the tumultuous events of the twentieth century stymied the development of this nascent literature. Xu Zhen (1898–1967) and a handful of others followed in Tang Hao's footsteps during the first half of the twentieth century, but real progress would have to wait until after the disruptions of the Second World War and the Cultural Revolution.[21]

At the very beginning of this next period, starting in the early 1980s, much of the literature produced on the history of the martial arts within mainland China was mixed at best. Texts tended to be repetitive, formulaic, and ideological. However, during the early 1990s a notable shift began to occur. As popular interest in the Chinese martial arts increased, there was greater demand for high quality publications and studies. Some of this research was driven by individual localities seeking to explore their own history and promote both local prestige and tourism. The rest tended to be published by university professors, sometimes at collegiate level sports training programs. A steady stream of books and journal articles emerged from about 1990 onward.[22] Some of the more important examples of this trend include Ma Mingda's 2003 work entitled *Wuxue Tanzhen* (*Seeking Facts in Martial Studies*, in two volumes), Zhou Weiliang's 2003 *Zhongguo Wushushi* (*Chinese Martial Arts History*), and the encyclopedic 1997 publication *Zhongguo Wushushi* (*Chinese Martial Arts History*).[23]

Stanley Henning has written a valuable review of this newly emerging Chinese language literature. He highlights three of the top authors in the field (Ma Mingda, Zhou Weiliang, and Cheng Dali) as well as exploring various trends and approaches to the topic.[24] In many ways the current project most closely resembles the historical research of Zhou Weiliang. Like Zhou's research, it contextualizes the practice of the martial arts by examining the cultural, social, and economic systems that surround them.

While there is currently a flowering of scholarship in the area of Chinese martial studies, the present volume makes an important original contribution to this literature. Most of the recently published works focus their attention on national (and sometimes ancient) history. By contrast, the current study claims that the traditional fighting arts are best understood through the lens of modern regional and local history. A national-level approach can impose a degree of uniformity onto discussions of development and motivations that obscure exactly the sort of variance that is most useful to students of social history.[25]

Modern public martial arts instruction did not arise at the same time in all areas of China. In some places it was well-established by the end of the nineteenth century, in others it was not commonly available until the 1920s. Simply extrapolating what happened in Shanghai or some other major city and then imposing that framework onto the rest of the country neglects much of what is most significant about this story. National-level historical narratives that focus on the reforming agendas of the Central Guoshu Institute or the earlier Pure Martial Association (sometimes referred to as Jingwu) often commit this error. Rather than asking which modern martial arts school arose first, students should instead be investigating why these institutions emerged earlier in some places than in others. Doing so naturally turns our attention to regional conditions and requires an understanding of how local society reacted to broader systemic pressures.

Most of these approaches also treat the study of Chinese martial arts history in relative isolation. This is not surprising given that this is a new discipline struggling for recognition. Chinese scholars are still attempting to lay a firm factual foundation, separating out what actually happened from centuries of accumulated folklore and legend.

Our research interests lay precisely at the intersection between the history of Chinese martial arts and the emergence of other important phenomenon such as globalization, economic development, and national identity construction. We have drawn on the Western social scientific literature to provide frameworks with which to think about these issues. Rather than always treating the martial arts as a dependent variable (the thing that is explained) any balanced historical investigation must be open to conceptualizing them as independent variables as well. Examining broader historical processes from the vantage point of these little understood social structures yields new and valuable perspectives.

The Chinese language scholarship that has had the greatest impact on the current study is that which focuses on local history and the emergence of Qing- and Republican-era martial arts institutions against the backdrop of economic modernity. Zeng Zhaosheng edited one of the first comprehensive collections on the history of southern Chinese martial arts in his 1983 volume *Nan Quan* (*Southern Chinese Boxing*). He later updated this research in what remains one of the best overviews of the history and development of Southern Chinese hand combat in his 1989 edited volume *Guangdong Wushu Shi* (*A History of Guangdong Martial Arts*). While giving a valuable overview of events in the province Zeng fails to treat Wing Chun (and events in Foshan more generally) with as much detail as one might like. As such we have also made extensive use of Ma Zineng 2001 edited work titled *Foshan Wushu Wenhua* (*Foshan Martial Arts Culture*).[26] Zhang Xue Lian has also offered valuable insights into the workings of the local branch of the national Jingwu Association in the 2009 monograph, *Foshan Jingwu Tiyu Hui* (*The Foshan Pure Martial Athletic Association.*)[27] Where necessary these sources have been supplemented with articles and books published by practicing martial artists which, when properly understood and evaluated, provide an invaluable window into the evolution of southern China's unique martial arts subculture.[28]

Many Chinese universities also publish journals of physical culture that include articles on the martial arts. Some institutions even host entire journals dedicated to Wushu. While most of their articles focus on state-sponsored Wushu and Sanshou (a type of modern Chinese kickboxing), occasionally important works on the traditional martial arts are also published. We have reviewed much of this literature and have drawn on it where necessary. For instance, Zhou Weiliang has published an important article critiquing the "southern Shaolin" tradition in Hangzhou Normal College's *Journal of Capital Institute of Physical Education*. Yimin He, addressing the question of regional economic development has also painted a remarkable picture of life in nineteenth-century Foshan in an article titled "Prosperity and Decline: A Comparison of the Fate of Jingdezhen, Zhuxianzhen, Foshan and Hankou in Modern Times."[29] While some of the journal literature is excellent, the quality of other pieces can be uneven. Care must be taken when evaluating sources.

The Chinese language literature is not the only place where we have seen important developments in the last decade. The martial arts are also attracting increased academic interest in the West. The recent publication of a number of books and articles on the social meaning of these fighting systems has contributed to the emergence of "martial arts studies" as a new interdisciplinary research field.

In general this literature seeks to understand the martial arts as socially constructed institutions rather than purely technical systems. The evolution and significance of these structures can be studied from a variety of perspectives including history, anthropology, critical and gender theory, media studies, and the social sciences. Research on the emergence of kung fu as a global phenomenon has made important contributions to the development of this more theoretically informed approach to understanding the martial arts.

Predictably, anthropologists were some of the first Western scholars to realize the potential of this field. Martial arts classes and clans provide ideal units for ethnographic analysis. Daniel Miles Amos was an early pioneer in this area, completing a doctoral dissertation in Guangdong and Hong Kong in 1983. His findings were finally published in a series of articles in the 1990s. More recently Adam Frank and Avron Boretz have published the results of their extensive ethnographic analysis of Taijiquan associations in Shanghai and the role of martial identity in southern heterodox religious (and sometimes criminal) communities.[30]

The Chinese diaspora and the broader Asian cultural sphere have also provided martially minded anthropologists with new areas for exploration. After extensive fieldwork in Malaysia, D. S. Farrer published *Shadows of the Prophet: Martial Arts and Sufi Mysticism*. His in-depth investigation of a Silat school and its connections to transnational Sufi networks provides valuable tools for anyone interested in investigating the connections (supposed or real) between Asian martial arts and religious identities.[31] Ethnographies such as these are a rich source of observation and data that can be mined by various types of social scientists and historians.

Western historians have also discovered the rich potential of Chinese martial studies. Douglas Wile's 1996 monograph *The Lost Tai-Chi Classics from the Late Qing Dynasty* was the first English language historical study dedicated exclusively to a Chinese martial art tradition published by a university press.[32] The author's analysis of a wide variety of documentary resources, as well as his sensitivity to social, political, and economic questions helped to demonstrate the intellectual viability of martial studies as a research area.

Brian Kennedy and Elizabeth Guo have made a number of contributions to the English language literature on the Chinese martial arts. Their 2005 volume on the history of Chinese hand combat training manuals provides a very readable introduction to the field. Likewise, their 2010 study of the Jingwu Association discusses a critical topic for any student of twentieth-century martial arts history. For the most part, the work of Kennedy and Guo consists of translating existing Chinese language sources rather than undertaking fresh theoretical investigations. Still, given the state of the Western literature this is quite helpful.[33]

Another historically inclined author is Andrew Morris. In 2004, he released a study of the development of sports in Republic-era China. Only a single chapter of his extensively researched book dealt directly with the martial arts, but his detailed analysis of period sources and journals has proved to be an invaluable resource for anyone writing in the field.[34]

Meir Shahar's volume on the Shaolin Monastery has gone beyond the mark set by Kennedy and Morris. Rather than simply translating existing sources and arguments, Shahar actually undertakes a challenging research program and presents what may be the single most informative work on the ancient Shaolin martial arts tradition written in any language. Again, from our current perspective the most laudable aspect of this work was his attempt to place the Shaolin Temple within the political, religious, and social landscapes that framed its existence.[35]

One of the pressing problems facing Western students of Chinese martial studies has been the lack of reliable translations and commentaries on the classic hand combat works. These texts and manuscripts are, after all, the primary source material of the field. Even Chinese language readers may have trouble locating reprints or microfilms of some of the more esoteric documents.

However, as interest in all aspects of China's martial history grows, the body of texts available to Western students is expanding. Investigators of such northern arts as Taiji, Bagua, and Xingyi Quan are the most fortunate as the body of literature surrounding these traditions is the best developed. A number of classic texts and handbooks have been translated and published in the last decade.[36] The work of the prolific writer, thinker, and martial artist Sun Lutang (1861–1933), who did as much as anyone else to craft the modern understanding of the relationship between Taijiquan, Xingyi, and Bagua, is now available in English.[37] Stephen Selby has also provided detailed translations and commentaries on traditional archery texts in his 2000 Hong Kong University Press study, *Chinese Archery*.[38] In addition to philosophical and technical discussions, careful readers can also detect interesting historical and social data in each of these works.

Unfortunately, there are fewer "classic" texts dealing with the martial arts of southern China. One important exception to this is the *Bubishi*. While this manuscript tradition is normally venerated in Japanese martial circles, the underlying text itself deals with White Crane and other boxing techniques from Fujian province where it was originally authored. This work is full of folklore and period discussions sure to be of great interest to anyone studying the emergence of the modern martial arts in southern China.[39]

Students of the ancient antecedents of modern hand combat systems have also seen an increase in the number of primary texts in translation over the course of the last decade. In addition to General Qi Jiguang, the contributions of fellow military officer Yu Dayou and Shaolin student Cheng Zongyou have recently become available in English translation for the first time through the efforts of a group of dedicated martial arts historians and historical fighting enthusiasts in Singapore. The sudden availability of these important texts is sure to benefit the growth of Chinese martial studies in the West.[40]

A number of shorter theoretical works, seeking to understand trends in the development and spread of Chinese hand combat systems, have also been gathered and published in edited volumes. Those interested in the links between military history and the modern Chinese martial arts would be well-served by Nicola Di Cosmo's *Military Culture in Imperial China*. Thomas A. Green and Joseph R. Svinth have also published a collection of articles, some of which are quite relevant to our current project, titled *Martial Arts in the Modern World*.[41] Most recently D. S. Farrer and John Whalen-Bridge have released an interdisciplinary collection of essays titled *Martial Arts as Embodied Knowledge: Asian Traditions in a Transnational World*.[42] This volume's introductory essay is deserving of careful study as it lays out the case for the emergence of martial studies as an independent and uniquely interdisciplinary research area.

The academic interest in the martial arts, and Chinese hand combat traditions in particular, has been on the rise in the West. Established authors and highly respected presses are beginning to publish in this area. Cambridge University Press's *Chinese Martial Arts: from Antiquity to the 21ˢᵗ Century* by historian Peter Lorge clearly signals the growing importance of this area of study.[43] In this ambitious work, Lorge attempts to survey the complete history of Chinese hand combat traditions ranging from military to civilian arts, stretching from the Bronze Age to the current era of globalization. His work is detailed, well-researched, and conceptually noteworthy. Lorge addresses a number of difficult questions surrounding the meaning and evolution of the "martial arts."

While comprehensive works such as this offer new readers a valuable entrance to the literature, we continue to believe that highly focused studies of local history which provide a longitudinal examination of a single region, or even a single city, are the most likely to demonstrate how these traditions actually functioned within the broader context of

Chinese society. As such, the current volume relies on a single, highly focused case study. In the future other scholars might produce similar works focusing on different regions and arts. This would be a sustainable growth path for the literature and the current project aims to inspire exactly that sort of research.

When attempting to understand the social significance of the martial arts, it is not enough to only examine these structures as an "embodied practice" or a historically given technical transmission. While the traditional fighting systems are often presented within a complex framework of physical teachings, embodied experiences are never entirely self-interpreting. Rather, students look to a rich tradition of myths and symbols to make sense of their interactions with the martial arts.

In the current era these symbols are conveyed not just through oral teachings, but also by movies, television programs, video games, and wuxia novels. Martial artists are often avid consumers of these products, so it is not surprising to discover that they can shape their subjective experiences in significant ways. Of course, most non-practitioners are totally reliant on these media representations when formulating their basic ideas and beliefs about the martial arts.

Film and cultural studies scholars have made a number of contributions to our understanding of the evolving global significance of these fighting systems. Stephen Teo's 2007 study *Chinese Martial Arts Cinema: The Wuxia Tradition* provides a valuable window into the ways in which these films have shaped the current discussion of the martial arts.[44] In his monograph *From Kung Fu to Hip Hop: Revolution, Globalization and Popular Culture*, T. M. Kato delves further into the relationship between popular culture and the martial arts.[45] Readers interested in the continuing social significance of Bruce Lee's films should see *Theorizing Bruce Lee: Film—Fantasy—Fighting—Philosophy* (2010) and *Beyond Bruce Lee: Chasing the Dragon through Film, Philosophy and Popular Culture* (2013) by Paul Bowman.[46] It is unlikely that Wing Chun would enjoy its current global popularity without Bruce Lee's explosive rise to superstardom in the 1970s. Those interested in the ways that this art has been portrayed on film should also see Sasha Vojkovic 2009 volume *Yuen Woo Ping's Wing Chun* published by Hong Kong University Press.[47]

More central to the current study is the evolving literature on wuxia, or swordsmen novels, produced in China, Hong Kong, and Taiwan between the late nineteenth and middle of the twentieth century. Criticized by May Fourth intellectuals and various social reformers, this genre has proved to be remarkably popular and resilient. While some of these novels dealt with prominent debates at the national level, other stories popularized local martial arts practitioners (such as Wong Fei Hung and Leung Jan), turning them into folk heroes and enshrining their styles within southern China's imagined past. This type of storytelling had a noticeable impact on the folklore of a number of hand combat styles and it seems to have contributed to the popularization of such central myths as the destruction of the Shaolin Temple.

John Christopher Hamm surveys much of the earlier and more local literature in his 2005 volume *Paper Swordsmen: Jin Yong and the Modern Chinese Martial Arts Novel*. Petrus Liu looks at the evolving social discourse surrounding wuxia fiction and argues that these works offered a sophisticated critique of the variant of modernization theory being promoted by many intellectuals as the solution to China's developmental dilemmas during the Republican era.[48] Both of these discussions contribute to our understanding of the popularity and subjective meaning of Wing Chun as a social institution in southern China during the volatile twentieth century.

Having briefly reviewed the state of both the Chinese and English language literatures, it is now possible to place the current volume within the framework of the existing scholarly discussion. Drawing on this literature, we advance the most detailed and reliable account of the development of martial arts in Guangdong province to date. To better understand these social processes we focus extensively on events in two cities, Foshan and Hong Kong, during the late nineteenth and twentieth centuries. The development and popularization of Wing Chun, culminating in Ip Man's export of the art to Hong Kong, is our primary case study.

We argue that it is not possible to understand the evolution of these traditions without looking at the social, political, and economic systems in which they are embedded. The southern Chinese martial arts have never been just one thing. Over time various groups have sought to use these institutions as vehicles to navigate China's evolving social landscape.

The martial arts have functioned as tools for framing personal and community struggles within this dynamic system. Specifically, in southern China hand combat traditions have provided society with a way of understanding its relationship with the nation while still preserving a space for regional pride and autonomy. Although paradoxical on purely historical grounds, students of Chinese martial studies can attest that there are good reasons why so many inhabitants of Guangdong and Hong Kong "remember" Wing Chun (mediated by the images of Bruce Lee and Ip Man) when imagining their collective past.

Part I

Hand Combat, Identity, and Civil Society in Guangdong, 1800–1949

Chapter 1

Growth and Disorder

Paradoxes of the Qing Dynasty

Originally we were humble people and good subjects, but we became pirates for a variety of reasons. Because some of us were not careful in making friends, we fell in among robbers. Others of us were unable to secure a livelihood or were kidnapped while trading on the rivers and lakes ... In addition, as a result of the famine of the last couple of years, people had nothing with which to maintain their livelihood and as time went on could not help but pillage in order to live. Had we not resisted officials and soldiers, our lives would have been in danger. Therefore, we violated the laws of the empire and wrecked trade. This was unavoidable.

—Petition presented to Bai Ling, 1810[1]

Introduction

The creation myths of the Chinese martial arts are full of mysterious mountain temples, ancient military heroes, and long lost truths. In current debates nothing serves to answer questions about a style's "authenticity" as quickly as an argument about its great antiquity. For instance, local lore dictates that many of the modern styles of southern China (including Wing Chun) are descended from the Southern Shaolin Temple, or strongly influenced by its students.

While the famed temple has turned out to be a literary creation, China does have an ancient and vast martial history. It is little wonder that so many modern martial artists look to the past to validate their work. Ancient schools of wrestling, sword dancing, and archery existed during the Bronze Age and Early Imperial Period. The biographical legends of great swordsmen and assassins passed on by the Han historian Sima Qian have helped to shape the idea of "martial virtue" throughout Chinese history. Many discussions of the Chinese martial arts begin with an extensive investigation of these ancient traditions.

They may also spend chapters exploring the military literature and accounts of the rise of unarmed boxing during the Ming dynasty. This was the era when the ancestors of what we currently think of as the modern Chinese hand combat methods were first being brought together and popularized. If one is interested in the actual connection between the historic Shaolin order and the martial arts, this is the era to investigate.

The archeological exploration of southern China is certainly a fascinating subject. And historical records do indicate that there were distinct schools of boxing in the region during the latter part of the Ming dynasty. Yet the story of the modern Chinese martial arts really begins in the Qing dynasty, a few hundred years later.

The idea of boxing as a popular pastime, a valuable form of military training, and a pathway for self-cultivation first emerged in the late Ming dynasty. Most of the older forms of the art practiced in the south do not seem to have survived the transition between dynasties, or the other social disruptions that the region was subject to, without undergoing fundamental change.

The roots of southern Chinese hand combat, as it exists today, can be found in the unique forms of social and economic organization that emerged during the Qing dynasty. While practitioners drew on an extensive body of preexisting techniques and theories, these were reshaped and embedded in a new set of social institutions to create the traditions that we now think of as "martial arts." Much of this project happened in the eighteenth and nineteenth centuries, with the pace of change accelerating towards the end of this era. In fact, the period of 1840 to 1911 is particularly important in the emergence of the region's unique martial traditions.

The Qing dynasty, founded by northern Manchu tribesmen, was the last and best documented of all China's imperial governments. In reviewing its records we see essentially two different periods. The first, lasting from the establishment of the dynasty until roughly the turn of the nineteenth century, was characterized by political stability, the expansion of the economy, and a sustained population boom supported by ever-increasing harvests. The one hundred years of the next period (from roughly 1800 onward) continued to see an expansion in both market size and population, but now these same factors worked against the state, causing internal strain and ultimately political collapse.

In 1600 China enjoyed a higher standard of living than any other state in the global system. Yet in the space of slightly more than three hundred years this position of dominance eroded. The Qing dynasty was ultimately bought down by its own inability to deal with increased domestic pressures and to recognize the growing imperialist threat posed by the West.

These national developments had a critical impact on the world of civilian martial artists. Intellectual ferment at the end of the Ming dynasty helped to create many of the basic ideas that are still taken for granted in hand combat training.[2] At the same time, this tended to be an elite-driven process that probably could not sustain the enthusiasm needed to bring Chinese martial arts into the modern era. To really understand the evolution of the modern schools that exist today we must consider how hand combat training became a mass phenomenon, particularly in Fujian and Guangdong Provinces. What forces created both the supply and demand for the rapid expansion of a new set of martial arts styles in southern China during the late nineteenth century?

We can better understand both sides of this equation by taking a closer look at the evolving demographic, economic, and political world in which these new styles (including White Crane, White Eyebrow, Hung Gar, Choy Li Fut, and Wing Chun) first emerged. The decline in agricultural wages and expansion of both national and international trade networks ensured that urban population centers would swell throughout the nineteenth century. Workers, paid in cash, had both the leisure time and resources to devote to martial arts training. Being a member of a martial arts school also provided urban employees with a set of connections that could be very helpful in times of unemployment or illness. This newly monetized economy also allowed for a rapid expansion of the pool of professional martial arts instructors.[3]

The turn toward rebellion, banditry, and even the threat of foreign invasion in the late nineteenth century increased both the demand for martial arts training and the number of individuals ready and willing to provide it. The development of local militia units had a profound effect on the region's social structure and even on the Qing state. New ideas about unarmed combat spread through these networks. Both the political turmoil and the new economic reality of the late nineteenth century led directly to the emergence of the first truly "modern" Chinese martial systems and schools.

The following chapter proceeds in three parts. The first briefly reviews the early history of the Qing dynasty, providing a framework for the detailed discussions to follow. In the second section we turn our attention to China's place in the growing international trade system and the threat of Western imperialism during the last half of the nineteenth century. Many of the most important events reviewed in both the first and second sections actually begin in southern China, our area of geographic interest. Lastly, we turn our attention to Guangdong Province and ask what life was like in Guangzhou and Foshan, two cities that are central to the emergence of Wing Chun and many other southern styles in the 1840s and 1850s. Both of these cities were shaped by the domestic and international conflicts of the nineteenth century, including the First and Second Opium Wars and the Red Turban Revolt.

We argue that the southern hand combat schools that emerged in the late Qing period were essentially adaptive structures responding to the needs of their day. As the power of the central government declined, local gentry found themselves forced to master the martial disciplines so that they could train a militia and maintain social order. As peasants were increasingly forced off the land and into urban work environments, they found themselves facing a new set of threats and lacking any traditional support structure. Practical self-defense was a real concern for this new class of urban dwellers. The outbreak of numerous rebellions, conflicts, tax revolts, and secret society uprisings throughout the nineteenth century ensured an emphasis on brutal practicality that still sets a number of these southern systems apart from other martial arts today.

The Qing in Late Imperial History

The Manchurians, who created the Qing dynasty, were a farming people who lived north of the Great Wall of China. In the generations immediately before the invasion of the south their leaders founded a new independent state, created a script for their spoken language, translated many Confucian texts, and with the help of a number of Chinese citizens (slaves, long-time residents and hired advisors) created their own parallel court structure complete with ministries and administrative processes. Before they ever seized Beijing, the future leaders of the Qing dynasty had already solved one of the great problems that plagued all of the "northern" conquerors. How does one integrate both his own political aspirations and Han Confucian tradition into a single set of governing institutions? By the time they breached the northern frontier, the Qing already had an efficient state structure in place. This gave them an advantage over the various generals and warlords then vying for the throne.

The Manchu invasion was initially aided by a number of Chinese officers who decided that the new dynasty offered a better chance for peace and stability than the rump Ming state. After quickly overrunning the northern half of the country, opposition to Manchu expansion centered around the Yangtze River basin and half-hearted attempts to prevent the Manchurian armies from crossing this natural barrier.[4]

The Qing responded with a carrot-and-stick strategy. They promised peace and social continuity to those forces that aligned themselves with the new state (including jobs in the civil service or opportunities to take "special" national exams), and utter destruction to anyone who opposed them militarily. In between these two extremes were a large number of former Ming officials who would not immediately serve the Qing, but who did not put up an organized resistance either. In dealing with this group, the Qing used diplomacy, engaging in public works projects to attempt to demonstrate that they had received the "Mandate of Heaven." The regime even asked dubious scholars to audit their progress or compile important academic works of great cultural value as a way of demonstrating their virtue and ability to rule.

It took the Qing fifteen years to hunt down the last Ming pretenders to the throne, and a little longer to put down the last of the independent generals and warlords that inevitably emerged in these periods. The most important, and famous, of the Ming loyalists was the pirate king Zheng Chenggong, more commonly known in the West as Koxinga (1624–1662). He is also a central figure in many of the region's later Triad and martial arts legends. As such, it is important to know a few facts about his actual life and career.

Born in Japan to a Japanese mother, Koxinga was the son of Zheng Zhilong, a powerful merchant and pirate who controlled a vast fleet of ships. The Zheng family remained loyal to the Ming dynasty. However, when one of the last remaining Ming princes took refuge in Fuzhou, Fujian Province (a clan stronghold), Zheng Zhilong refused to support a proposed counteroffensive against the Qing forces. The government managed to capture and kill the isolated Ming prince in short order. Worse yet, Zheng Zhilong actually accepted a Qing offer to become the governor of Fujian and Guangdong Provinces, leaving the "family business" of conquest and piracy in the capable hands of his son Zheng

Chenggong. This greatly disappointed the Qing who had assumed that the entire Zheng clan was included in the deal. Zheng Zhilong was taken to Beijing as a hostage and later executed.

The younger Zheng continued to publicly support the Ming dynasty, though he could not send material aid to the sole remaining claimant to the throne in the far southwest. Instead, Koxinga focused on consolidating his own power base, retaking Taiwan from the Dutch in 1662, and using the island as his base of both commercial and political operations. The local tropical landscape finally accomplished what the Qing could not, and Koxinga died of malaria at a relatively young age. He was succeeded by his son Zheng Jing (1643–1682), who abandoned all pretense of Ming loyalty and concentrated solely on piracy and conquest.[5]

While the political loyalties of the Zheng clan are in reality far from clear, what is certain is that the Qing took them quite seriously as a military threat. After protracted negotiations failed to persuade Koxinga to follow his father's example in swearing loyalty to the empire, major military forces were dispatched to crush the rebellious pirate kingdom. In a sign of growing exasperation the Emperor actually ordered the forced evacuation of coastal Fujian and Guangdong (in 1661 and again in 1662) in an attempt to contain the threat posed by Koxinga's fleet. The "Great Clearance" lasted almost a decade and it had a major effect on the local landscape. It imposed a substantial hardship on the people of southern China. When the coastal ban was finally lifted in 1669, the government had trouble convincing people to return to the emptied regions. They even had to offer monetary inducements to recruit settlers.[6]

Some theories claim that the Hakka linguistic minority moved into the eastern and coastal areas of Guangdong following the Great Clearance. This minority group would come into violent conflict with the Cantonese speaking majority during the "Punti-Hakka Clan Wars" that lasted between 1855 and 1867.[7] Out of necessity, the Hakka people developed a number of martial arts, including Hakka Quan, Southern Praying Mantis, Bak Mei (White Eyebrow), and Dragon Style, which share some important characteristics with Wing Chun. Like Wing Chun they too began to emerge into the public view (usually in Guangzhou rather than Foshan) in the later nineteenth century. We will discuss these systems in greater depth in a later chapter.

Given all of this initial turmoil, it is remarkable that by the 1680s there was essentially no elite opposition to Qing rule. This is an important point to emphasize. The common refrain of "Overthrow the Qing, Restore the Ming," used by so many revolutionary groups in the later nineteenth century, *was not* a survival of a continuous anti-Qing movement lasting throughout this era. It had nothing to do with imaginary anti-Qing secret societies created in the image of an overly romanticized Koxinga. Rather, this is yet another example of how groups attempt to use history to legitimize their current policy grievances, and in so doing re-imagine the past.[8] While a calamity, the Ming-Qing transition was no more difficult, and in fact was probably smoother, than many other dynastic changes.

The early years of the new dynasty saw innovative and efficient government and a rapid growth of the state in terms of its economic wealth, land mass and overall population. It was also a time of remarkable political stability with no major internal conflicts arising throughout the 1700s. The fact that there were only three emperors, all gifted and dedicated individuals, probably accounts for much of the success of this early period.

Kangxi (r. 1661–1722) assumed the throne when only fifteen and proved to be a dynamic and vital leader. He loved to hunt and travel throughout the realm (often under the pretense of inspecting major public works projects). He ensured that Han Chinese scholars were brought into the government. At the same time, he expanded and solidified the inner-Asian border, reaching agreements with Russia and taking control of Mongolia and Tibet. He was open to Western learning (brought by Jesuit missionaries) and was more interested in Western ideas about mathematics and science than probably any other emperor.

Yongzheng (r. 1722–1735) had the shortest tenure of the three. Already middle-aged when he assumed office, Yongzheng focused his efforts at putting the nation on a sound financial footing. This included such projects as creating a new uniform tax code and curbing the power of the Manchu hereditary military elites.[9] Yongzheng also helped to oversee the reconstruction and rehabilitation of the Shaolin Temple in Henan.[10]

Qianlong (r. 1735–1795) benefited from the vigorous reforms of both of his forbearers. He attempted to play the part of the perfect sagely emperor and was a visible proponent of Confucian neo-orthodoxy throughout the land. He was also deeply concerned with questions of what we might now call "national identity" and tried to root out and destroy any work that referred to the Manchu people as being "alien" or "un-Chinese." In fact, it seems entirely possible that these two projects were linked, being two different aspects of his attempt to strengthen the state through the creation of a new, coherent, cultural identity.[11]

Confucian philosophy was favored precisely because it facilitated this sort of linking of identities through bonds of responsibility. Heterodox religious movements (whether Buddhist or Daoist) were problematic in that there was no separation of "church" and "state" in traditional Chinese thought. The Emperor was the head of both the cult and the kingdom. Millennial Buddhist or Daoist arguments about the need for religious reforms, or warnings of the dawning of a new kalpa (a Buddhist aeon), could not be made without at the same time questioning the emperor's ability, or right, to rule "all under heaven." Political and religious legitimacy were inseparable. Qianlong became concerned that Shaolin might be harboring heretics during the 1750s within this *specific* ideological context. Direct political revolt by the monks was never really a fear.[12]

While the regime's incentive to act against heterodox groups is easily understood, the ultimate wisdom of the policy is still being debated. In a number of cases state persecution turned relatively peaceful sutra reading societies, frequented mostly by devout senior citizens, into militant organizations forced underground in order to survive. By disrupting the ties between these new religious movements and other aspects of Chinese society, the government may have actually made them *more* susceptible to political radicalization, and hence a greater threat to the state than they ever would have been on their own. At the same time, some organizations were genuinely dangerous and needed to be controlled. From the time of Qianlong onward, the government took an increasingly hard line toward even moderate Daoist or Buddhist organizations and did everything in its power to advantage a neo-Confucian outlook.[13]

Qianlong's religious policy also seems to have been part of a broader conservative movement that dominated elite thought during much of the Qing period. Ebrey notes that some Han literati blamed the sensual excesses and cultural "confusion" of the late Ming for the state's invasion and defeat by the Qing. This conservative turn in Chinese life was complex and affected areas as diverse as family law, poetry, classical painting, and the economy.[14]

On the one hand, it was likely advantageous to the development of hand combat as it brought about renewed interest in martial matters among a certain class of young gentlemen.[15] Ensuring the physical "strength" and safety of the nation was seen as a Confucian virtue in this context. Nevertheless, to the extent that it turned China's gaze inward at precisely the same time that the European powers were beginning to expand aggressively into Asia, this conservative shift was probably detrimental to the dynasty's ultimate survival.

Whatever its long-term consequences, the cultural and political stability that the Qing brought was a great material benefit to the Chinese people. In 1651, just a few years after the inception of the dynasty, Fairbank and Goldman estimate China's population as being roughly 150 million individuals. By the middle of the nineteenth century the population had climbed to 432 million. By the 1970s that number had increased to 700 million.[16]

It should be noted that while the number of mouths to feed was increasing throughout this period, the amount of farmland was more or less fixed. While it was possible to reclaim land from lakes through elaborate construction projects, and hills could be further terraced to allow for more efficient use, these projects can take a long time and yield relatively little new farmland. By the early nineteenth century all available land was under cultivation. Sustained population growth was only made possible by increasing the per acre yield through the more intensive use of irrigation, fertilizer, and human labor.

At some point, as the land-labor ratio skews in favor of the latter, we must hit a point of diminishing returns for each additional unit of farm labor. By the mid-Qing the average family was only farming an acre or two. This drove the efficiency, and ultimately the wages, of agricultural workers down. There were simply too many hands trying to work too little land. While the population increased throughout this period, it is more difficult to guess when standards of living actually rose.[17] For a great many people, standards of living probably dropped during the middle of the nineteenth century, leading to the paradox of economic growth without development.[18]

This demographic shift had a dramatic effect on Chinese society. The peace and prosperity of the eighteenth century contributed almost directly to the Malthusian misery of the nineteenth. As farm size decreased, more sons were left without a livable inheritance. Increasingly, these individuals were pushed into elaborate systems of tenancy, but even that was not a secure existence. Large numbers of young men with few prospects of marriage found themselves entering urban areas looking for jobs in handicraft industries, or as dockworkers or porters. Others, especially in the south, took directly to the sea becoming sailors, fishermen, smugglers, or pirates. Trade with the West, centered in Guangzhou, was one bright spot in this otherwise bleak economic picture. Wealth and employment was created along the southern trade routes, though not even this could absorb all the surplus labor. These demographic and economic factors contributed directly to the breakdown of the Confucian social order that the state was trying so hard to promote.

Rebellion in the Qing Dynasty

As standards of living dropped, old social structures were disrupted, and the government found itself powerless to aid the ever-growing population in times of famine or natural disaster. Unmet expectations led to rumors that the "Mandate of Heaven" was slipping away, or that the state was facing an "end of days" millennial, or demonological, crisis. Such fears would lead to an escalating pattern of rebellion and violence throughout the nineteenth century.

The first of the serious outbursts was the White Lotus Rebellion (1794–1804). This uprising was started by a millennial Buddhist sect that was popular with the poor peasants living in the hilly and highly inaccessible regions of Hubei, Sichuan, and Shaanxi Provinces. The government had to develop a novel strategy that employed newly constructed walled villages, forced population transfers, and demanded a reliance on popular militias rather than the official Manchurian "Banner Armies," to overcome this threat. Suppressing the violence took years and cost tens of thousands of lives.

In 1813, members of another Buddhist sect, the Eight Trigrams, rebelled closer to the capital. At least 100,000 rebels actually managed to seize several cities, and they even entered the Forbidden City in Beijing, before the uprising was put down in bloody fashion. Up to 70,000 people may have died in the Eight Trigram uprising and its aftermath.[19]

This uprising also bears careful consideration as it is characterized by large-scale collaboration between religious sectarians and martial artists. This trend becomes more common as the nineteenth century progresses. One of the three leaders of the revolt was named Feng Keshan ("King of the Earth," 1776–1814?). He was a professional martial arts teacher and practitioner of Meihuaquan, or Plum Blossom Fist. While minimally interested in the religious ideology of the group, Feng was devoted to revolution and he was able to mobilize an entire network of followers through his martial arts associations. Plum Blossom boxing was commonly demonstrated and taught in the markets in Shandong and Henan Provinces. Its study was quite widespread.[20] Practitioners made use of "plum blossom poles" to perfect their footwork and balance (a training aid also used in Wing Chun). Shahar notes that this was one of the styles being taught at the Shaolin Temple.[21] While there is no evidence linking Feng Keshan to Shaolin, he is a good example of the sort of individual that the government was worried about in their eighteenth-century redesign of the monastery.

Martial artists in the Eight Trigrams movement also relied on special magical techniques to make themselves invulnerable in battle. Government records indicate that many of them practiced a technique known as the "Armor of the Golden Bell." In order to perform the technique one first had to burn incense, write a charm on a piece of paper, burn the paper, mix its ashes with water or wine, and then drink the mystical concoction. A series of ritual taboos were associated with the practice, but if correctly performed this technique was said to make one impervious to swords, spears, and in some cases even firearms. Esherick notes that the technique seems to have originated with wandering Daoist priests (who sometimes taught martial arts as part of their profession).[22]

This example further serves to illustrate exactly why the government feared the mixing of popular religious movements and the study of martial arts. Heterodox beliefs in invulnerability magic simply made the mix all the more volatile and dangerous. Religious sects would occasionally use martial arts groups as recruiting devices, but it is not always clear how close the relationship was between these two aspects of the organizations. Perhaps this is one of the reasons why there is still so much confusion about the relationship between martial arts and Chinese religious practice today. Even in the nineteenth century it was a very complicated and fluid subject with many different groups and styles coming to various accommodations.[23]

As great as the destruction was in these early uprisings, their numbers pale in comparison to the death toll generated by the Taiping (or "Great Peace") Rebellion. Spreading across much of China between 1850 and 1864, this conflict saw the destruction of six hundred cities and the deaths of up to 20 million individuals. The inspiration for the rebellion came from the south in an area that had seen much social disruption, both in terms of the Opium War and penetration by Christian missionaries. A collapse in the price of tea and the opening of new trade ports also conspired to put huge numbers of southern laborers out of work in an area best known for its secret societies, lineage feuds, and simmering ethnic tensions.[24]

Hong Xiuquan (1814–1864) mobilized and shaped these latent social tensions. An educated individual of Hakka origin, he had failed to pass the civil service exam. This is not surprising. Even though the total population had skyrocketed, the number of positions in the civil service remained fixed. By the late Qing, only 1 percent of applicants actually passed the national exams. This lack of social mobility among the educated elite was yet another source of tension and resentment in the nineteenth century.

Leaving behind his original ambition, Hong became a charismatic religious leader. In his first major vision (1837) he was visited by an old bearded man and a younger middle-aged figure who greeted him as "younger brother." Hong was instructed by the pair to fight demons.[25] As ter Haar has argued, the concern with a demonological apocalypse was a regular and growing feature of Chinese popular religion in the late eighteenth and early nineteenth centuries.

In the traditional Chinese view, best articulated by the "Classics of Mountains and Seas," the term "demon" was quite flexible. It could refer to explicitly other-worldly beings, such as those found in Buddhist cosmology, but it was also applied to the strange, barbaric, and misshapen subhumans who were thought to live beyond the "four mountains" and "four seas" that defined the ordered realm of China proper. Given that the state had been invaded from the north, was being ruled by a foreign dynasty, and that a new set of imperial powers were making their presence felt along the eastern and southern coasts, Hong's China was quite literally a land beset by "demons."[26] It did not take much of a religious imagination to see apocalyptic events on the horizon if something was not done.

If this were all that had happened, it is likely that Hong's movement would simply have ended up like many of the other once popular, but now forgotten, millennial Buddhist and Daoist sects of the later Qing. However, after running across a missionary pamphlet he had received several years earlier, Hong decided that the two men in his vision had in fact been the Christian deities, and that he was Jesus's "younger brother" tasked with a special mission for China.

Hong then turned to Christian missionaries to learn the basic technology of their religion, including new ways of worship, baptism, and prayer. He was attracted to the strict fundamentalist strain of the Old Testament, especially the parts about monotheism, destroying "idols," and the need for moral rejuvenation, including the banning of drinking, opium smoking, and the practice of female foot binding. His earlier demonological concerns were likewise reworked and the Manchurians now became the physical incarnation of the Christian "devil" that he had been sworn to destroy.

By 1851 Hong had 20,000 supporters whom he ordered to collectivize their property. He declared himself ruler of the "Heavenly Kingdom of Great Peace" and made known his intention to overthrow the state. His forces scored a number of victories in their early years and ethnic Hakkas, secret society members, and other actors who had fared poorly under the Confucian order, swelled their ranks. In 1853, they took the city of Nanjing which was defended by a force of 5,000 Banner troops. All the ethnic Manchurians in the city, including upward of 35,000 elderly men, women, and children, were rounded up and executed by gruesome means including drowning, burning, and bleeding, befitting their status as "demons."[27]

In Nanjing, Hong set up a new government which immediately called for land equalization, equality between men and women, and a new social system based on both his teachings and unique reading of the Christian Bible. Nevertheless, the situation stagnated through a combination of greed and incompetence and not much more was accomplished over the following decade. They failed to win gentry support for their social reforms, and while the Taiping government appealed to Western Christians for aid it was decided that they were only superficially Christian. The Western powers found them entirely too brutal and corrupt to support. Great Britain, which had tried to maintain neutrality for most of the conflict, ultimately sided with the Qing dynasty. For instance, when the Taiping army tried to seize Shanghai in 1860 and 1862, it was the Western powers that organized the defense of the city. In this later period, the Taiping military and civil leadership factionalized and they did not fight as effectively as they could have given their immense numbers.[28]

The rebellion was ultimately put down through the efforts of Zeng Guofan, a civil servant who managed to personally raise an army in his home province of Henan. Following the pattern established in the Opium War, he recruited local Confucian scholars as his officers. These individuals had a clear stake in the system and would likely fight to defend it. The turn toward a local, gentry-led, militia system was yet another manifestation of the conservative bent in late Qing political thought.

These local scholars were responsible for recruiting, training, and drilling the peasant-soldiers. This was often a major logistical undertaking as weapons had to be produced, food and rations needed to be stored, and insurance systems had to be put in place. Confucian schools often served as drilling grounds or the headquarters for the various units, leaving no doubt about the values that the militia was to fight to uphold.[29]

It took a decade, but ultimately Zeng's army defeated the Taipings, captured Nanjing, and quite literally left no survivors in their wake. This form of military organization, developed a few decades previously in Guangdong to deal with the British, and then perfected in the campaign against the Taipings, remained common throughout the nineteenth and early twentieth centuries.

In the early Qing period, a rough balance of power had been established between the central government (which created policies), the local gentry (who carried them out) and the masses (who paid for all of it in taxes, and might revolt if pushed too far). Alliances might be formed between any two of these groups on a given issue, assuring that no one player was able to exploit the system as a whole. This three-way balancing act was one of the things that reinforced the social and economic stability of the early Qing era.

The success of the militia movement fundamentally reordered Chinese society. As the Banner armies consistently failed in combat, the central government lost an important power base for dealing with the rest of society. It was clear that they could no longer offer basic defense or security, let alone timely famine relief. As these tasks devolved to the local gentry (who did have the wealth and connections to carry them out) the imperial government lost power and China became increasingly decentralized. In the south the gentry also tended to be the local landlords. This increase in their political influence capped off the demographic boom that allowed them to raise rents and amass huge amounts of economic power. Both the Qing dynasty and the non-educated population as a whole were the long-term losers in this power struggle.[30] Martial arts instructors, mercenaries, private security guards, and those who could offer their services to these new structures were among the winners.

The Taiping Rebellion is one of those few defining moments that clearly changed the course of a nation's history. With 20 million dead, it was, and is likely to remain, the largest and most destructive civil war in human history. It is interesting to compare it to the roughly contemporaneous American Civil War in order to better understand China's military thinking and level of technology.

Fairbank and Goldman characterize the American Civil War as history's first truly modern war, and the Taiping Rebellion as the world's last, and bloodiest, traditional conflict. Let us begin by parsing out exactly what the authors mean by this. Some of their insights will have important implications for our later discussions of armed conflict between China and the West.

At the start of the Taiping conflict, in the early 1850s, both sides were woefully under armed by modern standards. Most soldiers in both the rebel and Imperial armies were armed with only a spear and a sword. The cavalry was weak and lacked sufficient horses and, while there were a number of cannons on the battlefield, they were a hundred years behind their European counterparts. Both sides used matchlock muskets, but neither army could equip more than 20 percent of their forces with these firearms. Under these conditions, most engagements ended in hand-to-hand combat, and the higher *esprit de corps* of the Taiping units was often a deciding factor in their early victories.

After a few years the situation in China looked very different. Large numbers of muskets, and even cap-lock rifled arms, began to make their appearance. Western advisors and mercenaries were increasingly employed by both sides to improve the performance of their artillery. As the battlefield got hotter, both armies discovered the advantages of fighting from entrenched positions, just as was the case in the American Civil War. While spears, bows, and swords remained fixtures on the battlefield, the Imperial and Taiping armies of the 1860s looked, on the surface, much more similar to their Western counterparts than they had at the outset of the conflict.

Yet the quality of the weapons alone did not define the effectiveness of the Chinese military. Cutting-edge rifles and cannons could be bought in large numbers and deployed quickly. Whole ordinance factories could be purchased for a price. Yet other critical pieces of the puzzle were still missing. There were no academies to train Chinese artillery officers to the same level of expertise as their European counterparts. There was no dedicated medical corps following the Imperial army. While China did set up factories to make advanced weaponry and ammunition, it did not have efficient market and transportation structures to move this material around the country. Nor did it have the engineers to make the factories run effectively.

China did not fail in its competition with the West because its soldiers did not know how to use rifles. By the second half of the nineteenth century firearms were a well-entrenched aspect of China's martial life. Soldiers, mercenaries, bandits, and private security firms all had and used firearms. Deeper institutional factors, not specific weapons technologies, were responsible for China's problems with the West. While it is tempting to turn to quick, single-variable explanations of China's inability to deal with the threat of imperialism, any such theory is bound to fail. Technological, economic, social, and political factors all conspired to complicate China's global position. Students of martial studies must remember that China's modern schools of hand combat were all created in the era of firearms.

Western Imperialism and the Qing Response

One domestic disaster after another monopolized the attention of the Qing dynasty for much of the nineteenth century. However, the realm also faced a new foreign threat unlike anything it had yet seen. China responded inadequately to the challenges of Western imperialism because, in the late eighteenth and early nineteenth centuries, it did not yet understand the full scope of the global transformation that was then underway. Whether it liked it or not, China, through its trade in silk, tea, cotton, sugar, porcelain, spices, silver, and later opium, had become a critical player in the international global economic system. The great powers would not, and could not, continue to ignore it. The once central realm of the "Middle Kingdom" was about to find itself on the periphery of a much larger and more dangerous commercial world.

The ultimate roots of China's failure to come to terms with the Western world might lay in Confucianism's utter disdain of merchants, commerce, and anyone whose actions are motivated by greed rather than a desire for public service. No "independent" markets existed in imperial China. Instead, the state attempted to tightly control trade and then use the profits that merchants generated to advance public goals.

While there were always groups of Confucian scholars who specialized in financial matters, in general, both the Ming and Qing dynasties woefully neglected the management of their currency and trade situation. Though earlier dynasties had mastered sophisticated financial technologies like paper currency and deposit banking, neither the relatively weak Ming nor Qing states were even able to mint and circulate their own silver coinage. Taxes were paid with "ounces" of silver whose value in copper currency fluctuated significantly. [31]

Further complicating the economic situation was the fact that the Qing had banned all private international trade as being too socially disruptive. All foreign trade was routed through the "tribute" system in which a foreign power would send a delegation to Beijing bearing extensive diplomatic "gifts" (really exports), and after making a public show of accepting the Emperor's beneficent leadership, would in turn receive a rich cargo of Chinese "gifts" (imports) in return. The number of tribute missions was often limited to once a year, or once every three years.

At base, this was a political rather than a primarily economic system. It was important for the Chinese to awe their guests with their superior silks, ceramics, and other goods. The system worked well in terms of restricting the overall flow of trade and cementing relationships with other minor Asian powers. It also meant that China did not profit as much from its trade as it could have since it was always running a structural trade deficit. Lacking access to open lines of communication and the news that markets always bring, the Chinese government was left unaware of the scope and depth of changes in the world economic system.

While the tribute system may have been sufficient for managing relationships with minor states like Korea, it had real limitations when it came to dealing with the major European powers and their desire for trade. Great Britain in particular developed an insatiable thirst for Chinese tea and porcelain to serve it in, and English merchants discovered that they could sell Western cloth, yarn, and other consumer goods as well. However, the Qing government drastically restricted the scope of this trade, limiting all English trade to the southern port city of Guangzhou (referred to by the English as Canton). European traders were not allowed to actually live in the city, but instead occupied a number of "factories" (really warehouses and offices) in their own quarter during the trading season. Each foreign ship that arrived was indemnified and assigned to a family in the Canton Cohong (the merchant guild) for processing.

The British sent a diplomatic mission in 1793 led by Lord George Macartney that attempted to convince the Emperor to accept an official diplomatic mission and open trade practices based on published tariff rates, already a standard practice in Europe and the Americas. In effect, the United Kingdom was inviting the Chinese state (an important trade partner) to join the international community. The Qianlong Emperor dismissed the offer claiming that China already had "all things," and as such could have no possible need for European goods.[32]

This statement was not entirely accurate. The Chinese government wanted one British good desperately. That was silver. The government had an almost insatiable appetite for foreign silver as a means of compensating for its declining tax revenues and as a way to continue to support the military (which was very expensive, if not entirely effective). Importation of European goods were restricted not because the Chinese people were not interested in them, but to force England to continue to pay for all its imports in silver (most of which was mined and minted in Latin America), thereby creating a structural trade imbalance that stretched across three continents.

In the early days of the Chinese trade, it is unlikely that this mercantilist policy had much of an impact. But by the nineteenth century Chinese silks, porcelain, and tea were major trade goods all over the world. As an ever-greater percentage of the world's silver supply was funneled into China, the UK began to face the very real prospects of a currency crisis. This monetary imbalance set the stage for the Opium War.

Unscrupulous British merchants had discovered that there was one good that Chinese markets were willing to buy from the West, despite a number of government injunctions. That was the addictive drug opium, grown in large quantities in India. By 1838 the British were shipping 40,000 chests of the substance to China a year, almost all of it entering through the Pearl River Delta and Guangzhou.

The Chinese government was appalled. Opium created major social problems as addiction rates soared. That foreign merchants would attempt to win personal profits by destroying the health of the nation seemed to confirm all of the Confucian warnings against commerce. Further, the trade in opium totally reversed China's position in the global silver market. Now, rather than being a net importer of silver, the state was becoming a net exporter, finding itself facing exactly the same monetary dilemma as the United Kingdom a few years earlier.

In the late 1830s, the imperial court decided to do something about the opium trade in the south. They sent new officials to the region who, on their behalf, arrested large numbers of Chinese collaborators and drug addicts. They also seized and destroyed huge amounts of the drug. Foreign merchants were forced to sign pacts that they would no longer trade in opium in exchange for the right to trade in China at all.

While this was not a huge problem for some merchants, those that specialized in the opium trade were facing financial ruin. The major opium trading firm Jardine, Matheson and Company sent representatives to London to lobby for war, and even offered to loan the government ships and navigators to force the Chinese markets open.

Despite the conclusions of many Marxist historians, the British government was not overly swayed by these arguments and it did not go to war to secure the drug trade. After decades of neglect, there were many diplomatic, monetary, and trade matters at stake. War was seen as the best option for forcing a confrontation with the Chinese in which they would have to come to the bargaining table and deal with the English as equals, rather than through the insulting tribute system. The opium conflict was simply the straw that broke the camel's back.

Whatever the political justification, both sides sensed the inevitability of conflict and started to prepare for war in 1839. Chinese officials installed large numbers of cannons in the forts that protected the Pearl River, and they laid chains across the estuary leading to Guangzhou, anticipating that the brunt of the attack would fall there. Local gentry across the Pearl River Delta received reluctant imperial permission to assemble and train peasant militias that were only too willing to "expel the barbarians." Unfortunately, these countermeasures were not entirely successful.

The more experienced British simply sailed further upstream, seized two other port cities, shut down trade on the river, and disembarked troops who threatened Guangzhou itself. Sensing defeat local Chinese officials agreed to negotiate, concluding the first of what would come to be known as the "unequal treatises." Local officials ceded Hong Kong to the British and agreed to pay them the cost of their expedition (calculated at 6 million Mexican silver dollars). They also allowed British merchants to take up residence in Guangzhou itself and agreed that in the future there should be direct diplomatic meetings between officials.

This was an agreement that ultimately satisfied no one. The Emperor exiled the Governor for even allowing the war with England to come to a head, and the official who negotiated the treaty was immediately arrested and hauled to Beijing in chains. The Chinese insisted that the new governor who had been appointed was not constrained by the agreements of his predecessors. The British commanders in the region were not amused by this new approach to international law and spent years attempting to impress on the Chinese government the need to live up to their prior treaty agreements, no matter who happened to be in office. The question of whether or not foreigners could take up residence in Guangzhou became particularly charged and led to the emergence of what was later known as the "Entry Crisis."

For their part, the British public felt that not nearly enough had been done to secure their country's commercial position given the vast expense of mounting the expedition in the first place. The next year, in 1841, they sent twice as many soldiers (10,000), seized several coastal cities including Shanghai, and besieged Nanjing. The Qing dynasty was forced to sign another (although not the last) treaty at bayonet point. The Cohong was to be abolished, a public tariff of 5 percent was to be imposed on all goods, "Most Favored Nation" trade status was to be honored (essentially forcing free trade on the Chinese), British subjects were only to be tried under British law, and the total Chinese war debt was raised to 21 million ounces of silver. China was also forced to open five additional ports to British trade. Soon other European powers were maneuvering for treaty ports of their own. Even Japan was able to seize territory by the end of the nineteenth century.[33]

Given the ultimately disastrous outcome of the Opium Wars, one would not think that great narratives of national strength would arise from this period. Nevertheless, some saw reason for hope in the growing village militia movement, which really got its start in southern China. Guangdong Province, because of fierce competition for scarce land and other resources, had a long history of family lineage organizations (which could own land corporately) raising militias and carrying on armed feuds with each other.[34] Instability in the economy made unemployment a real problem, and it was not uncommon for unemployed, or underemployed, workers to supplement their income with either banditry on land or piracy along the coasts and rivers.

The local gentry had experience in raising and training militias to deal with these problems. The threat of foreign invasion, and the clear incompetence of national Banner troops, who often caused more damage to the countryside than they prevented, strengthened this movement and won it carefully circumscribed imperial approval. For its part, Beijing was simply happy to see the raising of reliable troops that it did not have to pay for, thereby lowering overall budget expenditures.

The militia movement received a major boost from the "San Yuan Li Incident" in May of 1841. The historical record is mixed as both sides claim victory, and while Chinese folklore records the incident as a major victory with huge numbers (possibly "hundreds") of causalities, the British remember it as only a minor skirmish that happened in the middle of their march out of Canton after having, once again, defeated the city.

On May 24, as part of the 1841 campaign, the British military commenced its second attack on Guangzhou in as many years. The Chinese government had recently increased the number of cannon forts around the city. However, once the British infantry succeeded in overrunning these positions they were able to bombard the Chinese with their own artillery. The city surrendered once again (paying 6 million ounces of silver this time) and in an attempt to limit damage British commanders ordered their army not to enter the city, but to instead withdraw from the region since the dispute had now been settled.[35]

As the British forces marched out of the region, local militias continued to gather in anticipation of the already concluded battle. Having missed the main engagement, outlying hamlets and villages continued to send their men to rallying points. At the same time Chinese Banner Army reinforcements from other provinces began to withdraw from the region as well. Rumors of rape and pillage started to circulate throughout the countryside. In all honesty it seems that the Qing army was at least as responsible for any irregularities as the better-disciplined British forces, but the Chinese population held the "black" units of the English army (actually composed of ethnic Indians) in special contempt. All the while local militia forces continued to gather.

On May 30th a force of 8,000 militia members attacked a British column and forced it take up a position and engage them. The Chinese militia was armed mostly with spears, short swords, and shields. The majority of British troops appear to have been armed with late pattern Brown Bess muskets. The British counteroffensive was initially successful. However, the weather turned, and in the pouring rain the flintlock mechanism on the muskets failed to ignite reliably, crippling the effectiveness of the British troops.

Showing a stunning lack of leadership the militia forces, which clearly had both the numerical and tactical advantage, did not strike. Instead, its officers decided to hold back waiting for more reinforcements. There is every possibility that if the Chinese had attacked during the rain they would have massacred the British troops, who would have been no match for the well-drilled militia. Spears are greatly superior to bayonets and rifle butts in this sort of close quarters combat.[36]

The delay in the battle instead allowed the British to deploy units of Indian soldiers armed with the more modern and effective Brunswick rifle. The Brunswick was designed as a replacement for the venerable Bakers rifle of Napoleonic War fame. It employed a belted ball system where ridges on the lead ball fit into two shallow groves in the barrel that provided the rifling. This system could be difficult to load in the hands of inexperienced troops, and those who did not actually use it often criticized the Brunswick, probably unfairly. In the hands of well-trained troops the rifle seems to have performed well. More importantly, the Brunswick rifle did away with the old flintlock ignition system and replaced it with a "modern" enclosed cap that was impervious to the rain.³⁷

Once the Brunswick-armed troops deployed, the encircled unit was rescued and the army's main camp was secured. British military reports indicate that in total one soldier died during the "San Yuan Li Incident," and fifteen others were injured. To the extent that the action is remembered at all, it is probably most significant as a successful test of the Brunswick rifle system. The only objective lesson about the militia system that one can glean from the actual battle records is that a unit will be no more competent than its leaders, and good Confucian scholars do not always make the most aggressive field officers.

If the study of martial arts has taught us anything, it is that history rarely stands in the way of a good story. Perhaps buoyed by their own small losses, rumors and glorious retellings of the events began to circulate in the Chinese camps the next morning. In official reports to Chinese officers, the number of reported British deaths rose to a dozen. Among the militia units themselves there was talk of a hundred dead or dying British soldiers, all the victims of the superior martial skill and righteousness of the village militias.

Soon what had been a resounding defeat at Guangzhou followed by an aborted engagement against an already withdrawing foe was recast as a great military victory in which the people of China took their fate in their own hands and "expelled" the barbarians even when the Qing could not. These rumors made their way back up the chain of command and were actually believed.³⁸

Beijing probably "learned" exactly the wrong lessons from the San Yuan Li Incident. For the most part the gentry-led militias were more effective than the Banner armies. Yet the belief that an uprising of "the people" could expel the foreigners was dangerous. It probably colored perceptions of the imperialist threat, and may have hindered the formation of more effective national strategies of economic and military reorganization.

Certainly indulging this fantasy during the Boxer Uprising (1898–1901), when the court decided to support a violent anti-foreign uprising, led to disaster. Backed only by an underfed and unorganized "peasant army," the Dowager Empress literally declared war on the entire industrialized world in an attempt to "expel the barbarians" from China. All of this ended with very predictable results. Within a few weeks of mobilization, the Western militaries had massacred the poorly led peasant Boxers, forced the court to flee in exile and imposed previously unthinkable demands on these Chinese people.³⁹

The Pearl River Delta: Conflict and the Spread of the Martial Arts

Our historical overview has brought us repeatedly to the Pearl River Delta region in the mid-nineteenth century. Events that were triggered in this region, such as the Opium War and the Taiping Rebellion, marked the path by which China would enter the modern world. They also defined the energetic, dynamic, chaotic, and often quite bloody backdrop against which most of the modern southern schools of kung fu would emerge. Even if a specific art had antecedents in the Ming dynasty, this cauldron both shaped these systems and created an immense demand for martial instruction.

Two things set this geographic area apart from the rest of the China. The first of these is the centrality of trade and commerce, rather than subsistence farming, to the local economy. While trade happened on some scale everywhere, the cities of Foshan and Guangzhou constituted one of late imperial China's truly great commercial centers. Second, southern China has a number of unique cultural and linguistic institutions. Perhaps none was more commented on at the time than the ubiquitous "lineage associations," each with its own family temple. The strength of Guangdong's lineage associations determined much of the character and quality of life in the province throughout the nineteenth century.

Let us first begin by exploring the general economic background of the province, and the commercial economy that came to be concentrated in Guangzhou. Guangdong Province is bordered on the south by the Pacific Ocean and on the north by a tall and imposing range of mountains that make overland travel and trade with central China difficult. A number of streams and tributaries divide these tall mountain valleys and combine to create the Pearl River that empties into the ocean near present-day Hong Kong. In the process of flowing to the sea the river deposits the sediments that it is carrying, creating the rich farmland that characterizes the "Pearl River Delta" region.

For much of China's early imperial history Guangdong Province was a sparsely inhabited hinterland. The area was lush and fertile, making it possible to harvest two rice crops a year, but the cultural and military authority of the Chinese state did not extend much beyond the walls of the administrative center in the provincial capital. Most of the tribal peoples who lived in the region did not speak Chinese and were not considered imperial subjects. Guangzhou's easy access to the Pacific did make it a major trade hub, and much business was conducted with the Middle East. The city even had an "Arab quarter" to accommodate all of the foreign merchants.[40]

Slowly, Chinese cultural influence spread throughout the region, and the population began to increase. Both of these processes accelerated during the Ming and Qing dynasties, when the importation of new technologies and new food crops, specifically sweet potatoes and peanuts, made it possible to increase the food supply by planting marginal hill land that had been previously ignored. In 1787, the population of Guangdong Province was estimated at 16 million individuals. By 1812, that number had risen to 19 million, and by the 1850s (our main period of interest) there were over 28 million individuals living in the region.[41]

Similar trends were at work in other places in southern China. Fujian Province went through a large population boom, and actually ended up exporting people to Guangdong throughout the Qing dynasty. Nevertheless, by the mid-nineteenth century there was no region of China more densely populated than the Pearl River Delta. In 1850, there were 284 people per square mile across the entire province (much of which was mountainous), and the average individual farmer could only work about one-quarter acre of land. A booming population and severe land scarcity would lead to recurring social tensions throughout the nineteenth century.

Given the extremely high value of land, most peasants in the rich alluvial delta region switched from growing staple grains (mainly rice) to cash crops during the nineteenth century. The most important of these crops was silk, which was produced through an innovative process in which patty fields were converted to mulberry plantations. Fish ponds, in which carp were grown for commercial sale, were then placed under the trees. The fish waste could be used as fertilizer for the mulberry trees, which in turn produced leaves that fed the silk worms. The cocoons were processed into raw silk thread on some farms; others would simply sell them to intermediaries. Silk farming (sericulture) was important in the regions around Foshan, and this cash crop was a vital source of income for many farm families. Still, the wide-scale shift to cash crops meant that Guangdong could not feed itself and was dependent on rice imported from other areas of China to meet its basic needs. The high cost of food was another factor contributing to social instability later in the Qing dynasty.[42]

By the mid-nineteenth century Guangdong's economy was entirely trade dependent. Over half of all imports received in Guangzhou were basic foodstuffs including rice, beans, and bean cake, on which much of the population depended. Other imports included European wool yarn, cotton thread, cotton cloth, and large amounts of opium. The local economy's top exports were silk garments, raw silk, black tea, sugar, and tobacco.[43]

The ever-expanding flows of trade imposed both costs and benefits on the local population. The greatest benefits were economic. Many jobs were created in the tradable goods sector, and there was always a great demand for porters, sailors, and factory workers in Guangzhou. Foreign ideas and fashions inevitably seeped into the local environment creating a vibrant, if not always peaceful, atmosphere.

Unfortunately, the centrality of trade also brought social instability and unemployment when the global tea or silk markets suffered reverses. The delta's importance to world trade also made it one of the first targets of European imperialism during the Opium Wars. Piracy remained a serious and persistent problem throughout much of the nineteenth century.

Some pirates were simply bandits in boats that attempted to attack and ransack other vessels. Occasionally, freebooters would form larger fleets that would work cooperatively and could be quite dangerous, at times attacking and destroying fortified towns. One particularly industrious set of pirates actually disguised themselves as imperial customs officers and began collecting duties from local merchants.

Perhaps no social problem has been as pervasive and destructive in Chinese history as banditry. Given the importance of waterborne transportation and communication to Guangdong's economy, we should not be surprised to see piracy filling this traditional niche. An examination of the Guangdong provincial archives, captured by Lord Elgin and currently held in London, shows that pirate attacks were probably more common than land-based bandit raids throughout the first half of the 19th century.[44]

The other defining characteristic that set the South apart was the strength of its clans and "lineage associations." Clans and lineage structures certainly existed in other parts of China. Yet in Guangdong Province a change in ritual observance had made it possible for these family groupings to act almost like corporations, buying and holding huge amounts of land, and occasionally coming into both legal and physical conflict over resources with other lineage groups. Visitors to the south frequently commented on the strength of these local lineage associations.

A lineage association is fundamentally defined by the existence of a central temple or hall that holds the tablets listing the clan's ancestors. Imperial law dictated that commoners could only venerate up to four generations of their own ancestors in home shrines. However, during the Ming dynasty the creation of temples dedicated to an important clan ancestor (often a civil servant or degree holder) became popular. Old ancestral tablets, no longer used in home shrines, could then be moved to this central hall where they took on a new social, rather than strictly religious, significance. The creation of this central communal space allowed many distantly related branches of the family to share the same ritual observances, and it generally strengthened clan identity.[45]

The clan temple was supported with specially held land that could be rented out to tenant farmers, and the revenue generated was then applied to things like maintaining the sanctuary, paying for the education of clan members, or paying their expenses when they traveled to take the civil service exams. Relief funds for the poor, disabled, sick, and injured were also funded through these land holdings. In many instances the profits were simply plowed into the acquisition of ever greater amounts of land.

The economic relationships created by these lineage organizations were not always benign. Often the clan's land was rented to the poorest members of the lineage who could not afford farms of their own. They would sometimes be charged usurious rents for the privilege of farming the clan's land. In his study of the local agricultural economy, Lin argues that much of the worst landlord-tenant exploitation in Guangdong actually happened within families that were ostensibly related to one another through the clans.[46] Thus, the lineage system, while unifying individuals around a common corporate identity, also tended to create "class" tensions between the leading families of the lineage who collected the rents (and were almost always members of the gentry), and the poorer members of the group who paid them and had little chance for social advancement.

Lineage associations also came into conflict with each other as they fought over land and water rights. Clan wars were actually quite common throughout southern China during the nineteenth century. Lineage associations had their own militias and it was not unusual for these paramilitary forces to clash. If a member of a rival clan was killed in the conflict, and the state was brought into the affair, the offending clan would often turn over a "forfeit," one of its members who was already wanted for another crime, to take the fall for the group as a whole.

One of the things that made clan conflict so destructive in Guangdong was the active participation of the gentry in the planning, training, executing, and covering up of these events. This group's command resources allowed violence to be sustained on a greater scale than was seen elsewhere. In other parts of China the links between the clans and the local gentry were much weaker. In the south these two sets of institutions became tightly intertwined.

If disputes began to escalate it was common for clans to hire outsiders, such as mercenaries or secret societies, to fight for them. The frequency of clan-based violence was one of the things that actually kept the clans together, despite the internal economic exploitation that they facilitated. No one wanted to abandon the support and physical protection that they afforded in a violent environment. Lineage associations became the single-most important institution of mass social organization in Guangdong.[47]

Geomantic rules dictated that there were a limited number of auspicious sites for the building of temples, and many of the smaller and weaker families simply could not afford to buy a building site. Nor did they have much in the way of resources to pool to begin with. The institutional strength and aggression of the larger clans impeded the social mobility of these smaller families by driving up the price of land, effectively trapping them in an economically subordinate position. These facts notwithstanding, there were a surprisingly large number of fully fledged clan associations. The medium-sized commercial town of Foshan had a whopping 420 lineage temples by the mid-nineteenth century.[48] It was this social and military organization, already embedded in every clan structure, which allowed for the creation of the larger multi-village militias.

The Opium War actually damaged the lineage association system in some subtle but important ways. The creation of larger militias allowed gentry from one town to work closely with their counterparts from another city, and to see how much they really had in common. Likewise, peasants from different areas were given a venue in which they could compare notes and discover how much they had in common as well, especially compared to the literati-landlord officers who commanded them. In short, the creation of larger military units allowed for the creation of a proto-class consciousness that upset the balance of power within the existing clan structures.

Increasingly, the gentry seized control of lineage organizations through their role as militia leaders, and they used these military forces to shape society to their ideological and economic liking. At the same time, disaffected peasants were less likely to associate with lineage structures. They turned instead to other groups, especially secret societies, for protection, support, and a sense of belonging that the traditional clans could no longer offer.[49]

The term "secret society" covers a lot of ground in Chinese history. There have always been many different sorts of illicit organizations that pop up in diverse times and places. These groups can be built around criminal, religious, or political goals and they may have been more or less active in their opposition to the state. For instance, the White Lotus Society was critical to the overthrow of the Yuan dynasty and the creation of the Ming regime.

During the nineteenth century secret societies once again become a critical problem, particularly in Guangdong and Fujian. The most famous of these groups was the Tiandihui, or the "Heaven and Earth Society." A number of other groups existed as well and they are often referred to collectively as the "Triads." Secret societies play a prominent role in the stories surrounding many southern kung fu styles, but they are often romanticized beyond the point of recognition in these accounts. Luckily, there is now vibrant academic literature on the history and sociology of these groups that portrays them in a much more realistic light.[50] Students of martial arts history would do well to ground themselves in this more rigorous literature before accepting much of what is commonly repeated on the subject.

Murray, Ownby, and ter Haar all agree that what set the secret societies of the nineteenth century apart from their predecessors was the emergence of a new institutional framework. Sometime late in the eighteenth century the old Chinese custom of forming sworn brotherhoods (for whatever purpose) through blood oaths was combined with the equally important tradition of village-level mutual support societies. Again, these support groups could be formed for a wide variety of purposes, ranging from mutual aid in the face of banditry or extortion, to pooling money for small business loans. The original Triads emerged out of a combination of these two traditions.

A large number of these newly formed secret societies turned to banditry and even rebellion, but this was probably a reflection of the breakdown of the local social and economic order in the early nineteenth century rather than an expression of any long running political agenda. As both ter Haar and Antony have demonstrated, the distrust of the Qing dynasty seen in the rhetoric and mythology of these groups can be traced directly to apocalyptic religious movements within popular culture that emerged late in the eighteenth century.[51] The calls to "overthrow the Qing" heard throughout the nineteenth century are more complicated in their origin than many modern martial artists realize. Nor does it appear that any of these groups had any serious plans to "restore the

Ming," other than perhaps to declare themselves the spiritual inheritors of the Ming political legacy.[52]

One of the things that is most striking about nineteenth-century secret societies is that, despite the fact that these groups had many different names and origins, they all shared a broadly similar creation myth. This narrative places the origins of the secret societies within the walls of the Shaolin Temple. A variety of investigative documents allow us to reconstruct multiple versions of this story, and the initiation rituals that accompanied it from the early and mid-nineteenth century.

New initiates into the Triads were instructed that in 1674 the monks of the Shaolin Temple (whose location varies between accounts) received a request from the Qing government. The Emperor asked them to assist in the conquest of a group of Western barbarians. In acknowledgment of their help, he granted the monks a special seal.

Sixty years later a local official saw and coveted the valuable imperial seal while visiting the temple. He convinced the new Emperor that the monks were a threat and that they were planning a revolt. The Manchurian Banner Army surrounded the temple and, with the help of a traitor whose identity again varies depending on the version of the story being told, managed to burn the monastery to the ground. One hundred eight monks escaped with the seal through a burning hole in the side of the temple wall. This act is often depicted as a fiery "rebirth."

The Banner troops gave chase and picked them off one-by-one as they fled. A small group of survivors came to a river, and a bridge mysteriously appeared, allowing them to cross. This same bridge is also a pivotal symbol in the initiation ritual enacted by new members of the Triads. The Qing army (which had now taken on all of the characteristics of a supernatural demonic entity) continued its onslaught until there were only five monks left. They escaped onto a high mountain and there discovered (again circumstances vary) an incense burner floating on a stream with the following inscription, "Oppose the Qing dynasty and restore the Ming dynasty."

The inscription on the heavenly treasure serves to emphasize that, while the monks had been loyal citizens, they were betrayed by the very power structure that they tried to serve. While they were now rebels, no one could accuse them of being disloyal. This would have been a familiar sentiment to many of the new recruits joining secret societies in the mid-nineteenth century. They too must have felt let down by their clans and communities. To restore proper order, the monks received divine sanction to battle against the government which they had once supported.

In the story the monks are then joined by a number of other mysterious individuals, the five "Tiger Generals," each of which stands at the head of a heavenly army tasked with fighting demons (the Qing) and a mysterious boy who is identified as a Ming prince. Unfortunately, the great battle with the Qing army ends in defeat. The brotherhood of monks is forced to flee, this time splitting up and spreading their message throughout southern China where they once again seek to raise a secret army.[53] In short, the founding myth of the Triads is a "fall from grace" story, utilizing the Shaolin motif, which holds out the promise of a future restoration of good order within the kingdom.

New members would be given this account as they were initiated into a local group or cell. Parts of this story were ritually and theatrically enacted, and a blood oath was administered. At the end of the ceremony all of the entrants received a new name (Hong), showing that in a very real way they were creating their own artificial lineage structure, complete with ancestral tablets and sacrifices. It is remarkable the degree to which ancestral lineages permeated popular thought in Guangdong Province. Rather than rebelling against these structures and the ideology that supported and upheld them, those on the fringes of society attempted to use myth and ritual to appropriate the social power of these institutions for their own anti-systemic purposes.

Triad novices would then receive a printed piece of yellow silk or paper testifying that they were members of the groups and entitled to certain rights. Which rights they received was often a function of how much they paid for their initiation. Those who paid the least were protected from exploitation by the group, and might be asked to join certain "business ventures" in the future. If you paid more, you might receive the necessary training and books to carry out initiations yourself, and make a substantial profit by doing so.

Legal records demonstrate that many people joined secret societies hoping to make money by selling initiations.[54] This does not necessarily mean that they disbelieved the story that they were spreading. Instead, the secret societies operated almost as independent franchises might today. This flexibility in their structure was one of the things that allowed them to spread so quickly. It also ensured that large-scale coordinated actions between cells would be tricky as there were no firm lines of vertical communication.

Nineteenth-century secret societies and martial artists both made use of the myth of the Shaolin Temple. However, the two groups did not use the story in quite the same way. Hand combat schools had no elaborate initiatory rights of passages comparable to the theatrical reenactments that we see in the Triads. The elements of the story that are the most important to secret society members—the imperial seal, mysterious bridge, incense burner, the appearance of the five Tiger Generals, and the revealing of a lost Ming heir—are all completely missing from the simpler accounts given in martial arts traditions.

How these two variants of the Shaolin myth relate to each other remains a critical puzzle. It has often been noted by scholars that when comparing two different versions of the same document, the one that is shorter and less clear in its meaning is almost always the older tradition. This is a counterintuitive finding. We are used to thinking of things as having existed in some perfect state in the past, and as they are passed down from one set of hands to another, elements are lost or confused.

It turns out that this expectation is the problem. When documents are transmitted, either orally or in written form, there is a very strong temptation to resolve or "clean up" any points of ambiguity in the original text. Resolving these problems inevitably means expanding the text, and over a number of generations, these expansions can become quite extensive. When faced with two texts or coexisting traditions, scholars often taken the shorter and less developed as being the primary source.

Ter Haar has attempted to undertake a historical study of the relationship between the versions of the Shaolin myth circulating in the secret societies and the hand combat schools. He notes, for instance, that the oldest references that we have to the "Heaven and Earth Society" dates to the 1786 Lin Shuangwen rebellion in Taiwan. The first written references to the Shaolin myth among secret societies do not appear until the 1810s. Of course, there was always a certain amount of overlap between the world of professional martial artists and organized crime. A number of the leaders of the Red Turban Revolt were noted martial artists. Ter Haar draws on these facts and concludes that the secret societies borrowed the preexisting mythos of the burning of the Shaolin Temple from martial arts schools in the early nineteenth century. Although he devotes more time and energy to investigating the Triad narratives than the martial ones, his conclusions still deserve careful consideration.[55]

While secret societies had been an unpleasant fact in Guangdong Province for some time, increased economic pressures and frictions within lineage associations during the mid-nineteenth century swelled their ranks. Disenfranchised members of society's lower classes either turned to bandit groups in the hills or joined secret societies in urban areas. The outbreak of the Taiping rebellion only exacerbated the situation.

While Guangdong was not directly affected by the fighting, the conflict drastically increased the province's tax burden as it was expected to contribute to the war effort.

Just as the government was making greater demands on society, its losses on the battlefields made it look increasingly weak. Rumors that the "Mandate of Heaven" had been withdrawn began to circulate. This combination of lost prestige and increased extraction led directly to the outbreak of tax revolts across the province.

The trouble really began in April of 1853. Emboldened by the general sense of chaos, Triads in Guangzhou (the provincial capital) began to operate in the open, kidnapping merchants, extorting rich families, posting anti-government placards, and even imposing their own "taxes" directly on the citizens of the city. Collusion among low-level clerks and runners was a real problem that further impeded the government's ability to respond to the crisis. The suburbs of the capital became active combat zones characterized by heavy barricades, militia patrols, and fortified armed households.

The first major tax revolt also occurred that April when city officials began to demand more than their normal "cut" from the powerful (and criminal) gambling guild. In retaliation the gamblers formed an alliance with the "Small Sword Society" (one of the numerous Triad groups in the region) and immediately clashed with the government. After one inconclusive battle, the newly formed rebel group advanced rapidly up the eastern branch of the Pearl River, cutting off communication between the capital and the town of Huicho.

The presence of rebels in the area inspired the local clans to renew their own tax protests, and the poorer lineages openly aligned themselves with the secret societies. Ye Mingchen, the governor general, was afraid of the tax revolt spreading. This would cripple not just Guangdong but the Empire as a whole at a time when its finances were already badly stressed. The imperial resistance to the newly created Taiping government was basically being funded by Guangdong's tax revenues. A sustained revolt in the south might have devastating implications for Beijing. For this reason the Governor ordered that an example be made of the offenders. Almost immediately things spiraled out of control.

Banner troops slaughtered entire villages throughout the region, killing men, women, and children indiscriminately. This carnage only turned the remaining population against the government. A professional smuggler and secret society member named Ho Liu vowed to avenge his brother's murder during the initial tax revolt. He named himself the

"Avenger of Sorrow" and began to raise an army in the volatile eastern highlands. In 1854 he ordered his troops to attack the county seat of Tungkuan (Dongguan). News of these events spread like wildfire and almost every secret society in Guangdong went into open rebellion. Bandits, more interested in spoils than politics, streamed out of the hills and attacked both cities and towns throughout the province. The Governor General's rash action in the eastern highlands had precipitated the Red Turban Revolt.[56]

During the first month of the uprising, armies led by secret societies captured a number of cities and towns to the north, east, and west of Guangzhou. It was clear that the capital was in danger of being cut off from communication with the outside world. Possibly the most ominous event was the fall of Foshan, a city approximately fifteen miles to the southwest, which sat at the nexus of two major tributaries of the Pearl River.

While surrounded by rich farmland, most of which was dedicated to sericulture, Foshan was a predominantly commercial and industrial city. There was no formal census in imperial China and this complicates population estimates, especially for smaller cities. The government registered entire households for tax and labor conscription purposes. David Faure, who has probably done more research on the history of this city than any other Western historian, reports that in 1752 the city had approximately 30,000 households. Following the conventions of the day, and assuming an average household size of six individuals, that would place the population of Foshan somewhere around 180,000 persons.[57] Wakeman, in his account of the crisis that gripped the city in the 1850s, places its population in the 200,000 to 300,000 range. This seems like a reliable figure, and even the most inflated estimates do not imagine the city as having more than half a million residents at the time of the revolt.[58]

While often overlooked today, in the nineteenth century Foshan was considered one of the four most important commercial towns in the entire country. It served as a secondary manufacturing hub that supplied the goods necessary to sustain Guangzhou's increasingly urban population while processing other commodities for international and domestic consumption. Its major industries included the production of cotton textiles, rattan, brassware, cassia, silk, and pottery (which was particularly well-regarded).[59] However, its most important industries all centered on the iron works. The city sat near a rich ore deposit and produced a wide assortment of goods including cast-iron pots and stoves, nails, wire, and even steel blades. Foshan held the imperial iron monopoly and thousands of merchants were forced to travel from across the country to buy its wares.⁶⁰ There were also armories and cannon foundries in Foshan that made it a strategic target for both the government and the rebels.

Unlike other farming towns in the region that were organized around a single lineage structure—where all the residents usually shared the same surname—Foshan was a "temple town." The city itself surrounded the Beidi Temple, dedicated to the Northern Emperor and later to the Perfect Warrior. This sanctuary (often called the Ancestral Temple) was the central hub of urban life. There were also a number of specialized markets spread throughout the city and industries tended to cluster in neighborhoods.

The original inhabitants of Foshan had a reputation for being independent and willing to fight to defend themselves. In 1449, the town was attacked by the rebel general Huang Xiaoyang. The various neighborhoods mustered a local defense and actually managed to drive him off. In 1452, the Emperor awarded Foshan the title "Neighborhood of Loyalty and Righteousness." These events are often noted as the foundation of the town's unique martial heritage. The twenty-two leaders of the resistance were commemorated with their own special hall built beside the Beidi Temple.⁶¹

Foshan itself likely began as a collection of markets that expanded as the region's commercial interests grew. It was not an administrative or political center and, as such, the town was never walled. Given its location, wealth, and strategic industries, this lack of permanent fortification was a cruel quirk of fate.

The city seems to have undergone rapid population growth in the first half of the nineteenth century with a number of its residents emigrating from other places in Guangdong and Fujian Provinces to do business. This is illustrated by the fact that there were a great number of "hometown" guilds in Foshan that catered to these expatriate businesspersons.⁶² Note for instance that Leung Jan, a seminal figure in the history of Wing Chun, and Wong Fei Hung, an equally important figure to Hung Gar, both moved to Foshan in order to establish medical practices.⁶³ This pattern seems typical of the transient and professional demographic that made up much of the city's population during the later Qing.

Foshan is probably best known as the "home" of Cantonese opera. Also known as Guangdong opera, this dynamic and vital style of performance is set apart by its use of elaborate costumes, large repertoire, interest in martial based stories, and performance in the local dialect. This last characteristic has tended to limit the appeal of the art form.

At the same time, Cantonese opera has shown dynamism and a willingness to innovate that often makes it a subject of interest among serious opera fans.

There are records of opera performances in the Guangzhou/Foshan area from the Han dynasty onward. However, the late Ming was the critical era in forming the opera traditions that were still present in the 1850s. Yuan-style opera, with its ten different types of characters, was still popular in Foshan and more emphasis than usual seems to have been put on military stories. There is even a local tradition that operatic performance played an important role in the city's defenses during the Ming period. One story relates that when Huang Xiaoyang attacked the city in 1449 the local officials encouraged the residents to dress in military costumes and march back and forth beating drums all day, thereby hiding the relatively small number of regular troops actually stationed in the city. The *Foshan Patriots Archive* (Daoguang Period) contains another, more enigmatic, story dealing with the same period:

> When Huang Xiaoyang attacked again many villages in other places were destroyed. However, the people in Foshan built wooden fences and defended [the city for] several months. The enemies saw a giant figure with Yuan style clothes and a huge sword in his hand. The enemies were frightened by the giant and escaped. It can be said that those Cantonese opera actors in Foshan defeated some of their enemies by "performance."[64]

The implication of this story seems to be that the people made a giant figure of a warrior, dressed in a Yuan-era opera costume, which demoralized a group of invading soldiers. The creation of giant, sometimes fearsome, puppets is a common aspect of popular religion in southern China. These figures are sometimes paraded through the neighborhood in military processions as part of a temple's regular cycle of observances. Whatever the reality of these events, it is clear that by the Qing dynasty they were part of a robust local folklore tradition claiming that through "psychological operations" operatic imagery had helped to save the city in its time of greatest need.

Many costumes, plays, and historical records relating to the Cantonese opera were lost in the fires of the Red Turban Revolt. Yet some facts remain, and the later Qing incarnation of these same traditions allow us to make some fairly reasonable guesses as to what life on the

"Red Boats" was really like. To begin with, while the best opera performers had a chance to gain substantial fame, the Confucian class structure relegated them to the absolute bottom of the social world. People were thought of as belonging to the "better classes," composed of civilians, soldiers, merchants, and salt manufacturers, or the "mean classes," including slaves, laborers, boat people, prostitutes, and actors. This was an important distinction as members of the "mean classes" could not sit for the civil service exams, and thus one of the major avenues of social mobility was closed to them and their children.[65]

It was a common practice for theater groups to buy young children (almost always boys) from impoverished peasant families. These boys would then be subjected to years of often harsh training in acting, singing, and martial arts—the basic skills of the opera world. Traditionally, both masculine and feminine roles were performed by male actors. Huang Renhua has attempted to reconstruct the original Cantonese opera canon, and has found that the vast majority of the plays performed (probably between 60 and 70 percent) were "action-based" performances that prominently displayed martial arts feats. The remaining 30 percent of plays tended to revolve around vocal performance.[66]

Given the intense competition between various opera troops, and the centrality of martial arts to these performances, different actors competed with each other to bring new and innovative combat techniques to the stage. Often these actors would seek out famous kung fu teachers and become accomplished martial artists in their own right. Lin Yu, in his volume *Traditional Guangdong Opera Art* states that, "The southern [operatic] tradition is full of showy forms, such as Fist, Sword, Staff, 108 Style Fists, Six and a Half Point Pole, Monkey King Staff, Nunchaku, Broadsword, Sudden Thrust, Monk Stick, Buddha Palm, Double Whips, Sword Whip, Long Thread Fist, Flower Fist, Triple Forks, Double Spears, and Cynanche Spear."[67]

Opera performances often became centers for gambling and other illicit activities. In fact, these antisocial associations were one of the reasons why the neo-Confucian gentry tended to persecute opera troupes. Travel was also dangerous as there were bandits on the land and pirates in the water that might harass opera companies or attempt to charge them "tolls." Nor were these groups likely to receive much sympathy or support from the already overstretched government. This combination of practical need and intense competition between troupes helped to make the Cantonese opera scene a veritable incubator for southern martial arts.

One of the more common theories of the origins of Wing Chun revolves around the opera companies.

> Yat Chan Um Chu (Yi Chen), a high ranking monk on Mount Heng in Hunan Province,[68] taught Cheung Ng (Zhang Wu or "Tan Sao Ng"), a fighting actor in the Xiang-Kun opera troupe. Tan Sao is a style of Wing Chun and it can be often seen in Cantonese opera. The Qing government wanted to arrest Cheung Ng and he had to run away and hide in Foshan's Qionghua Hall.
>
> Cheung Ng taught Wing Chun to Wong Wah Bo, a fighting actor of the Cantonese opera. Wong Wah Bo taught it to Leung Jan, and then Wing Chun was spread throughout Foshan. Because Cheung Ng was both a martial arts master and professional performer, he integrated unarmed combat, singing, performance and other skills to reform Cantonese opera.
>
> At first, his singing style was not different from Chin opera, Yiyang opera and Kunshan opera. He combined some other local operas styles and added in martial arts. His opera was special for the integration of Wing Chun, Shaolin martial arts, Taiji, Eagle Claw and Chi Kung.[69] Guangdong opera acquired its distinguishing features from then on. Cheung Ng (Zhang Wu) was then worshiped as the "Lord of Fighting Actors" of the Cantonese opera.[70]

Cantonese opera in Foshan organized itself through a professional guild. During the reign of Emperor Jiajing (1522–1566) a central meeting place, called the Qionghua Guild Hall, was constructed in Dajiwei. The building was used to train local performers, as well as providing a space to organize and manage the different opera troupes. A stone stele was erected near the river that read "Qionghua Ford" and this was the launching point for the boats that carried the traveling opera troupes throughout the province.[71] By establishing a central guildhall where offerings could be made to the gods and "ancestors" of the art, Foshan essentially claimed to be the home of Cantonese opera.

Like other marginal and commercial groups, the opera troupes began to come under increasing pressure from the government in 1853 and 1854. Li Wen Mao was a well-known member of the Fenghuangyi troupe in the 1840s and early 1850s. He was said to be a strong individual and had a good voice. Li was most famous for playing the role of Zhang

Fei, a brave but uncivilized hero in the *Romance of the Three Kingdoms*. Li's original loyalties and connections with revolutionary politics are unknown, but a legend states that in 1853 an official of the Taiping government in Nanjing sent an agent to Guangdong seeking to stir up the various anti-government groups. This agent's diplomacy gave Li Wen Mao a chance to meet with Chen Kai, a local chief of the Heaven and Earth Society.

Nothing happened that year. The following year, in 1854, Li and his troupe were performing in Foling when they became entangled in a serious dispute with tax collectors. For reasons that are still not entirely clear, Li went into open rebellion and began to organize the local opera companies into a fighting force.

Readers should recall that as these events are taking place in Foling, rebel armies are encircling and threatening Guangzhou. One of the most damaging of these attacks was directed by Chen Kai, who assembled a secret society led army and actually managed to seize Foshan itself. Li Wen Mao is supposed to have organized his army according to the different types of roles seen in the opera, creating three different types of troops: Civil Tigers, Brave Tigers, and Flying Tigers. They then marched to attack the capital from the west, with Li Wen Mao attempting to coordinate the various rebel armies that were applying pressure from the north, east, and south.[72]

Large numbers of impoverished and disaffected peasants rapidly swelled the ranks of the rebel armies in Foshan. It is clear that tens of thousands of individuals joined Li and Chen's rebel efforts. Lei puts the ultimate size of their army at 100,000, but given the moderate size of Foshan's total population, that number seems exaggerated.

Li's troops turned the rebellion into a revolutionary performance. They went out into the streets and fought in operatic costumes, recalling the role of performance in Foshan's earlier battles against outside oppression. By adopting the personas of easily identifiable folk heroes, they argued symbolically that it was they, and not the government, that represented the forces of social order and justice that the long-suffering people of the region yearned for.[73]

Nor was this the only time that fighters dressed in opera costumes would take to the streets. Ter Haar reports that costumed fighters were also seen, to a lesser degree, during the Small Sword Uprising that gripped Shanghai in 1854. The mode of dress used in opera costumes at the time emulated older Ming, rather than Qing fashions, making them a ripe symbol for any group claiming Ming restoration as their objective. He also points out that the secret societies had traditionally viewed their initiation rituals as theatrical performance, blurring the lines between political, religious, and theatrical ritual. Given this background, the appearance of elaborately costumed rebels is probably less paradoxical than it first appears.[74]

Most of the fighters did not dress up as the lords and ladies of the *Romance of the Three Kingdoms* before taking to the barricades. Historical sources relate that many of the rebels simply donned a red scarf or turban, leading to the rebellion's popular name.[75] Even this much simpler uniform calls on a symbolic repertoire that tends to undercut an easy political reading of this uprising.

Modern historians have tended to find the origins of the secret society initiation rituals not in political causes, but rather in Daoist practices meant to exorcise or ward off demonic attack. A piece of red cloth was often worn around the head during Triad initiation rituals to demonstrate that the candidate was descending into a liminal space. Daoist priests, shamans, and spirit mediums often wore a red sash for the same reason, usually when performing a ritual from the vernacular Popular Religion. Rebel forces throughout Chinese history had depended on red headgear to illustrate the divine life giving power concentrated within each soldier.[76] Given the widespread concern over the "demonic" nature of the Qing, the choice of color works on the spiritual, historic, and political levels. It is not clear whether the revolutionaries themselves were drawing the same cultural distinctions between these realms that Western readers might today. It is this blurring of categories that explains why the appearance of opera-costumed rebels gripped the popular imagination in such a powerful way.

For all of the discussion of the "opera uprising," the occupation of Foshan was actually carried out by Chen Kai and the secret societies. Much to the government's distress, they began their administration of Foshan by lowering the tax rates. The governor's great fear was that Chen and his rebels would forge ties with the workers and managers of Foshan's strategically important armories and cannon foundries. If Chen managed to procure large numbers of modern weapons and made contact with the rebel forces encircling Guangzhou, the provincial capital would surely fall.

While it was clear that the official government troops were unable to stop Chen's advance, the fifteen miles separating the two cities was the heartland of the militia movement that had come to prominence during the San Yuan Li Incident a decade earlier. In the meantime the area's militia network had been allowed to decay but, realizing the gravity of the situation, the local gentry worked quickly to rebuild the old fighting force. The government in Canton funneled them what resources and reinforcements they could spare, including a number of modern cannons.[77] While Chen and his rebels held undisputed control of the waters, they were never able to exercise the same degree of control over the surrounding countryside. They simply could not fight their way through the entrenched conservative militias that dominated the rice patties and mulberry groves separating Guangzhou and Foshan.[78]

This delay allowed the government to turn back a number of the advances and establish a more comfortable security perimeter around the capital city. The imperial forces then directed their attention to Foshan. On November 10, a large body of imperial troops disembarked from war junks, joined the local militias from the countryside, and attacked the town. The battle was a stalemate, leaving the rebel forces in firm control of Foshan.

A week later, the government struck again with a similar attack. This time Chen's rebels were better prepared. They managed to get behind the advancing imperial troops and capture the heavily armed war junks that the government had used as transports. Chen then fired the ships' cannons into the rear of the government forces, as they were being simultaneously bombarded by Foshan's own artillery from the front. At least 1,500 government troops died in the ensuing crossfire, and the rebels scored what may have been their most impressive victory of the uprising.[79]

The November battles are important because they once again serve to illustrate the changing nature of Chinese warfare in the nineteenth century. While the average village militia member was probably armed with a spear, a pair of short swords, and a rattan shield, battlefield conditions were rapidly evolving. Ultimate victory depended on one's ability to deploy muskets and cannons, while carefully managing tax policy and public diplomacy on the home front. The martial arts training of the rebel soldiers was clearly not the only skill they depended on to survive, nor could it ensure final victory.

It was the more mundane task of political leadership that ultimately defeated the secret societies of Foshan. Chen had succeeded initially by promising lower taxes. Yet, as the campaign dragged on, expenses began to mount. In January of 1855, the rebels began to demand increased "contributions" to the cause. When a tax collector ventured into a particularly independent section of the city he was seized by the citizens and held until he promised to reduce the tax rates. After being released he returned with a body of armed men, set fire to the entire neighborhood, and proceeded to kill anyone caught fleeing the inferno. The slaughter lasted for two days and the population of the city turned decisively against the rebels. When imperial forces approached the city on January 17, they faced no resistance from the local (now solidly pro-government) population. They found a mostly empty and burning city and discovered that 20,000 rebel soldiers had managed to flee into the hills.[80]

Li Wen Mao's fight took a slightly different path than Chen's. Li and his three "Tiger Armies" did take part in the unsuccessful campaign against Guangzhou in 1854. However, rather than returning to Foshan, he ultimately led his troops to Guangxi Province (immediately to the northwest of Guangdong) and took over the city of Guiping in 1855. Li signaled his dynastic intentions by adopting the reign title "Hongde," meaning "Great Virtue" and, in an act of supreme irony, crowned himself the "King of Peace and Order."

In the following years Li went about setting up his own civil and military services (complete with a public examination system), creating legal codes and tax laws, and even minting his own money. Li quickly abandoned any pretext of "restoring the Ming" and instead emphasized the degree to which his regime was a re-establishment of Han ethnic power. Nor did Cantonese opera fare all that well in the new utopia. Li Wen Mao became just as distrustful of the popular medium as the Qing had ever been, and his regime adopted a number of laws strictly regulating performances. This environment sapped the art of its vital energy.

Li's kingdom was short lived. He was injured during an attack on Guilin in 1858, and was forced to retreat into a mountainous area where he ultimately died of his wounds. Chen Kai, who had abandoned Foshan a couple of years earlier, took command of the remaining troops and continued the struggle. In 1861, Chen was finally captured and Li's kingdom formally ceased to exist. While not as powerful as some of the other lords of the Taiping Rebellion, at its height Li's "Country of Great Success" encompassed territory in Guangdong, Guangxi, Hunan, and Guizhou Provinces, an impressive feat by any metric.[81]

The end of the Red Turban Revolt did not mark the end of the turmoil in the Pearl River Delta region. In 1855, both the governor's imperial troops and the local gentry embarked on a great "pacification campaign" designed to bring the countryside to heel. Rebels, and suspected rebel sympathizers, were hunted down and summarily executed. The initial number of executions was in the tens of thousands.

The scope of the purge expanded with time. Actors and performers were arrested and killed, as well as those who may have aided the rebels simply by having paid them "taxes." Vagabonds and homeless individuals were also massacred en masse. Informants were often those with a score to settle, and village elders routinely volunteered "trouble causers" within their own communities for execution. In short, the neo-Confucian forces of "order" used the purge of the countryside as a pretext for declaring war on the lower classes and forever asserting their control over the region's economic and political future. As many as one million individuals may have lost their lives in the events following the conclusion of the Red Turban Revolt.[82]

Conclusion

Cantonese opera paid a heavy price for its involvement with the rebellion. The Qionghua Guildhall was burned to the ground in 1855. A large number of local performers who had not followed the rebels into the hills were slaughtered and dumped into a mass grave at Tieqiufen (Ironhill Tomb). All public performances in the local vernacular language were banned, though Mandarin opera groups were apparently allowed to carry on. The opera ban lasted for ten years. When re-legalized in 1871 the new guildhall was built in Guangzhou rather than Foshan.

Many actors were forced to look for alternate employment. Some became performers in related traditions, like puppetry or storytelling. Others took to wandering or gave up the profession entirely. It is against this bleak backdrop that Wing Chun first comes into the public view. Its verifiable history begins when a Foshan doctor named Leung Jan takes in a former opera performer named Leung Yee Tai and his colleague Wong Wah Bo. In gratitude, they pass on their martial knowledge, acquired over the course of their careers in the Cantonese opera.

Understanding the events of the 1840s and 1850s sheds a great deal of light on the practical concerns that shaped many late Qing hand combat systems. It is impossible to engage meaningfully with these martial traditions without first appreciating the environment in which they arose. Guangdong's history of violence and revolution casts a long shadow over the remainder of this volume.

Chapter 2

Setting the Stage

The Evolution of Guangdong's Martial Arts, 1800–1911

> Graceful Staff Flying above the Dragon's Wiggling Tail.
> Strong Fist Releases out, the Tiger Raises his Head.
>
> —Martial Couplet composed by Chan Heung, 1848[1]

Introduction

The exploration of the martial landscape of the Pearl River Delta during the late Qing and early Republic periods begins with two deceptively simple questions. Given that the practice and development of hand combat is always a somewhat specialized pursuit, exactly who studied martial arts? Why did these individuals choose to invest scarce resources in these efforts when most of Chinese society explicitly rejected martial pursuits?

There is no single solution to this puzzle. The answer varies according to whether one chooses to examine the countryside, with its peasant militias and banditry, or the city, with its more urban social and economic structures. When discussing martial arts in Guangdong the question of ethnicity invariably raises its head. The Hakka and Cantonese peoples both lay claim to a distinctive set of arts, each with its own practices and traditions. Therefore, how one answers this question also varies dramatically over time.

The late Qing and Republic periods are notable for being eras of rapid change, and this was especially true for the Chinese martial arts community. These shifts happened throughout the province but were especially notable in relatively urban areas undergoing the move toward modernization. Economic and social changes radically altered the ways that martial arts were taught, and even which arts would survive and be passed down to the present day.

As new groups entered the marketplace for instruction, the social meaning and purpose of the traditional martial arts evolved. What had previously been a means of personal or community defense increasingly became a nationalist and state-dominated project to build up a common identity and strengthen the resistance against foreign imperialism. At the local level, national political disputes drew Foshan's various martial arts associations into conflict with one another over issues like the "April 12th Incident" and the growing strength of the labor movement.

Over the course of the next two chapters we will further explore this tension between the development of martial arts on the local level and their subsequent manipulation by national organizations with more ambitious agendas. During the late Qing and Republic periods, the growth of various martial arts institutes and voluntary associations allowed these practices to reach a more urban, middle-class, and educated audience than they ever had before. Yet it was still not clear what sorts of values these schools would champion.

Wing Chun did not emerge in a vacuum. It was developed in dialogue with other hand combat systems and in response to broader social trends. By properly setting the social and historic stage we hope to throw additional light on how this unique art developed, and why it has continued to succeed when so many other southern combat systems have languished or vanished altogether. To do this we must first investigate the evolution of Guangdong's various martial arts schools in much greater detail.

Who Studied Martial Arts in Guangdong Province, 1800–1911?

Our prior discussions of the persistent problems of banditry, lineage feuds, and political unrest have already offered us a few hints as to who studied the martial arts. In many ways the answer is most clear for the countryside where, in particularly conflict prone areas, practically everyone would have been forced to take some interest in community safety. As law and order broke down in the increasingly acrimonious nineteenth century, the central government became more comfortable with passing the costs of neighborhood defense on to the local gentry. In practice this led to an explosion in the number of gentry funded and led militias from the 1830s onward.²

This is not to say that the militarization of the countryside was a new phenomenon. Peasant life in China was always characterized by disputes over land, water rights, and other scarce resources. In the Pearl River Delta region, with its history of strong lineage associations, these disputes often escalated and led to long-running private feuds between warring clans. Many of the larger clan associations even had small private militias. Both Wakeman and Kuhn point out that these were the basic social structures that were later combined to construct the larger, official, gentry-led militia groups. In times of extreme stress, such as the periods of military activity directly before the first and second Opium Wars, it is hard to imagine that practically the entire male peasant population of key strategic areas was not put under arms. During these intervals large numbers of martial artists were hired to work either as military trainers or mercenaries.

If the British were the threat that galvanized the local gentry into creating large militia organizations in the first place, the most pressing dilemma that these populations faced was actually much more local and had nothing to do with imperialism. Old fashioned banditry and piracy continued to be the scourge of the countryside up to the 1950s. Individual villages were often left to fend for themselves. Throughout the country it became common practice to hire young men or militia members to guard the fields at night lest all the crops be stolen by bandits from neighboring villages.³

The problem with the decentralization of law and order through the adoption of the militia system was that it became impossible to enforce good discipline across such a broad cross section of society. Both Esherick and Kuhn have demonstrated that the line separating the "militias" from the "bandits" might be as thin as a single bad harvest or local catastrophe. With little in the way of centralized relief, starving villages could easily turn on their neighbors, becoming in essence "bandit towns."

Individual young men who inherited no land and had no prospects of getting a legitimate job often turned to salt or opium smuggling (both were thriving industries in Guangdong) which in turn led to full scale banditry. In fact, hiring these youths as "braves" or militia members was one way of controlling local lawlessness. When it became too expensive for the government to continue to maintain these poorly trained and undisciplined forces, the "soldiers" often chose to apply their new found skills in fields of criminal endeavor. Again, this basic pattern continues from the nineteenth century all the way through the end of the Republic period.[4]

All in all, Guangdong's countryside tended to be a highly militarized place. Lineage feuds, persistent banditry, the fear of imperialism, and increased reliance on local militias all ensured that a constant stream of new recruits would have to be trained in the "martial arts." These arts were not always similar to what we might recognize today. Individual lineages or militia associations would be responsible for hiring their own instructors. These were often former members of the Qing military and what was taught was sometimes a mixture of various skills chosen for their practicality and ease of use rather than any single coherent "style." In most cases the village militias would not have had access to firearms, and most of the emphasis was placed on training with simple weapons, in particular the pole, spear, rattan shield, and sword. Boxing was occasionally taught as well, though possibly not as often as many modern readers might assume.

Of course there were exceptions to this general pattern. Some local militias were lucky enough to find talented instructors with a complete training philosophy and system of instruction. The famous Hung Gar practitioner, and sometime Foshan medical expert, Wong Fei Hung appears to be one such case. For all of the fame that he has achieved in the popular media, it is often forgotten that the real Wong was basically a recluse for the last few years of his life and very little reliable information about him has survived. It appears that as a young man Wong studied to take the military service exams. At one point he was selected as a military instructor by General Lie Wing-Fok of the Qing Fifth Regiment in Guangzhou. Later he was appointed as an instructor of the local militia association.[5] This sort of training is probably typical of what was available in the local countryside.

Martial instruction was less commonly sought in urban areas, but the types of practitioners one might encounter, and their motives for practicing the martial arts, were much more diverse. This greater diversity notwithstanding, securing a livelihood continued to be a major motivating factor. Perhaps the most numerous practitioners that might be encountered in large cities were regular Qing military troops and law enforcement officers. These might take the form of ethnically Manchu Banner troops, or the more numerous, if no more reliable, Han Green Standard Army. European observers noted that martial arts practice continued to be the major form of drill seen in the Chinese military during the last years of the nineteenth century. As a result, combat between Chinese formations tended to devolve into a long series of simultaneous duals, rather than the more disciplined firing and marching formations favored by the European armies of the day. Of course, anyone hoping to gain a commission in the Imperial military would have to demonstrate excellence in both mounted and standing archery as part of the official military examination system.

Discussing the use of traditional martial arts by Qing Banner troops, one European observer in Guangzhou wrote:

> The worst of this pointless and dismal foolery [martial arts] is that it is taught to what the Chinese are pleased to call their army instead of anything really wholesome or useful. The people look on with amazement and admiration at the antics of the idle and dirty vassals who lounge about what by courtesy and a huge stretch of the imagination are called guard houses or barracks. "Ah," they say, when they see those useless persons jumping over each other's heads, or turning summersaults in the air, "here are valiant men! You won't find an enemy who will get the better of them!"[6]

Even though the formal military had more or less abdicated the countryside to the militias and bandits by the end of the dynasty, the same was not true of the major urban areas. As such, martial arts instruction was often seen as a route to a career as a soldier, or possibly an instructor, as we saw with Wong Fei Hung. Without a doubt the military was the largest employer of martial artists in the region. The need to deploy additional forces during the disturbances of the nineteenth and early twentieth centuries often led local authorities to hire "braves" who could supplement (or more often than not replace) the less reliable official troops.

While the military, and the possibility of military careers, may have been a major draw for martial artists in the provincial capital of Guangzhou, it had much less of a presence in Foshan. Foshan grew up as a series of production centers and markets surrounding a central temple complex. It never had much in the way of political influence, and hence had no important officials in residence. Few troops were ever posted there. The town was not even allowed to build walls since it was not a municipal center. The lack of easy access to local military careers probably had an important impact on the overwhelmingly civilian nature of the arts that developed in and around Foshan.

Of course the absence of the formal military did not obviate the need for protection. As a wealthy manufacturing and handicraft center Foshan found itself targeted by both secret societies, which might try to extort local businesses, and bandit gangs along the roads and rivers. These groups routinely harassed the shipping that was the lifeblood of the local economy. Such problems were not unique to Foshan, or even Guangdong. The increased social disorder of the late Qing period proved to be a major headache for merchants across China. Their universal response was to invest in private security.

This spending had an immediate effect on the local landscape. Pawnshops that were responsible for extending loans and credit to local farmers, often on usurious terms, resembled multistory stone fortresses that loomed over the countryside and could easily sustain themselves in the face of a bandit incursion or tax revolt.[7] Yet imposing architecture is not enough to ensure safety. Private security guards were also hired to protect both businesses and residences. These same individuals would also be used to collect debts.

Security guards rarely had access to expensive firearms; for them, a working knowledge of hand combat systems was a vital job skill. Such work was not particularly well paid, and the social status of guards in this section of the private security industry was often quite low. Readers may recall that the rags-to-riches story of the famous Foshan pharmacist and medical mogul Leung Caixin (1763–1855) begins with the promising young man being badly injured in the course of his duties as a lowly security guard. Only after being taken in by a local doctor does he recover from his injuries and go on to produce the patent medicines that would ensure the wealth of his clansmen for generations.[8]

Of slightly higher social status were private escorts and bodyguards. Government officials and rich merchants often hired local martial arts masters to accompany them on journeys or to act as a full-time security detail, effectively becoming part of the patron's household. Such individuals were often former military men or highly recommended civilian martial artists.

Much of the oral folklore of the Yuen Kay San Wing Chun lineage focuses on one such individual named Fung Siu Ching. Not much is known about Fung Siu Ching, other than Sum Num's assertion that he was the second instructor of his Sifu, Yuen Kay San. Most accounts state that Fung first learned the art of Wing Chun from "Painted Face Kam," a Cantonese opera performer and contemporary of Leung Yee Tai and Wong Wah Bo. Later he became an officer in the imperial army in Guangzhou. After retiring from formal military life he is said to have become the private bodyguard of the governor of Sichuan province at some point during the late nineteenth century.[9] While the exact facts of the case are impossible to verify, the general career path that this story illustrates was quite a common one. The study of civilian martial arts might lead to a job in the military, and, if you were lucky, this could result in a more lucrative retirement position in the field of private security.

Both night watchmen and bodyguards were beholden to the wishes of their employers and easily replaced. More romantic and prestigious still were the many "armed escort companies" that began to appear in the Ming dynasty and reached their full flower in the closing years of the nineteenth century. Goods and merchants were at their most vulnerable while traveling either by road or boat, and armed escort agencies tried to provide a certain level of peace and commercial stability as the government's ability to ensure law and order evaporated.

These firms were usually financially backed by powerful merchants (and in a few cases by court officials) who had an interest in the flow of goods and silver. While in the middle of the Qing dynasty the agencies mainly guarded tax payments (with the Court being their primary employer), by the nineteenth century shipments of goods, grains, and even people were routinely protected by these firms. Every major city and town had multiple competing agencies. Given its heavy reliance on trade and relative affluence, the colorful banners of private security companies must have been a common sight in and around Foshan.

Over time these agencies developed a shared institutional structure that was more or less uniform across China. The chief executive officer of each company was often a local martial arts master of good standing in the community. While not normally of gentry rank, he had to have a positive reputation with the local gentry and merchant class, as well as a cordial relationship with the local government, if he wished to attract customers. Just as important, his martial reputation had to be such that people were confident in his ability to safely deliver the goods. Still, the boss was mostly responsible for running the company and being its public face. He did not usually participate in field activities.

Under this figure was a secondary leader known as the Chief Warden. The Chief Warden was also expected to have a reputation for honesty and martial prowess. In actual fact, this position usually went to a retired minor military official or a former clerk who had good relations with the local government. Due to the particular nature of the armed escort business it was important to be trusted by the local officials. The Chief Warden often acted as a political "fixer" and ensured amicable relations with the administrative world.

Beneath the Chief Warden was the Head Warden. This individual was usually a no nonsense martial artist, responsible for training the other wardens and common guards. The Head Warden was also responsible for leading operations in the field. When actually in transit, the wardens acted as the last line of defense for guarding the goods or travelers. The common guards were sent ahead to clear and scout the road.

In practice, armed escort companies avoided conflict whenever possible. They often relied on the fierce reputation of their firms to deter trouble, and if approached by bandits were likely to attempt diplomacy or inducements as a way of defusing the situation. Only if this failed were they going to fight.

All of the wardens were trained martial artists and they openly displayed their arms. While wardens may have carried polearms and swords to let the locals know they meant business, in an actual fight they were just as likely to unsheathe a rifle or a Colt repeating revolver as a sword.[10] One of the truly interesting things about the late armed escort companies is that they represented an era in which martial arts, firearms, and careful diplomacy all coexisted.

At their height in the 1880s there were literally thousands of armed escort companies across China, and perhaps a dozen of the larger agencies achieved a great deal of public fame. Some of the larger agencies had many hundreds of employees and branches in half a dozen major trade centers. As such, the armed escort business was a major employer of civilian martial artists.

By the early 1920s the tides of history had changed and most of the major firms had disappeared. In the end they were done in not by the adoption of firearms, but by the creation of a banking system that allowed for the circulation of paper notes (meaning merchants no longer had to carry large amounts of silver) and the advent of safer and faster railroads and steamship lines.[11] In only a decade what had been a thriving industry, central to the Chinese economy, vanished thanks to the development of a more modern infrastructure.

Other civilians in and around Foshan also found martial arts to be a valuable job skill. As much as the noted Chinese historian, Tang

Hao, despised any suggestion of a connection between traditional or Daoist medicine and martial arts, the plain historical truth is that many practitioners of medicine also studied hand combat and saw it as integral to the success of their professional practices. If nothing else, it was probably good advertising.

Medicine was a prosperous, some might even say over-represented, industry in Foshan. The editors of *Foshan Wushu Wenhua*, when discussing the connections between medicine and martial arts, speculate that Foshan's manufacturing-based economy may account for the town's high concentration of traditional doctors in the nineteenth century. Many of the most important industries, such as the iron works, the textile mills, and the ceramic kilns, involved working in close proximity to dangerous equipment, open flames, or hazardous chemicals at a point in time when worker safety was an almost nonexistent concept. Not surprisingly there was a huge demand for "bone setters" and other trauma specialists as workshop accidents produced a steady stream of broken limbs and burns. Alternatively, the profits that these businesses generated provided a source of revenue for everyone from the most serious herbal doctors to traveling salesmen hawking patent medicines in the streets.[12]

The perceived connection between the subtle body energies in a martial and medical setting made kung fu practice a common way to advertise ones therapeutic prowess. Martial arts instruction could also provide a secondary line of income if one chose to take on any students. Ip Chun, the eldest son of Ip Man, humorously recalls growing up as a child in Foshan and seeing street performers demonstrating tricks and "hard qigong" feats in an attempt to entice the crowd into buying their patent medicines. At the time such sights were very common and Ip Chun recalls how he looked down on individuals who would travel from place to place demonstrating and selling their martial skills. Of course, the last few decades of his own life have been mostly dedicated to traveling from seminar to seminar, demonstrating his father's art. He notes that readers should be cautious in their judgments of others.[13]

On the other end of the social spectrum from these street vendors we have luminaries such as Leung Caixin. This individual started life as a lowly warehouse guard, but after a serious injury found himself apprenticed to a local doctor. He went on to create a number of locally famous medical elixirs and created a strong, clan-based, pharmaceutical empire.

While he eventually became incredibly wealthy he never forgot the martial arts. Leung built a school to teach the Confucian classics to the children of his clansmen. However, local history also records that he built a martial arts training hall and invited multiple masters to come and teach over the years. Apparently he believed a strong foundation in the martial arts was necessary to fully inherit and understand the family medical business. Training in martial skills also allowed one to take the military service exam, an important pathway for social advancement. His grandson (by adoption) Leung Mengzhan applied himself to both areas of studies and became an important imperial degree holder after passing the national military service examination held in the capital. This clan's meteoric rise from obscurity to wealth and status, in only three generations, wonderfully illustrates the sort of social mobility that Foshan's dynamic economy made possible in the early years of the nineteenth century.[14]

Between these two extremes we see another class of medical professional who also valued the martial arts. The owners of smaller, if still successful, medical businesses in Foshan also seem to have taken a keen interest in pugilism, both to demonstrate their grasp of esoteric human physiology and to attract customers. Some of the most important figures in Foshan's martial history combined both the medical profession and martial arts instruction.

Wong Kei Ying was a prominent Hung Gar practitioner who was reputed to be a student of Luk Ah Choi. Wong went on to become an important exponent of the Hung Gar style and was crowned one of the "Ten Tigers of Canton" by Republican-era newspaper writers and martial arts novelists. In 1847 his son, Wong Fei Hung, was born. Wong began to instruct his son in the martial arts at the age of five. Not much is known with certainty about the pair and it has proved virtually impossible for scholars to separate the truth of their lives from the abundance of stories, films, and novels that have grown up around them.

It is often said that as a child Wong Fei Hung and his father performed in the streets to make a living. One of the few facts that appears relatively certain is that as a young adult Wong Fei Hung ended up working for the military in Guangzhou. After retiring he opened or inherited the Po Chi Lam clinic at Renan Street in Foshan.

While kung fu films tend to portray Po Chi Lam as a famous martial arts school, Wong seems to have supported himself through the strength of his medical business. He did accept students and teach classes. Nor is there any doubt that he was involved with the local martial arts community. Still, it appears that he made a living as a bone setter and herbal doctor, though clearly his reputation as a martial artist was a great asset in the town's already crowded medical marketplace.[15]

A generation earlier, Leung Jan (1826–1901), perhaps the single-most important figure in the history of Wing Chun, also worked as a medical doctor in Foshan. There is substantial debate among the various lineages as to the name of his original clinic. The Ip Man lineage tends to assert that he practiced medicine at Jan Sang Tong (Mr. Jan's Hall) on Fai Jee Street in Foshan.[16] Other lineages claim the clinic's original name was Hang Chai Tong (Apricot Forest Hall).[17]

It is often asserted that Leung Jan became famous due to his many victories over his various opponents in "challenge matches." While there are contemporary references to Leung Jan which place him in Foshan in the mid-nineteenth century, there are no reliable period references to his many supposed challenge matches. Instead, Leung Jan appears to have become relatively wealthy and well-known based on the strength of his medical practice. He took few if any students. It is interesting to note, for instance, that the local money changer, Chan Wah Shun, who worked outside his clinic for years, is often said to have been shocked to learn that Leung Jan was a hand combat master.[18] It seems hard to reconcile these accounts of Leung Jan's extreme reticence with the more modern rumors of his many glorious challenge match victories.

The same Chan Wah Shun (c. 1836–1909), a rough contemporary of Wong Fei Hung, also mixed the medical and martial professions. Chan, who later studied both medicine and Wing Chun with Leung Jan, is best known for being Ip Man's first martial arts instructor. He came to teaching rather late in life.

After Leung Jan's retirement, Chan Wah Shun opened both an herbal clinic and a martial arts school of his own. Unlike his teacher, who preferred to keep a low profile, Chan Wah Shun was the first individual to openly teach Wing Chun in a "modern" commercial setting. Leaving aside the matters of lineage and timeline, it is very interesting to note that the two earliest historical figures in the Ip Man lineage both made a living as traditional doctors who taught martial arts on the side either as a hobby or, in the case of Chan, as a secondary source of income.

Soldiers, private security firms, and some traditional medical experts all relied on martial arts to make a living. Of course other less prestigious members of society also developed these skills to ensure their economic survival. While martial arts folklore is full of stories of mysterious wandering monks and priests, the majority of such figures that one would meet tended to be less impressive. Itinerant monks and priests could often be seen selling patent medicines or magical charms in the streets, and sometimes they would use martial arts displays to attract customers. These individuals were universally regarded as riff-raff and were subject to a fair amount of harassment by the state, which took a dim view of such activities.

Also disturbing to the state were the secret societies that preyed on local merchants, forming the urban counterpart to rural banditry. We have discussed these groups at length in a previous chapter, but it should be remembered that secret political and criminal organizations often used martial arts societies as a front to recruit possible members and to conceal their activities. Again, this was a pattern seen throughout China. Perhaps the best academic discussion of it is found in Esherick's masterful study of the origins of the Boxer Uprising.[19]

The same pattern that he observed in Shandong is evident in Guangzhou and Foshan as well. In his detailed study of the Red Turban Revolt, which swept the area in 1854, Jaeyoon Kim conducted an investigation of the backgrounds of each of the leaders of the movement. While Li Wen Mao's martial skills are often remembered, it should be recalled that he was basically a professional singer and an *amateur* boxer. However, Kim found that six of the other leaders of the rebellion were actually professional martial arts instructors.[20] And some of them, including Chen Kai, were also known members of local secret societies. The event of 1854 makes it clear that there was a connection between at least some professional martial artists and local criminal organizations.

Not all students of the martial arts sought to make a career out of their skills. As the Qing dynasty wore to a close the pace of economic change and social dislocation increased in both Guangzhou and Foshan. Facing global trade pressures, we see major shifts in employment and population patterns in both cities. Furthermore, the slow expansion of the industrial sector created the demand for a new type of worker, not the highly trained artisans who had been the backbone of the previous handicraft economy, but a less skilled generalist.

As workers flocked from the countryside to the city they increasingly turned to martial arts associations and schools. At first this was a minor phenomenon, but by the final years of the Qing dynasty it foreshadowed a major shift in who studied martial arts and how they were taught. While the full fruits of this transition would not emerge until the 1920s and 30s, the foundation of those developments was being laid at the local level throughout the nineteenth century.

Lin Boyan, a Chinese scholar, observed that the poor peasants streaming in from the countryside often had some training in martial arts, and they took these skills and interests to the city with them. He notes the cases of dozens of Guangzhou factories where workers set up their own private martial arts schools, often going to some lengths to import or hire an instructor.[21] This proved to be a critical turning point in the modernization and mass commercialization of Chinese martial arts. Nowhere was this shift more apparent or important than Foshan where, by the end of the nineteenth century, a fairly substantial percentage of the town's working-age male population had some sort of an association with a martial arts group or related organization.

The end of the Qing and the start of the Republican period represent an era of immense change for Chinese martial arts in general and the styles of Guangdong province in particular. In only a decade traditional employers like the Imperial Army and the armed escort agencies disappeared while the growth of the working and middle class created a new urban market for high quality, inexpensive, martial arts instruction.

Not all arts were equally successful in transitioning from traditional modes of transmission to the modern marketplace. Different social and organizational structures would be needed to succeed in this new environment. Yet the upheaval and dislocation within Chinese society actually created opportunities for new styles and types of associations to emerge. Ironically, it was at this moment—when the pundits predicted the imminent demise of the martial arts as being something that was just too backward, superstitious, and "Chinese" to survive in the modern era—that they began to adopt the new organizational structures that would allow them to not just survive, but also to thrive, in a globally interconnected world.

This environment would not influence only the development of Wing Chun. It had a major impact on all of the southern styles that it came in contact with and competed against. We cannot understand Wing Chun in isolation from either its social context or the changing mix of styles that surrounded it. We now turn to a detailed study of the development of Foshan and the Pearl River Delta from roughly the turn of the nineteenth century until the fall of the Qing dynasty. Special attention will be paid to how the martial arts styles in each period reflect the economic and social changes that were rolling forth.

The Early Period: Middle of the Qing Dynasty to 1800

Guangdong Province underwent rapid economic and population growth throughout most of the eighteenth and early nineteenth centuries. By

1800 the area had long since recovered from the trauma inflicted on it during the coastal evacuation at the start of the dynasty. Both trade and agriculture were prospering. New food crops such as sweet potatoes, which could be grown on marginal land, allowed the population to expand steadily throughout the period. At the same time, prime arable land in the region around Foshan transitioned to silk farming. As silk became the region's most important export crop, land prices, and rents, began to rise precipitously.[22] Areas that had once been dedicated to rice paddies were replaced with mulberry groves and small ponds, giving the district its distinct appearance. While picturesque (and good for China's balance of trade), the loss of local growing capacity meant that Guangdong, one of the most fertile regions in China, actually had to rely on imported rice for much of the year.

The urban areas of Guangzhou and Foshan tended to be even more dependent on regional trade and industry for their well-being. This period also represents the apex of Foshan's local economic influence. At the dawn of the nineteenth century it may have had up to 500,000 residents, supported important iron and ceramics industries, and was a major center for regional trade and commerce.[23] Still, there was nothing in the way of actual "industrialization" and many of the industries that did exist depended on highly skilled labor organized through a series of guilds. In some ways the situation was analogous to what one might find in a major European town during the Renaissance.

Most of the residents of Foshan and Guangzhou were ethnic Han individuals who spoke Cantonese, yet the province as a whole was far from ethnically or linguistically homogenous. The Han River Valley and area around the port of Shantou had been settled by a group of immigrants, the Hoklos, from Fujian Province (immediately to the north) hundreds of years before. The Hoklos spoke a dialect similar to that of southern Fujian Province but not intelligible to the Cantonese speaking populations of the western and northern branches of the Pearl River. More recently the areas surrounding the Mei River and the eastern branch of the Pearl River were settled by another group of northerners, the Hakka. Again, this group spoke its own dialect and was forced to settle the less fertile areas and high mountainous regions by the other groups that had a prior claim on the better land.[24] Tensions between these groups were rife, and the Hakka would fight a low-level civil war with the majority Cantonese population throughout much of the 1860s.[25] As such, the ethnic distinction between the Punti (Cantonese speakers) and Hakka people is immediately relevant to the discussion and classification of Guangdong's various martial traditions.

Scholars and practitioners have invented a number of different typologies that claim to classify China's diverse martial arts. None of these is totally reliable, but they are commonly used. For instance, styles are often described as being "northern arts" characterized by their strong emphasis on kicking, or "southern" boxing styles, which supposedly focus on the hands. Alternatively, arts are said to be either "external" or "internal," "hard" or "soft," and, most confusingly of all, "Shaolin" or "Wudang" in origin. We generally believe that such labels obscure as much about the connections between the various arts as they reveal. Nevertheless, the current discussion requires us to introduce yet another mode of classification. When discussing the indigenous arts of Guangdong (and to a lesser extent Fujian) Province local commentators make a broad distinction between the "Hung Mun" and "Hakka" styles.

The Hung Mun arts are those that are practiced by the dominant Cantonese community.[26] The great majority of these schools employ the common mythos of the burning of the Shaolin Temple, and anti-Qing sentiments, somewhere in their founding legends. In fact, it is precisely these shared stories that define the Hung Mun martial arts group in sociological terms. All of the major family styles, such as Hung Gar, Choy Gar, Lau Gar, Li Gar, Mok Gar, and Fut Gar share this common story. Later styles, such as Choy Li Fut and Wing Chun, also make use of the same mythos. Of course the vast majority of this "revolutionary" rhetoric was always strictly symbolic and ritualistic in nature. While a few associations, such as the Hung Sing school of Choy Li Fut in Foshan, did seem to develop anti-systemic tendencies, the majority of these movements were, in practice, either apolitical or pro-status quo.[27]

The Hakka styles, in contrast, do not share a single unifying mythos. Many of the various styles have their own distinct legends or history. These styles also share a number of common traits with the schools of boxing seen in Southern Fujian Province, such as narrow high stances, triangular footwork, and an interest in short bridge formation and close range combat. Kicks often tend to be low and inconspicuous compared to what one sees in northern or even Hung Mun styles.

As the name implies these styles developed within the Hakka ethnic group and it seems likely that their practical, often brutal, efficiency is a direct result of the constant feuding between these communities and their neighbors for much of the nineteenth century. The initial development of these arts seems to have centered on the eastern branch of the Pearl River and the Mt. Luofu region. In fact, Mt. Luofu was the home of a number of regionally significant temples and it is referenced in the history of multiple styles found in Guangdong Province. Modern examples of Hakka styles include White Eyebrow, Dragon, Southern Mantis, and Chuka Shaolin (sometimes referred to as "Phoenix Eye Fist" in honor of its preferred striking weapon). While these specific styles emerged onto the public stage after 1920, their antecedents in the East River Valley are much older.

It should be noted that the preceding taxonomy has its weaknesses. While it may be true that in the distant past some Hakka arts were taught only to students of the same ethnicity, this has never been the case for the majority of the modern Hakka styles that are still seen today. Dragon and White Eyebrow were created and assumed their modern form in Guangzhou in the 1920s and 1930s. Their respective promoters actively sought government backing and tried to advance their arts as part of a *universal* revival in Chinese strength and martial culture, regardless of the ethnicity of perspective students.[28]

Likewise, as these once insular arts began to be taught to the dominant Cantonese community on a massive scale, they tended to adopt Shaolin motifs and creation tales. The martial arts masters of the early twentieth century understood the need for good branding and appear to have been willing to meet the expectations of their students. For instance, the current Chuka Shaolin creation myth shares a number of interesting similarities with Wing Chun's, including a nun who escapes the destruction of Shaolin, lives in a "White Crane Cave," and aids young orphan girls with bandit problems by teaching them her special form of hand combat.[29] This should not surprise us since the 1930s was the great decade of martial arts myth-making and storytelling. Yet the progressive spread and adoption of the Shaolin story tends to undermine the sociological difference between the Hung Mun and Hakka schools.

These objections notwithstanding, there do seem to be some broad similarities between arts traditionally classified as being members of one system or another. The distinction between the two schools also raises an interesting puzzle that is relevant to our current discussion. In sociological terms, Wing Chun is clearly a Hung Mun art. It makes use of the Shaolin motif; it developed along the western branch of the Pearl River and was practiced (so far as we know) exclusively by members of the majority Cantonese speaking community.

Yet the physical structure of the art, with its close boxing, bridge seeking, and narrow stances shows many similarities to the Hakka styles, particularly Southern Mantis and Chuka Shaolin. Some of the smaller styles found within the Hakka region, such as Shi Pan Village Boxing, also bear more than a passing resemblance to Wing Chun. So how is it that Wing Chun came to resemble the Hakka branch of martial arts evolution, when the other major arts that were practiced in the same town, Choy Li Fut and Hung Gar, seem to epitomize the Hung Mun style?

We will have to independently trace the development of both of these movements in our investigation of Guangdong's martial arts to solve this puzzle. The differing economic fortunes of the urban delta region, containing Foshan and Guangzhou, and the much more rural East River Valley, occupied by the Hakka, resulted in slightly different patterns of hand combat evolution throughout our period of investigation.

Early Development of the Hung Mun Styles, Prior to 1800

The evolution of hand combat in the Ming and early Qing eras is an immense topic encompassing both national and local trends. We believe that martial arts history is best approached as a branch of local history, and the local history of southern China generally seems to be less well-documented than that of the north. Southern style boxing shows a greater variety of forms, strategies, and concepts than the northern arts, yet the deep histories and original creators of these forms have been lost to the historical record and replaced with more recent myths. Still, it is clear that the history of unarmed combat in the region goes back just as far as it does in the north.

By the late Ming, unarmed boxing styles had firmly established themselves in the popular and military cultures of Guangdong Province. According to Xiaozhi Lu, at least a dozen boxing styles were practiced in Guangdong at this time including Zhoa Fist, Xi Fist, Wen Fist, Zhang Fist, Mysterious Fist, Bawang Fist, Monkey Fist, and Boy Praying to Bodhisattva style. The same source also lists a number of defensive patterns of hand combat including Mainzhang Defensive Fist, Jiuneihong Fist, 36 Methods of Attack and Defense and, lastly, the 72 Methods of Offensive and Defensive Fist.[30]

Little to nothing is known about any of these styles today other than the occasional scattered references. A number of the names are suggestive of trends in the wider martial arts world, such as the popularity of pictographic monkey boxing throughout China.[31] Others, such as the allusion to the "boy praying to the Bodhisattva," are reminiscent of later developments in the region, such as the repeated references to the "three prayers to Buddha" seen in the Wing Chun system.

These forms went into rapid decline at the end of the Ming dynasty, and by the restoration of social normalcy in the middle of the Qing, appear to have been totally replaced by a new cluster of styles with their own approach to hand combat. While it is impossible to say much about the earliest stratum of Guangdong unarmed martial arts, it seems likely that these systems provided much of the raw material from which other styles would later emerge.

The situation improved in the second half of the eighteenth century. Again a dozen major styles are believed to have existed in Guangdong. The most important of these were the "family" styles: Hung, Lau, Choy, Li, and Mok Gar. In general, these arts emphasized boxing and centered in the Pearl River Delta region, the most populous and wealthiest part of the province. Of course it was also the area which saw the most conflict between clans over land and resources. In that sense it is likely significant that each of these styles is named for a specific clan, a naming convention that does not appear to be as dominant in the region's earlier Ming era arts. This trend may reflect the growing strength of the lineages association in this period.[32]

While these arts are often grouped together in modern discussion, there were (and are) significant differences between the five family styles. For instance, Mok Gar is unique in that it emphasizes kicking and leg work. It was also found along the East River, near Huizhou, at a fairly early date. The ultimate creators of these fighting systems remains a mystery, but in mythic terms each of the five family styles is traditionally attributed to "Jee Shim," a survivor of the Shaolin destruction discussed in the introduction.

It is interesting to note that the family styles really emerge and become quite popular between 1790 and 1820, about the same time as the first secret society rebellions in Fujian and Guangdong. This is also the time that the story of the burning of the Shaolin Temple is first recorded in the interrogation records of imprisoned rebels. Circumstantial evidence indicates that it was via the influence of these early arts that the central mythic motif of the Hung Mun system was established and the legend of the burning of the temple was spread to later styles like Choy Li Fut and Wing Chun.

Early Development of the Hakka Styles, Prior to 1800

Unfortunately the early development of the Hakka system is even less well-documented than its Cantonese counterpart. What is known is that by the middle of the eighteenth century the area of the East River near Boluo and Huiyang had become a central location for martial arts practice and innovation. The styles that later emerged in this area share certain characteristics including specific forms and names of movements and postures. This has led some martial artists to postulate the theoretical existence of an older art named "East River Fist." This name was chosen due to the geographic locations of the arts in question, and the fact that the "East River" is explicitly referenced in the names of forms and movements that were preserved in the modern local styles (specifically Dragon and Southern Mantis). The similarities in names and movements across the various regional styles naturally led some students to hypothesize the existence of an archaic, ethnically Hakka, system of hand combat.[33]

One must be exceedingly careful in making these sorts of generalizations as there are other, equally effective, ways of predicting convergence between modern martial arts styles. Still, it may be useful to postulate the existence of a common pool of fighting techniques in the East River Valley that differed substantially from the techniques advocated by the nascent Hung Mun system. This would help to explain how the Hakka and Punti arts took on their unique characteristics at a relatively early date.

As we get closer to the nineteenth century the picture once again becomes clearer. Within this area certain clans became well-known for their fighting prowess. The most important of these were the Lam, Chu, and Lee families. Each of these groups developed a reputation for their unarmed boxing, ability to strike vital points (dim mak), and staff or pole fighting methods.[34] Each of these clan names is also important to the subsequent development of martial arts in Guangdong Province. It is interesting to once again note the use of kinship-based naming systems. This is probably due to the rising importance of surname associations and the resulting conflicts both between and within them.

Early Regional Influences and the Process of Institutionalization

What sort of outside influence, if any, is evident in Guangdong's martial arts at this time? The orthodox Wing Chun mythology places the genesis of the art at the Shaolin Temple, either in Henan or possibly Fujian Province. While we have already noted that the Southern Shaolin Temple is most likely a myth, there still might be truth to the legend that these arts came from the east. Fujian Province tended to be more densely populated than Guangdong and its ports were easily connected with its neighbor to the south through trade and commerce. Fujian was also subject to many of the same pressures that we have already seen in Guangdong, including pervasive banditry, piracy, ethnic tension, and a weak central government. As the eighteenth and nineteenth centuries wore on, a large number of individuals immigrated from over-crowded cities and towns in Fujian, drawn by Guangdong's quickly growing economy and the promise of lucrative work. Thus, Fujian seems the ideal place to focus our search for wider regional influences.

Some of Fujian's most historically significant exports were the secret societies, including the Heaven and Earth Society, carried by refugees and immigrants from the end of the eighteenth century onward. Like the Hung Mun styles, these societies adopted the myth of the burning of Shaolin as a recruitment tool. They too spoke of five ancestors who had escaped the tragedy. It seems certain that at some point in the past these five ancestors became confused with the various family styles and the fantastic tales of martial monks that were already circulating among martial artists.[35] This fusion led directly to the martial arts mythology that would arise periodically: at the end of the nineteenth century, in the 1930s, and then again in the 1970s and 1990s.

Perhaps no art has been shaped by these trends more than Hung Gar. Here we must differentiate between the relatively old "village" styles of Hung Kuen and the later, reified lineage created by Wong Fei Hung and his disciples in Foshan, Guangzhou, and Hong Kong. When most people think of Hung Gar today it is only the later incarnation that comes to mind. But, in reality, modern Hung Gar is probably so far removed from its roots as an eighteenth-century family style that to uninformed observers it would appear to be a different art altogether. So what then is the origin of the system?

The only evidence we have of this early period is mythic, but here the legends are actually quite suggestive. Hong Xi Guan (est. 1734–1808) was said to be a tea merchant with revolutionary sympathies, born in Zhangzhou, Fujian. He became a member of the Heaven and Earth Society and a lay follower at the supposed southern Shaolin Temple. Some accounts state that he even became a student of the legendary Abbot Jee Shim. Of course the same venerable monk makes an appearance in the Wing Chun legend.

After the temple's destruction the Abbot Jee Shim hid on the Red Boats of the Cantonese opera companies and visited Guangdong three times. He taught the opera singers martial arts but, after this third trip to the area, he decided that his style was too unstable. He then developed a new art with wider low stances, returned to Fujian, and taught it to Hong Xi Guan and his wife, Fong Wing Chun. In his travels as a revolutionary and merchant, Hong spread this art through the southern tip of Fujian, along the Guangdong coast, and then finally to the outskirts of Guangzhou where it took root, eventually becoming the Hung Gar that we know today.[36]

We have already reviewed some of the individual elements of this myth. What is of interest to us here is the idea that Hung family boxing may have originated in Fujian Province. A group of researchers from the Taiping Institute, a nonprofit group dedicated to researching and recording the history of traditional fighting arts, investigated this story. They did so by traveling from Guangzhou to Zhangzhou and examining a number of areas where traditional village style, Hung Kuen, was still practiced. The researchers found that as they moved north the style became both simpler and softer. The most "primitive" version of Hung family boxing was practiced in southern Fujian Province, and the style was not seen at all farther to the north. Given that styles tend to become more elaborate through time as new forms are added to fix perceived problems, this does lend a certain credibility to the hypothesis that Hung family boxing may actually have first emerged in Fujian before moving south later in the eighteenth century.[37] This is critical because Hung Gar later went on to influence many of Guangdong's other hand combat styles. There are even some similarities between village Hung Kuen and Wing Chun.

Fujian's martial arts seem to have been more developed in the seventeenth century than their Guangdong counterparts. White Crane Boxing, perhaps the premier pictographic school to emerge in Southern China, spread and split into a number of major subtypes, indicating that it had a large base of support. One of the interesting points about the history of that art is that it claims it was also created by a woman who went on to be a successful instructor in a large school with a number of important students.

This is an important innovation and not as common in early periods as one might suspect. In order to have a professional teacher, students must have money (or large amounts of surplus rice) with which to pay their dues. Students must also have the leisure time to pursue these studies. And lastly, students will probably not seek out civilian martial arts instruction if they have already been pushed into a gentry-led rural militia.

The development of martial arts schools is really dependent on the growth of economic systems that one is more likely to see in prosperous manufacturing-based towns or cities. Given that the rapid urbanization of Fujian preceded that of Guangdong, it is not a surprise to see these sorts of schools appearing there first. Throughout the eighteenth and nineteenth centuries Fujian exported martial arts instructors to Guangdong. Both the Cantonese and Hakka arts that developed farther to the south were greatly influenced by these trends. It is actually hard to overstate the influence that Fujian's martial schools had across the entire region.

The only areas in Guangdong that could support similar schools prior to 1800 would have been Foshan and Guangzhou proper, but even there the economy had not reached the peak levels that it would achieve in the 1830s and 40s. One would thus predict that the province's martial arts would have been transmitted in a more traditional manner. The majority of individuals learned a collection of techniques (not even a coherent style) through militias or formal military instructions. Teachers in trades that utilized martial arts, such as pharmacists and doctors, opera singers, and armed escort companies, would pass on their more sophisticated bodies of knowledge only to those in their own organizations. Consequently, it is interesting to note that the traditional Wing Chun narrative incorporates two of these professions.

In both the countryside and the city, individuals with considerable skills might be approached by those wishing to find a tutor for either themselves or their children. Such individuals could often be convinced to teach in exchange for material support and a place to live. This is probably what Leung Jan offered his teachers in exchange for Wing Chun instruction. In all of these cases teaching is handed down through a specific family line (such as a son who inherits his father's medical practice) or through a more or less "personal" master-disciple relationship.

This traditional mode of transmission makes sense when it is remembered that martial arts were primarily a way of making a living. Given that these skills were valuable precisely because they were rare, one would not want to spread them too widely. Lacking a currency-based economy and mass urban markets, it was essentially impossible to capitalize on the interests of large groups of people even if one wanted to. Put simply, the types of martial arts schools that exist today are artifacts of the economic institutions that we possess.

Zeng, in his comprehensive study of hand combat organizations in *Guangdong Wushu Shi* (*A History of Guangdong Martial Arts*), finds no evidence of formal voluntary martial arts associations in the province prior to the 1840s, after which their numbers quickly begin to escalate.[38] It was during this period that the province's economy entered an era of rapid economic adjustment. Fujian, having gone through similar changes earlier, might have already begun to develop "commercial" structures for teaching its martial arts.

If these conclusions seem surprising, it might be worthwhile to consider the view of the martial arts that we get from one of the most important novels in Chinese history, *Heroes of the Water Margin* (sometimes titled *All Men are Brothers* or simply *Water Margin*). The earliest extant copies of this text date from the mid-sixteenth century, or the late Ming period. The novel follows the exploits of a group of bandits and the officials, some righteous and others corrupt, who seek to deal with them. Action is central to all of the various storylines in the book, and it goes without saying that all of the 108 major heroes are described as unimaginably brilliant martial artists.

It is interesting then to read the story and consider where each of the major characters gained their great abilities. The majority of the heroes learned their martial arts while in the military. Many of the bandits picked up their remarkable skills as part of their lawless lifestyle. There are even allusions to a few members of the local gentry who collected talented martial artists and taught some of their skills to their own retainers. But of the 108 heroes profiled in the book, *not one* of them learns their martial arts in a formal school with a Sifu and fellow students.[39] This was simply not part of the experience of most martial artists in the Ming period, and evidently the same traditional patterns of instruction held firm for both the Hung Mun and Hakka Styles through the nineteenth century. In the next section we will consider why these traditional patterns of instruction began to change and how this impacted the character of Guangdong's martial arts.

Urbanization and Market Driven Reform: Guangdong's Martial Arts, 1836–1900

The third decade of the nineteenth century saw a sudden spike in Guangdong's population of martial artists, and the beginnings of a rapid transformation in how these fighting styles were learned. Two events underpinned this shift. The first was of immediate importance at the time, but the second, a less obvious innovation, had far-reaching implications for the future practice of civilian martial arts in southern China. Both of these events played themselves out in the Pearl River Delta.

The obvious source of militarism in the 1830s and 1840s was the sudden increase in imperialist aggression (particularly by Great Britain) in the Guangdong region. Open conflict erupted between the two states in 1839, during the Opium War, discussed in Chapter 1. Nor was this conflict a surprise. Both sides sensed the rising tensions and attempted to shore up their respective positions well before the start of actual hostilities.

Officials and generals in Guangzhou began building signal forts, modernizing the artillery, and constructing gun emplacements. The one thing that was not seen during this time period was a substantial increase in the size of the Banner or Green Standard armies, or even much in the way of an attempt to modernize them. The imperialist threat in the south was never a central concern of the Qing regime in Beijing. Throughout most of the nineteenth century they regarded the various internal disruptions and rebellions as a more pressing danger and consistently underestimated the true magnitude of the risks posed by European, Japanese, and American interests. The central government even cut the size of the regular military units, rightly regarded as ineffective in an actual fight, in an attempt to set the national budget in order.

As a result of these policy choices, local militias in Guangdong received government backing and became a major force in the fight against the British in their repeated attempts to attack Guangzhou. The throne granted special permission to the gentry to convert or establish a number of Confucian schools to help manage local militias. These structures served as administrative offices out of which the gentry coordinated the budgeting, training, and operations of local militia groups.[40]

One of the often overlooked consequences of this decision was that the Qing dynasty, for the very first time, abrogated the strong restrictions that had prevented the gentry from ever forming or joining voluntary associations. Most voluntary associations during the Qing dynasty were in fact illegal. There was no concept of "freedom of association" in Chinese society and the state used its broad restrictions on voluntary associations as a way to forestall rebellion.

These rules were often observed in the breach by peasants or merchants. Commercial guilds sometimes received government recognition, though often the state found it more useful to simply ignore the guilds and let them know that if they stepped out of line they would be shut down. This had the effect of forcing the owners of voluntary associations to anticipate the state's wishes and comply without ever being asked. All in all, this was a reasonably effective, and usually benign, system of social management. Likewise, the peasants were rarely harassed about their mutual aid or insurance societies. Religious organizations, like sutra reading groups, were always more of a concern to the state, though local officials would often simply ignore them unless directly ordered to do something.

This same forbearance was never extended to the gentry. In exchange for their lofty social status they were without exception banned from voluntary associations (other than the literary societies), and their behavior was monitored to make sure that they complied. The state was much more concerned about a gentry-led revolt than a merchant-led one, so its restrictions were tougher. Even innocuous reform efforts, such as the creation of an anti-foot binding league, could earn the wrath of the state.[41]

The participation of the gentry in the militia movement had always been limited in the past. Their lineage associations might maintain a small standing army, yet the gentry had to be careful of too closely aligning themselves with these groups. As major landlords they might attempt to organize their peasants into a crop-watching society, but you could not formally extend these institutions to neighboring estates.

The imperial order to create networks of militia changed how the gentry of the Guangdong related to the state in ways that the Qing never fully anticipated or grasped. Both Wakeman and Rhoads have argued that this fundamentally altered the balance of power within society and contributed to the growing political consciousness of the gentry and richer merchants.

These changes also promoted the acceptance of martial values among a certain segment of the gentry. After all, there cannot be a more Confucian value than self-sacrifice for the defense of the state. The central role played by members of the so-called "new gentry," such as Ip Man and Yuen Kay San, in the promotion and preservation of Wing Chun during the 1920s and 30s, was possible only because of fundamental social shifts that had begun almost a century before.

The second major event of the 1830s was an affair of the common people and it went largely unnoticed at the time. In 1836, an individual by the name of Chan Heung announced the creation of a new martial arts system called Choy Li Fut. By the end of the century it would become the most popular hand combat system in Guangdong and have schools in every major county and town of the province. In fact, Wing Chun, Hung Gar, and most of the Hakka arts developed in the shadow of Choy Li Fut. This fact is usually overlooked by students of Guangdong's martial arts since the popularity of the style declined precipitously after 1949. However, it is impossible to tell the story of the development of the province's civilian martial culture without first starting here.

Chan Heung (ca. 1806–1875) was born in King Mui village, located in what is now the city of Jiangmen.[42] His village was situated in the Pearl River Delta, about 30 km due south of Foshan. As with most martial arts that arose in the nineteenth century, few facts about the development of Choy Li Fut are known, and the rest of the history of the system is supplemented with myths focusing on the survivors of the Shaolin Temple.

Chan is said to have been a talented martial artist who first learned his craft with his uncle, Yuen Woo. Oral folk tradition claims that Yuen Woo was a secular disciple at the mythic Southern Shaolin Temple, and this explains his remarkable martial arts skills. Chan is said to have studied with his uncle until he reached the age of seventeen. At that point his uncle approached one of his "kung fu brothers," Li Yau San, and asked him to instruct his nephew. Li is also said to have been a graduate of the Shaolin Temple, and reportedly instructed Chan for another four years.

At the end of this time Chan's story morphs from the merely improbable to the impossible. Li suggested that his young student travel to the famous Mt. Luofu along the east branch of the Pearl River and seek out instruction by the Buddhist recluse known as Choy Fok. Unfortunately, this monk had already decided to retire from the world and had publicly declared that he would not accept martial arts students. Instead he would only teach and cultivate the dharma.

Upon locating the recluse Chan managed to convince Choy to accept him strictly as a religious disciple, but he continued to practice his martial arts every night in secret. This pattern continued until one night when Chan was practicing his kung fu by kicking stones high into the air and then smashing them into bits before they hit the ground. Suddenly the monk appeared and asked if that was really the best that he could do. The monk motioned to a very large stone and asked Chan to kick it 12 feet through the air. Chan mustered his strength, kicked the small boulder as hard as he could and barely moved it the required distance. Without speaking, the monk approached the rock, slipped his foot under it, and effortlessly sent it sailing through the sky.

At that point the monk agreed to accept Chan as both a martial and religious student and instructed him for another eight years. At the age of twenty-nine Chan decided to return to the world. After this point his life story becomes substantially more mundane.[43]

Chan named his style Choy Li Fut in remembrance of the sources of the new tradition. The "Choy" referred to the Choy Gar taught to him by the monk. The "Li" is a reference to the Li Gar that he learned from Li Yau San. The "Fut" denotes that this is a "Buddhist" art with its roots in the Shaolin Temple, as well as remembering the contributions of his uncle who had taught him Fut Gar. He publicly revealed his art in 1836. Chan was first hired by the Chen village in Shunde County as a coach and militia instructor. Shunde was a rich and well-connected area, and it would appear that this is when his reputation as a martial arts instructor began to spread.[44]

The outbreak of the Opium War gave Chan another opportunity to prove himself. Oral folklore recounts that he went to Guangzhou to join the army and fight the British. These traditions pose some interesting questions. The major militias in Shunde had to stay in place as the entire region was strategically significant. It is also the same area where local gentry-led militias would stop Chen Kai's forces and prevent them from reinforcing Li Wen Mao's siege of Guangzhou in 1854. This critical action broke the forward momentum of the Red Turban Revolt. It is even possible that some troops trained by Chan may have been involved in that action.

It seems unlikely that Chan actually joined the Green Standard Army and there are no other indications that he sought a formal military career. Of course, one could not join the Banner Armies as they were composed of ethnic Manchus. Instead Chan was probably hired as a "brave" or mercenary. The governor-general oversaw the hiring of many such mercenaries and they played a vital role in the stiffening of the various militia units that defended the city. Experienced martial artists and fighters were very much in demand, so it seems entirely likely that someone like Chan Heung would have been caught up in the action.

Period sources discuss the training and deployment of these troops, including their use of local martial arts. The May 1840 edition of the *Asiatic Journal and Monthly Register for British and Foreign India, China and Australia* includes the following notice on page 327:

> Governor Lin has enlisted about 3,000 recruits, who are being drilled daily near Canton in the military exercise of the bow, the spear and the double sword. The latter weapon is peculiar to China. Each soldier is armed with two short and straight swords, one in each hand, which being knocked against each other, produce a clangour [sic], which, it is thought, will midate [sic] the enemy.

A more detailed discussion of these events was provided by the British Naval Officer J. Elliot Bingham. The "double swords" noted in both accounts are the direct ancestors of the hudiedao (or butterfly swords) that are still used in Wing Chun, Choy Li Fut, and Hung Gar today. The hudiedao and staff (which lay a foundation for the other polearms) are usually the first weapons taught to students of the region's arts. It is interesting to note that these are the same skills that formed the core of nineteenth-century militia training.

> March the 21st, Lin was busy drilling 3,000 troops, a third portion of which was to consist of double-sworded men. These twin swords, when in scabbard, appear as one thick clumsy weapon, about two feet in length; the guard for the hand continuing straight, rather beyond the "fort" of the sword turns toward the point, forming a hook about two inches long. When in use, the thumb of each hand is passed under this hook, on which the sword hangs, until a twist of the wrist brings the grip within the grasp of the swordsman. Clashing and beating them together and cutting the air in every direction, accompanying the action with abuse, noisy shouts and hideous grimaces, these dread heroes advance, increasing their gesticulations and distortions of visage as they approach the enemy, when they expect the foe to become alarmed and fly before them. Lin had great faith in the power of these men.[45]

The years after the Opium War saw a rapid growth in banditry, secret societies, and rebellion. The Taiping Rebellion changed China's political landscape when it broke out in 1850. Despite the Choy Li Fut movement's reputation for revolutionary behavior, Chan is said to have initially resisted pressure from his students to support the new "kingdom."

It is often forgotten today that the Taipings had their own unique religious ideology. They were violently opposed to both Buddhism and Daoism, burning temples as they attempted to purge the countryside of any sign of "heresy." Chan apparently considered himself a committed Buddhist and wanted nothing to do with the group.[46] It is thought that a good number of his students did not share these same reservations.

In or around 1848, Chan expanded the scope of his operation and started to create branch schools throughout the region. The first wave of new instructors was composed of his various disciples.[47] It is no coincidence that this sudden expansion from a traditional master and his disciples to a network of institutionally linked commercial schools occurs just as bandit gangs and secret societies are mushrooming in anticipation of Guangdong's own descent into chaos and civil war. Demand for hand combat instruction was reaching an all-time high.

The first of Chan's many disciples to take up instruction was Lung Ji Choi, who set up a school, under Chan's authority, in Guangxi Province. At this point Choy Li Fut ceased to be a village or country style and took on its more institutionalized and networked characteristics. The second branch was opened almost immediately thereafter by Chan Din Yao and Chan Din Fune in Foshan. The Foshan location functioned for between four and five years, and then, like everything else, it went up in the flames of the Red Turban Revolt. Still, it is remarkable that Choy Li Fut was being taught publicly in Foshan about fifty years before the appearance of the first Wing Chun schools.

What role, if any, the early Foshan school played in these events is unknown. We do know that Chan Din Yao and Chan Din Fune do not show up on the list of known rebel leaders provided by Kim.[48] Of course, this is not definitive proof. They may simply not have ranked highly enough in the rebellion's hierarchy to warrant mention, or possibly some of their students participated in the rebellion without their teacher's approval. Yet even this seems unlikely.

Many current students of Choy Li Fut wish to claim that their school was involved in all such revolutionary activities, but given the fact that most of the other branches of Chan's movement appear to have operated with relatively little difficulty throughout southern China, the logical conclusion would be that the state simply did not see them as a threat. It should be remembered that the Red Turban Revolt was followed by a brutal and violent "white terror," which claimed literally hundreds of thousands of lives. Those groups that the governor or military saw as "trouble causers" (such as the Cantonese opera companies) quickly lost their heads. At this time Chan's Choy Li Fut organization was operating very much in the open, and there is no evidence that the government ever sought to attack its schools or execute its leaders.

For whatever reason, Chan Din Yao and Chan Din Fune did not reopen the Foshan school immediately after the rebellion. Zeng, in *Guangdong Wushu Shi*, claims this is because one of the pair lost his eyesight.[49] A more likely explanation might be that such activities were frowned on in recently pacified Foshan, and martial artists, like Cantonese opera singers, had to wait for tensions to die down before publicly resuming their trade. While the return to normalcy in Foshan seems to have been slow in coming, in 1867 Chan sent another disciple to reopen the school, now titled the Hung Sing Association.

This individual was named Jeong Yim (c.1814–c.1893) and, while he proved to be the single most important figure in the reestablishment of Choy Li Fut in Foshan, almost nothing solid is known about him. The dates of his birth and death are unclear with some traditions claiming that he lived for thirty-three years, while others assert that he died in his eighties. What is certain is that he was a disciple of Chan Heung and he reopened the Hung Sing school under his authority in 1867. While most of the biographical details of his life are clearly legendary, the product of later martial arts novels and serialized newspaper stories, it does appear that Jeong was responsible for giving Foshan's Choy Li Fut its unique character. It is also interesting to note that Jeong was a rough contemporary of Leung Jan. Wing Chun, as we know it today, began to emerge just as Choy Li Fut consolidated its regional dominance.

Current popular accounts of the founding of the Hung Sing school often state that the government in Guangzhou was horrified to learn that the "revolutionary" organization was about to be reopened, so it sent soldiers to try and stop this by any means necessary. As a result Jeong Yim had to train efficient fighters quickly and in secret. Only after they had mastered devastating combat skills were more advanced forms added. These assertions are simply absurd and are likely a self-serving historical myth created at a much later time (when the idea of "revolutionary action" was genuinely popular) to bolster the school's reputation.

Rather than training a secret network of deadly revolutionaries, Jeong Yim and his later successor Chan Ngau Sing (1864–1926) appear to have been successful precisely because they were quite open and public. While it is certainly possible that there may have been tensions with local government officials, it is impossible to imagine that an organization as large and high-profile as the Hung Sing Association could have operated without at least tacit government approval. As we will see in the next chapter, the government was more than capable of shutting the school down when it actually wanted to.

Jeong Yim opened his public school at 15 Ya Bang Street. The location is still present and it is known today as the "Hung Sing Ancestral Hall."[50] The organization grew and spread beyond its original confines. By 1920 (at the peak of its popularity) the Hung Sing Association had thirteen branches and roughly 3,000 members in Foshan alone.[51] Given that the town's total population at this point in time was about 300,000 individuals, we estimate that at least 4 percent of all working age males under forty were associated with or in some way connected to the Hung Sing Association. This organization would eventually transcend its role as a simple martial arts school and become an important player in Foshan's larger social and political landscape.

We can speak more specifically about how the Hung Sing Association operated under Jeong Yim's successor, Chan Ngau Sing. When Jeong died (probably in the early 1890s) a number of his top students left to take up teaching careers of their own elsewhere in the region. The school went into a period of decline after losing its venerated leader, and Chan looked for some way to bring about a revival of local interest in Choy Li Fut. He was extremely successful in doing this, though some of the myths and legends that were created in his era are likely responsible for obscuring the earlier phases of the art's history in Foshan.

Chan took over the Hung Sing organization during a period of rising nationalism and discontent with the Qing government. The handicraft economy of Foshan was slowly industrializing, and workers were increasingly squeezed by the new system of trade and production. Unemployment was a real problem, and the fear that China would be partitioned by the foreign powers, much as they had just divided up Africa, was pervasive throughout Guangdong. If the Hung Sing school was to succeed, it needed to be able to thrive in this more volatile and politically conscious environment.

In comparison to his predecessors, we know slightly more about Chan as an individual. Chan was a rough contemporary of Chan Wah Shun. He originally worked as a copper and brass smith and studied Hung Gar with a local teacher for about four or five years. Some say that he challenged and was defeated by Jeong in or around 1873. He then joined his school and remained Jeong's student until the older master died. Other biographical accounts, favored by Doc Fai Wong's lineage, state that his original teacher simply left China and recommended that Chan continue his studies with Jeong instead.

It was Chan who, in the 1890s, first established the Hung Sing Association's famous "three exclusions" policy. Chan claimed that he would not teach anyone who was a high government official, anyone who was a local bully, or anyone who did not have a legitimate job. These last two points were specifically designed to exclude hooligans and enforcers from the various secret societies.

If one wanted to join the Hung Sing Association, he had to be gainfully employed, usually as a worker in a local shop or factory, or sometimes as a small merchant. Of course, if he were not employed, he would not be able to pay the tuition. This school was a strictly commercial venture. Second, he had to be recommended by someone who was already a member of the association, and his application needed to be approved by the "chairman." In reality, the Hung Sing Association was a very large public school that would teach basically anyone who paid his dues on time. Nevertheless, by publicizing the "three exclusions" Chan was able to maintain the image of a more select, tightly knit, organization.

Best of all, this image could be maintained at very little cost as it was not really necessary to exclude anyone. How many gangster chiefs or high government officials even wanted martial arts training in the first place? In reality, the purpose of the "three exclusions" was to make the organization more welcoming to the working-class clientele that Chan sought to attract. Again, professional martial artists during the late Qing understood their new base of urban consumers and had no problem with the idea of branding and marketing their schools. Chan appears to have been something of a genius in these areas. His tenure saw the creation of numerous branch schools across the city.

In addition to the famous exclusions, Chan also advanced a ten-point code of ethics for his members:

1. Seek the approval of your master in all things relative to the school.

2. Practice hard daily.

3. Fight to win (but do not fight by choice).

4. Be moderate in sexual behavior.

5. Eat healthily.

6. Develop strength through endurance (to build a foundation and the ability to jump).

7. Never back down from an enemy.

8. Practice breathing exercises.

9. Make the sounds ("Yik" for punches, "Wah" for tiger claws, "Tik" for kicks).

10. Through practice you cannot be bullied.

As this list makes clear, urban violence, especially at the hands of secret society members, was a problem for workers in Foshan in the later parts of the nineteenth century. The Hung Sing school promised relief from that, both through gaining new defensive skills and, just as importantly, through membership in a large mutual support society. New applicants to the Hung Sing Association are referred to in the Chinese language literature as "apprentices" and it is clear that individuals turned to the organization for more than just martial arts instructions.[52]

Workers away from their home village, and those who could not join the more powerful clan associations, joined schools like Hung Sing for both a network of contacts and mutual support. The Hung Sing Association even maintained its own cemetery, a major charitable undertaking by the standards of the time.[53] And given the relatively large percentage of Foshan's workforce that was involved in this organization, it is not hard to see its potential as a collective bargaining device in the increasingly acrimonious world of labor relations.

Given this outline of basic facts, we can now ask some deeper questions about the Foshan Hung Sing Association as it existed in the closing decades of the Qing dynasty. To begin with, what sort of basic organizational forms do we see here? This is a critical question since Choy Li Fut was one of the first martial arts in the region to be taught commercially on a wide scale in public schools. As stated earlier, there was not much of a historical precedent for this in Guangdong, though something similar had already taken root in Fujian Province. So what sorts of preexisting social forms and institutions were adopted to create this new generation of commercial urban schools? Given the centrality of the Hung Sing Association to the local martial arts environment, if we can answer that question for this organization we might be able to uncover the basic social structures that underpinned the entire generation of schools and associations that followed it.

A few possibilities immediately present themselves. It is often asserted that Guangdong's martial arts of the Hung Mun group (including Wing Chun) have their roots in anti-government secret societies. The founding mythology of these schools claims as much. It is conceivable that the new generation of martial arts schools were modeled on secret society chapters. One should also remember that membership in the societies spiked in the late nineteenth and early twentieth centuries; at exactly the same time we see an explosion in the number of public martial arts schools.

This theory, often implicitly advanced by practicing martial artists, has a number of critical shortcomings.[54] To begin with, complex ritualized initiation ceremonies, including the use of blood oaths and divine theater, were always at the heart of the secret society experience. These things are totally missing from the sorts of martial arts schools that developed in the nineteenth century. Furthermore, one could become a master of a secret society, and even found a new chapter, simply by paying more for your initiation. No actual skills had to be conveyed in the process.[55] Yet martial arts schools are centered on the mission of conveying physically embodied skills. The one thing they absolutely must have is a functioning teaching structure. While the ritual transfer of esoteric knowledge was important, secret societies never really operated as schools.

This is not to say that there was not substantial overlap between the world of martial artists and that of gangsters and secret society members. Clearly there was. Secret societies might even use martial arts schools as recruiting devices. However, it is interesting to note that these individuals always kept the two bodies institutionally and organizationally distinct. There was never any sense that a commercial martial arts association and a secret society were the same thing, or even shared a common organizational structure.

Another possibility is that this new generation of martial arts schools is modeling its organizations on the powerful clan and lineage associations that dominated life in Guangdong. Many things suggest this. Most martial arts schools set up shrines in which incense sticks were burned in memory of the founders of the school. The names of these founders were inscribed onto what can only be called ancestral tablets. Furthermore, the nomenclature that dominates life in all southern hand combat schools is drawn from popular neo-Confucianism. The teacher is not referred to by a professional title. Rather he is called "Sifu" which indicates both father and teacher. Senior students are referred to as "older brothers" while junior students are "younger" brothers or sisters. All of these factors taken together make it abundantly clear that martial arts schools functioned as an artificial family, complete with elaborate kinship structures.[56] This is one of the ways in which they succeed in bestowing a new identity upon students.

Yet this theory also has its limitations. To begin with, the familial aspect of modern Chinese martial arts is the most obvious at the local level, within individual schools. As soon as one starts to look at broader hand combat associations, the parallels to large clan structures begin to break down. Furthermore, no matter how traditional a martial arts instructor attempted to be, a public school remained a voluntary pay-for-play space. The sort of social control that was possible in the traditional Chinese family was never a possibility in the martial arts marketplace. Nevertheless, the power that familial and kinship ideas conveyed probably had a transformative effect on martial arts students. It is also clear that many martial arts instructors appropriated the language and structure of kinship systems and used them to advance their own goals.

It is also possible that the militia structures that dominated the countryside helped to inspire the new public schools. Chan Heung, Wong Fei Hung and many other hand combat teachers originally started off as soldiers or drill instructors. Yet it is remarkable how little impact this seems to have had on the martial arts associations of Guangdong Province. While most schools have a respectful atmosphere there is no sign of military style discipline. Ranks, either from China's ancient or modern military traditions, are totally absent from what is a self-consciously *civilian* project. The militarism that dominates many of Japan's martial arts is simply absent from Guangdong's hand combat tradition.

We propose that martial arts historians, when searching for the social origins of modern public schools, might wish instead to consider China's rich tradition of merchant guilds. Foshan was a major commercial center and the city was home to literally hundreds of guilds. These guilds oversaw and regulated the manufacturing process in many industries, including the training of apprentices, and often dominated the social lives of their members.

The guilds of Foshan fell into three categories. The first of these might be thought of as "hometown guilds." These organizations were basically social clubs that offered a place to stay and entertainment to individuals who originated from a common area. Such guilds were most common in Beijing where there was a great need to house temporary visitors coming to sit for the imperial exams or to meet with officials. In

Foshan, it was mostly businessmen from other areas of southern China who made use of the hometown guilds. Such organizations usually had an executive board and a chairman who was a locally prominent and wealthy citizen. Given the nature of these clubs they tended to be lax in the regulation of their members.

More important were the "masters' guilds" for different industries. There might be a chopstick maker's guild, a basket weaving guild, and a sword manufacturers guild hall all on the same block. These organizations regulated the local industry, set prices, and oversaw the training of new apprentices. The richer guilds often had an extensive social presence which might include official recognition by the local government, the building and maintenance of a local temple to facilitate common worship by its members, and charitable projects such as running schools or cemeteries. Since these organizations usually contributed to the good order of the community, and were apolitical in nature, they were often approved of by the government. Of course care always had to be taken not to offend local officials.

Lastly, there were the "journeymen's guilds," again organized by industry. Rather than being dominated by the masters and shop owners, these guilds were often founded by workers who were employed in these shops and industries. More skilled than apprentices, yet not rich enough to go into business for themselves, these individuals were often forced to accept the pay and working conditions that the masters set. Not surprisingly, they attempted to organize themselves to promote their own collective bargaining power. Journeymen's guilds might also provide valuable networking opportunities for those looking for employment, and even rudimentary unemployment insurance. Given their involvement in strikes and their connection to both social and market disorder, these organizations were often banned by the government.[57]

One possibility is that in an effort to renew its membership the Hung Sing Association moved to fill the void created by the absence of effective journeymen's guilds. Chan Ngau Sing may have even nudged things in this direction, and thus inspired the strategies that other local martial arts schools would adopt as well. While not itself a guild, it is clear that his association provided many of the same services. It gave workers a place to meet, network, and search for employment. Martial arts practice promised safety and health benefits in a marketplace without any form of unemployment insurance. And as we move into the 1920s in the next chapter, the Hung Sing Association begins to play an undeniably important role in the evolution of the local labor movement and Communist Party in Foshan.

Examining early martial arts schools through the lens of guilds might resolve some other questions as well. For instance, what is the role of religion in Chinese martial arts? Authors from Tang Hao to Kennedy and Guo have decried the emphasis placed on religion and spirituality by modern students. These authors see spirituality as, at best, a distraction from the fundamentally practical nature of hand combat and, at worst, a delusion.[58] Still, there is an undeniable aspect of religious practice in many southern forms of martial arts. Everything from neo-Confucian ancestral altars, to spirit possession techniques in traditional Southern Mantis lineages, to involvement in the more esoteric aspects of lion and unicorn dances, touches on traditional Chinese ritual and spirituality.[59] How then should we understand these connections?

Chinese guild culture provides one clue. Christine Moll-Murata relates that all of the early sources on Chinese guilds note that they shared a common religious practice. In fact, this was one of the major benefits that guild membership provided, and the more prosperous guilds might even build entire temples to facilitate worship (and meeting) by their members. These temples might be dedicated to previous guild members and gods that were seen as important to the craft in question. Thus the chopstick maker's guild might have its own temple or altar dedicated to a specific deity.

Naturally, there is nothing particularly spiritual about the making or use of chopsticks. The creation of a temple, and a common pattern of worship, does nothing to change this. The goal was never to sacralize eating utensils; what was a secular activity remains so. A common pattern of worship does something else. It helps to create a sense of shared identity while designating a specific private space where the new collective can be enacted. The point of the religious ritual is not to produce a better chopstick; it is to create a tighter and more focused community, more dedicated to each other, and better able to carry out the social functions of the guild. This understanding of religion in defining the communal is one of the most fundamental insights that we gain from the writings of Emile Durkheim and Fustel de Coulanges, director of the École Normale. Nowhere are their insights more clearly demonstrated than in Chinese popular religion where a community is quite literally defined as those who burn incense together. By creating an altar one creates an organization.

Religion, which was largely phrased in a familial context, did play a vital part in the early martial arts schools. Its function had little to do with hand combat itself, focusing instead on the problem of creating and binding together a new type of community. It would then stand to reason that what is needed in Western martial arts schools today is a new way of creating group identity, not a blind adherence to ancient ritual forms. A more detailed discussion of the parallels between Foshan's commercial guilds and early southern martial arts schools is beyond the scope of this volume, but it is an area that deserves additional study.

Chan's efforts to revive awareness of Choy Li Fut found an attentive audience. The late 1880s and 1890s saw an increase in popular interest in martial arts in Guangdong, both as a way of strengthening the country and as a form of fashionable entertainment. This transition is most evident in the world of commercial literature. Throughout the late 1800s periodicals like *Dianshizhai Huaboa* (*Decorative Stone Studio Illustrated News*) ran colorful stories about martial artists. Many of these tales featured female heroes, such as the case of three beautiful sisters who could jump back and forth on plum blossom poles (set over iron spikes), but could not find any male suitors due to their intimidating martial ways.

Other stories featured prostitutes who were martial artists, or women who used boxing skills to rescue their hapless husbands. This should not be taken to mean that women took up martial arts en masse in the late nineteenth century. The popularity of such accounts, written by male authors for a predominantly male audience, seems to derive its impact from the unexpected, but still relatively safe, reversal of gender roles.[60]

One also wonders if this sudden interest in the image of female martial artists might be a popular response to Western imperialism in the late nineteenth and early twentieth centuries. The classic assertion that "soft" could overcome "hard" was certainly reinforced in these stories, albeit in a fanciful way. This, in turn, underscored the essential value of Chinese culture and identity in the face of an existential challenge from the West. Douglas Wile has argued that these same sorts of insecurities may have colored the emerging emphasis on "softness" and "internal training" in Taijiquan at a more elite social level in northern China at roughly the same time.[61] This literary interest in female warriors expanded during the Republic of China period. The Wing Chun creation myth, which is unique in its inclusion of two central female protagonists, needs to be understood as both a reflection of this general trend and a commentary on the underlying concerns and insecurities that fueled it.

The anonymous publication of *Shengchao Ding Sheng Wannian Qing* (*Everlasting*) in 1893 provides one of the most popular early martial novels published in Guangdong, and the first to discuss the burning of

Shaolin and the rivalries between the various survivors. In fact, Hamm has argued that the "old school" of martial arts fiction that arose in the wake of *Everlasting* really centered on the glorification and promotion of local heroes and local identity, through the medium of martial arts. Incursions by northern, Mandarin speaking, martial artists was apparently just as galling to the readers of these early novels as the advances of British merchants.[62]

Hand combat's late nineteenth century wave of popularity was not destined to be long lived. The Boxer Uprising, in which a group of martial artists, cultists, and peasant youth attempted to "save" the empire by besieging the foreign legation in Beijing, delivered a true body blow to China's indigenous fighting systems. In the wake of the failed uprising the government was forced to pay huge war reparations to the Western powers, notably impoverishing the country.

The cautious governor in Guangzhou immediately restricted the martial arts in an attempt to forestall any local groups from taking it upon themselves to also "save" the nation, thereby giving the foreign powers a chance to seize parts of the Pearl River system or to partition southern China. Ip family tradition records that the years following the Boxer Uprising were a time of disorder and banditry, and Wing Chun was not being openly taught in Foshan.[63] The Hung Sing Association, the largest martial arts school in the town, was officially shut down by the government in 1900.

At this point Chan Ngau Sing left for Hong Kong where he tried to make a living selling vegetables. After an altercation with a local policeman, similar to the one that Ip Man would report decades later, Chan was arrested and deported back to Guangdong.[64] Luckily, by 1905 the situation had calmed and it was possible to resume open martial arts instruction. The Hung Sing Association likely reopened its doors around this time. But things could not stay the same. The first decade of the twentieth century was the start of China's great period of revolution and upheaval. Once again, martial arts schools were forced to evolve in order to survive in the rapidly changing environment.

Other Public Martial Arts Associations in Guangdong, 1836–1900

Throughout the nineteenth century Hung Gar and Choy Li Fut were the most popular arts in Guangdong. While Choy Li Fut pioneered the development of public schools and broader regional associations, it was not the only tradition to develop new types of institutions. New forms of martial arts organizations quickly spread as economic reform and upheaval penetrated the countryside.

The Hakka styles took a little longer to embrace these innovations, but in time they did as well. Huizhou County saw a lot of martial arts activity in the second half of the nineteenth century. Not surprisingly, much of the institutional innovation happened as violence between the Hakka and other ethnic groups spiked in the 1860s, leading to an increased demand for hand combat instruction.

The Lin Jia Martial Arts Institute was founded in 1862 in Lianghua Xu, Huidong. It was created by Lin He (1831–1908).[65] Lin was a native of Huiyang. He started to learn the local arts when he was fourteen, and at the age of seventeen he claims to have studied with a former monk from Fujian Province who had given up his vows and returned to secular life.

There is a possibility that Lin was hired as some sort of military officer in Haifeng County, but the majority of his career was spent as a civilian martial arts instructor. Local tradition also claims that, after resigning from the military, Lin traveled to Mt. Luofu, where he studied either Chan Buddhism or, according to other sources, a more advanced form of martial arts. After leaving the Luofu area he returned to his home, established the Lin Jia Martial Arts Institute, and began a public teaching career. To commemorate the origins of his art he posted the following couplet in his school "First to learn from Shaolin, then from Huizhou."

The art that Lin originally taught was likely Luo Shan Fist or Hu Shi Boxing, also known as Shi Pan Village Boxing. This style remained popular in the area for some time, and can still be seen today. The Lin Family Martial Arts Institute has survived for 120 years and has produced a number of well-regarded masters. It preserved important elements of traditional Hakka arts and passed them along to later styles, such as White Eyebrow and Dragon.[66]

In 1886, another long-lasting martial arts institute was established in the extreme southwest of Guangdong Province, at the Shijing port of the Hainan district in Xuwen County. This coastal region was also involved in trade, but it did not do the same volume of business as Guangzhou, and its economy developed even more slowly. The students who established the organization, named Ying Wu Tong (Ying Wu Hall), were all seafaring merchants. Being constantly harassed by pirates they decided to learn martial arts for their own protection. Indeed, pirates and bandits continued to harass trade throughout the 1880s and thousands of armed escort companies thrived around the country.

The local merchants established the Ying Wu Tong on the grounds of Tin Hua Temple.[67] Temples were one of the few public spaces found in traditional Chinese towns and cities. As such, they were often the site of martial arts schools. This does not necessarily indicate any sort of theological relationship.

Reportedly, over 300 students enrolled at the school, but no local martial arts teachers were available. The community had to recruit instructors from other areas of the province. The fact that there was now a marketplace for such skills in the Pearl River Delta, as well as Fujian to the north, made this possible. We should also take note of who these students were. Typically merchants did not study martial arts during the Qing dynasty, and they certainly did not form large voluntary associations to do so. The Ying Wu Tong demonstrates that the profile of the average martial artist was evolving rapidly in this period. By the 1890s these trends could be seen in even relatively under developed areas.

The Xuwen Martial Arts Association has had a fairly continuous, and colorful, existence. In the 1930s it is remembered for using a combination of spears, swords, and primitive field artillery to defeat a prominent local bandit. During WWII the group used its knowledge of the sea and skill with small wooden boats to harass the local Japanese naval presence. As late as the 1980s, former students of the third and fourth generation of the organization were still teaching local children the arts that they had learned and perfected in their own eventful youths.[68]

If the Hung Sing Association was the prototypical commercial public school, the Ying Wu Tong illustrates a different, but no less important, evolutionary pathway. This organization was unique in that it truly belonged to its students. It was the students who hired instructors, arranged their pay, and rented space for their activities. Rather than being a vehicle for a single teacher's commercial exploitation of his art, it was a genuine voluntary association, open to the public, dedicated to addressing local concerns. This combination of boxing school and civic center would become essential to the mass popularization of martial arts in the 1920s and 30s. In some respects the Xuwen school foreshadows the development of the national Jingwu movement discussed in the next chapter.

Another public martial arts association was created in Guangdong at the very end of our current era of study. Established in 1898 (at roughly the same time that Chan Wah Shun began to teach) it was named the Dongguan Martial Arts Institute. Like the Ying Wu Tong, its development was a result of increased local demand for martial arts instruction. The 1880s through the 1890s was a time of heightened popular interest in martial arts, so we should not be surprised to see a jump in the number of public schools across the province.

As in Xuwen, the locals were initially forced to bring in martial arts instructors from outside the region. The first instructor hired was named Gao Dao and he came from Fujian Province. Gao was a master of Five Animals boxing (in this case Dragon, Snake, Tiger, Leopard, and Bear) and taught a number of weapon forms. Total enrollment in the early phase of the school was about thirty students. However, the government forced the organization to close following the outbreak of the Boxer Uprising.

The local population resurrected their martial arts institute in 1911, an era of rising national consciousness. This time they hired an instructor from Lianjiang County named Huan Jin Biao. Huan taught the family styles (Hung, Lau, Choy, Li, and Mok Gar). However, this incarnation of the school was short lived. Perhaps a total of sixty students received instruction.

A third phase of the school began in 1933 under the leadership of Mo Cai Zhang. Mo had been a student during the first and second phases of the association and presumably he taught what he had learned. However, the Japanese invasion in 1938 once again disrupted instruction. It is estimated that the school had about eighty students during this time.

In 1946, the school was briefly reopened, but it collapsed almost immediately. Two years later another effort was made to reestablish instruction. This time 100 students enrolled, and the instructors, Xu Cai Dong and Hu De Wen, were both natives of Zhanjiang. The communist takeover of Guangdong in 1949 forced the association to close its doors yet again.[69]

The Dongguan Martial Arts Institute provides us with a cautionary tale. Unlike the Hung Sing Association and the Ying Wu Tong, it was never really able to put down deep roots in the countryside. Crisis and calamity easily disrupted the Institute's work. Its history demonstrates that popular demand for martial arts instruction is not enough to ensure that a public school or voluntary association will survive. Solid institutions grounded in the local community, and a steady supply of financial and political support, are also necessary to deal with risk.

It is difficult to develop these resources at the purely local level. Small communities are easily disrupted by even a single crisis event. More effective ways of spreading risk are necessary if a martial arts association is going to survive through the decades. That is part of the reason why we see a turn toward both stronger political backing and the creation of larger, nationally franchised, martial arts institutions during the Republic of China era. Yet it is important to realize that these better known national movements are building on foundations that were first laid down in the nineteenth century. Guangdong's hand combat community clearly demonstrates how this process of social change and evolution progressed.

Conclusion

There is no easy answer to the question of who studied hand combat in nineteenth century Guangdong. The period was one of sweeping change, both in the countryside and urban areas. The martial arts are always embedded in larger economic and social structures. When these structures are transformed, the modes of instruction seen within civil society must also change.

The types of public martial arts schools that we have today are an outgrowth of a predominantly urban, monetarily based, economy that gives teachers an incentive to spread their art widely across a great number of students. This sort of instruction was first seen in the south in Fujian, but by the 1860s these new institutions were making inroads in the more urban and developed areas of Guangdong Province. These markets fundamentally altered how the martial arts were taught and the types of students who would seek out instruction.

Commercial guilds likely provided a social and institutional template that was readily adopted by the new generation of schools in Guangzhou and Foshan. These marketable organizations were further strengthened through the adoption of pseudo-kinship identities and norms. Understanding the connection between guilds and martial arts schools clarifies some important points about how these early associations functioned and why, as we will see in the next chapter, they became involved in the region's contentious labor politics. It may also allow us to better understand how the broader society viewed these schools and the place they accorded them within China's rapidly evolving civil society.

Indeed, the evolution of Guangdong's martial arts community in the late nineteenth century provides students with a clear vantage point to examine broader questions about the nature of change and reform in the closing years of the Qing dynasty. If martial arts scholars truly wish for greater critical engagement with the disciplines of history, anthropology, sociology, literature, and political science, then they must demonstrate that the evolution of hand combat illuminates important themes of interest to these fields. The preceding discussion has suggested that the study of popular hand combat associations can offer rich insights into the evolving social and economic lives of China's working class, an important group that is often neglected in national histories.

A more detailed understanding of the evolution of southern China's hand combat systems also has much to offer students of traditional martial arts. It is not enough to simply mimic the movements of others. One must instead internalize and focus on the core concepts of the art, attempting to fully address the problems that its founders sought to overcome. In practice one cannot succeed unless you look beyond the pointing finger of specific techniques. It is vital to understand the environment in which an art arose.

Guangdong Province could be a cruel place at the end of the Qing dynasty. Violence, interpersonal as well as communal, was a fact of life in both the cities and the countryside. Nor was this an idyllic age of martial honor and spirituality, conveniently situated before the invention of firearms, as imagined in so many kung fu movies and novels. In truth, arts like Choy Li Fut, White Eyebrow, and Wing Chun all evolved and assumed their present form in an era when both bandits and security guards carried guns, union members clashed violently with strike breakers, and organized crime and drug smuggling were major social issues. The philosophies and principles of these arts emerged in response to both these specific problems and larger debates about nationalism, modernization, and imperialism.

In Chapter 3 we continue to track the evolution of hand combat in Guangdong. Foshan's martial community will become increasingly involved in contentious local politics while, at the same time, intellectual reformers take up the question of what role these arts should play in the national identity. The emerging martial marketplace forms a sort of microcosm in which central themes in modern Chinese social history play out with startling clarity.

Chapter 3

Northern Tigers versus Southern Heroes

Local Identity, National Reform, and the Golden Age of Guangdong's Martial Arts, 1911–1949

I don't oppose playing ball in the least, but I do oppose this feverish consumption of foreigners' goods. This is exercise, but it is the exercise of the gents and ladies of the leisured classes. If you want to exercise your body, is a blade not enough? Is a sword routine not enough? Are wrestling or boxing not enough? Of China's eighteen types of martial arts, not one is incapable of drenching our entire bodies in sweat, stimulating all the body's blood, tendons, and bones.

—Warlord Feng Yuxiang, 1927[1]

Introduction

The years between the fall of the Qing dynasty and the Communist Party takeover in 1949 were the golden age of Guangdong's martial arts. Nevertheless, it was common in that period for journalists and intellectuals to publicly question whether China's traditional methods of hand combat could possibly survive in the modern era. This gloomy speculation proved to be totally disconnected from reality. There was, in fact, an immense demand for martial arts instruction among China's growing urban populations.

Displaced peasants from the countryside streamed into cities where they joined martial arts schools seeking mutual protection, support, and a reaffirmation of their local and national identity. The market for urban martial arts instruction, introduced in the previous chapter, simply exploded in the years following the creation of the Republic of China. This vibrant outpouring even inspired local practitioners to create, or publicly reveal, some of the most popular "traditional" martial arts practiced in China today. Regional journalists and authors got in on the act and, by the 1920s and 1930s, they were mass producing martial arts-themed articles, novels and radio programs that would fundamentally reshape how people thought about the history, culture, and mythology of these combat systems.

At the same time a second, very different, martial arts revolution was afoot in northern China. Intellectuals and national reformers from the New Culture Movement believed that China could not be made safe from imperialism without a massive overhaul of almost all aspects of its ancient civilization. This concern even extended to the realm of physical culture and exercise, a topic that China's self-appointed cultural guardians had been studiously avoiding since the end of the Ming dynasty. Much emphasis was placed on the importation of Swedish calisthenics and German drill exercises as a way of "strengthening the nation," both spiritually and physically.

Fortunately, growing disenchantment with the policies of the Western powers allowed some martial artists to claim possession of a unique tool that could both improve the health of China's masses, and create a unified, powerful sense of national identity. The Japanese, a perennial source of inspiration for Chinese reformers, had already demonstrated that martial arts could promote nationalism and national strength. If Bushido could power the Japanese empire, surely China's rich martial heritage could strengthen and invigorate the state. Of course, the traditional arts would have to be subjected to a vigorous reform and modernization process in which the local, the superstitious, and the particular would be stripped away in favor of the universal, the scientific, and the easily franchised.

Many groups were part of this later trend, but two were clearly dominant. The 1920s was the decade of the Jingwu Association. These urban reformers, businessmen, and journalists created the first, truly national, martial arts brand. They were able to spread their message of "national salvation" to the major urban coastal areas of the state. The Jingwu Association demonstrated that new groups, such as the middle class, intellectuals, and even women, could benefit from the practice of martial arts. They were so successful that in the 1930s the national government decided to launch its own Guoshu (or "national arts") movement. The state also sought to reform hand combat and to create a universal program practiced throughout the country. These innovators hoped to strengthen the bodies of citizens while at the same time ensuring their absolute loyalty to the National Party and Chiang Kai-shek.

Guangdong's martial artists were buffeted by these two competing forces. On the one hand, the local market in hand combat instruction was thriving. It rewarded traditional exponents who could claim a link to China's ancient past, a past that seemed to be slipping away. New styles and "lost" lineages, backed with stories of wandering Shaolin monks and mysterious qi powers, sold quite well. In socioeconomic terms, this movement tended to be more working class in its orientation (though there were notable exceptions) and, while urban, it retained some links to the countryside. There was also immense pressure on at least some martial arts schools to take a stand on issues that were relevant to their members, such as the value of regional identity, resisting imperialism, and the growth of the labor movement in Foshan and Guangzhou.

On the other hand, there were the national reform movements centered in Shanghai and Nanjing which claimed that the martial arts had to be fundamentally reformed if they were going to survive in the modern era. The direction of their proposed alterations did not always line up with existing market pressures, but the reformers were envisioning a vast new project that would involve literally the entire nation. More ominously, the movements that conveyed these messages were dominated by northern styles and masters who had little time for the exotic schools of kung fu that they encountered in the south. If these forces prevailed, the coming age of martial arts would be overwhelmingly urban, middle class, and nationalist in character. The stage was set for a conflict, and it was the clash of these two very different cultural currents that would define the golden age of martial arts in Guangdong Province.

Ip Man, then a student of Wing Chun, stood at the crossroads of these two pathways. He was an exponent of a small southern style, little known beyond his own home town. At the same time he was well-educated, relatively well off, and connected to the local GMD machine through his job with the police department. The debates that swirled around him would not just affect what happened in Guangdong in the 1930s, they would reemerge in Hong Kong in the 1950s and have a profound effect on the development of modern Wing Chun.

The following chapter will examine each of these major themes in turn. It begins with a discussion of the development of the local market for martial arts instruction in Foshan and Guangzhou. Social and political conflict had a major impact on many martial arts schools during this time period, and some could not resist the lure of aligning themselves with a specific faction or political party. While this often brought short-term economic benefits, the long-term consequences of such decisions could be disastrous. We then turn our attention to the Jingwu and Guoshu movements, two attempts to harness popular interest in martial arts for larger commercial, national, and statist goals. While there were major differences between the two groups, in some ways both expressed the same basic drive for national unification and reform. It is particularly interesting to ask why the Guoshu movement failed to establish itself in Guangdong, given that the Jingwu Association had been quite successful in exactly the same areas. Lastly, we consider how the ideology of the Guoshu movement may have affected Ip Man and the way he taught Wing Chun after arriving in Hong Kong.

Creating Southern Heroes:
The Local Market for Martial Arts Instruction

Hung Mun Styles

The period between the Boxer Uprising and the collapse of the Qing dynasty was a decidedly mixed decade for southern China's martial artists. By about 1905 the official repression of martial arts schools eased. This allowed the Hung Sing Association to resume its activities in Foshan, now with genuine revolutionary aspirations. Sun Yat-sen, the father of modern China, decided to capitalize on the widespread suspicion that the ethnically alien Qing were planning on selling China, piece by piece, to the Western imperialists. The idea was ludicrous but, in an era when conspiracy theories seemed plausible, the rumor gained traction.

The general atmosphere of fear and impending collapse allowed Sun Yat-sen to create a number of revolutionary organizations and raise huge amounts of money from the overseas Chinese population. Most of his early plots were not very successful, but they were notable for the degree to which they relied on secret societies as muscle. These groups, in turn, made active use of the Shaolin mythology in an attempt to gain popular support and maintain their social coherence.[2]

This period of revolutionary fervor also saw increasing levels of political radicalization within the Hung Sing Association. Records indicate that prior to the 1911 uprising a number of Hung Sing members and leaders joined Sun Yat-sen's Revolutionary Alliance. These included Li Su and Qian Wei Fang who were both instructors within the organization.

Li and Qian supported Sun Yat-sen's "democratic revolutionary" movement in Foshan and Shunde. They drew their political support from the same demographic groups that the Hung Sing schools tended to recruit from—local workers, clerks, and small shop owners. Li Su was active in Huang Xing's uprising in Guangzhou and then, on November 10, 1911, led his followers against the government troops that were stationed in Foshan.[3]

While the Chinese reformers initially favored either a constitutional monarchy or a republic, these hopes soon faded. Various military officers and strong men began to seize power around the country, and there was even an abortive attempt to institute a new dynasty. More troubling was the increasing level of political division within the reform movement itself. The disastrous results of the Versailles Treaty, ending WWI, brought the most basic goals of the new country into question.

While the Chinese state did not commit combat troops to fight in Europe, they did send a Labor Corps of over 140,000 persons to assist the British army. The understanding of the Chinese government was that, in return for this assistance, the German concessions in northern China would be returned following the end of hostilities. Instead, the allied powers conspired with the Japanese delegation and assigned the concessions to Japan in the final agreement. President Wilson publicly opposed the deal and famously advanced his "14 Points" and "Right of Self Determination." The anti-colonial implications of these declarations were ignored by the Europeans, setting the stage for many of the future conflicts that would consume the twentieth century. The Chinese deeply resented Wilson for being politically weak and failing to push the British to honor their original agreement.

At this point, a number of Chinese intellectuals decided that republican democracy was a fundamentally flawed form of government and nothing to be emulated. In their search for an alternative they began to study the basic principles of Marxism. It wasn't long before the Soviet intelligence agencies learned of this and sent handlers to China to aid in creating Marxist study groups and, eventually, two different political parties both modeled along Leninist lines. They were named the Guomindang, or National Party (GMD), and the Chinese Communist Party (CCP). These two institutions, sometimes in alliance, more often in conflict with each other, have dominated the nation's political destiny up to the present day.

While the Soviets obviously preferred the idea of a communist neighbor, their own doctrines of historical progression argued that China first needed to become a consolidated, and industrialized, capitalist state before the "proletariat" had any chance of achieving class consciousness. National Party leadership would advance this process. At some future date the real Communist Party could then step forward and lead a revolution. The Soviet government armed and advised both groups, contributing in no small way to the almost unfathomable brutality of the 1920s, 30s, and 40s.[4]

By 1922, these larger processes were starting to be felt in Foshan. In January of that year the Communist Party formally established a "Foshan Taskforce" charged with creating a local cell. The task force was composed of four individuals, two of which, Qian Wei Fang and Liang Gui Hua, were members of the Hung Sing Association. The mutual interest that initially linked the two organizations was the question of labor rights and collective bargaining. The Communist Party was pushing to develop a full-scale labor movement in the region.[5] Given the Hung Sing school's previous involvement in the issue, its political radicalization, and its ability to rally large numbers of militant workers, the two organizations were ideal allies in the struggle against local capitalists and factory owners.

In the fall of 1922, the communist cell established the Foshan Federation of Trade Unions and named Qian Wei Fang its director. In 1925, the Federation was reorganized and named the Worker's Congress with Qian Wei Fang again serving as the director of the Foshan branch. This group launched a number of strikes against both firms in Hong Kong and local businesses, and in particular those who attempted to employ so called "yellow trade unions."[6] These firms recruited their own martial arts association, referred to locally as the "Yi" schools, to organize their resistance to the Communist Party. The clash between the "She" (or Hung Sing) and "Yi" schools over labor relations was volatile and came to define the martial culture of Foshan during the mid-1920s.[7]

These conflicts had an important impact on the internal structure of the Hung Sing Association. New offices were created for those who were responsible for leading the various pickets. Most of the organization's quite considerable membership ended up joining the Worker's Congress, swelling the union's membership. One wonders how much of the anti-Manchu rhetoric in that era's kung fu storytelling is really a metaphor for these much more concrete disputes. Yet there were substantial dangers in aligning oneself too closely with any one of China's warring political factions.

Early in 1927, Chiang Kai-shek launched the notorious "April 12 Incident" (also known as the "Shanghai Massacre of 1927"). In 1926, he had begun a major offensive against the northern warlords in a bid to unify the country. Up until this time, the communists and leftists had been in a nominal alliance with the rest of the GMD (which they had been instructed to join by their Soviet advisors) against the warlords. Worker's Militias and communist organizers proved to be remarkably efficient in seizing Shanghai and restoring it to Nationalist control. At this point Chiang began to worry that the communists were planning on asserting their control over his own government as well.

As a result, he broke off his northern assault and returned to Shanghai. There his agents made contact with the Green Gang and the Hongmen (two local secret societies) and convinced them to attack the city's workers and union members. At the same time, the GMD's army forcibly "disarmed" the Workers Militia and arrested all of the prominent Communist Party members they could find. A number of communists were officially executed, but many more were simply killed in the streets or "disappeared."[8]

The violence quickly spread to the Pearl River Delta. On April 14, local officials, with the backing of the yellow trade unions and the Yi martial arts schools, attacked the Workers Congress. Many Congress members were arrested or killed, effectively neutralizing Foshan's communist cell, at least for a while. After a failed uprising in Guangzhou on December 11, Qian Wei Fang, Wu Qin and other important Hung Sing members were forced to flee to Hong Kong and various locations in South East Asia. The Hung Sing Association was officially suppressed by the GMD and closed its doors.

This period marks the start of a rapid decline in Choy Li Fut's popularity in Guangdong. While it never entirely disappeared, it has also never come close to regaining the overwhelming dominance that it once enjoyed in both martial and political circles. The sad fate of the Hung Sing Association clearly illustrates our earlier assertion that it was the growth of the industrial working class, with money to spend and the need for some sort of collective support, which really drove the development of the first public martial arts schools in the Pearl River Delta.

While gone, the Hung Sing Association was certainly not forgotten. Choy Li Fut continued to be practiced in other schools throughout the province. It even enjoyed a measure of popularity in Hong Kong beyond the reach of the Nationalist government. However, it was really the growing market for martial arts fiction that made the now defunct organization immortal. Sometime in the 1930s, an author who wrote under the name Nianfo Sharen (nian Foshan ren or "One who remembers Foshan") composed a highly fictionalized and undated account of the school entitled *Foshan Hung Sing Kwoon* (*The Hung Sing School of Foshan*). This novel re-imagined the life of Jeong Yim claiming, among other things, that he was really the cofounder of the style. Additionally, it created the impression that the early period of the art's history in Foshan was much more revolutionary than was probably the case. The novel was successful and helped to preserve the memory of the Hung Sing Association, but at the same time, its fictional history came to replace the true origins and nature of the organization in many people's memory.[9]

Hamm, in his study of the "Guangdong school" of martial arts fiction, identified Nianfo Sharen as a pseudonym of Xu Kairu, an author who began to write in the 1930s in the style of Den Yugong. In 1931, Den began to serialize a number of novels in various Guangzhou newspapers. Some of them remain quite important and they often featured tales of the Shaolin Temple and biographies of local martial arts heroes. One of his most important works was *Huang Feihong Zhengzhuan* (*The True Story of Wong Fei Hung*). The novel inspired a host of imitators, each of whom sought out local masters from the past to fictionalize and promote. Xu was part of this movement.

These novels tended to idolize regional heroes as a way of protecting and bolstering local identity. Den and his school were the first to actually write their character's dialogue in Cantonese, rather than the more classical dialect that had been used in martial arts novels up until that point in time. Their characters tended to demonstrate and glorify the regional populations' reputation for feuding and quick tempers. Local readers took this as a sign of their heroes' virility and martial virtue.[10]

Many such novels were written and serialized in the newspapers of Foshan, Guangzhou, and Hong Kong throughout the 1930s, 40s, and 50s. Wing Chun, and its grand master Leung Jan, were even featured in a few of these works. While this school of popular writing did help to crystallize and give voice to an important regional identity, it also obscured and replaced aspects of history with romanticized fiction. Students of Guangdong's martial arts need to be very cautious in treating these novels as historical, rather than cultural, artifacts.

Once labor's ability to organize in Foshan was broken, it became impossible to rebuild the Hung Sing Association into what it had been. In 1936 and 1937 the Communist Party and Nationalists again declared a united front, this time to fight the Japanese invasion that was rolling across the face of China. Qian Wei Fang and Wu Qin returned from Hong Kong and began to teach a dadao, or "big knife," class to train an anti-Japanese militia. Unfortunately, they soon ran afoul of GMD authorities and were again forced to flee.

Wu Qin gathered perhaps 200 former Hung Sing members in Shi Ken village and formed the locally important Guerilla Warfare Second Team. This unit was placed under the direct command of the Communist Party. In May of 1942, Wu Qin was killed, not by the Japanese, but by an army led by the Nationalist general Lin Xiao Ya.[11] While Hung Sing branches continued to thrive overseas, the original association essentially ceased to exist in mainland China by the middle of WWII. Despite some efforts to rebuild after 1945, the school never managed to attract more than a few dozen students.[12]

While the Hung Sing Association clearly dominated Foshan's late nineteenth-century martial arts community, the situation during the 1920s was more complicated. This period, characterized by loosening political controls, increased local autonomy, and ever greater expectations of political and economic freedom, saw an absolute explosion in the number of voluntary associations throughout civil society. This same trend toward increased institutionalization is also evident in Foshan's martial arts community.

The second largest local organization in Foshan was probably the Zhong Yi Martial Arts Athletic Association, or the Zhong Yi Guang.[13] While the Hung Sing Association is fairly well-known, much less information is available on the Zhong Yi Guang (sometimes transliterated as the Cheung Yee Wui). As a violent rightwing group with a "special historical background," the Communist Party went to some lengths to suppress not just the membership of the faction but its historical memory as well. Nevertheless, it was of importance within Foshan's martial arts community, and local historians Xiao Hai Ming and Zou Wen Ping have been able to reconstruct some key facts about this organization.

During the last years of the Qing era, a resident of Zhangcha Village (now part of modern Foshan) named Zhao Xi organized the Xing Yi martial arts school. Not much is known about Zhao Xi's background.

Apparently he taught Hung Gar in his school, which was the first in the Foshan area to bear the "Yi" suffix. Zhao's organization grew quickly and he was able to franchise his reputation. There later appeared the Yong Yi, Xiong Yi, Qun Yi, Ju Yi, and Ying Yi schools, all associated with the original Xing Yi location. These six schools were said to constitute the larger "Yi" martial arts system. Researchers have determined that the schools taught both Hung Gar and Wing Chun, though they have not been able to reconstruct a full list of instructors.

Things are particularly opaque for the 1920s and 1930s. We have slightly more information about specific teachers in the late 1940s, prior to the communist takeover. Jiu Chao (1902–1972) taught Wing Chun at the Zhong Yi Association branch located at Kuai Zi Lane after the end of WWII. He was originally a native of Langbian Village in Nanhai County. Like Ip Man, Jiu came from a very wealthy family. He learned Wing Chun from Chan Yiu Min, the son of Ip Man's teacher Chan Wah Shun. Jiu also opened another martial arts school in Zhongshan and is said to have had more than 100 disciples between his two schools. Perhaps his best known student was Pan Nam.

It is interesting to note that Jiu enjoyed weapons practice and adopted a number of arms not generally associated with Wing Chun. He was supposedly an expert with both the five- and seven-section iron whip, the single saber, double jian, and the qi mei (or eyebrow) staff. The profile of his students also varied between his two schools. While his students in Foshan reflected the local economy's emphasis on handicrafts and trades, most of his students in Zhongshan were either farmers or fishermen. This is quite interesting since Wing Chun is not usually associated with the countryside during the mid-twentieth century.[14]

It is also believed that Cheung Bo (1899–1956) may have taught for the Zhong Yi Association. Rene Ritchie notes that Cheung Bo's lineage is not totally clear. He concludes that Cheung likely learned both Wing Chun and bone setting from Wai Yuk Sang, who was a doctor employed by the nationalist army.[15] Cheung Bo became a Dim Sum chef at the Foshan Tien Hoi Restaurant. He was close friends with Yuen Kay San and, in addition to teaching at his restaurant, he may have also taught at the "Hui Yi" martial arts school. Cheung was responsible for the early training of Sum Num, who he later referred to Yuen Kay San.[16]

Throughout the 1920s the Yi schools aligned themselves with local businesses, "yellow" trade unions, and the rightwing of the provincial GMD leadership. They clashed repeatedly with the Hung Sing Association over the various strikes and pickets promoted by the leftist organization. It would appear that the Yi schools were used as something like strikebreakers throughout this volatile decade.

During the early 1930s the Yi schools decided to formally unite and organized themselves as the Zhong Yi Martial Arts Athletic Association.[17] The organization was overseen by a number of locally prominent individuals including Zhao Xi, Guan Chao, Han Pei Kee, Liang Ming San, and Li Ming. The Association also expanded to include around a dozen separate branches. The various schools ranged in size from a few hundred individuals to a few dozen. Using rough averages we might guess that the total membership of the organization was around a thousand individuals, about one-third the size of Hung Sing Associations in the early 1920s.[18]

The membership of the Zhong Yi Association was more diverse than Hung Sing. Students included ordinary workers, businessmen, military personal, local politicians, and merchants. Membership dues were four pounds of rice a month, and membership was open to everyone who paid their dues on time. The organizational structure and discipline of the Zhong Yi Association was apparently fairly tight, but not as formalized as Hung Sing.[19]

The extant English language literature on Wing Chun contains only a few passing references to the Zhong Yi Association. This is not altogether surprising as the champions of Wing Chun who passed the art on to future generations, Ip Man and Yuen Kay San, both went out of their way to avoid becoming involved in the public martial arts community. This reticence on their part should be more understandable after the preceding discussion. One simply could not teach martial arts publicly in Foshan without entering a political and social minefield. In this sort of environment discretion definitely was the best policy.

There is a single possible exception to this. The biographical timeline of Ip Man's life compiled by Samuel Kwok (long-time student and associate of Ip Man's two sons, Ip Chun and Ip Ching) indicates that in the late 1940s Ip Man coached Pan Nam, a former Hung Gar student and important Wing Chun instructor in his own right, on the forms at the Zhong Yi Athletic Association. Unfortunately, Kwok does not go on to give any information about what the Zhong Yi Association was or what relationship, if any, Ip Man had with the organization.[20] Given the time period, one could speculate that this instruction may have happened at Jiu Chao's branch of the association. Leung Ting also relates a similar tale in his investigation of the origins of Wing Chun. He claims that in the year before Ip Man fled for Hong Kong he briefly instructed

Pan Nam at the "Shangsha Branch" of the Zhong Yi Athletic Association, but like Kwok he does not go into the story in detail.[21]

During the 1920s, as the labor movement in Foshan was developing, the Yi schools came to be controlled by two reactionary trade unions. They were the Foshan chapters of the Guangdong Provincial Trade Union and the Guangdong Machinery Trade Union. This suggests that perhaps the Yi schools were also recruiting workers and providing support in a similar manner as the Hung Sing Association, only this time with the backing of big business and the government. These unions were locked in a conflict with the Worker's Congress, and they involved the Yi schools in the violence.

A brief exploration of the unions sponsoring the Zhong Yi association may help to illuminate the social backgrounds and concerns of their shared membership. The Guangdong Machinery Trade Union was founded by Ma Chaojun. Ma was born in the last decades of the Qing dynasty and completed an apprenticeship in mechanics in Hong Kong. He was then sent to San Francisco for further technical training where, in 1905, he met Sun Yat-sen and was captivated by his ideas.

After returning to Hong Kong he formed a number of "workers' clubs" since formal trade unions were illegal. In 1909, he established an open union in Guangzhou but was forced to allow local factory owners to join the organization. Guangzhou was a more conservative place than Hong Kong, and those in power did not want to allow the creation of any major social organization that would not have the benefit of their input. Ma's union turned out to be rather conservative and it developed close ties with the GMD.[22]

It should also be remembered that mechanics were highly skilled workers. They earned considerably more than even skilled individuals in the handicraft industries. Those workers in turn might earn 30 to 40 percent more than unskilled individuals (coolies or rickshaw drivers), and even an unskilled worker might earn twice as much as a domestic servant. Generally speaking, a skilled worker would be able to support a family of six on a single salary. Unskilled workers usually had to employ their children to make ends meet.[23]

Despite the best efforts of the leftists to define all three groups as a single "working class," the material differences between various employees tended to skew their identities. Skilled mechanics were somewhat educated, highly trained individuals, who could afford middle-class aspirations. They enjoyed a good standard of living and did not socially or politically identify with unskilled workers. They had more disposable income to spend on martial arts classes and tended to sympathize with the right wing of the GMD, which was more in favor of business investment and trade.

Obviously these workers were fundamentally different from the less skilled, less well off, individuals that tended to join the Worker's Congress and the Hung Sing Association. Granted, these workers still made enough money to afford luxuries like strikes and somewhat less expensive martial arts instruction. They were by no means the poorest of the poor. Yet, by in large, they were the losers in China's involvement with the global economy. Their industries were threatened by foreign trade and investment and they did not have the buying power to take advantage of new imports.

The clash between the "She" and "Yi" schools was simply a proxy for the larger conflict between the Guangdong Machinery Trade Union and the Worker's Congress. This was not merely an ideological conflict. Rather, the massive strike and boycott of Hong Kong in 1925 revealed deep economic divisions within the reform and labor movements. Both the Hung Sing and Yi Associations fought for what was in their best economic and political interests.

More mundane martial rivalries and lion dancing also added to the enmity between the two groups. The Hung Sing Association controlled many lion dance teams, including the Luo Yong, Yue An, and Xie Lian groups. The Yi association owned the Zhao Jing group. Traditionally the Hung Sing schools danced the black-faced, seven-star lion, whereas the Yi schools adopted the red-faced, three-star lion. Fights often broke out between lion dance teams if one organization thought another was intruding on its turf. Conflicts between the peripheral lion dance associations tended to escalate and could end up involving the entire school.

The Yi schools continued to thrive after the destruction of the Hung Sing Association. The organization further consolidated its ties with the conservative wing of the GMD throughout the 1920s and 1930s. Nanhai County GMD party secretary, Zhang Qi Duan, was even named the group's president following its institutional reorganization around 1930.[24]

However, this same involvement in local politics would ultimately betray the Yi schools just as it had the Hung Sing Association. By binding themselves too closely to the GMD, the Zhong Yi Association only ensured that they would be totally suppressed once the communists seized Guangzhou and Foshan in 1949. While the Hung Sing school was at least remembered for its many revolutionary martyrs, the communists simply wrote the Zhong Yi Guang out of history.

Hakka Styles

The period from 1911–1949 was even more critical for the Hakka styles than it was for the Hung Mun. Since economic development and modernization generally came more slowly to the less fertile highlands occupied by this ethnic group, their arts were slower to adopt new institutional structures. Yet by the 1920s we begin to see a number of the most important Hakka styles making their way to Guangzhou and establishing themselves as modern public martial arts schools, open to anyone who can pay the tuition.

A complete study of each of these arts is beyond the scope of this chapter, but it is still helpful to review the development of two of the most popular styles, Pak Mai (often referred to as White Eyebrow) and Long Xi Quan (Dragon). These arts nicely illustrate the progression from traditional to modern modes of transmission discussed above. Likewise, they also demonstrate both the opportunities and dangers that come from forming a close alliance with the state, or individual political parties, even more clearly than the examples of the Hung Sing and Zhong Yi associations. It is also interesting to note that many of the physical movements and concepts in these styles bear more than a passing resemblance to Wing Chun.

Our prior review of the Lin Jia Martial Arts Association noted that, while the development of public martial arts schools progressed relatively slowly along the east branch of the Pearl River, there was always a great deal of interest in the subject. The last half of the nineteenth century had been traumatic for the Hakka people. They responded to regional and ethnic violence by developing a number of very effective fighting forms. Not all of these modes of instruction survive today, nor is it likely that this knowledge was always conveyed as part of a specific "style" as Chinese martial artists use the term today.

Still, we can identify two arts that were particularly popular in the area around Huizhou County. The Huidong Lin Jia Martial Arts Institute was still present in the local martial arts scene and promoting Lam Gar. Lee Gar, another Hakka art, was also quite popular with individual teachers and families in the region. These two arts together provided the basis for the emergence of both White Eyebrow and Dragon.

White Eyebrow was created by Cheung Lai Chuen (1880–1966). Cheung was born in Huizhou prefecture to the most junior branch of his clan. His father died at a young age, further imperiling the family's fortune. Cheung was often bullied by the other children from the more senior branches of the lineage. His mother decided that it was better to return to her own family in Huiyang.[25] These seeming reversals planted the seeds of Cheung's later success in life.

The boy was naturally driven to learn martial arts and was taken on as a student by Lam Sek, a well-respected local doctor who was able to train him in Lee Gar. At the age of thirteen the doctor recommended his student to Li Mung, a local Lee Gar master who ran a school. As an older teenager, Cheung became close friends with Lam Yiu Kwai (who would later found Dragon style). He also joined Lin He's school and began to study Lam Gar.

Lam Yiu Kwai (1874–1965) was also a resident of the Huizhou area. From a very young age he studied Lam Gar, first with his father (Lin Qingyuan) and then with his uncle, the famous Lin He. By all accounts both Cheung and Lam were excellent students. The oral traditions of both styles record highly improbable meetings with mysterious wandering monks who then adopted each of the boys to finish their martial educations. Lam Yiu Kwai is even said to have studied at the venerable Mt. Luofu.[26]

It is hard to know what to make of such stories. While it probably was possible to study martial arts on Mt. Luofu, it certainly was not necessary given the strong background that both boys already had. Further, both accounts are highly stylized. If all such stories are to be believed, eastern Guangdong and southern Fujian must have been carpeted with mysteriously long-lived, politically motivated, former Shaolin monks just itching to overthrow the national government by teaching local teenagers unarmed boxing skills. All of this is quite odd in an era when real anti-government terrorist groups had already demonstrated the effectiveness of improvised explosive devices and firearms for assassinating government officials. In reality, these stories are most likely advertising ploys designed to attract students and explain the origins of the new fighting systems that both Cheung and Lam would go on to create.

What is more certain is that in the 1920s both Cheung and Lam immigrated to Guangzhou in search of work and began to teach martial arts. Cheung appears to have gotten a job with the local government's salt monopoly office, which was running a low-level war against the numerous smugglers. This turned out to be an ideal platform for him to demonstrate his martial skills, and his reputation began to grow with the local authorities. Despite all of his revolutionary bluster, Cheung was strictly a government man. He sought out political contacts as stepping stones to success throughout his long career.

Lam Yiu Kwai also sought to make a name for himself in Guangzhou. Legend has it that he defeated a Russian boxer in a public challenge match, launching the young man toward local fame.[27] Once again, this account is very stylized. Nevertheless, there were a number of foreign wrestlers and boxers making the rounds in southern China, and these matches were a popular form of entertainment in marketplaces. Fighting challenge matches was also one method by which young martial artists could establish themselves, especially in a market that was already as crowded and saturated as Guangzhou's in the 1920s and 30s.

Both Lam and Cheung established a number of schools in the Guangzhou region. Cheung in particular is said to have managed an organization of up to eighteen schools teaching his "White Eyebrow" style. Lam named his style "Dragon Shaped Rubbing Bridges" and he too opened a number of schools. The two men also co-owned some schools. Both accepted a wide range of students, and they did more to popularize and prove the worth of the Hakka arts than practically anyone else.

Cheung, in particular, does not appear to have been satisfied with mere commercial success. He always sought government backing, or at least recognition, for his style. This was increasingly possible in Guangzhou during the 1920s and 30s as the government was getting into the martial arts business. At the national level the GMD was promoting a certain vision of traditional hand combat through the Central Guoshu Institute during these years. For a variety of political reasons that we will explore later, these formal intuitions never gained much traction in Guangdong and Fujian.[28] Still, provincial and local authorities in the south had their own reasons for promoting certain types of martial arts activities.

Militia groups were being formed by the GMD and they needed training and leadership. Likewise, the new police and military academies needed instructors. Occasionally famous martial arts masters from northern China were imported to fill these roles. Southern boxing techniques were not perceived as being up to the job. Cheung sought to challenge that perception wherever he could.

After being introduced to the Guangzhou Chief of Police, Lei Dat Ng (coincidently a native of the same home town), Cheung was appointed chief combat instructor at the organization's headquarters. This posting, along with his various business associations, allowed Cheung to build his list of contacts within the local government. After a meeting and friendly match with Col. Liu Chun Fan of the Whampoa military academy, Cheung was recommended as the chief civilian martial arts instructor. This appointment not only boosted Cheung's career, but it also helped to quell criticism that the national military academy, stationed initially in Guangzhou, was only teaching northern martial arts.

Cheung's activities at Whampoa seem to have focused on training civilian militia personal and leaders. He formed a "Big Sword Brigade" (of the type that would gain fame fighting the Japanese during WWII) and made a number of contributions to bayonet drill and combat training. These successes allowed Cheung to further branch out. He accepted additional teaching appointments at the Yin Tong Law Enforcement Academy and with Guangdong Province's secret intelligence service. In fact, it was his involvement with this last group that would forever color the way people think of White Eyebrow.[29]

Without a doubt the most powerful of Cheung's many disciples was Lieutenant General Kot Siu Wong of the GMD Intelligence Service. Kot's main assignment was to contain the growth of the Communist Party in Guangdong. By 1945, the leadership of the GMD realized that the communists were ready to make their move on all of the major urban areas of the country. In an attempt to minimize defections by the military, police, and citizens it was decided to enroll as much of the population as possible into the various triads and secret societies. The hope was that by insinuating itself into the web of relationships, initiation ceremonies, and blood oaths that held these criminal organizations together, the Nationalist government would be protected. Local secret societies were only too happy to oblige and would even replace the ancestral plaques of the Five Ancestors with pictures of Chiang Kai-shek. The people joined the secret societies en masse because not to do so was to invite retaliation as a probable communist sympathizer.

It was Kot's job to manage this leviathan and to make sure that it did not forget it's new, primarily political, agenda. Kot had been a member of some of the secret societies for years and was able to draw on his contacts to painstakingly form relationships and alliances with many of Guangdong's larger associations and gangs. In 1947, he invited the leaders of the local secret societies to a summit meeting on the campus of Kwok Man University in Guangzhou. He announced that they would henceforth be known as the Hung Fat San branch of the Cheung Yee Wui.[30] The new society then set up its headquarters at 14

Po Wa Road, Guangzhou. The historical record suggests that Kot Siu Wong was a patriot who truly believed that the popularity of the secret societies could help save the national government from collapse. All the same, his plan would unleash pain and exploitation on an untold number of people around the world.

When the communists seized the Guangdong in 1949, most of the members of the Cheung Yee Wui fled to Hong Kong. It should be recalled that Chiang Kai-shek used the secret societies to carry out massacres of the communists in 1927. Many martial arts masters, particularly those with ties to the GMD such as Cheung Lai Chuen and Ip Man, also fled at this time.

The sudden influx of many of China's most dangerous criminal organizations, along with waves of destitute refugees, quickly overwhelmed the British administration in Hong Kong. Throughout the 1950s the city seemed to teeter on the edge of social chaos. Kot attempted to reactivate his organization, but he was discovered and exiled by the British. They believed that running a secret war with the new communist government out of Hong Kong could only make a bad situation worse. Kot was eventually allowed to return to Hong Kong, and he did resurrect the Cheung Yee Wui. He grew to distrust his lieutenants and never managed to put a succession strategy in place. When he died in 1953, the organization split into warring factions, each led by a former lieutenant who saw himself as the natural choice for successor.

The vast majority of these sub-leaders immediately abandoned any political aspirations that the group may have once held, preferring instead to build vast criminal empires based on drug running, extortion, prostitution, and counterfeiting. The organization changed its name to "14k," apparently a reference to the original headquarters of the group in Guangzhou. It survives to this day as one of the largest and most ruthless criminal organizations on the planet.[31] 14k conducts illegal activities throughout Asia, North America, Europe, and even Africa.

The death of Kot and the degeneration of his organization proved to be an immense problem for Cheung. He had personally trained many of the leaders of 14k in his White Eyebrow style. The organization also provided material support and a comfortable existence for him when he first arrived in Hong Kong. Yet, rather than fighting the communists, his former students were now making his art notorious by terrorizing local business and refugees. White Eyebrow was quickly coming to be seen as a "forbidden art" and an absolute public menace. In fact, it is the distorted memories of this period that are the real source of the mixed reputation that the art still carries to this day, not the fictionalized accounts of the White Eyebrow Daoist from popular novels.[32]

While he was apparently torn by these developments, Cheung refused to publicly disassociate himself from 14k. He continued to enjoy the tribute and material benefits that came from being the group's martial "godfather." He may even have seen these as the just rewards of his lifelong work. Whether the victims of 14k would agree seems doubtful.

In the last period of his teaching career, Cheung attempted to repair his reputation by seeking out a new group of students. He chose wealthy businessmen with no apparent ties to organized crime. To his credit he did succeed in creating a number of lineages that could pass on his art without the taint of 14k's violent reputation.[33]

Cheung Lai Chuen remains one of the most complicated and interesting figures in the history of Guangdong's martial arts. He worked tirelessly to prove the worth of the local arts and helped to introduce the Hakka styles of the East River to the world. His is quite literally a rags-to-riches story.

The key to Cheung's success was government backing. While there was a great demand for martial arts instruction, government support proved the key to surviving the tumultuous events of the 1920s, 30s, and 40s. Yet, in the final analysis, Cheung is not an entirely sympathetic character. When many of Kot's old guard abandoned 14k, appalled by the brutal conduct of the younger generation of criminal enforcers, he chose to stay, damaging the reputation of the art he had worked so hard to create. The story of White Eyebrow demonstrates again the dangers of tying ones fortunes too closely to a specific political faction.

Cheung Lai Chuen makes a marked contrast with Ip Man. Both men were masters of local arts, and both associated themselves with the GMD. While Cheung attempted to promote himself as an instructor at various prestigious academies, Ip Man worked as a police detective and intentionally kept a low profile. Given his ties to the GMD and law enforcement, Ip Man must have had at least some contact with General Kot's organization. Yet, whereas Cheung relied on his old political contacts when he came to Hong Kong, Ip Man continued to hold himself aloof. It seems likely that the very real dangers of political entanglement had impressed themselves on Ip Man as he watched Foshan's martial arts community tear itself apart in 1927. This same cautious attitude guided his choices when establishing his own school in Hong Kong.

The Jingwu Association:
Martial Arts and the Construction of National Identity

Our discussion so far has focused almost exclusively on regional forces that shaped the evolution of martial arts in and around Foshan and Guangzhou. However, as the twentieth century matured a new group of actors began to emerge on the national scene. Their ideas and innovations would challenge the growth of regional martial arts movements around the country. Guangdong was no exception, yet the strong institutionalized presence of multiple local hand combat traditions had an important effect of how these national pressures were manifest and the sorts of reforms they could ultimately achieve.[34]

Throughout the early twentieth century intellectual life in China was dominated by calls for reform and modernization. Often these efforts took the form of "westernization" as the Chinese people attempted to adopt alien technologies and practices to quickly strengthen the nation and erase the lingering humiliation of foreign imperialism. These currents ultimately launched the May Fourth (or New Culture) Movement. Intellectuals called on their countrymen to abandon anything that was Confucian, backwards, superstitious, unproductive, or, in a word, too "Chinese."

Other writers, such as those who supported the "National Essence" school, took a more moderate approach. While still acknowledging the need for wide-scale reform, they were reluctant to replace Chinese values with Western ones. Instead, they sought institutions and ideas from China's past, such as those preserved in traditional boxing, which could act as a solid foundation to support both growing nationalism and a strong state.

There was a perception throughout the 1910s and 1920s that the Chinese people themselves had to be transformed, made stronger and more resilient, if the nation as a whole was to survive. Intellectuals who had ignored physical exercise suddenly adopted Swedish calisthenics, Olympic style sports, and American ball games, all as a way of curing the nation's physical and spiritual flaws. The nature of Chinese "physical culture" became a matter of national debate.

The one activity that most elite urban reformers assiduously avoided was the traditional Chinese martial arts. Their schools had left no written records and this supposed illiteracy made them beneath contempt. Traditional Chinese martial arts were almost always a local affair, prone to feuding among many competing factions. For that reason it was thought that they could not strengthen the identity of the nation as a whole.[35] Lastly, the failed Boxer Uprising of 1900 was still too fresh in the public memory. The Shandong peasants' heavy reliance on spirit possession, charms and magic seemed to confirm the worst suspicions of the new elite about the value of China's martial arts. They were a backwards superstition, one that had nearly destroyed the nation once and something that had to be excluded from the public sphere and forgotten as quickly as possible.[36]

The rhetoric of the May Fourth Movement presented its own paradoxes that a few cagey defenders of the martial arts realized could be exploited. To begin with, while the reformers generally promoted modernization and westernization, the failure of the allied powers to honor their agreements to restore the German concessions in northern China unleashed a wave of anti-foreign sentiment. This opened a space for a renewed interest in China's indigenous culture and a broader examination of what contributions the empire's past could make to the new nation's future.

The possibility of traditional boxing thriving in the modern world was probably more evident to the residents of Guangzhou's business community (where various systems of hand combat were growing quite quickly) than to anyone else. Yet it was Shanghai, a quickly emerging economic and cultural destination, which was destined to become the epicenter of the new martial arts reform movement.

The founding of the Shanghai Jingwu Athletic Association has been the subject of so many works of fiction that it is one of the most well-known of all martial myths. In 1907 Huo Yuan Jia (1868–1910) traveled from Tianjin to Shanghai. He was a teacher of Mizongyi (Lost Track Boxing). Huo had learned from his father who worked part time for a local armed escort company. Early in his career he acquired a reputation for defeating foreign boxers and Westerners who were traveling the countryside insulting the people. The actual facts behind these matches are hard to ascertain and it seems likely that at least some of his wins were actually by default. Other matches were likely the sort of highly publicized staged events that were popular in local marketplaces.

After accepting a challenge in Shanghai, Huo decided to remain in the city. In 1909 or 1910 (accounts vary) he was approached by a group of individuals (including Lu Wei Chang, Yao Chan Bo, Chen Gong Zhe, Zheng Zhou Chen, and Chen Tie Sheng) to became a founding member of, and instructor for, a new martial arts organization. The group was known at first as the Shanghai Jingwu Calisthenics School. Huo, who had been in poor health practically his whole life, died suddenly of a lung ailment (most likely tuberculosis), or of a reaction to medication that he was given. Due to the tense atmosphere of the time, rumors began to spread and eventually some members of the Jingwu School decided that he had actually been poisoned by his Japanese physician, Dr. Akino.[37]

It seems doubtful that much of the legend, popularized in the West by Bruce Lee in his treatments of the story, is true. Still, the young reformers and journalists who had founded the Jingwu Association realized that they were sitting on a gold mine. Huo was immediately declared the "founder" of the school and he became its first martyr to the excesses of rapacious imperialism. A cult of hero worship was constructed around his memory, and his story helped to spread the newly renamed Jingwu Athletic Association throughout China.

All that the Jingwu Association lacked at this point was financial backing. This came in the form of three of its very first members. Lu Wei Chang, Chen Gong Zhe, and Yao Chan Bo were three wealthy, highly educated, young businessmen. Lu and Chen were both members of important Guangdong merchant families living in Shanghai. As such, they were likely familiar with the success that modern commercial martial arts had enjoyed in the Pearl River Delta for decades. The two befriended Yao, a native of Jiangsu, and went on to create a number of companies and brands that bet heavily on, and invested in, the Jingwu Association. These included the Watson soft drink factory, the Hexing Photo Studio, the Central Printing Company, the Yufan Iron Mine, and an ill-fated business that imported textile spindles from England.[38]

It was the profits of these three young entrepreneurs that allowed the Jingwu Association to explode onto the national scene in the 1920s, spreading its message far and wide. Other commercial firms soon jumped on the bandwagon. The nationalist message of the Jingwu Association was in step with the various "buy Chinese" movements that were fashionable at the time, and the organization's publications turned out to be a great investment for the advertising dollar. The Association was also remarkable for its acceptance of women and genuine desire to promote female athletics. This openness allowed advertisers to reach a new demographic, the modern active woman.[39] In financial terms, the Jingwu Association was a success; it rode a wave of mass commercialism that had never before been seen in the Asian martial arts. Jingwu was the first truly national martial arts brand.

What was the message of the Jingwu Association? Basically, the organization claimed that it could provide "national salvation" through its martial arts instruction. This salvation would come in the form of a renewed spiritual commitment to the nation and the creation of bodies and minds that were tough and robust enough to sacrifice for the common good. Before this could happen China's martial arts would have to be purified of their superstitious and feudal heritage. Modern teaching methods were to be formulated according to efficient scientific principles. The organization's martial arts were meant to engage the body and to be spiritually healthy for the practitioner.

Standardization was also a central concern. Chinese martial arts had always been a local affair, the result of deep traditions or small-scale innovation. Traditional teachers constantly strove to tweak their arts or mythic narratives as a way of differentiating their product in a crowded marketplace. Jingwu went in the opposite direction. It aimed to create an art that was truly "national" in its scope and easily franchised by like-minded urban reformers. As with any franchise, producing a uniform product is essential to maintaining the brand's reputation and creating customer loyalty. While traditional teachers might hope to have dozens of students, branches of the Jingwu Association aspired to train groups numbering in the hundreds or thousands. Uniformity was the key to making this possible.

The spokesmen of the group roundly criticized local martial artists for their secrecy and petty lineage disputes. They claimed that only by sharing the best techniques between all styles could the "national art" be saved.[40] There was no room for the local, the particular, the traditional, or the mystical in the brave new world that the Jingwu Association, and its commercial backers, envisioned. Critics of the new organization, particularly those in Guangzhou and Foshan, could point to the group's many pamphlets and books and note that while the organization claimed to unite all of the nation's martial artists, its standardized curriculum taught only *northern* arts in all of its fifty-three branches. Southern boxing was apparently unworthy of preservation and reform.

The Jingwu Association drew most of its strength from the financial contributions of wealthy members and the volunteer efforts of its vast grassroots organization. It tended to be most successful recruiting among the urban, well-educated, and middle class. Its members were often students, intellectuals, government workers, or businessmen. By the middle of the 1920s it had powerful supporters spread throughout the country, giving it a certain geographic stability. However, the strongest support always came from the larger coastal cities in the east and south. It was the first Chinese martial arts organization to be truly national (and even international) in its reach.

The Jingwu Association also tried to cultivate personal contacts with political leaders whenever it could. Sun Yat-sen attended some important events and even graced their ten-year anniversary book with an introduction. Yet their strategy proved to be fundamentally different from that carried out by the Hung Sing and Zhong Yi Associations who tightly aligned their organizations, and membership, with a single political party.

Instead, the group appears to have sought patronage and favor from individual politicians wherever it could, but repeatedly maintained that their members should not become involved in politics.[41] Unlike the groups in Foshan, the Jingwu Association never sought to become part of the actual political process. As a result, the organization avoided the partisan radicalization that was so detrimental to martial arts in Guangdong. The association's political flexibility later proved to be a major asset. It was able to survive in one form or another up until 1966, when it was finally denounced and shut down during the early stages of the Cultural Revolution.[42] Very few of the other martial arts organizations discussed in this volume managed to survive the communist conquest in 1949.

Still, most historians date the passing of the Jingwu Association substantially earlier, to sometime around 1925 or 1926. While the central institutions of the Association may have survived in a reduced form, the national evangelizing mission that characterized the organization's golden years died when Nie Yuntai, an investor in the spindle importation venture, went bankrupt. The failure of this deal subsequently led to the bankruptcy of Lu Wei Chang, Chen Gong Zhe, and Yao Chan Bo, the three main financial backers of the movement. The national Jingwu Association had always relied more on contributions from wealthy patrons than local dues paid by members for support. The fact that it had been willing to greatly subsidize martial arts instruction was one of the reasons that the association had been so successful in the first place. Yet this strategy had the unintended consequence of leaving the organization's finances vulnerable to market shocks. The more grandiose aspects of the national movement could not survive this blow and basically disappeared.

Chen appealed to Chiang Kai-shek to back the crippled organization during his Northern Expedition in 1926. He refused, but not because he needed to be convinced of the power and potential benefits of a national martial arts program. Rather, the GMD had already begun to formulate plans for a new body, one that would be backed by the national government and be totally loyal to it.[43]

This is where most overviews of the Jingwu Association stop. However, the retrenchment of the national organization did not have much of an effect on the Guangzhou and Foshan chapters. Ironically, they continued to gain strength and influence throughout the 1920s and 30s. It is interesting to ask why.

The Guangdong branch of the Jingwu Association was the second to be opened (following the Hankou location) as the organization began to expand nationwide in the 1920s. It was formally established in April of 1919 and it continued to function until the Japanese invasion in 1938 forced it to suspend its normal activities. The local chapter's opening ceremony was held in the Haizu Theater and was attended by a number of local political, social, and military dignitaries. Li Fu Lin, Wei Bang Ping, Xiong Chang Qing, Chen Lian Bo, Jian Zhao Nan, and Yang Mei Bin were elected as "directors" of the new organization.

Typically, the key personal at a new branch (such as the athletics and martial arts director) would be appointed by the central organization in Shanghai. The local directors filled many of the minor offices. They formed committees to look after the mundane affairs of the chapter, such as finding suitable meeting places, buying uniforms, publishing lesson material, and promoting good relations with the community. In actual practice, the directors were also expected to be major financial bankers of the organization and often donated generously. This system effectively subsidized Jingwu membership for urban middle-class professionals, or those who aspired to become so.

The group was first located at the Ningbo Association building in Guangzhou. It later moved to a larger space at the Jianan Hall on Taiping South Road (now the People's South Road), and soon after to Lychee Bay in Xiguan. It finally found a more permanent home on Fengning Road (currently named the People's Center Road).

The original teaching staff was comprised entirely of northerners and included Chen Ji Xiu, who transferred from the Shanghai branch and served as the overall director of the martial arts program, Huo Dong Ge (the son of the famous Huo Yuan Jia), Li Zhan Feng, Zhao Lian He, Luo Guang Yu, Chen Zi Zheng, Yang Chen Lun, Sun Yu Feng, and Sun Wen Long. In a break with what seems to have been normal operating procedures, the Guangdong Jingwu Association was also allowed to appoint three martial arts instructors who specialized in southern hand combat methods. These were Lin Yin Tang, Kong Chang, and Li Bin. So far as we can tell, the same courtesy was not extended to any other chapters in the province and this did not have a substantive impact on the teaching curriculum.

The instructors covered a variety of styles. Chen Zi Zheng was a well-known exponent of Eagle Claw, a fighting art that was popular in the early Jingwu Association. Lou Guang Yu taught a northern variety of Praying Mantis, and Chen Wei Xian specialized in Yangtze River Fist. Li Hui Ting taught the "Flower Fork" form. Taijiquan was later introduced to the region by Jingwu instructors. It is not clear what specific southern styles, if any, became part of the local curriculum.

Three different class times were offered at the Guangdong branch and the school was more or less open for business from 6:00 a.m. until after 9:00 p.m. New students were required to learn ten basic forms from a variety of styles. As they progressed in their martial education they had more freedom to choose which forms they would study and could eventually select a specific style to focus on. One advantage to this system is that students were able to make a relatively informed choice about their eventual field of specialization. A total of 98 different traditional martial arts forms were taught at the Guangdong location including 32 solo unarmed sets, 35 solo weapons forms, and 31 additional sets that included paired unarmed or armed sparring.

Classes were offered at three different levels: basic, intermediate and advanced. After the completion of each level students were awarded a colored star to be placed on their uniform, replicating the three stars of Jingwu's official flag. The basic course ran for two years and it introduced students to a total of ten forms intended to improve basic fitness and provide a firm foundation for further study.[44] Students who mastered these forms and passed a rigorous examination, often proctored by instructors from other locations, received an "elementary level" certification. They were then free to advance to the more complicated material.

The "intermediate" level training also lasted two years. Students were introduced to more boxing and weapons forms. The student's progress was once again documented by a serious examination. Students who passed the intermediate level were then allowed to proceed to the advanced work. At this level students could choose to be instructed in the most advanced material including Lost Track Boxing, Sha Shou Jian, and Long Feng Shuang Dao (Dragon Wind Double Knives). Individuals also perfected their chosen style under the guidance of one of the official instructors. After achieving their advanced level certification students could then apply for jobs within the Jingwu organization or, more commonly, they were farmed out to local families, schools, or factories who were seeking martial arts instruction.

This educational pipeline was incredibly efficient. The Guangdong Jingwu Association could take an individual with no prior martial arts background and turn him or her into a competent certified instructor in only six years. The actual martial arts instruction that these graduates could provide was uniform and high quality. This success decisively demonstrated that the epic, often decades long, transmission processes seen in some traditional styles were not only unnecessary, but probably a hindrance to the overall survival of Chinese martial arts.

Jingwu's new streamlined methods created an explosion in the number of locally available, and reliable, martial arts instructors. By 1925, there were no fewer than 45 organizations and families in the Guangzhou area employing Jingwu coaches, who in turn trained around 3,000 students of their own. This was in addition to the thousands of students educated at the main Jingwu location.[45]

This intellectual respectability and efficient instructional process made hand combat attractive to new groups of students who had previously enjoyed only limited access to martial arts instruction. The new students were overwhelmingly urban, educated, and middle class. They were intellectuals, businessmen, shopkeepers, and government clerks. This was somewhat similar to the demographic that the Zhong Yi Athletic Association drew from. However, Jingwu students were decidedly better off than the working-class clientele that the Hung Sing Association served. In fact, there is a clear relationship between different modes of martial arts instruction and the question of economic class that has been ignored by much of the previous literature. Such class tensions, replicated and reinforced by the branding of the various martial arts societies, likely contributed to the hostilities that occasionally boiled to the surface.

It is also important to note that women contributed immensely to Jingwu's meteoric rise. Tall tales of mysterious sword maidens and Shaolin nuns notwithstanding, the truth is that very few females ever had access to martial arts instruction in late imperial China. Hand combat training violated too many gender taboos to be thinkable for most families and the widespread practice of foot binding, seen as necessary to ensure a daughter's marriage prospects, made the entire question moot.

Women tended to fare no better during the early years of the Republic. The reformers and guardians of China's growing physical culture movement turned their newly acquired scientific outlook against women's bodies and used it to justify the systematic exclusion of females from the growing arena of competitive sports and recreational exercise. While the scientific vocabulary was new, ideas about gender remained essentialist and traditional.

The Jingwu Association took a totally different approach to the question. Very early on they aligned themselves with the small but growing women's rights movement and claimed that not only was it possible for women to study martial arts, but in fact it was necessary to accomplish the organization's broader goals of "national salvation." If this required a major rethinking of gender roles and the social construction of ideas like "beauty," then so much the better.

Women responded enthusiastically to this message and advertisers and corporate sponsors, already seeking new ways to reach female consumers, realized that they had stumbled onto a major opportunity. Home products, overwhelmingly bought by females, found that it was very profitable to advertise in Jingwu's publications. Of the association's many contributions, there can be no doubt that the most important was its promotion of female martial artists. This development reflected the highly urban, educated, and reform-minded milieu in which the organization thrived.[46]

The Guangdong Jingwu branch also adopted an open policy to female members. Early in the spring of 1920, Chen Shi Chao (sister of Chen Gong Zhe), director of the Shanghai Jingwu Association's Women's Department, traveled to Guangdong to set up a Women's Exploratory Group. By the following year it had grown and was renamed the Women's Department. Leaders of the Women's Group also branched out and eventually established a Guangdong Children's Group to further spread the message of national strengthening and salvation through martial arts.[47]

The Foshan Jingwu Association

The success of the Guangdong Jingwu Association created demand for additional branches within the province. Additional chapters were subsequently established in Foshan (1920), Shantou (1923), and Guangzhou (1925).[48] All of these branches were established in the provinces' more prosperous middle-class areas. For all of its accomplishments, the Jingwu philosophy never really penetrated the hard-pressed countryside that remained more interested in establishing practical militias and keeping the bandits at bay than anything else.

Of these daughter institutions, the Foshan branch was clearly the most successful. In some ways its star even outshone the elder Guangdong organization. One might think this was no great achievement given what we already know about the popularity and long history of public martial arts instruction in the area. Foshan seems like it was tailor-made for the Jingwu Association. However, the new movement got off to a shaky start in the martial arts mecca. It was only the tireless work and sacrifice of a dedicated group of regional backers that allowed the chapter to gain local prominence at the same time that the national organization in Shanghai was slipping into insolvency and irrelevance.

The Foshan Jingwu Association was established in 1920, shortly after the creation of the Guangdong branch, but it appears that classes may not have actually started until 1921. Its headquarters were first located on Zhen Xi Street, and later moved to the Lotus Temple. As the organization expanded, it was forced to move again to the Lian Feng Paper Guild Hall on Chang Xing Street.

Wishing to bring the Jingwu Association to their home town, a group of local martial arts enthusiasts petitioned for the creation of a chapter and the Guangdong branch sent personnel to help establish the new center. The local movement was led by Ren Xiao An, who ran a fireworks store. Other early backers and "directors" of the Foshan Jingwu included Zhong Miao Zhen, Cai Mian Qing, Xiao Jian Nong, Huo Yong Min, Li Ming Kai, and Luo Da Qing.

Ren Xiao An served as the first director of the martial arts and athletics department from 1921–1923. He was responsible for managing and overseeing the various martial arts coaches and classes. All of the actual instructors were appointed by the central offices in Shanghai and specialized in the northern Shaolin styles that comprised the standardized curriculum. Yellow River Fist (a somewhat generic title used to denote northern Shaolin arts) was taught by Sun Shou Qing, Zhao Gui Lin, Liu Qin Gui, and Chen Hung Shu. Eagle Claw instruction was provided by Li Bao Ying and Liu Fa Meng. The Northern Mantis coaches were Luo Guang Yu, Yu Le Jiang, Chen Zhen Dai, and Fan Yong Zhen. Yangtze River Boxing instruction was provided by Yao Dian Xia. Taijiquan was first introduced to the town and taught by Ng Kam Chuen, Wu Gong Zu, Wu Tai Xie, Shi Zai Xian, and Yang Shou Zhong. Zhu Yu Ping was responsible for the Flower Fork form. The curriculum and pattern of instruction in Foshan was identical to the Guangdong branch.[49]

For all of its initial promise and imported staff, things got off to a slow start. While other areas of the country were just hearing the gospel of urban public martial arts instruction, Foshan had been practicing much of what Jingwu preached for literally generations. The area already had a vibrant, some might say excessively colorful, martial arts scene. Further, hand combat instruction was woven deeply into local culture and political identity.

It appears that many residents did not appreciate a group in far-off Shanghai sending martial arts masters to challenge their local teachers. The unmistakable inference to be drawn from the Jingwu program of the 1920s was that Guangdong's exotic martial arts community was exactly the sort of thing that needed to be "rectified" and subjected to the "scientific method." Local martial arts teachers and practitioners were not impressed by these claims.

The president of the Foshan Jingwu Association was not much help either. Zhong Miao Zhen was a jewelry store manager and appears to have hoped that the job of president would be mostly ceremonial. After all, these sorts of positions often were. Yet the unfolding situation in Foshan made it clear that stronger leadership was necessary. Zhong was either unwilling or unable to change the perception of his organization in the local community and what support he had in 1920 quickly dwindled. When he finally resigned in 1922, the Foshan Jingwu Association had only ten remaining members.[50] Nor had the organization done much better in recruiting ordinary students.

The situation led to a great deal of frustration among the underused contingent of teachers sent from Shanghai. At least one of them, a Northern Mantis master by the name of Yu Le Jiang, decided that he would recruit some students the old-fashioned way, by defeating local masters in public matches. These victories would definitively demonstrate the superiority of his northern art.

There are many contradictory accounts of Yu's resulting efforts. One version even appears in a pulp novel published in the 1960s. There is not even total agreement on which local master he fought.[51] Yet all of the various accounts of the match are clear that the town ended up selecting a Wing Chun practitioner to represent them. While it is impossible to know what actually happened, the older and possibly more reliable version of the fight unfolds as follows.

Yu was broadly dismissive of southern kung fu styles and made some public statements that caused tempers to flare. It was suggested that a challenge match should be arranged with a local martial artist to decide the issue. A pharmacist by the name of Lee Kong Hoi volunteered his friend, Ip Man, for the assignment, and Ip accepted the challenge. Never ones to miss a commercial opportunity, some local merchants decided to turn the match into a gala affair. They arranged for the fight to take place at a local theater where organizers could sell tickets and refreshments. The event was publicized and drew a large crowd.

Unfortunately for the crowd, both men had come to fight, not to put on a kung fu exhibition. Real fights, without extensive rules and safety equipment, rarely last long and tend to be not all that visually spectacular, at least not when compared to the popular imagination. Ip family lore states that Yu started by throwing his signature punches, and was quickly engaged and countered by Ip Man who simply off balanced him and threw him off the stage. Yu was hurt by the fall and may have broken some ribs. The fight was called off at this point. Ip Man had defended the honor of the Hung Mun styles, Yu had failed to advance the cause of the Jingwu Association, but the problems of the local merchants were just beginning.

They had promised the crowd a rousing fight, but the whole thing was over before most of the audience even knew it had started. The merchants convinced Ip Man to take the stage again, discuss his technique, demonstrate his hand forms, and generally stall until additional entertainment and lion dances could be arranged. The entire evening ended up as a neighborhood party, and Ip Man became known as a martial arts master within the broader community for the first time.[52]

It was clear to everyone that the Foshan Jingwu Association needed new, more dynamic, leadership. In 1922, Zhong Miao Zhen resigned as president and was replaced by the much more capable Liang Du Yuan. Liang was a local businessman with excellent organizational skills and a burning faith in the new group. He had suffered from ill health until he joined the association and began to intensively study martial arts. As his health improved he became an enthusiastic advocate of Jingwu's mission of national salvation. Liang would remain the president until the Japanese invasion in 1938.[53] Under his leadership, the Foshan branch finally gained a central place in the local martial arts subculture.

Upon taking office Liang Du Yuan began an aggressive policy of community outreach. Under his watch the organization opened schools and free medical clinics, hosted Western-style sporting events, published newspapers, and held classes on topics as diverse as music, painting, and public speaking. The broader Jingwu Association had always found it necessary to use these more accessible events to attract urban middle-class investigators. Those who stayed could then be convinced to enroll in martial arts classes.

The promotion of these other events, as well its vocal support of women's rights, illustrates Jingwu's affinity with elements of the New Culture Movement. While the later state-sponsored Central Guoshu

Institute is sometimes treated as a continuation of the process that Jingwu started, it tended to be much more conservative and statist in its approach to the martial arts. In practice, this meant placing slightly more emphasis on their roots in the "national essence" and less on social reforms.

The auxiliary programs of the Foshan Jingwu Association seem to have extended beyond the general pattern, and they turned out to be the key to the branch's success. During its first few years, the organization had been plagued by the perception that it was populated by outsiders who were hostile to the local community. What is more, that perception may not have been entirely incorrect.

Liang seems to have decided that the key to success was to embed his organization within the town by providing a wide range of subsidized opportunities to the middle class, such as roller skating expeditions or photography courses, and highly publicized charitable projects for the less fortunate. This allowed the organization to begin to build what sociologists call "social capital," or mutual bonds of trust and reciprocity. As people became more familiar with the group and its aims they came to trust it and viewed it as a part of local society.

Building these bridges proved to be absolutely critical. Not only did student enrollments begin to rise, but the Foshan branch secured sources of support and income that were not dependent on Shanghai. As a result, the collapse of the national Jingwu movement in 1925–1926 had little impact on the Guangdong chapters.

The Foshan Jingwu Association provided martial arts instruction for a number of local primary and secondary schools, and even founded a couple of schools of its own. These included the Yuan Jia Primary School, which followed the national curriculum but also taught martial arts on the side. The largest of their schools, Yuan Jia was founded in 1926. Earlier in 1924 the organization had created the Tao Jie Girl's School on Jin Xian Street, Liang Lane, with the aim of promoting female education. In 1946, the association expanded its educational offerings by opening the Yuan Jia secondary school. According to the association's records, by 1927 the Foshan branch had managed to place martial arts coaches in over seventeen local schools and was training over 2,000 students at these satellite locations.[54]

The organization also offered non-traditional students an opportunity to advance their educations. It began this effort by creating the Yuan Jia Civilian Night School located at the Great Market (later known as the Lotus Market). The aim of this institution was to promote literacy at little cost among the many employees, workers, and peasants who had come to Foshan but never received a basic education.[55] The creation of this night school would seem to indicate that while it remained a predominantly middle-class institution, the local chapter must have recruited at least some students from working-class backgrounds.

The Foshan Jingwu association could also offer very refined opportunities to its more sophisticated members. Huang Shao Qiang was a master of the Lingnan school of painting and a favorite student of the regionally well-known Gao Jian Fu. He perfected a variety of both Western and Chinese painting techniques and was a well-regarded teacher. In 1925, while he was teaching at the Foshan Municipal Museum of Painting, Huang decided to investigate the now rapidly expanding organization. He joined mainly to learn martial arts, but later became a fixture of the Foshan branch, holding painting classes and doing much to promote cultural opportunities for its members.[56]

Also, in 1925, the Foshan chapter began to publish its own newspaper, the *Jingwu Monthly*. The paper reported on local news in the club, discussed the theory of physical education, and editorialized on national salvation. It also carried lighter reading, including its own serialized martial arts novels, an entertainment review, and a discussion of literature and biographies that might be of interest to the membership. After publishing its first twenty issues, the monthly newsletter was reformed and re-launched as a weekly magazine.[57]

This community outreach, while vital, did nothing to weaken the Foshan chapter's dedication to promoting a centralized, scientific, vision of the martial arts. In June 1923, Ren Xiao An, the local Athletics and Martial Arts Director, stepped down and was replaced by an appointee selected by the central organization in Shanghai. They chose Li Pei Xian for this critical assignment. His story is worth examining in greater detail as he not only had an important impact on the way martial arts were practiced in Foshan, but it nicely illustrates the career pathways of a civilian martial artist instructor during the Republican period.

Li Pei Xian (1892–1985) was born at the end of the Qing dynasty in Xinhu, a town in the Jiangmen area of Guangdong. Li was interested in martial arts as a youth and learned Hakka Kuen. By 1916, he had moved to Shanghai where he joined the Jingwu Association and completed the six years of study necessary to become an instructor within that system. He studied Shaolin boxing with Zhao Lian He, Northern Mantis with Lo Kuang Yu, and Eagle Claw from Chen Zi Zheng. He also studied a large number of miscellaneous hand and weapons forms.

Li was hired by the Jingwu Association after receiving his advanced level certification and he later worked in their central offices in Shanghai. In addition to teaching martial arts, he also acted as a director in the dance and photography departments. In 1923, he was transferred to Foshan where he remained until 1938 when he left to organize an anti-Japanese Big Knife squad for the Guangzhou Martial Arts Association.

The fact that he was actually from Guangdong, spoke Cantonese, and had a background in a southern boxing style may have helped Li gain credibility within Foshan's crowded martial marketplace. However, his actual teaching activities did not deviate from the orthodox, strictly northern, teaching curriculum. One of his first reforms after taking office was to create a number of "small groups" within the broader student body of the Foshan branch. These structures were essentially study groups designed to keep students motivated and to provide mutual support and a sense of belonging. It is easy to see how these qualities, which are still essential to successful martial arts schools today, could become lost in the Jingwu Association's more megalithic teaching structures. These groups were a great success and more were created from 1924 to 1926.

Li also oversaw the successful introduction of Taijiquan to the Foshan Jingwu curriculum. This art has become popular throughout China, and the Pearl River Delta is no exception. The regional success of Taiji demonstrates once again the critical role that the Jingwu Association played in bringing northern styles of hand combat to the south. Li was also responsible for the martial arts columns published monthly, then weekly, in the branch's newspaper. In fact, he should probably receive much of the credit for the success that the Foshan Jingwu branch eventually enjoyed.

It is also worth noting that his career extended far beyond his involvement with this one organization. He became known as an advocate of Wu style Taiji in Guangzhou early in the communist era. In fact, Li quite successfully negotiated the change of regimes that ended the careers of so many other local martial artists. In 1957, he led the Guangdong martial arts team to Beijing to compete in the National Martial Arts Award & Observation Conference.

Two years later he was appointed the director of Physical Education Teaching and Research at the Guangzhou College of Traditional

Medicine. There he established a martial arts team that continued to campaign for the overall health benefits of China's traditional physical culture. In 1961, he began to offer courses in Qigong, in conjunction with the province's Department of Health, at a number of universities and high schools.

Li even appears to have survived the Cultural Revolution relatively unscathed. In 1960, 1962, and 1977 he released major works on Qigong and Taiji, all published by the People's Sporting Press. In 1982, he published an extended series of articles on Shaolin Boxing in *Wulin* magazine. In the years before his death he produced literally dozens of articles on different aspects of martial arts for various publications.[58]

Li's life story clearly illustrates the opening to the broader national culture that Guangdong's martial artists faced in the early twentieth century. Born in a relatively undeveloped area and educated in Hakka Kuen, this young martial artist went on to make a name for himself promoting Taijiquan and traditional medicine on the national stage. It seems unlikely that any of this would have been possible without the Jingwu Association. While its classes mostly catered to the urban and well-off, within martial arts circles it still filled the traditional role of providing a path for advancement to young men of talent who lacked resources.

The period from 1923 to 1937, under the dynamic leadership of Liang Du Yuan and Li Pei Xian, was the apex of the Foshan Jingwu Association. The organization expanded in size and scope and came to be accepted by the local community. Through the efforts of the Athletic Department, the various schools that it founded, and the many teachers it placed with families, companies, and area schools, the Foshan Jingwu Association was able to train thousands of students in the martial arts. It did all of this practically on its own, well after the decline of the national movement centered in Shanghai.

The great symbol of this period of achievement is the current Foshan Jingwu Building located in the town's Zhongshan Park.[59] Planning for the current structure began in 1933 and the idea quickly gained the approval of the Nanhai County government. The construction of the building itself was to be funded by donations from members of the local community.

The initial plan was to construct three linked structures that ran from east to west. The central building was to be the main public meeting space. It was to contain an auditorium for public performances, a kitchen, dining room, store rooms, and even a dark room for developing film. The eastern and western wings were to be connected to the central hall through side doors. The eastern wing included the organization's office space, a conference room, a drawing room, and some miscellaneous wardrobe and service areas. The western wing was supposed to have a music hall, a dedicated space for table tennis, public restrooms, and men's and women's changing rooms.

Unfortunately the group had trouble raising money during the turbulent 1930s. By 1935, only the central building, containing the main auditorium, had been constructed. This one section of the structure ended up costing over 30,000 Yuan. Over one-third of this money was donated by Lee Chi Ho, the descendent of Li Chung Shing Tong and heir of the "Foshan Po Chi Pill" fortune. Later, Liang Du Yuan, a prominent local citizen and the Director of the "General Department" of the Foshan Jingwu Association (which was responsible for the organization's accounting, communications and medical officers), donated the full cost of constructing the western wing of the complex. After its completion in 1937, it became the home of the organization's martial arts instruction efforts.[60] Li Pei Xian left the post of "Athletic Director" at about this time, and Lu Wei Chang, one of the original founding members of the Shanghai Jingwu Association, moved south to take up the newly vacated position.

During the Japanese occupation of Foshan and Guangzhou, the local branches of the Jingwu Association were forced to close down. The Japanese military used the newly constructed Foshan headquarters as a granary. The membership of the group scattered and its former leader Liang Du Yuan died in a Japanese bombing raid on Wuzhou, Guangxi.

The dynamic leadership that had characterized the group during the 1920s and 30s never returned after the end of the war. The organization was reorganized and a new group of directors were appointed. Unfortunately, a series of presidents were named who either lacked talent or resources and each quickly resigned. Huang Shao Bo was the last of these and he served until the takeover of Foshan in 1949. The single major accomplishment of the organization in this period was the opening of the Yuan Jia Secondary School in 1946. It housed the new academy within its own headquarters. This was important as schools across Foshan were being forced to close due to a spike in inflation and their inability to meet payroll. Still, it was clear that the association's martial star had fallen. The Foshan chapter finally closed its doors with the fall of the town in 1949.[61]

Year	Hung Sing	Zhong Yi	Jingwu
1836	Chan Heung Creates CLF		
1849	CLF School Opened in Foshan		
1854	Red Turban Revolt		
1867	Jeong Yim Reopens Hung Sing		
1893ca	Chan Ngau Sing leads Hung Sing		
1900	Boxer Uprising, Hung Sing Closed		
1905	Hung Sing Reopens		
1907			Huo Yuan Jia in Shanghai
1910s	Some Join Revolutionary Alliance	Zhao Xi Opens First "Yi" School	Shanghai Jingwu Formed
1911	Republican Revolution		
1919	May Fourth Protests		
1920s		Larger Yi System has Six Schools	Guangdong Jingwu
1921			Foshan Branch Opened
1922	Alliance formed with CCP		Rapid National Expansion
1922			Yu Le Jiang fights Ip Man
1923			Liang Du Yuan New Pres.
1925	Workers Congress; Massive Strikes		Li Pei Xian New MA Dir.
1926	Chan Ngau Sing Dies		Financial Collapse of
1927	Hung Sing closed by GMD	Active Conflict with Hung Sing	National Organization
1930s	*Foshan Hung Sing Kwoon* Published		
1931		Zhong Yi Association Formed	Golden Age of the Foshan
1933		Zhang Qi Duan President	Jingwu Association
1934		By the 30s and 40s Zhong Yi	
		Has about 12 Branches.	
1935			New Building Completed
1937	Hung Sing Briefly Reopens		Closed due to Japanese
1938	Anti-Japanese Units Formed		
1942	Wu Quian killed by GMD	Japanese Restrict MA Schools	
1945	Hung Sing Briefly Reopens		
1946		Zhong Yi Schools Reopen	Reopened but Leadership
			Weak
1948		Jiu Chao, Cheung Bo Teaching	
		Pan Nam Studies with Ip Man	
1949	Closed due to Communist Takeover	Zhong Yi Association Closed	Closed due to Communist
			Takeover

Sources: Henning 2003, Kennedy and Guo 2010, Ma 2001, Morris and Zeng.

Figure 3.1. Selected Timeline of Foshan's Martial Arts Societies.

Guoshu: "National Arts" in the Service of the State, 1928–1949

The success of the Jingwu movement did not go unnoticed, and its withdrawal from the national scene after 1926 left a strategic opening. The Guomindang (GMD), under the leadership of the militant Chiang Kai-shek, decided that the right sort of national martial arts organization could be a useful tool for both promoting nationalism and ensuring loyalty to the party. It decided that the Nationalist government would be the one to fill the gap left by the retreat of the civilian, and less political, Jingwu movement.

This process began with an unknown GMD bureaucrat selecting a new term for the "martial arts." A great variety of words and expressions have been used to refer to these combat systems throughout Chinese history. Apparently, it was believed that the first step in establishing control of the arts themselves was to create a single new vocabulary that would situate them within the realm of the state and national consciousness, thereby removing the taint of the particularistic and local.

In some respects the GMD picked up where the Jingwu Association left off. They, too, sought to elevate the martial arts out of the countryside and create a unified movement that was overwhelmingly urban, educated, and middle class. GMD functionaries also added party loyalty to their list of goals. However, they were unwilling to enthusiastically embrace some of Jingwu's more liberal tendencies.

A new name, Guoshu, meaning "national arts" was adopted by the government. The title proved to be quite popular, and martial arts associations and clubs across the country adopted it in mass. The reference to national strength and identity apparently played well no matter where one was or what the local political agenda happened to be.[62]

Getting these disparate martial arts organizations to actually adopt the substance of the GMD's reform agenda proved to be much more problematic. The Guoshu movement never really sought to create a single unified style; rather, what it wanted was political control and authority over the state's many exponents of traditional martial arts.[63] Not surprisingly, this bid for increased social control was viewed as a threat by the remaining communists, most of the unaligned warlords, and even some cliques within the GMD itself. Nor were China's many martial artists eager to lose control of their own associations and more locally focused agendas. And many reform-minded advocates of Western fitness practices continued to believe that the martial arts as a whole were just too backwards to save and the entire project was a waste of resources. Despite its official backing by the state, the Guoshu movement faced opposition on many fronts.

While students of Chinese martial history in the West are currently rediscovering the contributions of the Guoshu movement, with its unique institutions and ideology, it is important to state at the outset that this organization never succeeded in accomplishing its central aims. The new movement was, if anything, even less successful than the early Jingwu Association when it came to penetrating all of China's various regions and creating a truly national organization. The Guoshu movement had particular trouble establishing itself in southwest China. Even areas like Fujian and Guangdong, which were formally under GMD control, resisted its demands.[64] Discovering why this organization failed in precisely those areas where the Jingwu Association had many of its greatest and longest lasting successes will further aid our understanding of the martial arts environment in Guangdong during the 1920s and 30s.

The ultimate origins of the Guoshu movement are found in the efforts of a military officer named Zhang Zhijiang (1882–1966). At the time of the Northern Expedition, Zhang was serving as the commander of the warlord Feng Yuxiang's northwestern army. When Chiang Kai-shek arrived in Nanjing, Feng sent Zhang to the city to act as his personal representative with the central government. In addition to his successful political and military career, Zhang was obsessed with traditional martial arts. He credited their practice with curing him of a partial lower body paralysis that he had suffered earlier in life.

Zhang worked with Li Jinglin, a former warlord from Tianjin, and Zhang Shusheng, a military officer with whom he had a prior relationship, to propose the creation of a new national martial arts organization. The idea gained the immediate support of other high ranking officers in Nanjing and in 1928, by government decree #174, the Guoshu Yanjiuguan (Guoshu Research Academy) was launched with Zhang at the helm.[65]

As Zhang's project progressed, three semi-independent strategies emerged, all of which contributed to, and helped to define, the concept of "Guoshu." Some of these were formally institutionalized within the GMD, others were more loosely organized. The first of these programs to emerge on the national scene, and probably the most obvious to non-martial artists, was a series of semi-regular "national exams" or martial arts competitions.

The format of these events continually evolved through the late 1920s and 30s. In practice they appeared to be a combination of the old Qing military exam system and Western sporting competitions. The first of these events was hastily organized and was hosted in Nanjing from October 15–19 in 1928. The Nationalist government had just been inaugurated and the "exams" (really games) were viewed as a celebratory event. After three days of individual performances, the final 200 contestants were selected to take part in a massive, best of five rounds, sparring competition. On the final day of the competition the seventeen top finishers were granted the guoshi (national warrior) title.

Of course, all of these "national warriors" were male. It never occurred to the more paternalistic, less reform-minded, Guoshu movement to open a category for female competition. Under the leadership of the new Nanjing group, female martial artists lost much of the ground that they had gained during the Jingwu era.

The second, and final, National Guoshu Exam was held five years later in October of 1933. This meeting was better organized and a much more structured affair. The performance of individual boxing and weapons sets was eliminated as such practices were by then deemed too subjective and "unscientific" to be of any value in a modern sporting competition. Five weight classes (something that had not existed in 1928) were created and contestants had to compete in tournaments in at least three of the four disciplines offered (wrestling, boxing, fencing, and spear play).

Extensive rules were drawn up for each event, allowing judges to give penalties for "unsportsmanlike conduct" such as low kicks, eye gouges, attacking an opponent's back in fencing, or grabbing an opponent's spear in an attempt to deflect or disarm him. The cumulative effect of these changes was both to make the tournament safer (there had been a number of injuries and deaths in 1928), and to transform the harsh fighting disciplines into "civilized" sporting events suitable for an educated middle-class audience.[66]

A structure was put in place by which athletes could qualify for the National Examination by competing in a number of county and provincial tournaments. Titles were awarded to successful contestants at each level: first zhuangshi (hero), at the county level, then wushi (warrior) at the provincial level, and lastly guoshi (national warrior) for the top champions. The GMD instructed that tournaments were to be scheduled in every county in December, in every province in April, and the month of October was to be reserved for the national championship.[67] Given the tenuous political situation throughout the country it is unlikely that most of these events were ever held, but some certainly were. The overall effect was to emulate the Qing system of military degrees; the award structure nicely demonstrates the balance between traditional Chinese identity and modern Western methods that the Guoshu movement was trying to strike.

Unfortunately, the second National Examination failed to generate much interest within China's martial arts community. Realizing that there was a problem the organizers of the Exam scheduled it to partially overlap with the Fifth Annual National Games (where a number of prominent martial artists were already competing) to ensure that there would be enough contestants and spectators to make the venture worthwhile. Even in this relatively barren environment female martial artists were systematically excluded from the competition.[68]

While the examination system had great promise, it failed to become an avenue for success or recognition for most of China's traditional martial arts practitioners. The fact that these individuals were simply not showing up for the county and provincial level tournaments meant that new national standards and regulations had very little effect on local martial arts associations and schools. Of course, the examination system was not the only branch of the Guoshu movement to suffer from this problem.

The crowning jewel of Zhang's organization was a new national school dedication to the teaching and promotion of martial arts, the Guoshu Research Academy. Initially, the organization was split into two sections, one dedicated to teaching the "Shaolin" arts, and the other committed to teaching "Wudang" styles. Dividing the school's administration and staff by fighting systems turned out to be a fantastically bad idea. The two factions immediately went to war with one another.

Morris relates that Gao Zhendong (the Dean of the Wudang arts) and Wang Ziping (the Dean of the Shaolin disciplines) resorted to fisticuffs to resolve mundane administrative disputes. More menacingly, teaching instructors from each school, Liu Yinhu (Wudang) and Ma Yufu (Shaolin), attacked each other with bamboo spears.[69] Given that the central goal of the academy was to bring China's various martial arts factions together, to promote a new sense of openness and scientific reform, and (most importantly) to turn away from the superstitions and feuds of the past, the organizational structure of the institution can only be called woefully shortsighted.

It is unlikely that any deep ancient hatred really characterized the "Wudang" and "Shaolin" branches of the faculty. The great "rivalry" between these two fraternities is a product of martial arts myths, novels from the 1930s, and films from the 1960s and 70s. Mundane jealousies and limited resources seem to have sparked the actual conflicts.

Whatever the reason, it became apparent that the institution would have to be reformed if the Guoshu movement was going to survive. In July of 1928 the organization's name was changed to the Central Guoshu Academy. The staff was unified into a single faculty and new divisions for teaching, publishing, and general affairs were created.[70]

The saving grace of the Central Guoshu Academy was that it had a knack for attracting the very best individuals in the country. While all of its key instructors represented northern arts, each was an accomplished master and genuinely talented individual. This alone set the Academy apart from much of the GMD where individuals tended to receive appointments based on political connections rather than actual ability. The instructors that Zhang gathered really were among the best the nation had to offer. The quality of the scholars and administrators assembled by the Academy was usually quite good as well. Ma Liang, the famous educator, joined the school's staff, as did Tang Hao, the father of modern martial arts scholarship.[71]

The students selected for the Central Guoshu Institute were also undeniably talented. Two types of students were admitted. Sixty students, selected by regional and provincial programs, were admitted into the "Instruction Section" and trained to be coaches and teachers. The entire program could be completed in three years, but applicants were expected to already have a substantial background in hand combat. Students in this track studied a variety of martial and academic disciplines. Other students were sent to the "Training Section" where they were provided with similar instruction in the martial arts and academics, but could not earn a teaching degree.[72] Similar programs were then created at regional training academies around the country.

Stanley Henning, quoting an account by Ju Hao, a police officer from Jiangdu City who was sent in 1929 to study at the Jiangsu Provincial Guoshu Institute (a local school under the oversight of the Nanjing organization), gives us a good idea of what life was like for the students at the time:

I graduated from training at the Jiangsu Provincial Guoshu Institute, where I studied Xingyi Quan [Form-Intent Boxing]. . . . The training was divided into two parts, skill classes (in the field) and academic classes (in the class room). There were six hours of classes every day, four in the morning and two in the afternoon, one of which was an academic class. All of the remaining classes were in skills. The academic classes included physiology and hygiene, infantry drill, the Three People's Principles, and the origins and importance of Xingyi Quan.[73]

At first, female students were admitted to the academy and they were assigned a separate, if still rigorous, curriculum. This gesture turned out to be short-lived. After it was discovered that some of the male teaching staff had engaged in inappropriate behavior with some of the female students, the schools administrators decided that, rather than disciplining the offending staff, it would simply be better to expel all of the women. The nationalist and statist ideology of the Guoshu movement had no room for anything but strong *male* heroes.[74]

The curriculum of the Central Guoshu Academy also had an undeniably militant bent. In addition to martial arts classes, students were also expected to take classes in military drill, bayonet combat, military studies, and "party indoctrination." At the same time that the National Examination system was attempting to re-imagine Chinese martial arts as a modern middle-class sport, the Central Academy was creating a structure of unified military drill that could quickly be taught to the masses, unify them into a single fighting body, and ensure their loyalty to the GMD. One of the reasons that the Guoshu movement ultimately failed is that its various branches tended to work at cross purposes with each other. Of course there were other issues as well.

In February of 1929, the Central Guoshu Academy began to publish its plans to reform and regulate the practice of martial arts on a national scale. It distributed instructions for creating a vast number of provincial, municipal, and county level branches that would then oversee district and village level Guoshu associations across the country. Regional martial arts masters were to be recruited as teachers. They would be allowed to continue to practice their local styles, but were expected to give priority to teaching the national curriculum (again dominated by northern arts) that the Central Guoshu Academy created.

Financing and administration was also centrally planned and regulated. Additionally, every primary and secondary school in the country was ordered to begin instructing its students in the martial arts by 1930. A Central Martial Arts Physical Culture Specialty School was created in 1933 to help fill the demand for well-qualified instructors.[75]

What was envisioned was a massive movement that would have enrolled and militarized a large percentage of the nation's total population, ensuring their loyalty to the Nationalist government once and for all. The political implications of the proposed organization were immediately obvious and they limited the appeal of the Guoshu movement. China was far from unified in the 1930s, and the transparently political and statist aims of this movement ensured that the Guoshu schools would only survive and prosper in areas that were already firmly under Chiang Kai-shek's control. In practice, this restricted the reach of the program to some urban and coastal areas.

To illustrate this general problem Morris brings up the case of Shanxi Province. Martial arts had long been popular in the area, and a relatively large percentage of the local population participated in them. In fact, the province boasted a stunning 560 registered martial arts organizations (many of which had adopted the by then fashionable "Guoshu" title). Yet under the warlord Yan Xishan, not a single Guoshu club or class actually affiliated with the central GMD organization could be established in the province. While there were many public martial arts schools and associations in Shanxi, each and every one was a local affair.

The same pattern was seen in the South. Fujian and Guangdong were formally administered by, and loyal to, the GMD. Nevertheless they enjoyed a certain degree of local autonomy which regional leaders jealously guarded. Apparently, even this degree of friction was enough to keep the Central Guoshu Academy from establishing branches in major southern martial arts strongholds. Xiamen (Amoy) in Fujian continued to have a thriving chapter of the Jingwu Association throughout the 1930s, yet the Guoshu movement was never able to gain a reliable base of support in the city.[76]

Guangdong also proved to be a major challenge. The short history of the "Liangguang Guoshu Institute" nicely illustrates how even political disputes within the various cliques that composed the GMD could limit the success of the broader Nanjing reform movement. In October 1928, the governor of Guangdong, General Li Jishen (an important military figure in the GMD), observed the first National Martial

Arts Examination in Nanjing. He was impressed with what he saw and decided to sponsor a regional branch of the new Guoshu organization that would reform, administer, and promote the martial arts in Guangxi and Guangdong. He invited Wan Lai Sheng (who specialized in Six Harmonies and Shaolin Boxing) and Li Xian Wu (a Taiji master and native of Guangdong), two of the winners in the 1928 competition, to return to Guangzhou with him.

The local government quickly approved the governor's plans and Wan Lai Sheng was formally appointed the head of the new organization by the Eighth Army (commanded by General Li). Anticipating the creation of a large well-funded organization, Wan went about recruiting other martial arts masters to provide instruction. These included Fu Zhensong, Li Xian Wu, Wan Laimin, and Gu Ru Zhang (also known locally as Ku Yu Cheong). All of these individuals were well-known, talented martial artists. Gu Ru Zhang in particular had stood out in the 1928 National Exams. He would go on to be a major player in the promotion of Bak Siu Lam (Northern Shaolin) throughout southern China. These instructors, along with Wan, were known collectively as the "Five Southbound Tigers." The new institute was conscious of the need to recruit some southern stylists for the teaching staff and it hired Zhang Liquan, a White Eyebrow expert, among a handful of others.

The organization first opened its doors for business in March of 1929. It was located near the stables in East Jiaochang, Guangzhou. At first it hosted three, two-hour classes a day (8:00 a.m., 1:00 p.m., and 7:30 p.m.) with an initial enrollment of 140 students. Almost all of these individuals were local government employees. This did not satisfy the total demand for instruction, so two new one-hour class times (7:00 a.m. and 5:30 p.m.) were added to accommodate the work schedules of local civil servants.

As knowledge of the new group spread, demand for its services expanded. Following the lead of the Jingwu Association, the Liangguang Guoshu Institute would send teachers to offices, schools, or other groups who requested their services and could muster at least twenty students and the appropriate fee. Again, it was government agencies that took the lead in off-campus instruction. Within eight weeks a total of eleven classes were being offered at the group's headquarters and an additional nine special classes had been established at various government offices. A total of 500 students were being educated by some of the most talented martial artists in the country. Initially, enrollment was limited to men, but special classes for women were eventually created.[77]

Still, the student body was made up almost exclusively of low-level GMD functionaries and government employees, a single very narrow demographic. The school's extremely rapid growth also makes one wonder how many of its students enrolled because they were ordered to do so. Or perhaps they saw participation in the governor's new program as helping their chances for career advancement. While the new institute did a fantastic job of gathering some of the top talent in the nation, it never really succeeded in establishing deep roots in the local community, and it is clear that its influence never spread much beyond the government offices of Guangzhou.

Despite these shortcomings, or maybe because of them, the governor and the Liangguang Martial Arts Institute pressed ahead with their grand plans to radically reform the practice of martial arts throughout the province. They began by ordering the registration of all martial arts schools and organizations in Guangdong. This was followed up with a ban on the establishment of new schools or associations other than those created by the staff of the Guoshu Institute. Plans were also put in place to begin publication of a new martial arts magazine that would explicitly advance the nationalist "Guoshu philosophy."[78]

With the full power of the provincial government and the Eighth Army backing the orders, it is likely that in time these policies could actually have been implemented, at least within the more populous areas of the Pearl River Delta and Shantou. It would seem that General Li Jishen was quite serious in his desire to bring the local martial arts community to heel and transform it into a tool to be exploited by the state. In retrospect, it is hard to see how the execution of such a plan could have been anything but disastrous for Guangdong's flourishing indigenous martial arts community. While the Central Guoshu Academy was in some ways more flexible than the Jingwu Association, it was still an organization dominated by a handful of northern styles that fundamentally had no need for what they perceived to be the unsophisticated and eccentric boxing styles of the less civilized south. Deep pools of local knowledge and experience were about to be sacrificed on the altars of "national unity."

Political calamity intervened before implementation of the new policies could begin. In May of 1929, General Li Jishen resigned as governor and traveled to Nanjing with the intention of mediating a dispute between Chiang Kai-shek and the "New Guangxi Clique." The full history of the dispute between this group and Chiang need not detain us here. Basically, Chiang Kai-shek proposed reorganizing the military;

this threatened the leaders of Guangxi who then broke with Chiang. Negotiations between the groups went badly and Li Jishen was arrested and held until his eventual release in 1931. Li then drifted into the orbit of the Communist Party and out of our story.

The new governor of Guangdong, and leader of the Eight Army, was General Chen Jitang. Chen is often remembered for his reforms, building, and charitable projects. He paved the streets of the Guangzhou, built some of the most modern buildings in the city, and instituted a rudimentary social safety net. He tends to be remembered favorably in the region.

One of Chen Jitang's first reforms was to eliminate his predecessor's Guoshu Institute. It was possible that he saw the organization as a threat, or perhaps he did not want to align himself with a wing of the GMD that was so much under the influence of Chiang Kai-shek's vocal supporters. Whatever the real reason, Chen claimed to be acting out of a need to cut spending and put the government's finances back in order. The total budget of the Institute was around 4,500 Yuan a month, a substantial figure, but probably not outrageous given the scope of the assignments that had been tasked to the organization. The Liangguang Guoshu Institute folded after a mere two months of operation, a victim of internal politics within the GMD.[79]

The upshot of this rapid fall was that a number of prominent northern exponents were left unemployed and more or less stranded in Guangzhou. This seeming setback created new opportunities that spread the northern arts more effectively than anything the Guoshu Institute had ever managed to do. After all, most of the instruction that the school had offered was focused on a handful of civil servants. Chen's forced dissolution of the organization allowed its instructors to enter the much broader marketplace for private instruction. It was within these smaller commercial schools that northern styles, such as Bak Siu Lam and Taijiquan, really took hold and began to spread in the south.

Following the breakup of the Guoshu Institute, Li Xian Wu was hired by the Guangdong Jingwu Association as the Director of Academic Affairs. He later published a guide to Taijiquan that is discussed in Kennedy and Guo's review of martial arts training manuals.[80] Other former instructors introduced their own schools of Cha Quan and Bagua Quan throughout the region.

Gu Ru Zhang proved to be among the most influential of the remaining staff. Attempting to capitalize on the work that had already been accomplished, he sought to create the Guangzhou Guoshu Institute, formally established in June of 1929. Gu was selected as president. Wang Shaozhou was named vice president and Ren Sheng Kui, Liu Jing Chun, and Yang Ting Xia (the wife of Wang) all worked as instructors.

It seems likely that this new, smaller organization, had some level of official backing and that it fell within the broader Guoshu movement led by the Central Academy in Nanjing. The group was housed in the building of the National Athletic Association on Hui Fu East Road in Guangzhou. That said, the new institute did not continue the grandiose mission of its predecessor and it did not attempt to regulate or lead the local martial arts marketplace. It essentially became just one more martial arts school among many.

Gu inherited many of the civil servants who had initially enrolled in the older organization. He appears to have had a few hundred students at a time, and his organization continued the pattern of holding special classes for offices or institutions that could gather a large number of interested individuals. Yang Ting Xia taught the female students, and the organization as a whole offered instruction in Six Harmonies Fist, Form-Intent Boxing, Bagua Quan, Cha Quan, Taiji, Shaolin Boxing, and Northern Mantis. Various weapons forms were also taught.

The new organization appears to have been fairly long-lived and to have enjoyed some real success in spreading its vision of the martial arts. In 1936 (the same year that Chen Jitang was forced to flee to Hong Kong after throwing his lot in with the ill-fated Guangxi Clique) the Guangdong Province Athletic Association sponsored a martial arts exhibition at the Guangzhou Public Stadium. The Guangzhou Guoshu Institute performed for the crowd and received an award in recognition of its performance. The Japanese invasion of the area in 1938 forced the school to finally close its doors.[81]

Our entire discussion of the institutional aspects of the Guoshu movement in Guangdong has focused on Guangzhou. As the capital, and the GMD's main base of power in the province, it makes sense that this is where their central efforts would be located. At the same time, we must ask whether their influence spread to Foshan during the 1930s. Ip Man was active in the martial arts community during this period and was later employed as a police inspector by the local government. It is possible that the GMD's efforts to promote a different view of the martial arts may have had some impact on the development of Wing Chun.

At first glance it would appear that the various Guoshu-related groups failed to penetrate into the countryside even so far as Foshan. The smaller town never created or hosted a branch of the official Guoshu organization. This failure would seem to be an indictment of the whole effort. If it cannot even succeed in a town as seemingly friendly and saturated with martial arts as Foshan, where could this movement hope to take hold?

Yet it is possible that the situation may be more complex than it first appears. While the GMD never sent a large contingent of northern, Guoshu-approved, teachers, we should remember that something important did happen in the town around 1930. For close to two decades the "Yi" schools, which taught Hung Gar and Wing Chun, had existed in some form of loose federation that was backed by a number of local "yellow" trade unions. They were constantly coming into conflict with the Hung Sing Association, which backed the Communist Party in a number of disputes surrounding the development of the local labor movement.

The Hung Sing Association was closed by the GMD in 1927, following the infamous "April 12 Incident." Shortly after the founding and then the rapid dissolution of the Liangguang Guoshu Institute, Foshan's "Yi" schools came together to create a much tighter organization known as the "Zhong Yi Martial Arts Athletic Association" under a single unified leadership. Of the many ways of expressing the term "martial arts," the organization chose the new, government-approved term, "Guoshu."[82] This alone would not be evidence of any sort of relationship. Morris has already observed that as the term gained popularity it was adopted by a variety of groups that had no particular association with the Nanjing organization.[83]

Nevertheless, it is also important to note who assumed formal leadership of this new organization. Its president was none other than Zhang Qi Duan, the GMD party secretary for Nanhai County.[84] While all of the evidence remains circumstantial, the organization's history of backing the GMD, their acceptance of direct political leadership by the party, their choice of names, and their date of incorporation all point to the Zhong Yi Association having some sort of relationship with the local political establishment. Perhaps what the case of the Zhong Yi Association demonstrates is that local government officials were really more interested in having political control of martial groups than the details of the styles that they actually taught. Given that they were already backing a large and successful group in Foshan, it may have been seen as unnecessary to create another competing school.

If this interpretation of events is correct, the choice to simply work with the Zhong Yi Association represents a telling concession to the realities of the local martial arts market. Given the intensely local nature of most schools, it seems that any large-scale, top-down, institutional reform effort undertaken in the chaotic 1930s was doomed to fail. It was almost impossible for the state to assert its control over the vast network of private schools and associations that had grown up since the end of the last century, and it could only try in the unlikely event that it had the strong support of the local GMD leadership.

This is the central paradox faced by both the Guoshu and, to a lesser extent, the Jingwu movements. In their public statements they constantly claimed that Chinese martial arts were in danger; they had become irrelevant and were dying. They proposed the resurrection of the arts through a process of rigorous purification and modernization. Both organizations then sought to use this new movement to advance their own commercial, social, or political goals.

The irony was that the local martial arts were not dying, certainly not in Guangdong, and probably not in most other areas of the country. New commercial schools and organizations were growing at a dizzying rate, so much so that outside regulatory efforts found it essentially impossible to control the local supply of martial arts instructions. While some high profile groups struggled, the 1930s saw a steady rise in interest in the martial arts.

Newspapers in Guangzhou, Foshan, and Hong Kong all began to carry serialized novels glorifying local martial artists from the recent past. New radio programs, and later early films, hyped martial strength. Urban individuals became involved in these traditions in record numbers. The simple reality is that Chinese martial arts were more popular, and practiced by more social groups, in the 1920s and 30s than ever before.

In an era when China was undergoing rapid industrialization and change, the imaginary world of "rivers and lakes," with its martial codes and wandering heroes, seemed to reveal a window back onto something essential in the national character. Studying the martial arts became a way for urban educated youth to ground themselves in an identity and community of their own making. It reaffirmed both the past strength and future promise of the Chinese people.

Precisely what the details of this new identity would be was the issue at stake. In some senses, both the Jingwu and Guoshu movements were rushing to get out ahead of a transition that was already well underway and threatening to pass them by. As Hamm has already noted, the early martial arts novels of the "Guangdong School" tended to be firmly grounded in *local* identity and *local* pride. They glorified regional heroes and sold out as fast as they could be printed.[85]

Petrus Liu goes even further in his reading of this literature and asserts that period martial arts fiction was often more sophisticated than today's casual readers might suspect. Rather than being simple potboilers, these stories engaged with many of the pressing debates of the era. They maintained that authentic communities could be built on mutual responsibility and ethics rather than vertically imposed laws, rights, and governing institutions. Martial arts dramas were, in essence, an argument that communities should be structured around the concept of *minjian* (between people) rather than *tianxia* (all under heaven.)[86]

Nor was this debate confined to the printed page. As the previous review has illustrated, many of these tensions were playing themselves out in the competition between local schools and national martial arts institutions throughout southern China. In an era when Guangdong was basically an autonomous political region that Chiang Kai-shek sought to reassert his control over, such displays of parochialism could have important ramifications.

Realizing the essential impossibility of an institutional solution to the problem, a group of authors associated with the Central Guoshu Academy decided that the battle had to be fought on ideological grounds. Rather than trying to directly infiltrate the dense network of martial arts schools covering both the countryside and urban areas, they instead put pen to paper in an attempt to convince these groups to reform themselves. This ideological effort was the third strategy that supported the GMD's Guoshu movement.[87]

The writers and intellectuals that the Guoshu movement employed were just as talented as their martial arts instructors. We have already mentioned one of the organization's early leading lights. Tang Hao, a Japanese trained lawyer, worked tirelessly to promote the goals of the Guoshu movement, both as a martial artist and as a scholar. He was the first person to take up the academic study of China's martial arts in the modern era. His contributions to our understanding of the early history of Taiji and the development of Shaolin Quan are literally invaluable. His sharp pen exploded many of the myths that popular teachers and martial arts novels had promoted.[88]

At the same time, modern students must remember that his scholarship is not ideologically neutral. He sought to promote and justify his own populist vision of the "national arts" through his presentation of martial history. As a leftist thinker he wanted to rescue China's traditional fighting systems from the politically and culturally conservative mythmakers of the day so that they could be returned "to the masses."

Other writers tended to be even more ideological and philosophical in nature. These authors attacked those who saw the martial arts as hopelessly outmoded and superstitious, as well as local instructors who clung to traditional styles, mysterious lineages, and petty rivalries. They criticized anything that appeared "unscientific," or "superstitious," in the martial arts. These writers knew that it was precisely those elements that would stand out to the May Fourth reformers; therefore, eccentric and exotic practices had to be ended before they endangered the entire martial arts movement.

Of course, it should be remembered that the martial arts community was actually in no danger whatsoever. Again, stories of miraculous qi powers and wandering heroes were being snapped up by audiences just as fast as they could be written. Rather, it was the GMD's vision of a unified, modern, scientific, and politically pliable Guoshu movement that was in jeopardy.

Fundamentally, it was in danger because it was of little interest to anyone other than a handful of educated, mostly urban, reformers. The Hung Sing Association, the Zhong Yi Association, the various White Eyebrow schools, and a great many others had already discovered the secret to commercial success in Guangdong. The Jingwu movement had previously demonstrated what was necessary to succeed on a national scale. But rather than changing their message to fit these market realities, the reformers in the Guoshu movement sought to use the coercive powers of the state to reshape public opinion.

In 1934, a new martial arts journal, humbly titled *Seek Truth*, went into public distribution. It became a major mouthpiece for the Nanjing reform movement. In its first issue it viciously attacked traditional martial arts practitioners who "cling to factional views, siding only with their own and attacking all others, and cultivating slavish bigotry in all who enter. They are always bragging about themselves but never teach their secrets to others, selling their bunk to the fools who come to study with them, flaunting their artifice and dazzling all with their mystery and wonder."[89] One wonders how the movement could expect to gain any sort of traction among the traditional practitioners with this sort of rhetoric.

Stylistic questions aside, if traditionalism was what the Guoshu movement despised, what sort of future did their ideology envision for the martial arts? Authors argued that they should be displayed and taught in the most transparent way possible. This general rule applied to everything from discussions of the origins of the various styles to descriptions of how best to execute a punch or a kick. Scientific terminology drawn from modern physics needed to replace outmoded and superstitious ideas like the "Eight Directions" and the "Five Elements." Such terms were too backwards and closely linked to superstition to have any lasting place in the "national arts."

Further, there are only so many ways in which the human body can move, and some of these pathways must be more efficient than others. This means that when examined at the most basic conceptual level, one quickly discovers that there is a single truth that underlies all of the various hand combat systems. Schools needed to be willing to share with each other, and to discard what does not work, for the sake of national salvation. Such an approach to understanding the martial arts was fundamentally conceptual in nature, and it was more likely to appeal to urban educated students than the traditional methods of instruction which revolved around following and obeying one's master.

Even the traditional relationship between students and teachers was open to attack. According to the Nanjing reformers, the Chinese martial arts, when stripped to their core, were progressive and rational. It was only the confusion and ignorance of parochial martial arts practitioners during the late Qing dynasty that obscured this central truth.[90] Rationalization and reform could reveal it.

Conclusion: Ip Man and the Guoshu Philosophy

Much of this rhetoric will sound immediately familiar to Wing Chun practitioners. This style has remained a traditional art and it never came under direct state control. At the same time, it seems to have absorbed aspects of the revisionist attitude that the Guoshu movement worked so hard to promote in the 1930s and 1940s. Ip Man, the grandmaster of modern Wing Chun, seems a likely point of entry for these ideas.

We discuss Ip Man's background and his contributions to Wing Chun extensively in later chapters. For the moment it is enough to note that he was a well-off and highly educated resident of Foshan where he worked for the police department. In short, Ip Man is precisely the sort of practitioner that the Guoshu movement was trying to reach. He was the target audience of projects like *Seek Truth* or Tang Hao's attempts to reform our understanding of martial arts history.

Whether through direct study or social osmosis, Ip Man seems to have absorbed many of the ideas embedded in the Guoshu movement's critique of contemporary hand combat. When he began to teach Wing Chun professionally he immediately jettisoned the traditional vocabulary that was used to describe the directions and forces. Terms like "bagua" and the "five elements" were replaced with ideas drawn from physics. Extraneous movements and concepts that seemed to serve no purpose were dropped altogether. Mysticism, and even the culturally common concept of "qi," has little place in Wing Chun. His children consistently describe the contempt in which he held other martial artists who claim to have learned their styles from wandering monks or nuns. He had no time for stories of secret lineages or quasi-magical techniques passed on only to a single disciple. He saw all of these things as a form of psychological compensation for those who lacked faith in their actual skills.[91]

In some ways these attitudes are surprising. While Ip Man attempted to renew and reform Wing Chun, relying on modern scientific concepts, he was very much a traditional Chinese gentleman and not overly sympathetic to the West. He never dressed in Western clothing and never taught Western students. While he banished philosophical concepts from Wing Chun he was conversant in Buddhist, Daoist, and Confucian thought. Qi plays little role in most Wing Chun schools today, but Ip Man himself was not above internal training. Indeed, the "Siu Lim Tao" form that he taught can be readily adapted for such practice. Lastly, while he had little tolerance for stories of mysterious holy men and lost lineages, he was a master of an art that expressly claimed to have been transmitted by a mythical nun and to be a living link with the grandeur of the Shaolin Temple.

It seems highly unlikely that Ip Man's "scientific" approach to martial arts was embedded in the Wing Chun style that he learned from Chan Wah Shun in the closing years of the Qing dynasty. More plausible is the possibility that something about the new Guoshu ideology struck a chord with him, and while he never adopted all of the movement's recommendations, his teachings in the 1950s bear the unmistakable marks of debates that began in the 1930s.

Much the same can be said for his most notable student, Bruce Lee. Lee's famous criticism of the "classical mess," his constant lampooning of traditional stylists and his dedication to scientific methods of reforming the martial arts all seem to uncannily reflect the heated debates that raged throughout the 1930s.[92] His subsequent introduction of these concepts into the realm of Western martial arts makes a good deal of sense when one considers his teacher's background and the reforms that he had already made to Wing Chun.

While a more detailed discussion of both Ip Man and Bruce Lee's ideas will have to wait for another chapter, we can conclude with some certainty that the Guoshu movement enjoyed its greatest success as a literary and ideological school. The National Examinations failed to arouse interest among most martial artists. Likewise, the complex network of associations and schools envisioned by the reformers at the Central Guoshu Academy only succeeded when there was strong backing from a local leader, and for the most part this was missing in China's southern and western regions. These institutional aspects of the Guoshu movement never really managed to spread much beyond the coastal urban areas.

However, the movement's publications did succeed in advancing a coherent ideology. Even in areas like Guangdong, where the formal institutions of Guoshu had struggled, these ideas were able to gain a sympathetic hearing among other educated urban martial artists. Ironically, many of these ideas, now over eight decades old, are still considered insightful and cutting-edge when repeated in today's Western martial arts publications. The core insights of the Guoshu movement have both survived the test of time and helped to shape some aspects of Guangdong's martial arts community.

In the 1920s and 30s, the realm of hand combat became a microcosm for many broader debates and disputes within broader Chinese society. Questions as diverse as the value of centralized political control versus local autonomy, the significance of nationalism, and the role of women in the new China, all emerged and became central to the ultimate fate of southern kung fu. Some of these debates reinforced the strength of Guangdong's martial marketplace; others threatened its core institutions and identities.

Ip Man is unique in that Foshan situated him squarely at the crossroads of these two battling forces. He experienced a certain amount of pressure to fill the role of "martial hero," defending the *local* identity. These demands are illustrated by accounts of his duel with Master Yu Le Jiang of the Jingwu Association. However, as a well-educated martial artist and employee of the GMD he was exposed to the rhetoric and ideas of the Guoshu movement. How he balanced these two competing forces would have a major impact on Wing Chun's ultimate development in Hong Kong in the 1950s.

Part II

Conflict, Imperialism and Modernization

The Evolution of Wing Chun Kung Fu, 1900–1972

Chapter 4

The Public Emergence of Wing Chun, 1900–1949

> No matter which of the preceding stories are true Wong Wah Bo, Leung Yee Tai and "Painted Face" Kam were, without doubt, the first generation of Foshan's Wing Chun. They inherited the past, enlightened the future and made great contributions in the spread and development of Wing Chun in Foshan.
>
> —Huang Xiao Hui and Huang Hong, 2001[1]

Introduction

The traditional Chinese martial arts are richly embroidered in a deep symbolic language. Sacred mountains and grottoes are recurring themes throughout their folklore. Animals, both mundane and fantastic, are among the most frequently observed symbols. Northern styles showcase imitative forms that seem to channel the essence of the monkey, eagle, or praying mantis. Emerging from this menagerie are two of the most beloved martial images: the tiger and the dragon. An ancient tomb, in the same province as the Shaolin Temple, contains the very first artistic representations of a dragon and a tiger in the shell-inlayed floor.[2] The two animals are still associated with the area's Shaolin fighting arts today, over 6,000 years later.

This symbolic pairing is not restricted to the northern arts. In 1848, Chan Heung composed a martial couplet, which relied on the heroic qualities of these two animals, to be displayed in all Choy Li Fut schools.[3] Nevertheless, when discussing the martial history of the south a more fitting symbol might be the fenghuang or Chinese phoenix. Paired with the dragon, a phoenix represents the crescent moon and all the feminine or "yin" forces of the universe. When shown alone, its symbolic tenor changes dramatically; it becomes the king of all the birds, master of the sun, and the sacred animal assigned to be the guardian of the south. While the Chinese phoenix does not rise from its ashes the way that its Western counterpart does, it is immortal and often associated with the element fire. While it celebrates peace, its departure foretells oncoming violence.

Destruction by fire has been a reoccurring theme in our discussion of Guangdong's history during the late Qing and Republic periods. Yet, like a phoenix, the traditional arts survived to return once more at the end of each calamity, transformed to be sure, but with their essence and brilliance preserved. This same pattern is also discernible in Wing Chun's history. From the destructive fires of Li Wen Mao's abortive revolt emerged a changed social order that could support a new hand combat school. This system would go on to become one of the most widely practiced martial arts in the world.

In the current chapter we will see how Wong Wah Bo, Leung Yee Tai, and "Painted Face" Kam, three members of a local opera troop, transmitted their accumulated martial knowledge in the aftermath of the Red Turban Revolt. After a period of transformation and refinement Wing Chun burst onto the civic stage in the early Republic period, becoming one of the most notable local martial arts styles. It was both numerically and socially successful, being backed by some of the most elite political and economic elements of Foshan society. Throughout this period a number of individuals, rarely remembered or discussed in recent works, taught and refined the system. Yet many of these gains were fated to be lost in the 1949 communist takeover of the province and the later Cultural Revolution. While a few masters (mostly within the Yuen Kay San lineage) were able to remain active throughout this dark period, it was really Ip Man, a local notable who fled to Macao and then Hong Kong, who is most responsible for the current popularity of the art.

Wing Chun has maintained its essence through a pattern of continual renewal and revival. In order to survive it has transformed itself from a small private system to a prominent local art which enjoyed the backing of important economic and political forces. Yet, by the end of our time period, Ip Man will be preparing to strike out in a new direction, one that would both minimize his arts connection to its parochial past and lead to a truly global rebirth.

From Legend to History: The Origins of Wing Chun in Foshan

When discussing the early history of Wing Chun it is necessary to divide our "facts" into three categories. First are the relatively few pieces of information that can actually be confirmed through independent evidence. Second, we have the much larger category of assertions that seem "plausible," meaning that they fit with what we know about the period, though there is no direct evidence that speaks to them. Lastly, there are those assertions that contradict known events and can be falsified.

Prior to the era of Leung Jan, "plausibility" is the most that we can hope for. Most accounts of Wing Chun's origins claim that it was first brought to Foshan by Cantonese opera performers in the mid-nineteenth century. More specifically, three individuals are commonly named in these accounts. They are Wong Wah Bo, Leung Yee Tai, and "Painted Face" Kam.

The problem with these assertions is that there is no evidence, independent of the oral folklore of the Wing Chun community, which attests of the existence of any of these individuals. Traveling (and possibly rebellious) opera singers are an undeniably romantic image, and one that is employed by other martial arts in the area, notably Hung Gar.

On the other hand, Foshan was the hub of local opera activity in the early and mid-nineteenth century. There were a number of unemployed singers following the Red Turban Revolt, and it is notable that Leung Jan shares at least a clan affiliation with one of the named performers. For all of these reasons we consider it at least *plausible* that Wong Wah Bo and Leung Yee Tai contributed to the development of Wing Chun in Foshan. Painted Face Kam (a reference to the heavy makeup worn by performers) is a considerably more shadowy character who appears later in the Wing Chun folklore of only a few lineages (notably that of Yuen Kay San), and he may have originally been attached to the related, but distinct, art of Weng Chun (sometimes referred to as Jee Shim Wing Chun) practiced publicly in Hong Kong from the 1950s through the present.[4]

Given that so little is known about the very existence of these figures, it is not surprising that there is even less certainty about their character and individual histories. This paucity of evidence has not prevented a rich body of legend from growing up around them. Leung Yee Tai is often associated with pole fighting and is said to have been the individual who introduced the Six and a Half Point Pole form to Wing Chun. According to some accounts, this highly efficient form came directly from the legendary Abbot Jee Shim. Perhaps because of his association with the pole, it is often claimed that Leung Yee Tai was not an opera performer but a member of the barge crew who was responsible for using a long maritime pole to steer and propel the ship through shallow channels or canals.

Wong Wah Bo is said to have been a singer who specialized in martial roles. According to the Ip family tradition, it was he who inherited Yim Wing Chun's boxing system from Leung Lan Kwai (or in some versions from Leung Bok Chau). Wong Wah Bo and Leung Yee Tai were said to have been friends and to have traded their knowledge to create the art originally taught to Leung Jan sometime after 1855. Of course, all of these accounts must be treated with caution.[5]

The Red Turban Revolt represents a turning point for those interested in studying the local history of the Pearl River Delta region. Given the magnitude of the destruction and loss of life, it is quite easy to understand how lives and events that arose after this tragedy would be easier to track than those that occurred before it. And as we have seen in previous chapters, the role of Li Wen Mao and his army of opera singers made life especially difficult for Cantonese language performers who managed to survive the initial calamity.

Far-reaching social reforms were unleashed in Foshan and Guangdong as a result of these events. The national government, humiliated in the Opium Wars and hopelessly bogged down in the Taiping Rebellion, lost considerable respect in the eyes of local elites. It was no longer able to balance the competing demands of the parochial gentry, on the one hand, and the peasants and handicraft workers on the other. The political influence of the more plebian elements of society was diminished by the rebellion and white terror that followed, during which large numbers of "socially undesirable" people were slaughtered with impunity.[6]

Increased economic competition and changing patterns of trade further upset this delicate system by putting pressure on the large clan associations, one of the few social structures that united the different economic elements of local society. After the events of 1854–1855, increased power shifted into the hands of local elites who used this influence to create a social and political order that they could dominate. Later in the twentieth century, Communist Party organizers and historians alike would wonder at the conservative and generally reactionary nature of Guangdong Province. While it was the birthplace of many revolutionary leaders, those same individuals often found that they had to go somewhere else for their movements to begin to gain traction. It was the tumultuous events of the nineteenth century that set the stage for many of the revolutionary puzzles that would plague union organizers and political officers alike during the twentieth century. As we have seen in previous chapters, this highly polarized and reactionary class structure also had a very important impact on the development of local martial arts styles.

Given that opera singers could no longer function openly in the later 1850s, it is quite plausible that Leung Yee Tai and Wong Wah Bo might turn to a prosperous business owner for both financial and political support. This element of the creation myth makes a great deal of historical sense. If an art, such as Wing Chun, were to survive and prosper in late nineteenth-century Foshan, it would certainly help to have the backing of the newly empowered business and gentry classes.[7]

While the red boat actors are merely "plausible," we can be much more certain when examining Leung Jan (originally named Leung Tak Wing). Still, as the current discussion demonstrates, there are important limits to our knowledge. We know that Leung Jan was not the first member of his family to choose a medical career. It was his father who first opened a successful pharmacy and medical clinic on Fai Jee Street, an enclosed market in Foshan. It also appears that the father had two sons.

The eldest, Leung Tak Nam, became a successful merchant and businessperson. The younger son, Leung Tak Wing, was more interested in medicine and eventually inherited the family business. The name by which he was generally known, Leung Jan, was basically a nickname adopted for use among his mostly illiterate customers.

As a youth Leung Jan showed an interest in martial arts, and his father hired a number of instructors.[8] Given that public schools did not yet exist, these instructors may have become members of the Leung household. After his father's death Leung Jan inherited the business and went on to become a successful and notable doctor who was well remembered in local history.

Still, questions remain. It is not clear when Leung Jan took over the family business for himself. The dates of his birth and death are also debated by various sources. Leung Ting lists his birth date as 1816, and it is likely that he died in 1890 or 1891 in his home village of Gulao. If true, Leung Jan would have been 74 or 75 at the time of his death.[9] Other researchers disagree with these figures. Huang Xiao Hui and Huang Hong move his life up a decade, claiming that Leung Jan was born in 1826 and died in 1901.[10] These later dates seem to be more widely held, although it is not really clear which are most credible. If the later dates are accepted, Leung Jan would have been in his early thirties when he began his Wing Chun training. If Leung Ting's estimates are used, he would likely have been in his forties.

Another unresolved question focuses on Leung Jan's family situation and, by implication, how he viewed the teaching of his martial art. The standard Ip family account lists only three sons when discussing Leung Jan's life: Leung Bik (who later instructed Ip Man), Leung Chun, and Leung Ko.[11] In addition to his children only a single outside student is mentioned, Chan Wah Shun. This would seem to indicate a very traditional, lineage-based, approach to the martial arts. Or it could indicate a financially secure professional who saw no need to take on the headaches that come with public teaching.

Other researchers have taken issue with this. They rightly point out that, since we do not have birth certificates for any of these individuals, it is hard to say whether they existed at all. Perhaps Leung Jan had no children and taught only outsiders. Leung Bik might be a fabrication created by Ip Man to further his own reputation. Of course, Foshan would have been full of people who personally knew Leung Jan in the early twentieth century. It might have been difficult to pass off imaginary children to such a well-informed audience.

Leung Ting has gone in the opposite direction in his own research, and claims that Leung Jan had five sons. In addition to the three listed above there was also a Leung Gee (supposedly the second oldest son) who later immigrated to Vietnam and taught Wing Chun publicly in the local "Cantonese Association Hall." Leung Jan's fourth son, Leung Yuen, is reputed to be the only one who took no interest in the art and little is known about him.[12]

While there are a number of differing oral accounts of Leung Jan teaching other outside students, there is basically no way to confirm this information, and it may simply be the result of martial arts mythmaking. Huang Xiao Hui and Huang Hong provide a colorful list of other possible disciples including "Pork Gui" (a local butcher), "Big Mountain Tree" (an exceptionally strong individual), and "Hooligan Qi" (self-explanatory).[13] We can say with certainty that Leung Jan passed both his martial and medical knowledge on to Chan Wah Shun, and most likely to some of his own children as well. Beyond that we move into the realm of speculation.

Around his 70th birthday (most likely 1895) Leung Jan retired and returned to his ancestral village of Gulao in Heshan. Still active and interested in the martial arts, the now aged master began to teach a small group of local youth a modified version of this Wing Chun which focused on side-facing positions. This brief period of instruction became the nucleus of the Pin Sun Wing Chun system that is sometimes encountered today.[14] Leung Jan probably died in 1901, the same year in which China, and the traditional martial arts community, was rocked by the Boxer Uprising.[15] Ironically, these events led to the temporary closure of most of Foshan's martial arts schools.

In the words of Ip Man, "Leung Jan grasped the innermost secrets of Wing Chun and attained its highest level of proficiency."[16] While it remains unclear how many students he actually taught in Foshan, there can be no doubt as to which of his disciples was the most influential.

It was Chan Wah Shun (1849-1913) who transformed Wing Chun into a public art. In doing so he was following the trend previously established by local schools like the Hung Sing Association. This group taught Choy Li Fut and was the largest and most important public martial arts school in Foshan. While the school was reformed and reopened by Jeong Yim in 1867 (following the Red Turban Revolt) it was once more forced to close in 1901 due to the Boxer Uprising.[17] It is interesting to note that Chan Wah Shun's move into the public sphere happened just as the Hung Sing Association reopened its doors.

While Chan Wah Shun gained a fair degree of notoriety in local martial circles, there are still many unresolved questions regarding his early life. Leung Ting places his birth in the year 1833, while Huang Xiao Hui and Huang Hong favor the year 1849.[18] Given the importance of the events of the 1850s, this decade discrepancy has quite an effect on how one might imagine Chan's early life and formative years.

This uncertainty might be impossible to definitively resolve, but we may still be able to state which of the two scenarios is more plausible. If Chan Wah Shun was born in 1833 and he began to practice Wing Chun when he was twenty-five (as Leung Ting asserts) then he would have commenced his studies in 1858. Given that Leung Yee Tai and Wong Wah Bo probably did not seek refuge with Leung Jan until 1855 or 1856, this raises some difficulties. First, one wonders whether Leung could really have learned enough in two years to take on students. Second, in 1858 the opera ban was still in place and much of Foshan was in ruins. Given that Wong Wah Bo and Leung Yee Tai were both still around, and supporting themselves by teaching martial arts, it is not clear why Chan Wah Shun simply did not go to them (or one of their associates) instead.

If we accept Leung Ting's assertion that Chan was about twenty-five when he commenced his studies, but instead assume that he was born in 1849, he would have begun his training in 1874. By this time the opera singers would have moved on and Leung Jan may have had an opportunity to establish his reputation in local medical and martial circles. While either set of dates could work, this second possibility seems more plausible.

Chan Wah Shun enjoyed a varied career. He was born in Manin Village in Shunde.[19] As we have already seen, this was a generally conservative farming region characterized by rich landlords and strong local gentry.[20] It was also known for its robust militia organizations which hired such luminaries as Chan Heung (the creator of Choy Li Fut) to act as trainers and drill instructors.[21] We can probably assume that Chan was first exposed to martial arts as a child.

At the age of thirteen, Chan was sent to work at a rice shop in Foshan. Later he started a business as a moneychanger in the marketplace (where he first met Leung Jan) and acquired the nickname "Moneychanger Wah." While silver was the official tender, smaller transactions were carried out with copper or bronze coins. In any quantity these could be quite heavy, but Chan was known for his height and strength.[22]

Exactly how Chan was first introduced to Wing Chun is subject to some debate. The standard Ip family story is that he ran a money changing stall outside of Leung Jan's pharmacy. He was unaware that his neighbor was a martial arts master until one day (while taking shelter from the rain) he discovered Leung Jan teaching his sons and begged to be accepted as a student.[23] Huang Xiao Hui and Huang Hong instead claim that Chan Wah Shun was first taken on as a student by Li Hua (or "Wooden Man Hua") who was himself a student of Leung Jan. Chan studied with Li until his death, at which time he began to learn from Leung Jan himself.[24]

In addition to martial arts, Chan Wah Shun also inherited Leung Jan's medical skills. He eventually became an accomplished bone setter and herbalist in his own right and went into practice for himself. He even assumed many of Leung Jan's duties as the old master prepared for retirement in 1895. Ip family lore also claims that this is when he began to teach Wing Chun publicly. While Leung Ting relates a number of stories of Chan Wah Shun teaching students much earlier (usually while keeping the relationship secret from Leung Jan), the more common accounts state that Leung Jan did not wish to teach martial arts publicly, and hence Chan Wah Shun could not.[25] However, immediately upon his master's retirement Chan Wah Shun began to accept students.

Chan was the first individual to teach Wing Chun publicly, yet he faced a number of distinct challenges. To begin with, he suffered a stroke and retired in 1911, meaning that at most he only had a 15- to 16-year teaching career. Further, the Boxer Uprising in 1900–1901 caused general chaos and damaged the reputation of hand combat schools across the country. The provincial government closed martial arts studios throughout Guangdong in 1901 in a bid to prevent copycat attacks on foreigners. They quite correctly perceived that any provocation might give the British naval squadron stationed around Hong Kong a pretext to seize the entire Pearl River.

The legacy of the Boxer Uprising proved to be toxic to China's traditional hand combat community. At a time when the Chinese people were actively contemplating the future and far-reaching political and social reforms, martial artists appeared backwards, feudal, and superstitious. In short, the traditional modes of hand combat came to embody all of those values that the nation was moving away from. It would be another decade before a new generation of more urban and intellectual martial artists would arise and argue (successfully) that the traditional fighting styles could be a key element of China's modern identity.[26]

This historical background should help to frame our understanding of Chan Wah Shun's efforts to spread Wing Chun. Between 1895, when he first began to publicly accept students, and 1901, when the government suppressed martial arts schools and associations, Chan would have had at most five years to gather and teach his pupils. This is barely enough time to instruct a generation of students in the Wing Chun system. Other schools in the area resumed instruction somewhere between 1903 and 1905, so it seems safe to assume that this is probably when he reopened his doors as well. Chan Wah Shun only had a little over six years to train the rest of his disciples at a time when the popularity of traditional boxing was at an all-time low and his health was starting to fail.

When we combine this with the fact that Chan charged a considerable amount of money for instruction, it is easy to understand why, according to Ip Man, he only had about sixteen students. The small size of his school accurately reflects the marginal position that traditional modes of hand combat occupied at this point in time.

Little to nothing is certain about Chan's first period as a teacher. However, after the dust settled from the Boxer Uprising it is known that he approached a prominent local businessman and landlord named Ip Oi Dor (Ip Man's father) and rented space in the Ip family temple to conduct his classes. His students were not great in number but must have come from the better elements of society if they could afford the entrance fee of 20 taels of silver as "Red Envelope Money" and an additional 8 taels of silver in monthly tuition.[27] This was much more than the Hung Sing school charged its members, and it reflects the high degree of correlation between different hand combat schools and Foshan's radicalized class structure. Wing Chun truly was, and would remain for much of the 1920s through the 1940s, a rich man's game. Even with these structural restraints, the art gained more public exposure during this period than it had ever enjoyed in the past.

While Ip Man asserts that Chan Wah Shun taught as many as sixteen students, we have not been able to locate a list that is both complete and credible. Huang Xiao Hui and Huang Hong, in their chapter written for Ma, go farther than any other source by listing a total of eleven direct students. Their brief biographies of Chan's students and grand-students helps to paint a fascinating picture of life within Foshan's Wing Chun clan from the 1920s through the 1940s.[28] Given that Chan's teaching happened in two distinct eras, separated by an abrupt break, it is perhaps not surprising that it is so difficult to assemble a complete class roster. Following Chan's retirement in 1911, he returned to his native village in Shunde where, according to local tradition, he passed on a distinct version of his art that can still be seen today. Given his overall condition, it is unclear what Chan himself was able to convey. Of course, some of his other students were also in the area.

Chan's key disciples were Ng Chung So and Chan Yiu Min. Ng was one of his first students and perhaps inherited more of his master's martial genius than any of his other followers. Chan Yiu Min was the son of Chan Wah Shun. While there are a number of stories about the trouble he caused his father as a youth, Chan Yiu Min went on to open at least two successful Wing Chun schools, and he inherited his father's medical skills and practice.[29] We will explore the careers of both of these individuals later. Yet, as successful as each was, their lights did not shine the brightest. The disciple who would go on to make Chan Wah Shun famous was his youngest student, accepted shortly before his retirement. His name was Ip Man.

Ip Man: The Making of a Modern Wing Chun Student

Ip Kai Man (1893–1972) was the third of four children born to Ip Oi Dor and Ng Shui, a wealthy couple who lived in Foshan, on October 14, 1893.[30] His older brother was named Ip Kai Gak and his older sister was named Ip Wan Mei. He had a single younger sister named Ip Wan Hum. Ip Man's lineage within the Ip clan was quite prosperous.[31] His own family was heavily invested in land and business. Their holdings were spread between Foshan, the surrounding countryside, and Hong Kong, where they owned a number of firms.[32]

A few of the related families within the Ip clan lived together, virtually monopolizing a single street near what was then called the "Mulberry Gardens." As was the custom, these related families shared a single ancestral temple that was administered by a more senior lineage within the clan organization. In this case, the sanctuary was located behind the house of Ip Oi Dor and he was able to oversee its use and rent it out. Such revenue was often used by the various clans to finance their corporate worship, charity, and educational expenses.[33]

When Ip Man was about twelve years old (1905), Chan Wah Shun approached Ip Oi Dor and arranged to rent the family temple as a space in which to reopen his martial arts school. The young Ip Man was fascinated by what he saw. Even though he was being educated in the Confucian manner, appropriate to a child of his social standing, he would rush off after class to watch the strangely lyrical movements of the kung fu students in the family temple.[34]

He soon approached Chan Wah Shun and asked to become his student. This request would have put Chan in a difficult position. Ip Man was a very intelligent but apparently sickly child.[35] It must have seemed unlikely that this bookish youngster would make a great martial artist. Further, his father was not only rich and powerful, he was also Chan Wah Shun's landlord.

Even at the best of times Chinese martial arts lacked social respectability. Most students were from working-class backgrounds and while one might occasionally encounter well-off, educated practitioners, this was far from the norm. Filling the head of a small upper-class child with martial dreams must have seemed like an invitation for trouble. On the other hand, one could not simply snub the landlord's son.

Chan Wah Shun attempted to discourage the youth by telling him that rich, educated children did not make good martial arts students. But the boy was not dissuaded. Finally, in an effort to extricate himself from the situation, Chan said that he would only teach Ip Man if he paid 20 ounces of pure silver. It was inconceivable that any child would have access to this quantity of money. Twenty ounces of silver was enough money to buy a house, finance a marriage, or start a modest business. In today's terms this would be on the order of several thousand dollars.[36]

One can only imagine Chan Wah Shun's shock when the child appeared again the next day with the requested sum. After conferring with Ip Oi Dor, Chan was assured that it was the family's wish that their youngest son be taught martial arts. At that point Ip Man was accepted as Chan Wah Shun's sixteenth and final student.

Unfortunately, the relationship between the master and his new student would not last long. Chan Wah Shun was already advancing in years, and it appears that Ng Chung So was probably responsible for demonstrating and teaching most of the techniques to the young disciple. Still, Ip Man developed a deep respect for his teacher, and even after studying with Leung Bik in Hong Kong, never ceased to refer to him as "Sifu" (a term which implies both a "teacher" and "father" relationship.) This fidelity also reflects the values of his early Confucian education and upbringing.

Within a few months of accepting Ip Man, Chan Wah Shun began to have health problems and started the process of retirement. He ultimately returned to his native village after suffering a stroke. Prior to this he requested that Ng Chung So, his most prized martial disciple, complete the young Ip's training. Ng instructed him until he was fifteen years old.

Ip Man was sent to Hong Kong to attend St. Stephen's College in 1908. His family relied on help from Leung Fut Ting, a relative who lived in Hong Kong, to make the arrangements. St. Stephen's (opened in 1903) was a decidedly prestigious high school modeled on the best English boarding schools. It offered a Western-style education and English language instruction. Ip Man would later draw extensively on his own more modern education to explain Wing Chun concepts.[37]

The collapse of the Qing dynasty did much to discredit the traditional educational system. The various clashes with the West had demonstrated that European notions of industry and military science were essential to China's continued survival and prosperity. Further, the economic vibrancy of Hong Kong stood in visible contrast to the increasing stagnation of the once great trade centers of Guangzhou and Foshan. It was abundantly clear to the local merchants that political and social reform was necessary.

During the Republican period it became common for wealthy families to send their children abroad so that they could gain a modern Western education. This cadre of young elites, schooled in either Hong Kong or Japan, came to be known as the "new gentry." They bore the primary responsibility for the reforms that would bring the Chinese state and society into the modern era.

Hong Kong was an economically, socially, and ethnically complex place. Throughout the latter half of the nineteenth century the British-occupied island was the main bridge connecting southern Chinese society to the wider world. This meeting of different cultural expectations and norms was not always smooth, and British policies sometimes exacerbated the situation.

Fearing that local law enforcement might be unreliable, the British brought in additional soldiers from northern India (including areas such as Pakistan and Nepal) to serve as police officers in Hong Kong. This decision was particularly problematic since there was already a degree of racial tension and a history of violence between these groups.[38] Nor was this general policy confined to Hong Kong. It was a standard operating procedure throughout the British Empire.

Ip family tradition states that one day while walking to school Ip Man and a friend came across a "Pakistani" police officer beating a Chinese woman in the street. At this time Ip Man is reputed to have been eighteen years old, making it 1911, the same year that the Qing dynasty was finally overthrown. It is important to realize that the period surrounding 1911 was characterized by the emergence of very strong, sometimes violent, feelings of nationalism throughout China.

Supposedly, Ip Man and his friend confronted the police officer who then attempted to attack them. Drawing on his previous training Ip bloodied the man's face before he and his friend strategically retreated. The incident made enough of an impression on Ip Man's friend that he related the story to his family. An uncle, upon hearing the story, asked to be introduced to the young martial artist.[39]

Ip Man went to his friend's house and was surprised to hear that the older gentleman had heard of Wing Chun. However, he was disappointed with the reception that his demonstration of the forms received. Hoping to regain face he attempted to engage in "chi sao" (a type of two-handed training drill that resembles sparring) with the old man but was easily beaten and contained. Ip Man left his friend's apartment in shame. The experience shook his faith in his skills.

A few days later the old man attempted to invite the youth back, but Ip Man was too humiliated to return. He was convinced only when his friend revealed that his uncle was a Foshan native by the name of Leung Bik, the son of Chan Wah Shun's teacher Leung Jan. Realizing the opportunity that now lay in front of him, the young Ip Man returned to his friend's house and petitioned Leung Bik to complete his training.[40]

Leung Bik had fallen on hard times and accepted Ip Man's invitation to move in with him and become his teacher. Leung Ting has speculated that, in the approximately three years that Ip Man studied with Chan Wah Shun, he probably learned only Siu Lim Tao and Chum Kiu, the first two of the unarmed forms in the Wing Chun System.[41] If true, Leung Bik would have been responsible for teaching him Biu Jee (the third unarmed set), the Wooden Dummy routine, the Six and a Half Point Pole Form, and the Bart Jarm Dao, or double knives.[42]

Logically, this is possible and it would certainly explain how Ip Man completed his training. Of course, there are also other possibilities. Leung Bik may have taught Ip Man only a portion of this material, spending most of his time correcting his forms and getting his young student back up to speed. After all, it had been about three years since his last lesson in Foshan. Ip Man may have learned the rest of the system when he returned to Foshan and renewed his friendship with Ng Chung So.

Whatever the case, Ip Man was now in the position to compare the styles and teachings of two of the art's great masters. He related that the substance of the two men's systems was quite similar. What differed was how they went about teaching. Chan Wah Shun taught in a very simple style with metaphors drawn from everyday life. The more educated and refined Leung Bik used highly sophisticated traditional concepts and symbols in his attempt to explain the Wing Chun system. Hence, he was able to explain what he did in much greater detail.[43]

Unfortunately, this relationship was as brief as it was fruitful. Leung Bik lived with his student until his death in 1912, approximately one year later. Lacking any other students or children, the young Ip Man officiated at his teacher's funeral.[44]

Ip Man's activities in the following years are hazy at best. He was probably around nineteen or twenty when Leung Bik died. It seems likely that Ip Man stayed in Hong Kong for a few years after the death of his teacher and his graduation from high school. There are rumors that his older brother, Ip Kai Gak, attempted to arrange for him to attend college in Japan (a relatively common practice among aspiring members of the new gentry at that time) but the entire thing fell through for reasons that are now lost. Leung Ting states that Ip Man returned to his home town of Foshan when he was twenty-four.[45] If true, he returned in 1917.

Ip Chun relates that upon his father's return he discovered that the Wing Chun clan was not prospering. Of Chan Wah Shun's disciples only Ng Chung So was still teaching publicly. As Ip Man began to practice with his old friends, it was evident that his skills had increased considerably and he was now a force to be reckoned with. Luckily, changing trends in the north were about to unleash an explosion of interest in traditional hand combat systems that would greatly benefit all of Foshan's varied schools and associations.

The 1920s saw a flurry of martial arts activity in and around Foshan. The network of "Yi Schools" (later renamed the "Zhong Yi Martial Arts Athletic Association") started to expand. This reactionary organization promoted both Hung Gar and Wing Chun in its schools. At the same time the Jingwu Association, created in Shanghai in 1909, was spreading aggressively into the south, setting up branches in Guangzhou and Foshan in the early 1920s. The Hung Sing Association also became more popular and politically active in this period. As was demonstrated in Chapter 3, the traditional arts took on new symbolic meanings over the course of the decade and became associated with the quest to build a modern and unified national identity. This helped to restore interest in many of China's hand combat schools after the disastrous early years of the twentieth century.

Ip Ching relates how a Praying Mantis master from northern China, associated with the Foshan branch of the Jingwu Association, caused a local commotion by challenging the town's kung fu instructors who were, in his opinion, incapable of teaching authentic Chinese martial arts. The young Ip Man was selected to fight the challenge match and was successful in defending the town's honor. This event helped to galvanize Wing Chun's standing within the local martial arts community.[46]

While his reputation as a martial artist was growing, Ip Man expressed no interest in teaching during the 1920s or 30s. Nor did he show a particular interest in, or aptitude for, advancing the family fortune. Instead, he sought to live a comfortable lifestyle. His son, Ip Chun, relates that his father "sold all of his Hong Kong businesses so that he could have the freedom to do what he wanted. Much of his time was spent with Ng Chung So, practicing sticky hands [chi sao] to maintain his technique and researching higher levels of Wing Chun skill."[47] In modern parlance, the once promising youth had become a "kung fu bum."

The selling of the Hong Kong businesses had far-reaching effects on the Ip family. Possibly, political instability and the looming "Hong Kong Strike" might have made this seem like a wise decision. Yet the Ip investments were probably now less diversified and more concentrated in land holdings. Consequently, the family's income was more susceptible to shocks in the global markets for silk (a common local product), rice, tobacco, and tea. This was a problem because, while China (and the south in particular) had once enjoyed a virtual monopoly in these products, new sources were being cultivated around the globe. Higher quality French silk was replacing Chinese production as the market standard. Furthermore, the economic turbulence of the 1920s and the Great Depression of the 1930s would have a disruptive impact on an area of China now integrated into global market structures.[48]

Selling these businesses also made Ip Man less financially secure for political reasons. Investments in Hong Kong were guaranteed by the British government, while those in Foshan, Guangzhou, and Shunde were under the protection of the local regime. During the 1920s and 30s, China entered a period of political instability generally known as "warlordism." While the south was relatively stable compared to other areas of the country, the government and military did not always respect private property rights.

None of these storm clouds had yet fully gathered on the horizon, and Ip Man enjoyed a life of leisure throughout most of the decade. In the early 1920s he married the daughter of a prominent local gentry family named Cheung Wing-sing (or Zhang Yongcheng in Pinyin).[49] Together the couple had four children who survived to adulthood. Their two sons were named Ip Chun and Ip Ching, and the daughters were Ip Ar Sum and Ip Ar Woon.[50]

Ip Chun, the first son, was born in Foshan on July 31, 1924. He relates that his father was often quite strict with him (probably reflecting his own traditional upbringing) and saw to it that he began to learn Wing Chun at the age of seven. The following incident is quite interesting, and reveals what Ip Man may have been like as a father.

> As a boy he [Ip Chun] practiced the second form of Wing Chun, Tsum Kui, for a long time before going to show his

father what he had learnt. His father asked him if he thought it was good enough. Ip Chun had practiced very hard so he answered, 'Yes.' But as he stood in the Juen Ma (turning) stance, Ip Man said 'Don't Move!' He stepped forward and pushed his son. Ip Chun fell over. He thought he had been taken by surprise so he asked his father to push him again. The same thing happened.

Ip Man told his son to go away and practice for three months. At that moment Ip Chun made up his mind that he would practice not just his turning skills but all of the movements in the form, so that his father would not be able to push him over again.[51]

Modern folklore, perpetuated by the recent spate of vaguely biographical films (some of which enjoyed the advice and input of his still living family members), portrays Ip Man as a somewhat distant father who was criticized by his wife for not being more involved with his children. This incident indicates that there might be some truth behind this depiction. Pushing on a Wing Chun student to test the stability of the stance is quite common, and turning is a central concept to the second form. Yet leaving a child to practice a single movement for three months by himself, without oversight or guidance, is not.

It is also unlikely that this reflects Ip Man's own "traditional" training. With only three years of practice before moving to Hong Kong, then another one or two years of instruction from Leung Bik, it is evident that Ip Man himself must have moved through the entire system (comprised of six different forms and numerous exercises) quite rapidly. Given the quality and precision of his kung fu, this cannot have been achieved without constant oversight and practice with an experienced instructor. While he wanted his sons to follow in his footsteps, he did not appear to be interested in instructing them the same way in which he was taught.

Of course, it is also dangerous to read too much into accounts such as these. Traditional Confucian instruction often appears harsh or alien from a modern Western perspective, and there are a number of areas where such a teaching strategy may have been considered the norm. Still, the highly practical southern school of Wing Chun was not one of them. At this time, perhaps Ip Man was more interested in instilling "life lessons" than actually instructing his son in the details of the art.

The preceding review of the early years of Ip Man's life paints a fuller picture of both the individual and his environment than is generally provided. Wherever possible we have attempted to rectify contradictory timelines and shed what light we can on his actual personality. Further, when discussing Ip Man it readily becomes apparent that his insights into the essential nature of the art did not derive from his unique skills or the comprehensive nature of his knowledge of the Wing Chun system.

His repeated attempts to learn Wing Chun were actually thwarted by the frequent deaths of his teachers and the necessity of moving about to gain an education. Ip Man probably enjoyed fewer years of actual instruction than many of Chan Wah Shun's other students or grandstudents. Instead, what is most remarkable about Ip Man was his centrality to the unfolding story of Wing Chun. He stood close to the center of the social network that was responsible for developing and refining this art. He was in the unique position to know the details of both Chan Wah Shun's and Leung Bik's insights into the system. He knew most of the major Wing Chun practitioners of the 1920s and 30s and was acquainted with the entire breadth and depth of Foshan's martial environment. When combined with his dual traditional/Western education, Ip Man enjoyed an unprecedented vantage point from which he could analyze not only what Wing Chun was, but also how it worked. This knowledge would be invaluable when he did take up the mantle of "Sifu" later in life.

Chanting a Song in Spring Time: Foshan's Public Wing Chun Schools, 1920–1940

Most narratives of Wing Chun's history in Foshan focus exclusively on their subject (Ip Man or less frequently Yuen Kay San) before moving on to the events of the post-WWII era. From the standpoint of a cultural historian, this is a real weakness since neither of these individuals was in any way "typical" of the average Wing Chun practitioner, let alone martial artist, during this period. This misplaced emphasis undercuts our understanding of how Foshan's civil society developed in the Republican period, and it occasionally leads to historically false conclusions.

One of the more commonly heard assertions in the Wing Chun literature is that Ip Man was the first individual to publicly teach Wing Chun. This statement has been tossed around so frequently that it has become a sort of mantra. It is seen in all of the historical sources that we have used.

For such an assertion to be true certain historical liberties must be taken. Chan Wah Shun's mixed attempts at running a school need to be redefined as something much more exclusive and traditional than they probably were, and Ng Chung So needs to be altogether forgotten. Yet, this badly distorts the reality of life in Foshan's martial arts community.

There was a vibrant market in Wing Chun instruction during the Republican period. Hundreds of students actively studied the system in a variety of schools and classes. Some of these were associated with the Zhong Yi Association and others were not. In fact, it seems likely that Ip Man's own teaching style in the 1950s was affected by what he saw during this earlier period. In order to fully understand the emergence of modern Wing Chun it is necessary to temporarily set aside our discussion of Ip Man and turn our attention to some of the less well-known instructors of this period. This discussion should also enrich our general understanding of Foshan's martial marketplace.

While Chan Wah Shun never succeeded in building a large and thriving school, he was quite successful in cultivating a local reputation as a talented fighter and competent master. This reputation helped to advance the careers of a number of his key disciples in and around the Foshan area. Still, it is hard to say which of these students truly inherited the master's mantle. While Ip Man is sometimes criticized for refusing to select an "heir" to his system, the truth is that none of the historic Wing Chun masters seem to have thought this to be essential.

Chan Wah Shun's most influential student was probably Ng Chung So. While there are questions about the exact date of his birth, Ng was born in the closing years of the Qing period. His father owned a shop that sold ceramics, an important part of the local handicraft industry (Foshan is still famous for its ceramics), and the entire family was quite wealthy. His father was good friends with Chan Wah Shun and, when Chan began to teach, Ng immediately enrolled his two sons, Ng Siu Lo (the older brother, and hence Chan's first disciple) and Ng Chung So (the younger brother and second disciple). Apparently, in the earliest phase of his career Chan Wah Shun taught his two students in their own home.[52] These events probably occurred sometime between when Leung Jan retired (c. 1895), and the Boxer Uprising (1900).

The brothers resumed training after Chan Wah Shun reestablished his school in the Ip family temple. It is also clear that it was the younger of the two who enjoyed the greatest success. As Chan Wah Shun's health failed, he instructed Ng Chung So to continue to instruct and look after his youngest disciples. At this moment the informal leadership of the Foshan Wing Chun clan seems to have passed hands.

Ng Chung So followed in his master's footsteps and opened his own school on Shi Lu Tou Street ("The Entrance to the Rocky Road") in Foshan.[53] Leung Ting relies on local folklore and claims that Ng Chung So was in fact teaching in the back room of an opium den at that location. Supposedly, the establishment was under the control of Yiu Lam, the older brother of Yiu Choi (an important Wing Chun exponent) who was also known as "Bird-Fancier Lam." He goes on to inform his readers that opium smoking was socially accepted and not a matter of concern at this time.[54]

While romantic, and frequently repeated, these statements are questionable on a few counts. To begin with, there are no substantiated sources that back up this claim, though one might suspect that avoiding outside documentation would be a high priority of any gangster running an opium den. The very nature of this story makes it difficult to verify. At the same time, how serious opium smoking was depended entirely on who you were and under what circumstances you were caught.

It is certainly true that the GMD turned a blind eye to many illegal manufacturing and smuggling operations, preferring to tax criminals than actually putting them out of business. At the same time there was an immense anti-opium movement within civil society that marginalized the practice. The government even got in on the act with occasional crackdowns and highly publicized detoxification campaigns.

Generally speaking, opium use by the wealthy and powerful was seen as a less serious issue than its consumption by the working class. The army in Guangzhou went so far as to execute a number of its own soldiers for opium use.[55] As such, these claims are both more serious and more informative as to the social nature of Wing Chun than most commentators seem willing to admit.[56]

Whatever the truth of the drug charges, it is clear that Ng Chung So was successful in attracting a number of students. Following the general pattern, his students, like both himself and Ip Man, tended to be the rich scions of well-off families. This characteristic of his school, along with the earlier memory of Chan Wah Shun, cemented Wing Chun's place in Foshan's radicalized class structure.

Ng Chung So shared another similarity with Ip Man. He was not an effective money manager. He is said to have squandered much of his wealth feasting and drinking with his friends and associates. It is hard to know how reliable these accounts really are. The motif of the swordsman who disregards money but values friendship and honor above all else is a well-established stereotype in Chinese folk culture. When reviewing the biographies of historical martial artists, it appears that not only did they feel pressured to conform to these social expectations, but that such myths colored how they were remembered by their students and communities as well. It seems likely that poor investment choices and volatile local economic conditions contributed to his eventual impoverishment. Fortunately, Ng Chung So had built a vibrant school with many wealthy students and disciples. With their support he was able to weather the rough times toward the end of his life.[57]

Throughout the late teens and early 1920s Ng Chung So appears to be the only Wing Chun instructor who was teaching publicly in Foshan (other individuals were continuing to take on private students). When he returned from Hong Kong, Ip Man spent quite a bit of time practicing chi sao at his school with other students that his senior kung fu brother was responsible for recruiting and instructing.

Ng's efforts to promote and strengthen Wing Chun were a remarkable success, and he personally trained many of the teachers who would go on to prominence in his local community. Among his best known students we find He Zhao Chu (the son of a wealthy bakery owner), Li Shou Peng (a prominent local doctor), Zhang Sheng Ruo (son of a wealthy hardware store owner), Li Ci Hao, Luo Huo Fu (owner of a successful restaurant), and Liang Fu Chu (treasurer of the Ping Xin Restaurant). Additionally, the so-called "Three Heroes of Wing Chun," Yuen Kay San, Yiu Choi, and Ip Man, were all either associated with, or studied at, Ng Chung So's school.

As the popularity of Wing Chun has exploded, both after Bruce Lee's death and the latest spate of Ip Man movies, there have been numerous attempts to paint one individual or another (usually Ip Man or Yuen Kay San) as the "leader" of Foshan's Wing Chun clan and the true inheritor of the system from which all the others learned. Many of these arguments are transparently political, placing one lineage against another, and, more recently, martial artists on the mainland against those in Hong Kong. Unfortunately, most of these accounts promote a vision of what life in Foshan was like that is totally ungrounded and detached from reality.

At the most basic level, Wing Chun does not appear to have had specific "inheritors" and "leaders." Yet if it did, the "leader" of the

Wing Chun clan probably would have been Ng Chung So based on the fact that he was the one who kept the public face of the art alive, and actually invested the time and effort to train the next generation of instructors throughout the 1920s. Unfortunately, Ng Chung So's real contributions to the community are largely forgotten and he is rarely mentioned in current discussions.

After Ng Chung So, the most influential Wing Chun instructor of the era was probably Chan Yiu Min (1884–1942), the son of Chan Wah Shun. Born at the end of the Qing period Chan Yiu Min was greatly influenced by his father and went on to both teach Wing Chun and to practice traditional Chinese medicine. Leung Ting relates a number of local stories claiming that in his younger years Chan Yiu Min was quite problematic. He is said to have been lazy and to have spent his time carousing and gambling. In despair Chan Wah Shun decided to teach his medical skills to his son's wife, instead of to him, as he was sure that the knowledge would be wasted on his loutish offspring.[58]

While an amusing story, like much of the folklore that Leung Ting relates, there is really no evidence to back up this tale. In many ways his account sounds suspiciously like a typical prodigal son narrative. The little direct evidence that we have about the life of Chan Yiu Min actually paints him in a different light.

Like his father Chan Yiu Min was a native of Shunde, but he was born in Foshan. He began to formally study Wing Chun when he was eight years old (1892), just a few years before Leung Jan retired and his father started the process of opening a public school. After the death of his father, he opened a clinic called "Chan Ancestral Hall" on Xi Bian Lane where he practiced traditional Chinese medicine and taught martial arts. His father's local reputation was remembered and, as the traditional martial arts regained their popularity in the 1920s, he took on many students. In addition to his own children, he taught a number of individuals who would go on to become instructors themselves.

In 1932, Chan Yiu Min relocated and opened a second martial arts school in Wuzhou, Guangxi Province. Interestingly, his reputation had spread to the point that he had no trouble recruiting students in this new location. He died approximately ten years later at the age of 58.[59]

Jiu Chao (1902–1972) was a more important (though often overlooked) disciple of Chan Yiu Min. Jiu was born in Langbian village, Nanhai County. Like most of the early pioneers of Wing Chun he was born into considerable wealth. As a youth he studied Wing Chun with Chan Yiu Min in Foshan though it seems likely that he had previously been trained in Hung Gar. He excelled to such a degree that after 1945 he became a Wing Chun instructor for the Zhong Yi Athletic Association, which was then opening one of its many branches on Kuai Zi Lane in Foshan. This is an important piece of information as it indicates that at least some of the Zhong Yi's Wing Chun instructors were students or grand-students of Chan Wah Shun.

Jiu Chao proved to be a popular and successful teacher. He went on to open his own school on Taiping Road, Shiqi in Zhongshan. Huang Xiao Hui and Huang Hong indicate that between these two locations Jiu taught over 100 students, including Pan Nam, who would go on to become an important leader of the Wing Chun community in his own right.

Jiu Chao is also noteworthy for another reason. He may have been the most talented weapons expert within the Wing Chun clan during his generation. While Wing Chun is usually thought of as a boxing art, it does in fact have two commonly taught weapons: the long fighting pole and the double knives. Jiu's interests went well beyond these offerings. He also studied the shorter eyebrow-height staff, the five-section and seven-section chain whips, the saber, and the double jians (straight swords).

These exotic weapons skills actually became a part of how Jiu attempted to think about and demonstrate martial arts to the public. When opening his new school in Zhongshan he gave a demonstration in which he performed a routine with a very heavy and long pole made of pure iron.[60] The ease with which he could wield the immense weapon impressed the highly practical local farmers and fishermen and reportedly won him a number of new students.[61]

Jiu Chao also had numerous family relations who became involved in Wing Chun. His nephew, Jiu Wan (1921–1973), is also an important figure in the art's history. Jiu Wan was born in Foshan and initially studied Wing Chun with his cousin Jiu Tong (a grand-student of Chan Wah Shun). Later he studied with his uncle, Jiu Chao, and he even taught his own public classes in the Foshan Jingwu Association building in the late 1940s. Jiu Wan was one of the few local Wing Chun instructors to flee to Hong Kong following the communist advance (probably because he and Jiu Chao both worked for the police), and he later became an associate of Ip Man with whom he researched the higher levels of the art. The exact nature of their relationship is a matter of some controversy in the Jiu Wan lineage today. In Hong Kong, Jiu Wan created a large and successful school with numerous followers. His premature death in

1973 deprived him of the opportunity to fully emerge from Ip Man's shadow. Still, his career is remarkable in that it spans both the Foshan and Hong Kong eras of Wing Chun's development.

Another interesting, and seldom discussed, figure in this period is Lai Yip Chi (1901–1968 or 1970). While slightly younger than Ip Man, their basic life circumstances were otherwise similar. He claimed Shangtang in Nanhai as his home village, but was born in Foshan where his wealthy parents resided. His father was involved in a number of local businesses including the spice trade, noodles, kerosene, and selling secondhand clothes. The last business in particular suggests that he may have also had a hand in the local pawn shops. The Lai family owned a house on Chaoyang Street. They felt that their young son suffered from poor health so, at the age of thirteen, they retained Lui Yu Chai (a disciple of the now famous Chan Wah Shun) to strengthen and instruct their son.[62] Lai also learned quite a bit about bone setting from his teacher, who had also inherited Chan Wah Shun's knowledge of traditional Chinese medicine.[63]

This brings up a very interesting point. In many of the accounts from this period there is a clear connection between Wing Chun and bone setting. In Chapter 2 we saw that it was not unusual for traditional martial arts masters to supplement their income with some medical work, so in that sense this finding is not unexpected. Yet Lai was not the sort of student who was looking for gainful employment. Rather, in this earlier period, medical and martial knowledge were more closely tied within the Wing Chun clan than is the case today. It is therefore interesting to speculate as to why the martial aspect of this body of knowledge has managed to spread and propagate itself in the current global era, but the medical side has atrophied and virtually disappeared.

We suspect that one answer to this puzzle might be found in Wing Chun's complicated relationship with modernity. The simplicity and practicality of the art made it easy to teach and spread. Once Ip Man jettisoned the traditional conceptual framework of the five elements and the eight diagrams, he could then express the central ideas of the art in purely mechanical terms. This had great appeal to young reformers like Bruce Lee, and it made the art more accessible to Western students than something much more traditional, like White Crane or Xingyi Quan.

While the fighting side of the art could easily be quantified and discussed in terms of Newtonian physics, the same was not true of the medical aspect. Traditional Chinese medicine rests on a foundation of traditional Chinese philosophy. Once Ip Man "simplified" the art, it became much more difficult to convey its health and medical insights. Even though Ip Man had some expertise in these areas, few of his students fully inherited this knowledge. This body of skills has withered within the modern Wing Chun clan.

So many students today seek for a hidden or esoteric aspect of their art. This search is often directed toward obscure lineages and the propagation of what can only be described as highly dubious folklore. If there is a "lost" aspect of Wing Chun waiting to be rediscovered, it is probably the art's once close relationship with Chinese traditional medicine.

Despite his boxing and medical skills Lai Yip Chi never really considered setting up a school. Like Ip Man, he was wealthy enough that he did not have to work. Yet unlike Ip and Yuen Kay San, he appears to have actually taken up the family business. We know that as a young man in the late teens and early 1920s Lai worked as the manager of a pawnshop. As a matter of fact, the Pan Nam lineage claims that it was while attending a meeting of the Pawnshop Owner's Association that Lai attracted the attention of a mysterious character who would introduce him to an esoteric lineage of Wing Chun that differed in substantial details from what Chan Wah Shun taught.[64] Pan Nam claimed that it was this "secret" material that was the core of his own teaching style.

When the economy began to suffer at the outset of WWII, Lai found himself facing financial hardship. In 1941, he began to teach publicly for the first time. Paradoxically, he is said not to have charged his students for tuition. Instead, most of his students were actually working-class individuals from modest backgrounds who were employed as either delivery personnel or cotton blanket manufacturers. Given that Lai is known to have owned a transportation company at the time of the communist takeover, we suspect that at least some of these students were actually his own workers.[65]

This is fascinating because it once again suggests a connection between Wing Chun and the yellow trade unions that dominated Foshan's handicraft industries. As we saw in Chapter 3, the Zhong Yi Association was financially backed by the major yellow trade unions and supported their cause. Subsidized martial arts instruction seems to have been a perk of "union" membership in this period. An identical pattern is detectable in Lai's Wing Chun career. By 1941 the Zhong Yi Association would have been shut down by the Japanese. It seems likely that

Lai simply picked up the slack for his own workers, providing them with an additional job benefit while at the same time reducing the probability that they would be seduced by other forces.

If this speculation is correct, Lai's teaching career might be better viewed as an appendage to the Zhong Yi Association's efforts, rather than as a new or independent school. His activities may give us an interesting window into what the relationship between local martial artists and yellow unions looked like in actual practice. And, of course, there are echoes of Ip Man's later teaching career which will also be associated with local unions.

Unlike Ip Man, Lai Yip Chi either did not, or could not, flee the communist advance in 1949. He spent the rest of his life on the mainland and is remembered mostly for refusing to sell his precious antique collection to foreigners. As a result, some of his best pieces could be "donated" to the new people's museum. Likewise, Lai is said to have "donated" both his secret medical prescriptions and his extensive property holdings to the workers of China on the eve of land reform. Huang Xiao Hui and Huang Hong list his death as having occurred in 1968, but the details of his final years are unclear. Lai would have been 67 years old at the time of his death.[66] Leung Ting states that Lai Yip Chi was actually murdered by the Red Guards of the Cultural Revolution in 1970.[67] If true, he would have been 69.

All of the interwar instructors that we have so far reviewed are students or grand-students of Chan Wah Shun. This lineage appears to have produced more instructors and students in this period than any other. However, there were instructors in this era who claimed different lineages. Perhaps the most widely known and important of these was Cheung Bo (1899–1956). Cheung's memory has been preserved within the Yuen Kay San Wing Chun lineage as he was the first instructor of Sum Num.

A native of Zheng village in Sihui, Cheung resided and taught in Foshan. His early martial instruction is unclear. Huang Xiao Hui and Huang Hong state that he claims to have been instructed by an unnamed monk in Zhongshan County. While certainly a possibility, we have already discussed at length the credibility problems inherent in accounts such as this.

There is more agreement on his later martial education. Both Rene Ritchie and Huang assert that he was instructed by Wai Yuk Sang. Huang Xiao Hui and Huang Hong state that Wai was a Wing Chun boxer from Foshan and say nothing of his lineage. Ritchie digs into the matter further and concludes that Wai Yuk Sang was probably a professional doctor (and amateur martial artist) employed by the local division of the Republic Army. He goes on to state that there are rumors that Wai studied with Au Si, a pupil of Fung Siu Ching (a famous local martial artist from the nineteenth century). Alternatively, he notes that, given his teaching style, Cheung Bo might be related to the Gulao village system passed on by Leung Jan at the end of his life. Given these conflicting accounts, we conclude simply that Cheung Bo's lineage is not well understood.[68]

Cheung was employed as a dim sum chef at the Tien Hoi restaurant on Kuai Zi Street in Foshan. Ritchie relates that he ran a sort of informal school for members of his staff after hours at the restaurant. Again, this is actually a similar pattern of instruction to what we just discussed with regard to Lai Yip Chi. Cheung was also a friend and associate of Yuen Kay San and that is as far as most accounts of him generally go.

Huang Xiao Hui and Huang Hong suggest that this conventional interpretation understates the extent of his involvement with the art. In addition to teaching at the restaurant, Cheung ran at least two other classes. Apparently, he taught one group out of his home. They also note that Cheung was the chief instructor of the "Hui Yi" martial arts school on Xian Feng Gu Road.[69] Given the etymology of the schools name, it seems likely that this was part of the larger "Yi" network of schools (e.g., part of the Zhong Yi Association.) If true, this would be a significant piece of information. Not only would it provide us with another clue as to where the Zhong Yi Association was getting its Wing Chun instructors, but it would also cast a new and more politically significant light on Cheung's class for fellow restaurant workers.

The purpose of the preceding survey has been twofold. On the most superficial level we hoped to demonstrate that, far from Ip Man being the first individual to teach Wing Chun openly, there were a number of instructors running various types of schools throughout Foshan from the 1920s through the 1940s. Some of these schools were related to the Zhong Yi Association or a specific trade union; others were independent. A few were quite large; others were small part-time operations. While most of the first generation of instructors catered to young men from wealthy backgrounds, the profile of the average student diversified considerably as time progressed. We have seen that hundreds of students studied Wing Chun in Foshan under a number of competent instructors.

Rather than being absolutely exceptional, as so many accounts would have us believe, Wing Chun was simply one more aspect of Foshan's very large and thriving public martial arts marketplace.

We also hoped to shed light on a few interesting, often overlooked, individuals who were critical to Wing Chun's initial flowering in the pre-WWII period. This is an important exercise precisely because the current popularity of the art has led to seemingly unending debates as to the relative importance of Ip Man, Yuen Kay San, or (less frequently) Yiu Choi within the Wing Chun movement. Students and fans of the current crop of movies endlessly bicker over who was the true "leader" of the Wing Chun clan, or who had greater skill.

It should be quite obvious by this point that there was no leader in Foshan's Wing Chun clan, not within Chan Wah Shun's lineage and certainly not between the broader approaches to the art. Fans of modern Wing Chun often bring their own assumptions about what a "traditional" Chinese martial art should look like, or how a lineage should operate. They then attempt to impose those ideas onto the past. But as L. P. Hartley has remarked, the past is a foreign country, and people do things differently there. Perhaps, in the case of pre-liberation China, it would be more fitting to emphasize that they did things *very* differently indeed. Our stylized notions of "traditional" martial virtue owe as much to novels of the 1950s as to anything else, and such ideas had little impact on anyone's decision to hang up a shingle and start a school. As often as not, it was sheer economic necessity that drove an individual to declare himself a sifu or a master and to begin to act the part.

What we can gain from looking at the past is a renewed appreciation for how quickly Chinese civil society grew in the wake of the 1911 revolution. Prior to that event only the barest skeleton of a truly independent civil society existed in and around Guangdong. Yet a close examination of Foshan's martial arts community demonstrates that within three decades a vibrant choir of independent voices had emerged. It appears to have been wealthy merchants and the local gentry who were responsible for building many of these institutions, which were then slowly expanded to include different classes within Foshan's society.

This insight points to an interesting and often overlooked truth. While the martial arts schools of the Republican period could empower their students, providing a renewed sense of identity, important social contacts, and a sort of rudimentary safety net, they were also a mechanism of social control. These arts were actively cultivated to promote some readings of Chinese identity, but not others. Wing Chun schools promoted participation in some sorts of labor institutions, but not membership in the Communist Party. The company sifu created a more empowered worker, yet one that now had an additional reason to be respectful toward his supervisor or employer. In short, by joining martial schools, students became active participants in their own subjugation to broader social structures. Rather than being a truly independent realm, the land of "rivers and lakes" ultimately served as a safety valve that reproduced and furthered society's core social values.

While a vibrant civil society exists in the 1930s and 1940s, it does not appear to be as independent of underlying economic and cultural structures as we might expect in the West. Rather, civil and associational institutions, including martial arts schools, seem to have spread along a web of preexisting networks defined by traditional cultural ties. It was precisely this ability to create a set of power relationships within the emerging sphere of civil society that made martial arts such a contested area of Chinese life during the interwar years.

No discussion of the Wing Chun community in Foshan in the 1920s and 1930s would be complete without touching on one additional topic. When thinking back to the town's glory days, modern Wing Chun students immediately evoke the memory of the so called "Three Heroes of Wing Chun: Ip Man, Yuen Kay San, and Yiu Choi." And yet they have played only a minor role in our discussion of the public Wing Chun community in this period. Who were these "heroes" and how did they relate to Foshan's over-heated martial scene?

Obviously, readers will be familiar with Ip Man. As the major subject of this chapter we have already reviewed the details of his early life in an attempt to sort out what is actually known about his background from the wide variety of fanciful stories that circulate about him. Yuen Kay San (1887–1956) is also a familiar figure to most members of the Wing Chun clan. Born in 1887, he was older than Ip Man, but the two are reputed to have been good friends. As a child he lived with his wealthy parents on Chao Guan Lane. Yuen was the fifth child born in his family. His father was a wealthy industrialist who made a fortune manufacturing chemical pigments.

Most accounts indicate that his father hired Fok Bo-Chuen and later Fung Siu Ching to instruct his young son. These individuals are often said to have studied with "Painted Face" Kam at about the same time that Leung Jan was receiving instruction from Leung Yee Tai and Wong Wah Bo. Again, there is actually no evidence that any of these individuals existed, but the basic outline of the stories certainly seems plausible and fits with what we know about Foshan's late nineteenth-century history. Given his age, it seems likely that Yuen Kay San began his studies prior to the Boxer Uprising.

Like Ip Man, Yuen was a member of the new gentry. He never held a full-time job, though he may have occasionally served as a lawyer for the local government. Instead, he spent his time practicing and perfecting his kung fu. Yuen is thought to have fought in a number of challenge matches, but as we have already seen, the specific details of these events are very hard to reconstruct with any reliability.

Yuen showed little interest in teaching or passing on his art. He is known to have associated with Ng Chung So and Cheung Bo, most likely because these instructors provided a fresh crop of students for him to test his chi sao on, but he never taught a class himself. His only known disciple was Sum Num, originally a student of Cheung Bo's, whom he adopted as his protégé later in life. Rene Ritchie (1997) has done much to collect and publish the history and folklore regarding Yuen Kay San, as passed on by Sum Num and his grand-students.[70]

The third hero of Wing Chun was Yiu Choi (1890–1956). A native of Bao'an County, his father opened a pharmacy on what is now Fu Xian Road in Foshan. His store specialized in creams, pills, and medical powders. Commercial success once again made the family quite wealthy and provided Yiu Choi with both the resources and free time to feed his growing obsession with the martial arts.

As a young man he is said to have been renowned for his strength. He began his study of Wing Chun under Yuen Chai Wan, the older brother of Yuen Kay San. Eventually, the elder Yuen moved to Vietnam where he began to teach Wing Chun in the expatriate Chinese community.[71] Before leaving he recommended his young student to Ng Chung So who completed his training at his own school.

It was there that Yiu Choi befriended Ip Man and Yuen Kay San. According to Huang Xiao Hui and Huang Hong he instructed his own son and had five other disciples, but Yiu Choi never appears to have opened a school or taught publicly.[72] Instead, he and his brother opened the club in Foshan where Ng Chung So taught. When Ng retired from public teaching he moved in with Yiu Choi and spent his final years instructing his wealthy student and his son.[73]

Readers should be aware that the "Three Heroes of Wing Chun" title, under which these individuals are commonly linked, is a later fictional invention. It was never used in Foshan at the time of the current discussion. Given their wealth, vaunted social status, and kung fu prowess, these three young men provided ample fodder for later pulp journalists and novelists attempting to capitalize on the public's interest in local martial arts heroes. Yet, at the time, the actual contributions of these individuals to the development of Wing Chun were quite modest. None were forced by economic circumstances to take on students, and so they did not. While Ip Man would go on to be a prolific public teacher in the future, during the 1920s and 30s he was essentially a free rider, benefiting greatly from the efforts of Ng Chung So and others to build a sustainable Wing Chun community, but contributing little in return. Yuen Kay San was, if anything, more insular than Ip Man. It seems likely that he accepted challenges on behalf of the Wing Chun community, but tragically he was not as enthusiastic when it came to accepting students. Luckily, his one disciple, Sum Num, possessed a real talent for the art of promotion. If he had not, Yuen Kay San's legacy would likely have been lost. Lastly, Yiu Choi was the heir of an interesting branch of Wing Chun knowledge. While he did take on a small number of private students, his main contribution to the Wing Chun clan was actually to be a staunch supporter of Ng Chung So's tireless efforts to spread the art.

While Ip Man, Yuen Kay San, and Yiu Choi were all real individuals, and were in fact good friends, the "Three Heroes of Wing Chun" is a myth. The degree to which the real history of Wing Chun in Foshan has been replaced by pulp fiction and rumor is truly saddening. It is all the more tragic because the real lives and contributions of individuals like Chan Yiu Min, Lai Yip Chi, Jiu Chao, and Cheung Bo are even more interesting than the quasi-fictional exaggerations that have supplanted them in the popular consciousness. Only by understanding the nature of the Wing Chun community that these individuals built can we make sense of Ip Man's later attempts to reform and spread the system in Hong Kong.

Ip Man, 1937–1949: The Breaking Storm

Every account of Wing Chun's modern history mentions that Ip Man lost his fortune and was forced to take up a career teaching his beloved art. From his aging hands the style passed to Bruce Lee, and from his radiant image, to the world. In the modern mythology of southern China's martial arts this is seen as a sort of "fortunate fall," something that freed the old master from his past commitments and allowed him to pursue his actual passion on a full-time basis, passing on his great insights.

The truth behind this episode is much murkier than the platitudes. The late 1940s and early 1950s represented a period of wrenching transition that threatened to leave the older, more mature, Ip a shattered man. Nor are the exact details of this period always clear. It is often assumed that Ip Man's wealth was stolen either by the Japanese or the Communist Party. Obviously, there is some truth to both of these assertions. The Japanese occupation force did requisition large amounts of real estate in and around Foshan for their own purposes. Readers will recall, for instance, that the Japanese used the newly finished Jingwu building as a granary. And the communists were leading a "worker's revolution" which brought massive land reform in its wake. All of the local landlords and members of the gentry either voluntarily donated their property to the cause (as did Lai Yip Chi) or suffered their wrath.

At least some of the mystery surrounding when and how Ip Man lost his fortune seems to be deliberate. Being overly critical of the Communist government, and the 1949 Liberation, is still problematic for many Chinese writers today. We suspect that these sorts of political considerations have led Ip Chun and others to emphasize the role of the hated Japanese occupation in depleting the family fortunes and forcing his father's retreat to Hong Kong.[74] Yet this account is contradicted by clearly demonstrated historical facts.

Western students of Wing Chun have been less interested in defaming the Japanese and have instead turned their sights on their old Cold War nemesis, the Communist Party. While it is true that the 1949 takeover of Foshan does a better job of explaining the actual timing of Ip Man's flight to Hong Kong, the puzzle is still not complete. For instance, Ip Man was actually gainfully employed (possibly for the first time in his life) prior to his departure in 1949. Why after a lifetime of avoiding work had it suddenly become a necessity? Only a few other local Wing Chun teachers fled to Hong Kong. What exactly had Ip Man been doing that made his immigration both possible and necessary?

Overlooked in all of this is the role of the Nationalist Party or the GMD. When reading the history of this period, one cannot help but be struck how deeply divided this "government" really was. At times it can be difficult to distinguish the generals or cliques of officers within the GMD from the warlords whom they perpetually fought for dominance. Incompetence and an almost unimaginable level of corruption were the hallmarks of this administration on the local level. At the same time, it did play a crucial role in shaping the evolution, and the ultimate fate, of Foshan's martial marketplace.

At the most basic level Ip Man was probably responsible for much of his own financial hardships in the 1930s and 1940s. Throughout the earlier period of his life he had made a conscious decision to consume his resources rather than invest them. As we have already suggested, these decisions made his economic profile less diverse and more susceptible to both global market shocks and political interference.

These variables would become a major problem in the closing years of the 1920s. Sun Yat-sen had planned a major assault on the independent warlords who had established their own principalities in the north. It was set to take place in 1925. His death and the previously mentioned "Hong Kong Strike" (which was longer than expected) forced a delay. In 1926, the party's new military leadership was ready to advance. They moved the seat of government from Guangzhou to Wuhan and started the march north.

Unfortunately, things did not go exactly as planned. The left wing of the party, made up of communists and socialist sympathizers, grew in strength causing consternation in the GMD's more conservative quarters. This growing paranoia resulted in the Shanghai Massacre of 1927 in which many leftist elements were purged from the party or simply murdered in the streets.[75]

The violence inevitably trickled back to Foshan and led to full-scale conflict between the more conservative and right leaning "Yi" schools (who would later go on to form the Zhong Yi Association) and the enormous Hung Sing Association, which was backing the Communist Party. While the two groups had reportedly already come to blows over local businesses attempting to cross the picket lines of the Hong Kong Strike, this represented a major escalation of strife within Foshan's martial arts community. The Hung Sing Association was forcibly closed by the provincial government.[76]

Finances had also become a problem. The expedition would require enormous amounts of money, more than could be raised through the normal routes of taxation and licensing. At this point the GMD turned to the wealthy merchants of Guangdong for donations to advance the national cause. As the situation progressed it became clear that the forcible expropriation of wealth was not out of the question. There are many accounts that emerge from this period of the army literally ransacking houses and digging up gardens in an attempt to find hordes of buried silver.

This sort of expropriation has far-reaching effects. The immediate wealth lost is the least of these problems. More serious is the stifling effect that this has on the local business climate. Will merchants engage in innovative and risky trade practices if they believe the government may simply expropriate their profits? Will land owning peasants enlarge their irrigation systems or go out of their way to increase their rice yields if they suspect that their surplus will simply be requisitioned by the army? Put in these simple terms it is easy to see how unbalanced political institutions can lead to poor economic outcomes. When one adds the Great Depression into the mix, it becomes quite clear that Ip Man's money troubles, and in fact the decline of the entire local economy, probably began quite a bit earlier than is generally thought. Far from placing the entire blame on the Japanese or the Communist Party, the variables that need to be considered first are the economic policies of the GMD and Ip Man's own investment decisions.

While his fortune was diminished, Ip Man continued to live a leisurely life through most of the early and mid-1930s. He still did not need full-time employment. His second surviving son, Ip Ching, was born in 1936, approximately twelve years after his older brother, Ip Chun. Initially, the family lived in Foshan; yet, this domestic tranquility would not last.[77] In 1937, the Japanese attacked and occupied southern China. At this time the Ip family was forced to leave their home.

Still, things in Foshan were not as bad as in other areas under Japanese control. Hong Kong was more problematic. The initial Japanese assault ignored Hong Kong since it was a British territory. However, due to the allied economic embargo Japan later lashed out at American and British holdings in Asia. On December 8, 1941, the Japanese began operations against Hong Kong. By December 25 they had overcome all resistance and the allied forces in the area formally surrendered. This victory set the stage for numerous human rights abuses, all prefigured in the "St. Stephen's College Incident."

Ip Man's old high school, St. Stephens, was used as a field hospital during the Battle of Hong Kong. Immediately following their victory, a number of drunken Japanese soldiers stormed the hospital, shot two of the attending physicians, and bayoneted all of the patients who were unable to flee. The Japanese tenure in Hong Kong was marked by martial law, hunger, and frequent public executions. Luckily, it was easy to leave. Aware of the island's precarious lines of supply and communication, the Japanese actually deported many thousands of unemployed workers. Ip Man's sister, who lived in Hong Kong, sent her young son, Lo Man

Kam, to live with her brother in Foshan because conditions were much better there.[78]

It was around this time that Ip Man first began to experiment with teaching Wing Chun, albeit on a limited scale. In or around 1943, Ip Man was approached by two friends, Chow Wing Yiu and Chow Chang Yiu. These individuals owned a fabric and embroidery factory and they sought to hire Ip Man to teach their youngest brother, Chow Kwong Yiu. Much to everyone's surprise, Ip Man agreed to take the job.

Given the importance of "sensitivity training" in Wing Chun, it is best if new students have a variety of partners with whom they can work. This same principle holds for any number of arts that emphasize sparring or two-person drills. It was decided that a small class would be assembled that could meet in the largely empty factory warehouse. Lun Kai, another relation of the Chows, who worked at the factory, agreed to join the class, as did Chan Gee Sun, Lui Pak Ying, Chow Sai Keung, Chan Sum, and eventually Tsang So. Kwok Fu, one of Ip Man's better known students from this period, was employed as a junior clerk at a grocery shop next door to the factory. Eventually, he petitioned Ip Man to accept him as a student (he was already good friends with Lun Kai), and he became the last student accepted at the factory school.

Ip Man was hesitant to accept the title "Sifu." He asked his students not to use the more respectful term and instead to refer to him as Man Sok or "Uncle." Further, Lan Kai asserts that Ip Man never asked for any tuition from either himself or Kwok Fu. Leung Ting speculates that Ip Man must have realized that the two young men were relatively poor workers. Instead, the Chow brothers seem to have subsidized the class.[79]

Notwithstanding the informality and small size of the class, Ip Man's sudden decision to take up teaching inspired local gossip and possibly some controversy. This fact alone should cause us to be quite careful when extrapolating about the brilliant backgrounds of the so-called "Three Heroes of Wing Chun." Our perception of the importance of these individuals today is likely quite different from how they were actually viewed by their friends and neighbors at the time.

Ip Chun relates that after his father's decision to teach became public knowledge he was immediately challenged by a local Choy Li Fut Sifu named Wan Dai Han. While martial arts fiction is full of such encounters, in real life challenge matches appear to be somewhat less common. After all, any passing policeman or member of the Japanese military is likely to call such an encounter an "assault," no matter how one tries to spin it. Additionally, as we saw with the case of the earlier Jingwu master, walking into another instructor's school or neighborhood and issuing a challenge shows considerable disrespect. This can be very problematic for the one issuing the challenge, regardless of the outcome. Perhaps this is why in stories such challenges are almost inevitably issued by wandering adepts from far off places or unbalanced local teenagers. Such actions were never as common or taken as lightly as modern folklore or lineage apologists would have us believe.

Given all of this, it would have been easy for Ip Man to simply walk away from the challenge. He was not teaching publicly, he was not accepting tuition from his students, and he was not even calling himself a sifu. Yet once again he surprised the local community by accepting it. His son, Ip Chun, speculates that his father must have thought that this would be a good way to increase the profile of Wing Chun in Foshan's crowded marketplace. In short, the match might be good advertising. Tan Shan Chi, a local Chinese doctor, was recruited to act as the judge of the fight, and it was decided that this was to be a "friendly contest."

It is a remarkable fact that in all of our combined research we have yet to come across a single account where a great master or local hero loses a challenge match. Indeed, the fact that so many victors can occupy the same geographic space seems to make southern China something of a mathematical anomaly. According to Wing Chun tradition, Ip Man was able to evade the powerful distance strikes that Choy Li Fut is known for, and successfully counterattacked after employing his superior close range techniques. The judge, wishing to avoid any additional loss of face, immediately stepped in and declared the match a draw.[80] Of course, we do not have Wan Dai Han's side of the story. Whatever the actual circumstances or outcome of the fight, Ip Man continued to teach his small class, and public discussion of his activities abated.

Following the end of hostilities in 1945, the Japanese occupation force withdrew and southern China slowly began to return to a state of normalcy. Yet these recovery efforts were complicated by the fact that the civil war between the GMD and the Communist Party was just reaching the boiling point. Political instability continued to be a major issue. Nevertheless, shops and factories reopened as the economy began to emerge from its conflict-induced slumber. A number of martial arts schools and associations that had been forced to close by the Japanese occupation (such as the Foshan Jingwu Association and the Zhong Yi Athletic Association) reopened as the rhythm of local life was restored.

This return to normalcy spelled the end of Ip Man's first small efforts at running a school. His students dispersed as they returned to their homes or sought more profitable employment elsewhere. Ip Man had gained two years of valuable teaching experience, and he retained his relationships with a number of his students including Kwok Fu whom he would visit in the following months. Leung Ting asserts that Ip Man traveled to Kwok Fu's home village and continued to teach him until he found employment with the police.[81]

As the GMD struggled to reconstitute local governments it became evident that Foshan was in desperate need of law enforcement officers. In 1945, at the age of 52, Ip Man was hired for his first and only full-time job. Despite having no prior background in police work, he was named the captain of a unit of plain clothes (undercover) detectives. The job is reputed to have monopolized much of his time and to have taken him away from the world of Wing Chun.[82]

Exactly why he was hired and what he did during his career in law enforcement remains a mystery. It is said that Ip Man led the officers who broke up a kidnapping operation.[83] Leung Ting asserts that there are numerous other stories that relate to his time in the police force. Once again, they are impossible to verify.

One important issue that does arise when we consider the timing (1945–1949) and nature of Ip Man's employment is his relationship with the larger struggle between the GMD and the Communist Party. By 1945 the GMD was aware that the communists were preparing for a final push into the country's urban areas. Lieutenant General Kot Siu Wong of GMD Intelligence, stationed in Guangzhou, was tasked with ensuring the loyalty of Guangdong's police and military personnel. Communist agents were a major target of both the police and military. Kot attempted to organize the underworld secret societies and martial arts schools to resist this threat. In particular, he tried to convince or coerce practically the entire population of the Pearl River Delta to join the secret societies as he thought it would make them more resistant to leftist pressure.

As the captain of a detective unit in the second most important city in the province, Ip Man was basically a GMD intelligence asset from 1945 to 1949. While much of his time might have been spent tracking mundane criminals, it seems inconceivable that he could have remained totally unaware of Kot's policies. What he thought of them and what role, if any, he played in carrying them out, is unknown.

His sporadic involvement with the Wing Chun clan in this period does provide a few clues that might point us in the general direction. To begin with, accounts provided by his family indicate that Ip Man withdrew from his normal circle of friends in this period. While it may have simply been true that he was too busy to frequent Ng Chung So's classes, it might also have been awkward to continue to host a police officer in a reputed opium den (if there is any truth to the allegations). We do know, for instance, that Ip Man found time to begin to coach his second son (Ip Ching) during 1949.[84]

Ip Man trained a few of his subordinates and fellow officers in the police department. Jiu Chao, a Wing Chun teacher in his own right, was also hired by the plainclothes police squad at the same time as Ip Man. As we saw previously, he had studied Wing Chun with Chan Yiu Min, the son of Chan Wah Shun. He asked Ip Man to "correct his forms" during this period. We also know that in 1949 Ip Man was introduced to Pan Nam at a branch of the Foshan Zhong Yi Association. While the two were never formally teacher and student, Pan Nam also asked Ip Man to "correct his forms" and advise him.[85] The most significant aspect of this story is that it places Ip Man himself within the orbit of this little-understood organization.

These two examples would seem to indicate that, far from actually withdrawing from the Wing Chun clan, Ip Man may have felt it necessary to redirect his energies into different, more official, channels. After all, the Zhong Yi Association was strongly backed by the local GMD officers and it had a clear anti-communist orientation. It was the sort of place that one might expect a detective to be.

Still, after arriving in Hong Kong Ip Man struck out on his own. While he accepted assistance from a few personal friends, he did not turn to former law enforcement colleagues or to Lieutenant General Kot Siu Wong's newly resurrected anti-communist league for help. When the various puzzle pieces are fit together, the picture that finally emerges is of a man swept up in the great events of his day, someone who realized the importance of fulfilling expectations, yet who had no personal interest in joining an anti-communist crusade. In fact, Ip Man was willing to pay a price to remain independent.

While Kot and the GMD saw the traditional martial arts as a means to an end, for Ip Man, they were an end unto themselves. His focus never seems to have resided in the realm of politics, even though it was political revolution and calamity that shaped the major contours of his life. His son Ip Ching indicates that by 1949 he had become quite disillusioned with the Nationalist government that employed him.[86]

The last vestiges of Ip Man's world finally collapsed in the fall of 1949. A series of communist victories in the north pushed the GMD further south. After Nanjing fell the government was reconstituted in Guangzhou, very near Foshan. At that point Guangdong became a locus of confrontation. Guangzhou was overrun on October 15. Sometime prior to this Ip Man was informed that he had been blacklisted by the Communist Party, which was about to begin rounding up GMD officers.[87]

It is not known who tipped him off, but this turn of events was not surprising. His own disillusionment with the Nationalists notwithstanding, Ip Man represented many things that threatened the new political order. He was a member of the new gentry, a martial artist linked with a violent reactionary group, and as a police officer he had likely been associated with efforts to suppress the Communist Party in his area. Leaving his wife and most of his family behind, Ip Man fled his ancestral home, taking his oldest daughter, Ip Ar Sum, with him.[88]

Their first stop was Macao where they spent a few weeks with friends who owned a bird shop on Cho Doi Street. Following this brief respite they moved on to Hong Kong.[89] Within months the city would quite literally be flooded with refugees from across mainland China. The once wealthy and well-connected Ip Man found himself part of this surging throng of banished humanity.

Ip Man may have been luckier than most in that he at least retained his social network. He had some family in Hong Kong, but he turned to his personal friends for assistance. Lee Man, a prior associate, arranged for Ip Man to stay at the Restaurant Workers Union Association in Kowloon.[90] Kowloon was where many of the displaced homeless refuges would congregate in the coming months, and the neighborhood would gain a reputation for its poverty, vice, and organized crime.

It was exactly the sort of place where one would expect martial arts schools to thrive, but not yet. For close to six months the 57-year-old Ip Man waited. Perhaps he was regaining his equilibrium and sense of perspective after the shattering events of the last year. When he acted next it would be as a professional martial artist.

Conclusion

The Chinese phoenix is thought to be a harbinger of both conflict and peace. A gentle animal by nature, it settles and thrives only in tranquil and prosperous lands. When the country is divided, its departure is seen as a warning of evil to come. Likewise, the traditional Chinese martial arts of Guangdong Province were born out of periods of conflict, yet they needed decades of stability to spread and thrive. The periods from 1855 to 1900 and 1905 to 1937 represent two such eras. Foshan's martial arts were able to adopt new social roles and increase their presence in civil society, but in both cases calamity at the national level destroyed much of this progress and forced further evolution.

There is a real danger in looking back to the past to discover "traditional" Wing Chun. To put it simply, this relatively young art never existed in a static golden age. The very concept of "Wing Chun" is almost wholly socially constructed and it evolves considerably during the brief period discussed in this chapter.

At first "Wing Chun" existed only as an isolated individual practice which was created when a martial arts enthusiast named Leung Jan borrowed an extensive body of knowledge from the Cantonese opera and quite possibly the teachers his father had previously hired. He detached this knowledge from its original institutional purpose (assisting students studying for careers in the military, or protecting traveling performers) and reworked the system into something that could be passed on to a handful of students within his lineage.

The late nineteenth century was an important time for martial arts development in Foshan. Commercial schools were growing and becoming successful here long before they would be seen in some other areas of the country. Realizing the latent possibilities, Chan Wah Shun attempted to take Leung Jan's art and introduce it to the public, something his teacher had never intended. Due to the poor timing of the Boxer Uprising, and Wing Chun's early alliance with the wealthier aspects of Foshan's society, the art failed to thrive. Fortunately, it did manage to build up a core of dedicated followers that could become the teachers and masters of the next generation.

Realizing that the traditional Chinese martial arts could play a valuable role in creating a modern national identity, elites began to take a second look at these institutions in the 1920s. In this regard Foshan was unexceptional. Wing Chun schools allowed young members of the wealthy merchant class to meet and network. When tied to the yellow unions and the Zhong Yi Association they also provided an effective means of social control. Martial arts schools not only strengthened their students, but they also organized them. Groups like the Jingwu Association, the GMD, and even the Communist Party were willing to throw their support behind individual clubs and spread the gospel of the Chinese martial arts if it served their vision of "national salvation."

With this institutional backing, Wing Chun finally became a successful, if still local, martial art. Whereas Chan Wah Shun had a total of sixteen students, literally hundreds of individuals studied Wing Chun in a variety of schools throughout the 1930s.

Yet this success was predicated on a political, social, and economic framework that was not fated to last. The communist takeover of Guangdong in 1949 destroyed the basic social structures that were the foundation of Wing Chun's success. In the next chapter we will see how Ip Man reformed his art so that it could be successfully taught to different people in a highly urban environment without the sorts of institutional and social supports that it had once enjoyed. In so doing he weakened Wing Chun's conceptual and social links with its traditional homeland and paved the way for it to become a truly global art.

The story of Wing Chun's evolution is deeply entwined with Ip Man's own biography. It is important to understand why. In many ways his life mirrored the transformations that Wing Chun underwent in the volatile twentieth century. He was introduced to the art just as it was being opened to the public for the first time. He mastered the system as his friends and peers built schools that both advanced the art and enmeshed it in Foshan's destructive class conflicts. Finally, Ip Man himself would be the one to break with the old social patterns, simplifying the system and presenting it to the world as an independent structure.

He could do this not because he had studied Wing Chun longer than anyone else, or because he had more teaching experience. Ip Man certainly never claimed to be a "master" or to enjoy a position of authority within the clan. Rather, it was his placement at the center of the social network that had promoted Wing Chun, as well as his dual Confucian and Western education, which gave him the perspective that was necessary to solve the riddle of what this art would have to become to not just survive, but to thrive in its next incarnation.

Chapter 5

Ip Man and the Making of a Modern Kung Fu Master

> Who realized Ip Man's skill? All my training brothers respected Ip Man because he never hurt them, nor were they skillful enough to hurt him. Ip Man in the 1950s was the epitome of sensitivity; he could immediately read his opponent's intention.
>
> —Hawkins Cheung, 1992[1]

Introduction

No image is more central to the mythology of modern martial arts than the "little old Chinese man." Through years of practice and meditation this individual has attained not only self-mastery, but an almost mystical control of this environment. Such an adept is the ideal teacher, capable of revealing and cultivating his student's true potential. Individuals in both Asia and the West are often drawn to the martial arts precisely because they are attempting to find just such a mentor.[2]

Ip Man, whose early life was reviewed in Chapter 4, is often portrayed as exactly this sort of wizened sage. It is claimed that he was a gifted teacher who launched the careers of literally dozens of students, some of whom would go on to become quite famous in their own right. His best known pupil was the iconic Bruce Lee. Beloved by Western television audiences and an important reformer in the world of Hong Kong cinema, Lee left an indelible mark on global popular culture. His premature death, just as he stood on the cusp of true superstardom, propelled Wing Chun, a once obscure regional style, into the global spotlight.

This is the common summery of Ip Man's Hong Kong career encountered by most casual readers. Unfortunately, this brief sketch, repeated in so many magazine articles and books, obscures much about Ip Man and his role in the emergence of modern Wing Chun. For instance, given the inauspicious nature of his arrival in Hong Kong it must have seemed unlikely that he would become a well-known figure and symbol of "martial virtue" within the territory's hand combat community. How exactly did he go about building both a school and a reputation that could attract students from all walks of life? As we follow the twists and turns of Ip Man's efforts to reinvent himself, readers will gain a much clearer understanding of Hong Kong's martial arts subculture in the post-1949 period.

Given all of the famous kung fu teachers in the city, what attracted Bruce Lee, Wong Shun Leung, and a generation of angry, often near delinquent, young men to the school of an elderly, and by all accounts quite gentle, refugee from the mainland? Like many teenagers today these young men were looking for personal empowerment and transformation. In the martial arts they sought a type of social status and approval that Hong Kong's colonized status and limited economic horizons denied them. How Ip Man defined and negotiated his relationship with his sometimes volatile students, and the expectations of Hong Kong society more generally, will be the major focus of this chapter.

Rather than arriving in the territory as a fully formed "master," Ip Man was forced to adopt a number of teaching styles and institutions as his economic situation improved or deteriorated, and as social demands waxed and waned. At least three distinct eras are discernible in his Hong Kong career, each posing unique obstacles and challenges.

The image of violent machismo that Lee projected in his films was in many ways a natural continuation of the fears and insecurities that drove a generation of angry young men to Ip Man's doors in the 1950s. Yet, by the time of Lee's death in 1973, the Ving Tsun Athletic Association, the organization founded by Ip Man to carry on his legacy, was already moving in a different direction, seeking a new model of social discourse and accommodation in line with the emerging reality of life in the more prosperous Hong Kong of the 1970s and 1980s. Rather than Wing Chun being a single easily defined "object," this sometimes diverse body of practices, beliefs, and identity went through an almost continual process of renegotiation between 1949 and 1972.

In 1949 Wing Chun represented a conservative and reactionary force both supporting, and in turn propped up by, the Nationalist government in the Pearl River Delta region. Stripped of its social and political support, by the mid-1950s Wing Chun in Hong Kong had become a moderately anti-systemic movement. Ip Man's school allowed socially, economically, or politically marginal individuals to play out their own personal dramas of resistance without taking the more drastic measures of joining an actual "dark brotherhood." Finally, as Hong Kong's middle class became economically prosperous and began to demand widespread reforms from the territory's often dysfunctional society and government, Ip Man once again repositioned his school. This time he sought a formal rapprochement with the state while maintaining his independence from the growing network of government sponsored and approved martial arts programs. In this carefully choreographed negotiation one can see the lessons of the 1930s and 1940s being played out on a new stage. The evolution of Wing Chun provides us with a unique perspective from which to view the emergence of a truly independent aspect of civil society within Hong Kong.

Hong Kong's Economic Development, 1949–1972

We have already demonstrated that one cannot understand the emergence of a martial arts school, or any other institution in Chinese civil society, without first exploring the social and economic structures that created and sustained it. While our understanding of the Pearl River Delta is much improved, Hong Kong has always marched to its own beat. The area had been under British control since the Opium Wars, and it served as the main bridge between southern Chinese society and the broader global economy.

This chapter begins with a very brief discussion of Hong Kong's economic and social development during the twentieth century. The city went through a number of transformations that had a major effect on its social structures. Some of these changes created opportunities for Wing Chun to expand, but others led to social instability and slowed the spread of the art. The differing political, economic, and social structures within Hong Kong also conditioned the ways in which both popular and elite opinion viewed the martial arts. In this respect Hong Kong was quite different from the rest of Guangdong in the 1940s. While the Guomindang (GMD) promoted their version of martial arts as a tool to strengthen the populace and build national sentiment, the traditional arts were not as well received by the government in Hong Kong. With no incentive to promote a separate national identity, political and police forces tended to focus on the violent intersection of organized crime (the so-called "Triads") and popular martial arts instruction. The environment that Ip Man faced in Hong Kong was quite different from the somewhat protected and subsidized marketplace that existed in Foshan.

The evolution of Hong Kong's thriving economy is a topic of interest to scholars around the world and much has been written on this aspect of the story. Already, by 1900, it was replacing Foshan and Guangzhou as the main commercial port in southern China. Foshan had been a critical hub of domestic commerce, and Guangzhou had done a thriving business in international trade, yet these cities stagnated as their local waterways filled with silt and their highly regulated markets were overtaken by their *laissez faire* neighbor to the south.

Hong Kong also managed to achieve a level of industrialization that eluded the business communities further up the Pearl River. In the early twentieth century, just as today, industrialization was directly related to the overall level of "foreign direct investment." Such investments were basically impossible to initiate in Foshan and Guangzhou, yet British-administered Hong Kong proved to be an attractive destination for English, Chinese, and American businessmen. As Foshan's handicraft industries declined in the early twentieth century, Hong Kong enjoyed a burst of true industrialization.[3]

Still, its deep ports and strategic placement ensured that up through WWII Hong Kong would be mostly known as a port city coordinating both regional exchange and trade between China and its global neighbors. Financial institutions and banks were created to smooth these transactions and shipping remained the lifeblood of the economy up until the disturbances of the mid-twentieth century.

Following the collapse of the Nationalist government in 1949, Great Britain, the United States, and many other Western powers imposed economic sanctions on the People's Republic of China. The purpose of these sanctions was twofold. On a purely symbolic level they sought to demonstrate the West's resolve in the face of this new communist threat. More practically, they hoped to weaken the new government by denying it the efficiency gains and economic growth that accompany trade.

While these sanctions did convey the West's growing sense of animosity, they had no material effect on mainland China's economic growth during this period. In truth sanctions are rarely effective against continental sized economies, especially when the vast majority of citizens live in rural, basically self-sufficient, villages. The West had very little economic influence over China in the mid-twentieth century.

Ironically, these same sanctions had a devastating effect on the much more industrial and globally interconnected economy of Hong Kong. In 1949 the city experienced an extremely difficult year. It found itself overrun with refugees from the mainland. These individuals often lacked any form of employment or even shelter. At the same time the shipping industry was basically put out of business by the politically motivated economic sanctions that crippled regional trade. This is the scene that would have greeted Ip Man when he first arrived in the city.

Hong Kong began the process of fundamentally transforming its economy in the early 1950s. Some trade, specifically in agricultural products, remained. This was important as it kept food prices, and hence wages, down. Yet, increasingly, investment turned toward light manufacturing. Most of these new firms were quite small by contemporary standards, employing between a few dozen and a few hundred workers. Production was directed toward both domestic consumption and exports.

The period from 1950 on saw a steady growth of income and spending power throughout the city. At first this economic growth came slowly, but it accelerated rapidly in the 1960s and 1970s. Rising standards of living and wages allowed workers to spend more money on recreation and leisure, including tuition for martial arts instruction.

Despite this generally positive outlook there were a few periods of notable reversal. In 1962, mainland China opened its southern border allowing tens of thousands of refugees to flee, and many of these individuals ended up in Hong Kong. This resulted in economic displacement and confusion. More serious was the recession in 1967 when the start of the Cultural Revolution on the mainland led to strikes, uprisings, and violence in Hong Kong. These incidents will play a role in the story of Wing Chun's evolution in the post-1949 era.[4]

The territory's government in this period is often characterized as a relatively hands off, *laissez faire*, set of institutions. There is a large measure of truth to this view. The British administered the colony, but depended extensively on local civil servants. Economic liberalism was the order of the day. This contributed to the creation of a competitive marketplace of many small firms as opposed to the heavily state dominated process of economic development that unrolled in Japan and Korea (to say nothing of China).

Still, it is important not to overstate the case. Hong Kong's government was far from weak. It maintained extensive legal and social authority to regulate developments in civil society. From the perspective of many of the territory's martial arts schools, the strong hand of the state took the form of intermittent police harassment and overt discrimination. The government was also unafraid to intervene in the economy when it felt long-term structural adjustments were necessary. The state took aggressive measures to seize rural agricultural land, building new industrial neighborhoods in their place, as a way of dealing with the persistent problems of homelessness and overcrowding.[5]

The government also invested massively in primary and secondary education by building elementary and high schools across the city in a bid to educate its work force. Their efforts in this realm were so successful that the colony's small university system was unable to absorb all of the aspiring scholars that were produced. Many of Ip Man's students (including Bruce Lee) went overseas to pursue further education, taking his art to the United Kingdom, Australia, Canada, and the United States. Both of these factors, the fluid and evolving real estate market as well as the lack of university options, play a part in our discussion of Wing Chun's emergence on the global scene.

Hand Combat and Public Opinion in Hong Kong

In addition to understanding the basic economic challenges that Ip Man faced, it is also critical to know something about how elite, middle-class, and working-class individuals viewed traditional boxing in the 1950s, 1960s, and 1970s. The beliefs and expectations of these groups determined what was, or was not, possible. Their opinions framed the choices that Ip Man faced as he attempted to shepherd his art to maturity. While there are some similarities to the social attitudes that we have already encountered in Guangdong in the 1920s and 1930s, the situation in Hong Kong requires its own discussion.

Perhaps the greatest differences in social expectations can be found in the realm of elite opinion. In Guangdong, political elites subverted martial arts schools and secret societies, using them as tools against their rivals and the growing communist threat. While the average educated member of the "new gentry" likely took a dim view of traditional boxing, the work of intellectuals like Tang Hao and the publications of the

Central Guoshu Institute made it possible to at least mount an intellectual defense of the practice.

By comparison the elites of Hong Kong were much more hostile toward any form of hand combat training. The British rulers of the island were aware that the GMD had appealed to traditional boxing as a source of national identity and revolutionary fervor, yet these were hardly sentiments they were willing to foster in their own colony. Their opposition to traditional martial arts is far from surprising. The few references that we see in English-language newspapers are uniformly negative and dismissive, but for the most part the foreign press simply ignored the traditional arts unless they were implicated in some spectacular and bloody story of gang violence.

This hostile attitude extended far beyond the relatively small body of English civil servants and residents. Chinese members of the civil service, police force, and social elites were, if anything, even more hostile toward hand combat schools than their European counterparts. During the course of his extensive field research Daniel Amos found that most social elites, to the extent that they ever thought about martial arts, tended to describe a sliding scale of anti-social behavior with three major demarcations.

Most upper-middle-class respondents, and all law enforcement officials interviewed by Amos, claimed that there were strong links between private martial arts schools and organized crime. One study conducted by Hong Kong's police in the mid-1970s concluded that around 34 percent of all private martial arts organizations were either run by or associated with criminal gangs. These schools were a valuable asset for recruiting "muscle" in a criminal environment that was largely devoid of firearms. Hand combat schools also gave criminal elements a certain level of privacy and protection from surveillance. Finally, running martial arts schools was seen as a cushy retirement job for aging thugs who used their new positions to recruit impressionable youth into illegal Triad organizations.[6]

It seems that the figures were largely correct. However, estimates by other studies and individual law enforcement officers sometimes placed the correlation between organized crime and private martial arts schools much higher. Some police officials who granted Amos interviews claimed that up to 60 percent of all martial arts schools were controlled by criminal elements. In their opinion the mere existence of a private martial arts movement represented an existential threat to the security and safety of the community. While Amos concludes that these higher numbers are exaggerated, and probably do not reflect reality, they likely do represent the honest beliefs of social elites during the period of time at which Ip Man was active.[7]

Part of the inconsistency in the previous estimates has to do with how tightly one defines "organized crime." In Hong Kong any "Triad" organization, of any type, is illegal; yet clearly not all Triads are created equal. At one extreme there are the highly organized gangs that make use of Triad symbolism and stories yet spend their days running protection rackets and selling narcotics rather than "opposing the Qing." At the mid-level there are other social groups, which may be more politically subversive in nature (often anti-communist), who make use of the same imagery. Local teenage street gangs will sometimes adopt Triad symbols and initiations, and then typically go on to confront other gangs over turf. Lastly, there are individuals or very small cliques (not even large enough to qualify as a gang) who might adopt the Triad label for their own social or criminal purposes. Clearly these institutions are better distinguished by their differences than their similarities yet, under Hong Kong's criminal laws in the 1960s and 1970s, each of these groups was seen as a "Triad organization" and was pursued under the same set of criminal statutes. Membership in any Triad, of whatever type, was a crime regardless of the laws that this organization did or did not break.

Such sweeping measures were in large part a result of the allure that the "Triad" label held for displaced and marginal people in Hong Kong's society. Many Triad members were basically juvenile delinquents, alienated from a dominant society which provided them with few opportunities for advancement, looking to live out their own narrative of personal resistance in the symbolic, and yet always present, "land of rivers and lakes."

One highly discussed study, published in 1975, demonstrated that at the time there was a very strong relationship between traditional martial arts schools and juvenile delinquency. Agnes Ng, a social scientist, conducted an extensive statistical survey and concluded that youths who had already established some sort of criminal record were much more likely to enroll in hand combat schools than those who had never been involved in crime. In her sample set fully 20 percent of juvenile offenders had joined a hand combat school, whereas only 4 percent of those with a clean record had.

Amos was quick to point out that her study was not without problems. Most of the offenders she surveyed came from a working-class background, and the practice of martial arts was highly correlated with class status in Hong Kong during the 1950s through the1970s. Further, the non-offenders she surveyed had been middle-class students who were unlikely to have the time, freedom, or inclination to join martial arts schools in large numbers.[8]

These structural problems notwithstanding, Ng's study generated a good deal of interest and it was positively received by social elites at the time. As such, it remains an important measurement of social opinion. Leaders of martial arts schools must have been aware of these elite beliefs, if for no other reason than the near constant state of harassment in the press and at the hands of the police that many of them endured. Another of Amos' informants, an ethnically Hakka Southern Mantis master who ran a school in Kowloon in the 1960s and 1970s, felt compelled to declare:

> You know, many of my disciples, many young guys who do gongfu are called "delinquents" (fei zai) by people on the street. If someone doesn't know my disciples when he sees them on the streets he would consider them delinquents. I ask you, "How do you know a delinquent?" Is it only by appearance? Only because they have long hair? Bad guys are not all long-haired. Some are always dressed up and have a good appearance, but the police call all gongfu guys delinquents. The police used to just grab us and take us to jail. So we can't cooperate very well with the police in Hong Kong. Especially when you consider that the police are always rude, harsh, and impolite. A few years ago they would just seize you and they would beat you. Several of them would just beat you up. Even today I am sometimes questioned and body-searched by them.[9]

This statement illustrates the social tensions that were felt between those involved in the traditional martial arts and the upper levels of Hong Kong's society. The informant's concerns about police abuse were most likely justified. Nevertheless, there was also a fair measure of truth in the authority's assertion that martial arts groups, especially the less prosperous ones or those associated with specific temple organizations, were breeding grounds for local troublemakers.

Avron Boretz, another ethnographer, has studied the intersection of martial arts, popular religion, and the world of the "dark brotherhood" in both Taiwan and southern China. He notes that while all martial artists seem to live under a cloud of social suspicion, those who participate in schools or martial troops attached to local temple cults (such as the Southern Mantis master interviewed by Amos) not only draw from, but also tend to depend on, local toughs and small time criminals to fill out their ranks at festivals. Further, there are very good symbolic reasons why popular religious organizations would select individuals from these backgrounds when looking to conduct mock military processions, Lion or Qilin Dances, exorcisms, or public spirit possession rituals. Likewise, there are clear reasons why such problematic individuals would be drawn to these social and religious behaviors. As Boretz notes, all of these activities follow the basic logic of exorcism:

> Threatening substances and beings are generally classified as *yin*—that is, shadowy, insubstantial, female. Subduing such threats requires exorcistic power; which works, in turn, through objects and beings that are relatively more *yang* (bright, substantial, male) . . . But the most unusual aspect of Chinese exorcism is its distinctive use of the martial idiom. I posit that the martial, in turn, is a categorically male domain, and martial process, the mastery of innate male aggressivity (which implies, even as it represses and channels, a vigorous sexual potency) is then a sign of dominant masculinity. Thus, in the simplest terms, for men with few prospects for conventional social status and economic stability, violence, including the performance of martial ritual, becomes a viable medium for self-production.[10]

Boretz's carefully documented description of how these individuals are viewed within both the mundane and the religious community is beyond the scope of the current discussion. Yet his fieldwork suggests that there is still a strong relationship between criminality and some of the more "martial" aspects of modern Chinese culture.

So at one end of the spectrum social elites in Hong Kong perceived that there were a large number of small, unregulated, martial arts schools that had become a breeding ground for crime and disorder. Social bias and inconsistent definitions make it hard to measure what percentage of private schools were really fronts for organized criminal operations, but it is clear that some were. It is also clear that martial arts societies attracted marginal, often angry, youth in great numbers.

Such a situation could not be allowed to persist. The police made multiple attempts to crack down on the Triads and the martial arts schools that housed them. All of this culminated in new legislation passed in 1973 (the year after Ip Man died). Every martial arts school was now required to obtain a government license or it would be shut down. In order to get the license one had to submit a fee, record the names and addresses of all students, collect passport-type photos and submit these to the government upon request. If a criminal was caught making trouble the police would know immediately which school he was associated with, and that school faced retribution.[11]

If untrustworthy private schools anchored one end of the martial arts spectrum in the eyes of local elites, the other end was defined by the much smaller "official" world of martial arts clubs and societies. These included martial arts classes offered in high schools and colleges, as well as the schools who churned out opera students to supply the colony's thriving film industry. The leaders of these groups did not (for the most part) refer to themselves as "Sifu." Rather they adopted more modern, Western, titles like "coach." Their schools lacked the elaborate pseudo-kinship systems that both Boretz and Amos observed elsewhere. Martial arts instruction was conducted in a class, just like any other subject. Amos reports that students and teachers in these settings rejected the notion that there was anything traditional, spiritual, or mysterious about the martial arts. Rather, they were simply a set of skills that allowed one to perform a job (such as being an actor) that enriched society and earned a living. Not surprisingly, this attitude was strongly endorsed by the government. If martial arts were to exist at all, they had to support social goals and not the delusions of displaced young men seeking to transform themselves into modern day knights errant.[12]

In between these two extremes at least some elites were willing to admit the existence of a third, intermediary category. This last group was comprised of private individuals, involved in traditional schools, who were either prosperous or far-sighted enough not to be involved with Triad organizations or petty gangs. While still promoting a type of "play" that at heart was anti-modern and not in line with the state's interests, these individuals could perhaps be tolerated. As we have already seen, exactly what percentage of schools fell into this third, less sinister, category was a matter of dispute within the police department and elite circles.

Middle-class and working-class observers tended to have a simpler view of the martial realm. Amos reports that most members of Hong Kong's middle class did not approve of martial pursuits, but if they gave very much thought to them at all they simply assumed that one could not have a traditional martial arts school without being involved in the

Triads in some form or another. In a symbolic sense they may have been correct. In Chapter 2 we demonstrated that the myth of the burning of the Shaolin Temple, and the charge to "oppose the Qing and restore the Ming," were both universally held motifs among the Cantonese or "Hung Mun" martial arts styles. Given that the same myth and charge is at the heart of the traditional secret society initiation ritual, it is not hard to see why one might make a universal equation between the two groups.[13]

While some middle-class and wealthy citizens in Hong Kong practiced martial arts, as in most places in China, they were in the distinct minority. In fact, middle-class interest in the martial arts does not seem to have been as strong in the colony as it was in Foshan. The Jingwu Association set up a Hong Kong branch on Nathan Road in 1918, but it does not seem to have prospered to the same extent as the movement in Guangzhou and Foshan. Obviously, the central Guoshu Institute never set up programs in Hong Kong and, while a number of traditional teachers moved to the city prior to WWII, it seems that for the most part their students came from working-class backgrounds.

Studying the beliefs and opinions of the more plebian elements of Hong Kong's society in the 1950s and 1960s is more difficult. At the time few social scientists were asking working-class individuals for their candid thoughts on hand combat training. Luckily, much of the era's popular media has survived, and a brief survey of it suggests some interesting conclusions.

Traditional modes of storytelling and identity formation did retain a great deal of currency among Hong Kong's working and middle classes in the 1950s and 1960s. If working-class individuals were more likely to enroll in kung fu classes than their middle-class brethren, both groups were avid consumers of martial arts publications, novels, and movies. The first truly successful martial arts film was the pioneering "Burning of the Red Lotus Temple" released in 1928. Still, the genre did not achieve its recognizable form until 1949 when the first Cantonese-language film based on the exploits of Wong Fei Hung was released by Hong Kong's fledgling film industry. In the decade to follow, Kwan Tak Hing, who came to define Wong's screen presence, and Shek Kien, who played the part of an entirely fictional arch-nemesis, starred in 62 films. This remarkable output, along with earlier radio broadcasts, transformed the reclusive, often reluctant, martial artists from Foshan into a pop culture icon.

Kwan's films differed from both previous and later efforts in that they attempted to remain grounded in the gritty reality of southern

Chinese hand combat. Both Kwan and Shek were trained martial artists who relied on authentic styles, used real weapons, and eschewed the overuse of special effects or staged supernatural powers. Their efforts helped to set the stage for the later evolution of Hong Kong cinema, but their brand of film making remained firmly rooted in the realm of local storytelling focusing on homegrown folk heroes.[14]

As successful as these films were, Hong Kong's market for martial fiction was being transformed. In 1946 the territory had a total population of 1,600,000 residents. Following the victory of the Communist Party on the mainland that number swelled to 2,300,000. By 1960 the continuing flow of refugees had pushed the small area's population close to 3,000,000.

The original population of Hong Kong tended to be Cantonese-speaking businessmen, workers, and investors who were all part of the fluid and shifting southern Chinese commercial marketplace. For the most part these individuals did not consider Hong Kong to be their home. They continued to think of some place in Guangdong or Fujian Province as their home village, and many would return there after making it big or reaching retirement. Hong Kong was a place where the transient Chinese business community met equally transient European merchants and officials, all of whom were intent on making their fortunes and moving on.

The waves of refugees that poured into the city through the 1950s and 1960s permanently changed its character. These individuals hailed from all regions of China, many of them coming from northern and central areas such as Shanghai and Beijing. They did not speak Cantonese, and as the months turned to years, it quickly became apparent that they would not be returning home. Hong Kong, like Taiwan, became a nation in exile.

Nor were many of these exiles happy with their new home. At various points in the preceding volume we have seen tensions arise between the northern and southern variants of Chinese culture. Many of the new refugees saw their Cantonese hosts as ignorant hicks, incapable of grasping the true nuance and beauty of Chinese culture. In one particularly famous incident Mao Dun published an article denouncing Hong Kong as a "cultural wasteland." This feeling of alienation manifested itself in what was sometimes called the "central plains syndrome," a modernizing agenda seeking to establish national, linguistic, and social unity within Hong Kong's society. In short, it was an attempt to "improve" the native Cantonese residents of the area by removing everything about their identity that the new northern transplants found offensive or alien.

It is not surprising to find that the vast market for northern tastes quickly spawned its own media outlets, including radio stations and newspapers. Many of these publications focused on broader geopolitical issues and news from the mainland. Of course, like all newspapers at the time, they did not survive on their reporting alone. They also published contests, social essays, games, and serialized novels. These features were designed to build and maintain a loyal readership.

By 1955 many of these newspapers had begun to carry martial arts novels as well. The leader of this new literary movement was the creative and prolific Jin Yong. Writing for a variety of papers, including some that he later owned, he produced such classics as *The Book and the Sword* (1955), *Legend of the Condor Heroes* (1957), and *The Deer and Cauldron* (1972). These works, along with their many imitators, collectively defined a new school of martial arts fiction.

Their innovative aesthetic approach was everything that the Wong Fei Hung films were not. The works of Kwan and Shek focused on local folk heroes and the bitter vendettas and feuds of the Pearl River Delta. Jin Yong used the entire Chinese cultural sphere as his canvas, spreading his stories liberally throughout space and time. Whereas the audience of the early Hong Kong films delighted in the presentation of authentic local styles, Jin started with a few well-known historical names, such as "Wudang" or "Shaolin," and then let his imagination run wild. In his first work, *The Book and the Sword* (1955), his heroes use their special grasp of Qi to quite literally fly off the page.

John Hamm has argued that one cannot truly understand the narrative flow of Jin Yong's novels without first placing them within their proper social context. These were novels that responded to the needs of Hong Kong's immigrant population. Many of them can be read as extended meditations on the nature of Chinese society and identity in exile. The martial arts in these novels become a means by which the heroes enter the contest for control of the Chinese nation. When the protagonists are inevitably defeated, they retreat in exile, like the readers, to the far fringes of the Chinese cultural sphere. Hence, in Jin Yong's writing true martial virtue often emerges from the fringes of empire, but the focus of the action remains the contest for Han ethnic and cultural supremacy played out in the once and future landscape of the central plains.[15]

Given the immense popularity that both the early Wong Fei Hung films and Jin Yong's novels enjoyed, there must have been at least some overlap in their audiences. Still, these bodies of work were quite distinct and their differences are telling. Collectively they indicate that while there was a great deal of interest in, and support for, the martial arts among working-class individuals in the 1950s and 1960s, there was no consensus on which approach to them was the most valuable, or even what social meaning they conveyed in the modern era. Writers, film makers, and practitioners were still debating how the martial arts related to the community at large. In addition to the political and economic challenges introduced earlier, this ongoing discussion about the nature and value of kung fu would affect the evolution of Wing Chun's identity within Hong Kong's martial marketplace.

1949–1953: Creating a Foundation for Wing Chun

Ip Man's teaching career exhibits three distinct phases. Each illustrates the successive accommodations that were necessary as the art sought to find a place in Hong Kong's shifting social landscape. The first period begins with his arrival in 1949 and extends through 1953. This was a time of intense struggle and innovation that exhibits two trends. On the one hand, Ip Man drew on preexisting social contacts from Guangdong in his attempts to establish a school. Yet, traditionalism could take him only so far. In order to retain students he was also forced to innovate and adapt his teaching methods to meet the demands of this new, highly fluid, urban environment.

The second section of his career spanned from 1954 to 1961 when his school saw both its greatest growth as well as some serious setbacks. The rapid expansion of his organization, followed by reversals stemming from increased local conflict and personal scandal, forced Ip Man to carefully reconsider what image his art was projecting to society as a whole.

The last phase of his career began with the return of his sons, Ip Chun and Ip Ching, in 1962 and lasted until his death in 1972. During this final decade Ip Man retired from the daily tasks of teaching and turned his attention to institution building. These efforts found expression both within the Wing Chun clan and the broader traditional Chinese martial arts community.

The foundations for all of Ip Man's later accomplishments were laid in the early period lasting from his arrival in 1949 until the closing months of 1953. As we discussed in the preceding chapter, Ip Man fled Foshan along with his oldest daughter toward the end of 1949 after having been blacklisted by the Communist Party. He had previously been employed as the head of a plainclothes detective squad in Foshan during the last stage of the civil war. Following a brief stop in Macao, where he stayed with some friends, Ip Man proceeded on to Hong Kong.

There is little consensus on what actually happened after Ip Man arrived in Hong Kong during the closing weeks of 1949. A variety of figures have claimed to be the one who "discovered" the once great martial arts master, living as a homeless refugee on the streets of Kowloon, and then introduced him to the Restaurant Workers Union. Here he was able to secure lodging in a large communal room. Often Lee Man is credited with this discovery, though occasionally other individuals are named as well.

All of these accounts seem overly dramatic and probably include some exaggeration. While Ip Man may have come to Hong Kong with little money, he did have one asset that many other refugees lacked—an extensive network of social contacts. After all, he was not a total stranger to Hong Kong. He had been educated there and continued to reside in the city before returning to Foshan. He had owned multiple businesses in Hong Kong. Most importantly, he had both personal friends and family who lived in the territory. For instance, Ip Man's sister, who sent her son to take shelter with him in Foshan during the darkest days of WWII, was a resident of Hong Kong. When one takes these facts into account it actually seems rather unlikely that Ip Man would have spent much time in Hong Kong as a homeless beggar.

There is another, even more obvious problem with these stories. It is exceedingly unlikely that anyone finding Ip Man on the street in 1949 would recognize him as a "martial arts master." He had only taught a handful of individuals during WWII in Foshan. If anything he would have been recognized as a former police officer since that was the only public role that he had prior to arriving in Hong Kong. This element of temporal transference again indicates that these accounts probably include more than a little creative memory.

Ip Man appears to have come to the Restaurant Workers Union in Kowloon because of his relationship with Lee Man, who was then serving as the secretary of that body. The more interesting question is: Why did he decide to finally become a full-time martial arts instructor? He had showed little interest in this path in Foshan. It seems that Ip Man's age and legal status both played into his decision. As a recent refugee it is unlikely that he would have been able to continue his career in law enforcement.[16] Further, at 57 he had already reached an age when most people were considering retirement. It was not uncommon for individuals in other styles to take up teaching upon their retirement. Given his diminished economic circumstances, there was also the element of practicality to consider.

Ip Man told Ip Ching (his second son) that Chan Dao, a friend from Guangdong, was actually the first individual to suggest that he open a school and begin to teach Wing Chun professionally after his arrival in Hong Kong. Chan Dao, best known as the founder of Do Pai (or "The Style of the Way"), created his own martial art in Guangdong in the late 1930s by combining elements of Hung Gar, Jau Gar, Hap Gar, and Choy Li Fut. Ip Man's friendship with Chan Dao stretched back to the Republic period and the two continued to be on friendly terms through the late 1960s, when they were photographed together at a party.[17] Chan Dao had independently moved to Hong Kong and established his own school in the Sham Shui Po district of Kowloon. Given his advancing age and the encouragement of his friend, Ip Man finally decided to take up the mantle of "Sifu." This decision was reached sometime prior to April or May of 1950.

There are various accounts of how Ip Man announced his intentions to teach. The Restaurant Workers Union offered martial arts lessons to its members as a perk. Lee Man introduced Ip to Leung Sheung, Lok Yiu, and Lau Ming who were all union staff members. Leung Sheung (1918—1978) was already an experienced martial artist, having studied a variety of southern styles including Choy Li Fut, White Eyebrow, and Dragon. The group was impressed enough with Ip Man that they asked him to teach a course at the union, and Leung Sheung became Ip Man's first official student in Hong Kong. In May of 1950, Ip Man opened his first public class. It was a small group with a total of eight students. Leung Sheung, Lok Yiu, Lau Ming, Tsui Cho, Chan Kau, and Chan Sing Tao all enrolled. Later, eight more joined including Hui Yee, Lee Yan Wing, and Tsang Wing, making a total of sixteen.[18]

Unfortunately, the sorts of people who belonged to the Restaurant Workers Union were by their very nature highly transient. This made it hard to keep a class together. These students were also fundamentally different from the relatively refined leisure class individuals who studied Wing Chun in Foshan in the 1930s. It seems inevitable that Ip Man would have to adjust his teaching style and expectations as he attempted to move into a very different social environment.

In July of 1950 a second class was created. This one was founded with a total of thirty students, but again, attrition was a major problem. Eventually all of the students except for Leung Sheung and Lok Yiu withdrew. However, this class was notable for something other than its short duration. Group photos taken shortly after its creation clearly show that it contained a number of female students. This is the first time we have definitive proof of women studying Wing Chun. While the majority of Ip Man's students were male, throughout his life he did train a handful of women.

In November of 1950 Lee Man left the Restaurant Workers Union for another job. Like Ip Man, the new secretary, Chu Shong Tin, was also a refugee, having fled Guangzhou in the closing months of 1949. He also shared an interest in the martial arts.[19] The two got along well and Chu Shong Tin urged Ip Man to start a third class at a new location. Rather than meeting in the crowded Restaurant Workers Union office in Kowloon, the new class was to meet at the Kung On Branch Office in the mid-west of Hong Kong Island. This class started on January 1 with forty students, the largest initial enrollment to date. Luckily for Ip Man, attrition ceased to be as great a problem and he was able to finally build a steady student base.

The move to the main island seems to have been fortuitous. It must have been difficult to attract steady paying students among the refugees that were streaming into Kowloon. Not only were the students on the main island more reliable, but Ip Man could finally begin to expand his operation. He opened a fifth class (run concurrently with the fourth) that met on the rooftop of a building on Bridges Street. Another class for restaurant workers was inaugurated at the Wah Ying Restaurant on Stanley Street in the Central district of Hong Kong.[20]

In addition to a steady income, stable classes ensured that Ip Man's students would actually be able to gain some expertise in the system. Given the importance of word of mouth advertising to his business model (he never formally advertised his school), this was critical.[21] Specifically, as Leung Sheung and the other students began to build skills they quickly entered the world of roof-top challenge fights that were so prominent in this era of Hong Kong's history. Between 1951 and 1953 the initial successes of these Wing Chun pioneers attracted additional students.

Other aspects of Ip Man's reputation began to spread as well. Chu Shong Tin reports that his former teacher exuded a confident and stable Confucian glamour. This, combined with his easy sense of humor, attracted many young students who were looking for exactly such a mentor. Chu Shong Tin states quite openly that he idolized his Sifu and even moved into the Restaurant Workers Union Hall because of Ip Man's Confucian refinement and virtue.[22] It would appear that from the very start a variety of students were attracted to Ip Man and his teachings for slightly different reasons. Both his practical skills and the cultural values that he seemed to represent were sought after by the urbanized, and often displaced, youth of Hong Kong.

This diversification of his student base could not have been better timed. In 1953 Leung Sheung was defeated in a general election for union officers. Without his continuing support Ip Man lost the Restaurant Workers Union as a sponsor. As a result, he moved his main class to a new apartment on Hoi Tan Street. He also rented additional space where he taught evening classes and some of his advanced students at the Sam Tai Tze Temple (Temple of the Third Prince of Sea-Dragon) close to his new location on Yu Chau Street.[23]

While Ip Man was able to retain many of his earlier pupils, the move to Hoi Tan Street gave the new teacher a chance to further expand his student base. This move would ultimately free him from dependence on the internal politics of the Restaurant Workers Union. Yet, throughout the first period of his career, most of his students were far from wealthy.

When examining the students from this era another commonality appears. In addition to their trade, many of Ip Man's prominent early students share a common geographic or cultural bond. Leung Sheung, as we have already seen, was a master of the southern arts long before he met Ip Man. He already knew about Wing Chun and was simply looking for a teacher who could introduce him to the system.

A great example of how Ip Man built on these preexisting networks during the early stages of his career is his relationship with Jiu Wan. Jiu Wan (1921–1973) was the nephew of Jiu Chao, introduced previously in Chapter 4. Jiu Wan began to study Wing Chun with his cousin, Jiu Tong, who was a student of Chan Yiu Min in Foshan. Later he studied with his uncle, Jiu Chao, also a student of Chan Yiu Min. Various sources report that sometime between 1945 and 1949 Jiu Wan began to offer Wing Chun classes to the public at the Foshan Jingwu Association. Since Wing Chun was never part of Jingwu's official curriculum, it seems likely that Jiu was simply renting classroom space from the cash-strapped organization.

Jiu Wan followed his Uncle Jiu Chao into Foshan's police force, but he did not appear to have had a close relationship with Ip Man at the time. In 1949 he independently fled the Communist Party advance and eventually settled in Hong Kong. Jiu Wan got to know some of the employees of the Restaurant Workers Union and was introduced to Ip

Man. The two Foshan natives established a tight relationship and Jiu Wan followed his new teacher until his death in 1972.[24]

Another such student was Lee Shing (1923–1991). Lee was born in Guangdong Province. He was first introduced to Gulao (or side facing) Wing Chun by Fong Yee Ming (a grand-student of Leung Jan after his retirement from Foshan). As a young man Lee moved to Foshan where he had a chance to study with Ng Chung So. Sometime after WWII, Lee Shing moved to Hong Kong where he became friends with Jiu Wan. It was Jiu who introduced Lee to Ip Man in 1954.[25]

Jiu Wan, Lee Shing, and Ip Man represented the link with Wing Chun's mainland past. They were all familiar with how the art had been taught and propagated in Foshan prior to 1949. As such, Jiu and Lee quickly became aware of Ip Man's efforts to streamline both how the art was practiced and the ways it was explained and taught to a new generation of students. Despite these adaptations, both men remained staunch followers of their new sifu and continued to spread his vision of the art.[26]

Rather than relying on the complex philosophical frameworks of the eight trigrams and the five elements, Ip Man was explaining his actions in terms of physics and basic mechanics. He was dropping the poetic sayings that had traditionally been part of the Wing Chun teaching method, as well as pieces of equipment, such as the plum blossom poles, that were no longer practical for apartment dwellers.[27] Supposed secrets, like the "Five Elements Footwork" that had been part of the discussion of the second unarmed form (Chum Kiu) in Foshan, were unpacked and reintegrated into other places in the curriculum without the esoteric names and explanations. For that matter, Ip Man was the first Wing Chun teacher to adopt a formal curriculum to aid his teaching of the art. This helped to ensure that all students were being exposed to all parts of the system. In his new teaching method there were to be no secret techniques reserved only for the most faithful. If a student did not master all of the material in the curriculum it would be because he or she had quit or moved on, not because the teacher had withheld it.[28] This was a remarkably streamlined, modern, and egalitarian vision of martial arts instruction. It is also highly reminiscent of the arguments made by the Central Guoshu Institute in the 1930s.[29]

Ip Man also accelerated the learning process during the first three years of his teaching career. His goal appears to have been to get his students competently trained as soon as possible. Leung Ting speculates that this might have been a strategy for spreading the reputation of his relatively obscure art through success in challenge matches.[30]

This era also saw some of Ip Man's earliest efforts at building a larger institution to house his increasingly complex Wing Chun clan. After all, classes were mostly held in small apartments, on rooftops, and in public parks spread throughout the city. Ip Man even had students in Macao and back in Foshan. What was needed was a way to organize all of these students into a single body capable of financially supporting Ip Man and advancing the cause of Wing Chun. In 1953 Ip Man was photographed with a group of two dozen students under a banner that read "The Family of Wing Chun." A year later another group photo was taken of a body of students under a slightly updated banner that now read "The Family of Wing Chun: Foshan, Hong Kong and Macao." A year after that Ip was photographed with just the students from the Macao branch of his organization.[31]

While the Family of Wing Chun was later dissolved, it is the first evidence we have of Ip Man attempting to create a larger unified institution. This early group seemed to have enjoyed some organizational success and coherence prior to the setbacks of the mid-1950s. Ip Chun recalls that throughout the early 1950s he received regular remittances in the form of money orders that were derived from his father's teaching fees. These money orders were organized and mailed off by Leung Sheung. The payments stopped about the same time that controversy erupted in the Wing Chun clan in the middle of the 1950s.

While Ip Man's teaching career was starting to come together in the early 1950s, his personal life showed signs of escalating stress. Very little is known about his internal emotional landscape. Most acquaintances describe him as having an optimistic and somewhat irascible public face. Given some of the information in the more detailed accounts we can also conclude that he was occasionally unhappy and he missed his family. Ip Man had always been a family man, and even for someone as social and well-liked as he, exile is an isolating experience.

His relationship with his wife (Cheung Wing-sing) remains somewhat unclear. Ip Chun has discussed their marriage in a few interviews. He recalled that after the birth of his younger brother, Ip Ching, the family was not particularly well-off and often moved from place to place. But despite all this, his father and mother had a harmonious and graceful relationship. Their household life was characterized by the observance of customary gender roles. Ip Chun has described his mother as both virtuous and very traditional. She handled all of the household chores and saw it as her duty to be accommodating. Ip Man pursued his various hobbies and interests and was the public face of the family. While Ip Chun states that there were tensions and disagreements in his parent's marriage, he never saw them quarrel.

This picture of domestic harmony notwithstanding, one has to wonder how close Ip Man and his wife actually were on an emotional level. For instance, he apparently neglected to tell her that he was about to flee into exile, and let his eldest son (who had seen him off in Guangzhou) break the news to her. More interestingly, Ip Chun relates that the revelation that her husband would not be coming home anytime soon was received without any great concern by his mother.[32]

It may very well be that the gravity of what had just happened was not apparent to any of the parties involved. During the early 1950s Ip Man appears to have seen himself as making a place for his family in Hong Kong rather than accepting life without them. Chu Shong Tin reports that while generally upbeat and optimistic, traditional holiday celebrations such as New Years were hard on Ip Man and he complained about missing his family.[33] Further, the old Sifu was not sleeping well. Occasionally, he would walk the city until the early hours of the morning (often with a reluctant and increasingly sleep-deprived Chu Shong Tin in tow) before he could finally rest.[34]

Ip Man wrote frequent letters to his family and they were kept up to date on his address and location. When visiting him in July or August of 1951 Ip Chun had no problem finding his father at the Restaurant Workers Union, where he had just begun teaching. Evidently Ip Man was feeling confident about his career prospects as he requested that Ip Chun return to Foshan and make arrangements for his wife and remaining daughter to immigrate to Hong Kong. A short time later his mother and sister visited Hong Kong for a few days and were able to obtain the needed residency cards. Unfortunately, at that point they returned to Foshan. Apparently they needed to make further preparations before completing the move. His wife also still enjoyed a certain degree of luxury or comfort in Foshan and, given her somewhat distant relationship with her husband, may not have been enthusiastic about leaving.[35]

When Ip Man's daughter attempted to return to Hong Kong a few days later she discovered that the Chinese government had sealed the border. The realization that this new situation was permanent slowly dawned on individuals and families throughout the territory. Only then did the Chinese residents of Hong Kong appreciate their new status as a nation in exile. Ip Man's wife died of cancer in 1960 without ever returning to Kowloon.[36]

The first era of Ip Man's career was a period of struggle and adaptation. Between 1950 and 1953 we see his earliest attempts at building a school. He draws off of the advice from friends such as Chan Dao and taps into the preexisting social network of southern martial artists and Wing Chun practitioners. With the help of Lee Man, Chu Shong Tin, and Leung Sheung, Ip Man was able to secure the backing of a local labor union. Yet, in truth, his earliest efforts were not all that successful. High rates of student attrition were a serious issue. This led Ip Man to conclude that if his school was going to succeed it was necessary to seek a more diverse and financially stable student body. He also began to experiment with the style and pace of instruction in order to meet the demands of his followers and more effectively spread Wing Chun within Hong Kong's martial marketplace.

While Ip Man was eventually able to run multiple sets of classes throughout the city, something more was necessary to ensure his success. The working and middle classes were not all that interested in hand combat during the early years of the 1950s. They needed some reason to turn their attention back toward these traditional arts and to reconsider what role they played in their quickly evolving identities as inhabitants of the Chinese periphery. A tragic fire would fan the flames of change.

1954–1961: Ip Man and the Angry Young Men

John Hamm, in his careful investigation of Hong Kong's popular culture, notes that two stories dominated the headlines of the closing days of 1953 and the opening months of 1954. On Christmas Eve of 1953 a fire broke out in an area of Kowloon heavily populated with refugees. Fires are a major problem in any densely settled urban area. The Shek Kip Mei neighborhood, where the blaze was sparked, was particularly vulnerable because of the hastily built shacks, lacking any form of sanitation or electricity, which lined the streets. The fire burned for two days and caused a staggering amount of damage. Government officials noted that it was the single worst disaster in the city's history. Worse even than WWII. Close to 60,000 of Hong Kong's most vulnerable residents were left homeless and destitute.

Not all of the long-term effects of the fire were negative. The sheer magnitude of the human tragedy that had unfolded was a major shock to governments throughout the region. The American, British, and PRC governments came together in a rare show of solidarity with the Hong Kong administration in an attempt to extend humanitarian aid to the victims. For its part, the government of Hong Kong realized that it was now necessary to take much more proactive steps to extend its infrastructure, house the homeless, and fundamentally reimagine its relationship with the territory's expanding Chinese population. The fire proved to be a "wake-up call" in the truest sense of the phrase. Newspapers throughout Hong Kong carried extensive reporting on the tragedy, and this led to the mobilization of many groups and private charities within civil society. It was not long before the world of traditional martial arts found itself swept up in these events.[37]

The hand combat community in Hong Kong was facing a simmering conflagration of its own. In August 1953, a northern stylist by the name of Wu Gongyi (1900–1970) published an open letter declaring his willingness to fight any boxer from any style at any time or place. Wu, who was 53 at the time, was originally from Shanghai. He was the leader of the Hong Kong Jianquan Taiji Association. This group had originally been established by his father, Wu Jianquan (1870–1942), in 1937 after he fled the Japanese onslaught in the north. The Wu family Taiji lineage was quite prestigious. Wu Jianquan was the founder of the modern "Wu Style" Taiji lineage, and Wu Gongyi's grandfather, Wu Quanyou (1834–1902) was a disciple of Yang Luchan (1799–1872), the founder of "Yang style" Taiji. After 1949 Wu Jianquan permanently moved the headquarters of his late father's organization to Hong Kong.[38] Yet for all of his virtuosity he remained something of an outsider in his new homeland. The very fact that he, inheritor of the Wu Taiji style, found it necessary to issue such blanket challenges to southern martial artists suggests that he may have felt that he had something to prove.

Wu's inflammatory rhetoric did not go unheeded. Chen Kefu (35 at the time) led a White Crane school named the Taishan Fitness Academy in Macao.[39] Chen was a student of the much better known Wu Zhaozhong (1896–1967).[40] Wu was a native of Sanshui, a small town 15 km up the west branch of the Pearl River from Foshan, and an acknowledged master of the White Crane style. As a youth Wu studied with Zhu Ziyao in Jiangxi Province. During the 1920s he ran a school together with Gu Ru Zhang, an important northern Shaolin-style master in Guangzhou. In 1930, Wu moved to Hong Kong. Following the Japanese occupation of the city he moved once again to Macao in order to reestablish his school. In addition to his martial skills, Wu Zhaozhong was an author, a poet, an artist, and a practitioner of traditional Chinese medicine. Examples of his poetry and calligraphy are still sought at auction by private collectors today.[41] Given the stature of the teacher, it was quite significant when the student, Chen Kefu, took up Wu Gongyi's challenge.

The escalating war of words had been playing itself out for months in the Hong Kong press before the massive fire erupted in Kowloon. Hamm states that this rhetorical violence nearly became physical when supporters of both masters found themselves at a New Year's Eve banquet. This mass confrontation was the last straw, and on New Year's day, 1954, Wu and Chen signed a contract to fight in one month. Both sides went to some lengths to explain that the fight was not a duel (which would have been illegal anywhere) but rather the crowning moment of a martial arts exhibition to be held in Macao. The exhibition was to be a charitable event to raise money for a hospital and the victims of the Kowloon catastrophe.

It is interesting to note that the event was to be staged in the more free-wheeling Macao rather than British-controlled Hong Kong. Hamm reports that for years rumors circulated that the territory's officials would not sanction such a large and potentially explosive event. This refusal is in line with the general disdain for traditional hand combat demonstrated by elite members of Hong Kong's society and government.

Elite distaste notwithstanding, the ensuing fight generated a tremendous groundswell of enthusiasm among the city's mostly working- and middle-class citizens. Discussion, speculation, and wagering were intense in the weeks leading up to the match. Both masters displayed different styles and temperaments. Wu was both older and the more traditional of the two. Prior to the fight he retreated to a Buddhist temple to clear his mind, and he arrived at ringside wearing the long flowing robes of a traditional Confucian scholar.

While Wu had the advantage of experience, Chen was younger and stronger. His teacher's traditional background notwithstanding, Chen was almost a model of the modern, post-Jingwu/Guoshu, generation of martial artists. He studied a variety of styles including Japanese Judo and Western boxing in his quest for the most effective techniques. He jogged rather than meditated to clear his head, and he arrived at the ring wearing the robes of a Western boxer.

The two fighters differed in so many key respects that their conflict became iconic. Everything about what traditional Chinese martial arts had been, and what they were becoming, seemed to be on display when the referee presented the two opponents to the crowd. While existing footage of the match appears somewhat stilted by the standards of modern kickboxing or mixed martial arts, the two masters were determined to fight.

The contest was originally slated to last six rounds with no gloves and a wide range of allowable techniques. Much to the disappointment of the crowd, it was over in less than two. In the first round both boxers landed solid hits on their opponent's faces, leading to copious bleeding. This was compounded by the fact that neither martial artist seemed interested in guarding his face or attempting to slip or counter his opponent's punches. Neither individual seemed entirely comfortable in the ring and both lacked the basic experience and skills that would be considered necessary for such a high profile contest today.

The second round opened with a series of head shots followed by some kicks. At that point the judges stepped in and stopped the fight. Ostensibly they were concerned that if the contest were allowed to go on one or both of the fighters would be seriously hurt. Of course that is the entire point of a duel, but such norms did not fit easily into the realities of modern spectator sports. Amazingly, the judges declared the fight over without announcing a winner, or any official outcome.

The seemingly anticlimactic end to the fight turned out to be another boon for Hong Kong's daily newspapers. It allowed for weeks of speculation and discussion of what had *really* happened and what it all meant. While the outcome of Wu and Chen's match remained unsettled, some things did start to become clear. To begin with, there was a massive latent demand for, and interest in, the martial arts that was not being met in Hong Kong. Within weeks of the match martial arts schools were swamped with students, and newspapers, always looking for ways to increase their readership base, were beginning to push a new generation of serialized wuxia novels into the hands of an eager reading public. Jin Yong's first novel, *The Book and the Sword*, was a direct result of the interest created by the fight in Macao.[42]

This sudden increase in awareness proved to be more than just a passing fad. Jin Yong would go on to publish over a dozen novels and would become the top-selling modern Chinese author of all time in any genera. Likewise, the mid-1950s saw the start of a boom in enrollment in traditional martial arts schools that lasted well into the 1980s. The reemergence of hand combat in Hong Kong was more than a fad because it seemed to speak to a number of issues plaguing the territory's people, especially those at the lower end of the socio-economic spectrum. The duel between Chen and Wu reaffirmed the inherent strength and value of Chinese culture while leaving unresolved the issue of how it would evolve in the future. By turning the challenge match into a massive charitable event, the fight further demonstrated that the people of Hong Kong, even in a moment of great need, were not totally reliant on handouts. They could help themselves, and in that way maintain their dignity.

Moving the fight to Macao gave the entire proceeding a slightly subversive air. Interest in traditional Chinese martial arts once again became a way of establishing identity, of seeing who was truly in touch with their heritage. Participation in hand combat schools was an effective way of establishing individuality and resisting one's status both as a refugee and colonized individual precisely because the dominant social powers saw it as a subversive act. Press coverage in the early months of 1954 helped to establish a discourse that defined the traditional martial arts as a defense of not only the people's physical strength and security, but their moral and ethical "face" as well.

It goes without saying that this turn of events proved to be a much needed windfall for Hong Kong's entire hand combat establishment. Public schools, such as Ip Man's, enjoyed the benefits of all of this free publicity in the form of increased enrollment and enthusiasm. Novelists and movie directors started to increase their output of martial arts stories to meet a seemingly bottomless demand.

Still, this popularity would pose its own challenges. The new students who enrolled in Ip Man's schools were, in some ways, different from those that he encountered in the early years. Wing Chun would only succeed insofar as it could be adapted to meet the demands of this evolving clientele.

The volatile year of 1954 also presented Ip Man with more concrete challenges, such as navigating the reality of Hong Kong's perennially cramped real estate market. After Leung Sheung was defeated in a union election in 1953, Ip Man moved his school to the fourth floor of a Hoi Tan Street building. He also rented additional space at the Sam Tai Tze Temple. While this move probably helped Ip to begin to establish an independent student base, the situation was not ideal. Later in 1954 Leung Sheung managed to regain office in the Restaurant Workers Union, and Ip Man returned to teach classes at their building.[43]

Despite the frequent moves, Ip Man's classes grew quickly in this period. Students such as Wong Shun Leung and William Cheung, both of whom would go on to become leading lights in the spread and promotion of Wing Chun, joined the school at this time. Chan Chee Man, another student from the middle period of Ip Man's career, described what life at the school was like in the mid-1950s.

> I remember that I practiced Siu Nim Tao [the introductory form] for quite a long time, a month and a half just doing Siu Nim Tao. I remember Sifu always come around when I'm tired and say, "oh, go and play Siu Nim Tao again." I never complain that he teaches me too slow, never. Because at that time I really liked Ving Tsun. So every night we would go to the Union to practice from 7 to half past 9. After half past 9 Yip Man Sifu would go to the temple. At the temple, Sifu met the Tong Jong students, the older students to practice. So at the temple there was a wall, and there was another guy who taught another style of kung fu. So William Cheung at the time was very naughty, and another guy, I can't remember who. We used to climb up the wall and watch. How could other people learn this kung fu? We used to laugh and talk about it. So we are hiding on the wall, and then Sifu would walk by. So one of Sifu's Todai met him on the street and spoke to him. Yip Man Sifu got very angry, he goes in the temple and says, "who climb up the wall and watch people and say something?" I and William Cheung knew it was us. Since then Ip Man says no one is to climb up the wall.[44]

The previous story is very illuminating. It demonstrates that by 1954 Ip Man was teaching multiple groups of students, even if he was still holding his main classes at the Union. Many of these new students were much younger than the professional restaurant workers who had made up the bulk of his classes a few years earlier. In addition to the multiple evening sessions of class (both at the Union and at the temple) Chan Chee Man also states that Ip Man had an earlier morning session, but that this was much less well attended.[45]

Another interesting detail of Chan Chee Man's experience is how he was introduced to Wing Chun. Originally, Chan was a student of Choy Li Fut. He was also involved in a burgeoning youth movement that revolved around street fighting. Rather than simply brawling, these fights often took the form of "beimo," a type of semi-organized challenge fighting that occurred on the rooftops or in the cellars of various Hong Kong buildings. These matches lacked protective gear and time limits, often resulting in knockouts or other injuries, and were embedded in a larger culture of youth delinquency that various officials had already identified as a problem.

Chan Chee Man knew William Cheung and was aware that he was a Wing Chun student. Not knowing much about his style he challenged William to a fight, attended by about thirty of their mutual friends, and was soundly beaten. Chan was so surprised by the outcome that he decided to change styles. He was instructed by his old Choy Li Fut teacher that if he was going to study Wing Chun he needed to seek out Ip Man.

This youth culture of violence with its stylized challenge matches (while they did not have protective gear, they often had "rounds" and "judges") did much to accelerate the growth of Wing Chun. Prior to 1949, few residents of Hong Kong, other than southern martial arts aficionados, had ever heard of the style. During the 1930s and 1940s, Wing Chun never spread that much beyond the Foshan area. And, while Ip Man had succeeded in establishing a school, he showed very little interest in advertising his own business.

Wing Chun's reputation spread by word of mouth, and as often as not the mouths that were speaking were those who had seen Wong Shun Leung, William Cheung, or some other student winning a fight. Wong in particular built his reputation on being a vicious street fighter. His students claim that in his career he won between 60 and 100 matches (accounts differ). William Cheung, Duncan Leung, Hawkins Cheung, and Bruce Lee were all involved in the world of beimo to one degree or another. Ip Man seems to have even encouraged this behavior, to a certain degree, in the mid-1950s. He firmly believed that experience was a masterful teacher and that students should not be afraid of fighting. Speaking in an interview Hawkins Cheung recalled:

> Back in the 1950s, Yip Man trained us to fight, not be technicians. Because we were so young, we didn't understand the concepts or theories. As he taught us, Yip Man said "Don't believe me, as I may be tricking you. Go out and have a fight. Test it out." In other words, Yip Man taught us the distance applications of Wing Chun. First he told us to go out and find practitioners of other styles and test our wing chun on them. If we lost, we knew on what we should work. We would go out and test our techniques again. We thought to ourselves, "Got to make that technique work! No excuses!" We learned by getting hit.[46]

It seems quite clear that in the 1950s Ip Man explicitly taught Wing Chun as a fighting art. Ip Ching even relates a comical story in which his father took a student, who was afraid of fighting, out onto the street and attempted to provoke a conflict with a random stranger just to help his pupil move past his phobia.[47]

There was always an undeniably fiery and mercurial element to Ip Man's personality. Even as a senior citizen his youthful temperament would occasionally show through. Yet these elements did not dominate his personality or his public performance of the role of "Sifu." It would be a serious mistake to think that he was an overly violent individual, or that he ran a violent school. Nothing could be further from the truth. As a matter of fact, Hawkins Cheung provides us with some of the most valuable reminisces of life in the Wing Chun clan in this period. He points out that while Ip Man's students were often angry young men, he remained a model of calm and detached behavior.

> I always got pushed out when I practiced chi sao with my bigger seniors. Everyone who learned wing chun always wanted to prove that they were better than others. Most of the practitioners concentrated on the offensive side of sticking hands . . . Whoever was stronger would win. Egos ran wild and everyone wanted to be the best. . . .
>
> During that period I had a hard time. I thought of quitting a few times, until I finally went to the Old Man (grandmaster Yip Man). He always told me, "Relax! Relax! Don't get excited!" But whenever I practiced chi sao with someone, it was hard to relax, especially when I got hit. I became angry when struck. I wanted to kill my opponent. The sticking hands game became a fight, with both parties getting hurt . . .
>
> When I saw Yip Man stick hands with others, he was very relaxed and talked to his partner. Sometimes he threw his partner without having to hit him. When I stuck hands with Yip Man I always felt my balance controlled when I attempted to strike . . . He never landed a blow on his students, but he would put a student in an awkward position and make the fellow students laugh at the sight. He was the funniest old man . . . Yip Man never exhibited a killing attitude. The

students would swing their hands, and Yip Man would smile and merely control the movements.[48]

The preceding stories not only shed light on Ip Man's later teaching style, but they reveal a fundamental tension within the Wing Chun clan. The art, at its heart, revolved around the very real specter of violence. Kowloon in the mid-1950s was a violent place, and young martial arts students of the period insisted on making it even more so through their challenge fights and petty gang rivalries. It was the promise of becoming stronger and more formidable that attracted many new pupils in this period. Like so many students before and after, Hawkins Cheung and his friends came to Wing Chun seeking personal transformation.

Wong Shun Leung, William Cheung, Duncan Leung, Hawkins Cheung, and Bruce Lee were all restless young men who sought to perfect the art of Wing Chun to become tougher and more respected. Yet it is not always clear why this should have been the case. Martial arts were usually taken up by the working class and other marginal groups as a means of self-protection or employment. With the exception of William Cheung, none of these individuals were "marginal" according to the social definitions of the day. Duncan Leung, Hawkins Cheung, and Bruce Lee all came from wealthy backgrounds, not all that dissimilar to what Ip Man had enjoyed a generation earlier. Bruce Lee in particular had the privilege of being thrown out of some of the finest schools in Hong Kong on account of his reckless behavior and spotty educational attainment.

This new generation of students was younger and wealthier than Ip Man's pupils from earlier in the decade. Yet they were no happier and, by any measure, were poorly socially adjusted. All of these teenagers were a product of the post-1949 period. They were the result of a process of dual marginalization by the Chinese state on the mainland, and the British-controlled government that colonized the territory. While their families had succeeded, they were acutely aware of how limiting Hong Kong's horizons were. In fact, all of these individuals would end up leaving their homeland in order to achieve their greatest success and recognition. In retrospect, the frustration that these youths felt is understandable.

With little prior teaching experience, Ip Man must receive a great deal of credit for finding ways to reach his younger and more impatient students. When dealing with such pupils, Hawkins Cheung described how the elderly master would teach his students the entry and distance fighting techniques they wanted to know, and then allow them to go out and test them for themselves. Only when they discovered the inevitable shortcomings of such an approach were they ready to be introduced to the more sophisticated side of the art.

At the same time, encouraging one's students to go out and engage in illegal fights with other martial artists or street gangs has some drawbacks as a pedagogical strategy. By today's standards this would be considered unethical and illegal, and that is exactly how straight-laced Hong Kong society viewed it during the mid-1950s. Readers of modern martial arts history should not be confused by the glorified accounts of Wong Shun Leung or Bruce Lee's early exploits. These fights were dangerous affairs, and the individuals who participated in them, or promoted them, were criminals in the eyes of Hong Kong's law enforcement officers.

Ip Man thus found himself on the horns of a dilemma. It was unlikely that he would be able to totally control the actions of this growing body of younger, more "enthusiastic," students. And participation in illicit street fighting was helping to build the reputation of Wing Chun as a fearsome form of hand combat. Yet the increasingly aggressive tactics of Wong Shun Leung and the others were starting to pose a threat to the long-term welfare of the Wing Chun clan.

Modern accounts written from within the Chinese martial arts community tend to minimize the dark underside of the beimo youth subculture, but anthropologist Daniel Amos has noted how disruptive it was to his main informant, a Southern Mantis master in Kowloon during the 1960s and 70s named "Sifu Peng."[49] Master Peng's home village was demolished by the territorial government of Hong Kong to make way for a new housing project in the early 1960s. Peng, along with his family, were relocated to the "New Market Town" area of Kowloon in the mid-1960s where he was given a small apartment out of which he ran his martial arts classes (much the same as Ip Man).

Some of the other local schools viewed his arrival as a provocation. His students were involved in a series of challenge matches with another master and his disciples that lasted more than a year. After a final particularly bloody fight involving large numbers of students from both schools, the Hong Kong police descended on Master Peng's home. Even though it was determined that he was not the aggressor in this situation, both Master Peng and his students were detained by the police, subjected to intense interrogation, and photographed before being ultimately released.[50]

This incident clearly illustrates the dual dangers of youth challenge fights. First, an escalating pattern of injuries, defeats, and vengeance could lead to a virtual war breaking out between opposed schools. Second, too many injuries or arrests would bring down the police. As we have already seen, they strongly believed that there was a link between martial arts schools, Triad criminal behavior, and juvenile delinquency. As injury and enmity mounted, it became evident that what Wong and his friends were doing was unsustainable.

In 1956, a year of important developments, the seemingly nomadic Ip Man moved his school to a new location on Lee Tat Street in Yau Ma Tei. This was the actual gym that greeted such notable new students as Bruce Lee and Hawkins Cheung. Further, the local beimo culture escalated to a fevered pitch. Wong Shun Leung seems to have targeted a local Chu Southern Mantis clan for particular attention. Again, the pattern of violence between the two schools began to escalate uncomfortably. Eventually, outside mediation had to be employed to settle the situation.

Even after this dispute was resolved Ip Man's school, and its neighbors, did not enjoy peace. Youth fights flared up resulting in a general conflict with a local White Crane clan. Once again Ip Man turned to outside mediation to broker a peace. This time the new understanding between the two organizations was mediated by Mr. Chan Yuet Fat. While a member of the White Crane clan he was also the swimming coach of Wong Shun Leung's younger brother. The restoration of normal relations was celebrated with a large feast at the Mun Ting Fang Restaurant in Mongkok, Kowloon. The dinner was attended only by the senior members of both clans who took the opportunity to discuss their differences in a less public setting.[51]

The full ramifications of these fights were not confined to just the local martial arts community. A few years later, in 1958, Bruce Lee's mother determined that if her son stayed in Hong Kong he would end up in real trouble with the law. She encouraged him to immigrate to the United States and claim his citizenship (Lee had been born in the U.S. while his parents were touring with a Cantonese opera company). Eventually her husband and son warmed to the idea of a fresh start.

When Bruce applied for travel papers to leave the country he discovered that both he and his friend Hawkins Cheung were on a watch list of known juvenile delinquents. Lee attempted to go to the police to tidy things up, but whatever he said did not impress them, and evidently made things worse. Cheung's parents soon received a visit from the police to question them about their son's anti-social behavior and "gang activities." Fortunately, both the Lee and the Cheung families were quite wealthy and so, after paying off the police, their children were both allowed to leave Hong Kong to study in the United States and Australia.[52] Still, Lee and Cheung were not the major challenge fighters of this period, and the entire incident makes one wonder what sort of file the police were keeping on the much more violent Wong Shun Leung, William Cheung, and even Ip Man.

Other major developments also began to emerge in these years. Between the end of 1955 and 1957, a number of Ip Man's senior students left to establish schools of their own. The first of these was Leung Sheung, Ip Man's first and perhaps his best trained disciple, who branched out with his master's full blessing. Jiu Wan, who had previously taught Wing Chun in Foshan, and Lee Shing, also an experienced martial artist, began to take on students of their own. Like Leung they continued to acknowledge Ip as the master of the Hong Kong Wing Chun clan and retained an affiliation with his school.[53] While much less experienced, it appears that Wong Shun Leung and William Chun also started to teach a number of junior students during the 1950s. In fact, much of Bruce Lee and Hawkins Cheung's instruction was actually provided by their older kung fu brothers, intent on setting up their own studios.[54]

While Ip Man continued to run the "mother" school of the burgeoning Wing Chun clan, he began to take a less active role in the day-to-day details of instruction. Demonstrating forms and techniques was increasingly left to the senior students. There are a number of possible explanations for this. The most obvious would be that Ip Man had always considered his school to be a sort of retirement job. By 1957 he was 64 years old. After settling the Wing Chun clan's accounts with the other local schools and having seen some of his best students go on to open studios of their own, he may have simply wished to adopt the more supervisory role of "master." It should be remembered that in many, perhaps most, traditional kung fu schools the actual leader of the school rarely takes the floor to lead classes himself. Instead, he supervises from the sidelines, offering comments or criticism while the senior students provide most of the actual instruction. In that sense Ip Man seems to have been following a well-established behavioral norm.

Nevertheless, a few authors have portrayed this change in his routine in a less positive light. Rumors of drug use first emerged in our discussion of Ip Man and his relationship with Ng Chung So back in Foshan in the 1920s and 1930s. According to some sources, Ng conducted his classes in the backroom of a local opium den, and a number of wealthy Wing Chun practitioners from the period have been accused of using opium themselves. These charges are impossible to substantiate, and we have treated them as rumors. However, some of Ip Man's later students have stated that he either never stopped using narcotics or perhaps relapsed during the mid-1950s. He is rumored to have used either opium or heroin, both of which were increasingly expensive in Hong Kong.

Duncan Leung has made the claim that Ip Man would only teach his most advanced techniques (including the wooden dummy form) to those students who could pay him exorbitant sums of money to support his growing drug habit. Since Duncan Leung came from a very wealthy family he was able to buy a "secret discipleship" with Ip Man, and hence he learned the entire system which was rarely passed on.[55] Obviously, one must treat such accounts with caution. Not only does Leung make a serious criminal accusation without offering any supporting evidence, but he does so in a way that seems calculated to bolster his legitimacy within the Wing Chun clan. After all, if only he could afford to pay for the true teachings, why should students follow instructors from outside his lineage?

A single self-serving account would be easy to dismiss. However, Leung Ting relates a similar, if not identical, tale. According to him, Ip Man actually became involved with a woman who was supposedly a drug addict and generally a bad influence on the aging Sifu. Depressed by his lack of economic success and dragged down by a destructive relationship, Leung Ting claims that Ip Man started to take heroin. His involvement in his classes became erratic and many students left his organization. In order to raise the money necessary to buy drugs he sold sections of the dummy, long pole, and knife forms. Still, if one could simply buy the knife form, one wonders why so few of Ip Man's senior students took advantage of the opportunity. Leung Ting further comments that this was happening at about the time that Ip Man accepted Bruce Lee as a student. Lee later went to Wong Shun Leung and William Cheung because he felt that there was little actual instruction happening at the main school.

Leung Ting does not stop the story there. He goes on to include a redemption narrative. Realizing that his drug habit was destroying his school and his life, Ip Man is said to have locked himself in a bedroom for a week with nothing but a wall bag. As the pain of withdrawal mounted he punched the bag ferociously until both it and his fists were destroyed. It was his dedication to the practice of Wing Chun that helped to save the master from addiction. Free from his demons, Ip Man went on to be a much more active and energetic teacher in the last period of his career.[56]

While a more attractive story than Duncan Leung's, there are a number of problems with this account. To begin with, all of these events supposedly took place years before Leung Ting's actual association with Ip Man's Wing Chun clan. He could not have witnessed any of this for himself. Nor is he forthcoming about the sources of his information. As such, we are left with a rumor, and one that does seem to be tied to Leung Ting's persistent claims to have a "better" version of Wing Chun than Ip Man's other students from the prior periods.

Another problem is how little collaborating evidence there is for all of this. To use modern addiction parlance, there is not any evidence that Ip Man ever hit "rock bottom" before recovering from his downward spiral. And it seems unlikely that anyone could really beat a serious heroin addiction simply by being locked in a bedroom for a week.

There are also a number of detailed accounts of Ip Man's school and teaching from this period that fail to give any indication at all that his life was spiraling out of control. Hawkins Cheung, in a series of articles written for *Inside Kung Fu* magazine in 1991 and 1992, explained his relationship with Bruce Lee and his thoughts on Jeet Kune Do, the style that his friend developed after moving to America. Yet these articles are valuable to us because he paints an incredibly vivid and detailed portrait of what life was like inside the Wing Chun clan during the mid to late 1950s.

His description demonstrates that most daily instruction of the younger students was not handled by Ip Man himself. Yet he is not portrayed as being detached, self-absorbed, or stoned. Rather, Cheung recalls him walking around the classes, giving advice, correcting mistakes, and practicing chi sao with the senior students all while chatting about the day's news and exemplifying a charming sense of humor. The Ip Man portrayed in these articles is a brilliant teacher who, when faced with a cadre of angry young rich men, perhaps the single most difficult demographic to guide, found innovative ways to reach his students. While he did not handle the routine daily instruction, when there was a problem Ip Man was standing right there to offer sage advice and to help move students to the next level of understanding.[57]

While less detailed, and generally shorter, Darrell Jordan has collected a number of interviews with Ip Man's early students in his book

The Sound of Ving Tsun. Again, each of these individuals remembers their Sifu as someone who was very much present and a part of their learning experience. None of them portrays an individual spinning out of control.[58]

In short, it seems impossible to reconcile the assertions of Duncan Leung and Leung Ting with the eyewitness accounts of a number of Ip Man's other students at the time. The two sets of sources do not seem to depict the same reality. In one set of accounts Ip Man is begging for money to get high and actively selling his techniques, while in the other he is an island of stability with an uncanny knack for understanding the psychology of his students. Nor is there any evidence of Ip Man relapsing or using drugs in the last years of his career (the period on which we have the most actual information). In this case, it seems safer to go with the more conservative firsthand accounts rather than the later rumors published by Leung Ting and others.

While it is hard to know what to make of the rumors of drug abuse, Ip Man did face another much more public scandal in the middle of the 1950s that did disrupt his school and reputation. At some point around 1955, he entered into a romantic relationship with a woman (probably around 50 years old) from Shanghai. The identity of the woman is not known with certainty. It is known that she had an adult son named Shaohua, and that she was about ten years younger than her new partner. Ip Man never called her by any title (other than the "Shanghai Po" or Shanghai Lady) when talking with his students, and he never formally introduced her to his own sons when they eventually rejoined him in Hong Kong.[59] This strange silence notwithstanding, their relationship was a somewhat public and long-lasting one.

Ip Chun recalls that his father's mistress would often come to the apartment for lengthy visits during the days (even during classes), but that she never stayed overnight. Likewise, Ip Man often visited her at her place of residence. The relationship apparently lasted in one form or another from 1955 until 1968 when the Shanghai Lady finally succumbed to cancer. She was hospitalized at a remote hospice for the last month of her life. Ip Chun reports that, despite the difficulty of getting to her hospital in those days, he accompanied his father to visit her three times in the final weeks of her life. Despite this, his father never formally introduced the two and their conversations remained private.[60]

It is surprisingly difficult to find any firsthand accounts of Ip Man's extramarital affair, despite the fact that it was carried on in public for a number of years. There are few, if any, hints of her existence in the student descriptions of the mid-1950s and the 1960s. This might lead some readers to suspect that the affair was not considered to be a serious matter. After all, while second marriages had become markedly less common in the rapidly modernizing cityscape of Hong Kong, for a member of the gentry of Ip Man's generation, such relationships were not particularly rare. If Ip Man had been in business such a liaison would likely not have garnered much attention beyond his immediate family.

Yet, for Ip Man's followers and colleagues, this relationship was extremely important and embarrassing. It caused an uproar that led many students to simply walk out, and his reputation for "martial virtue" was tarnished. We have already seen that many of Ip Man's senior disciples left to set up their own schools in the mid-1950s, around the time that this affair came to light. Further, the elderly Sifu's economic situation was degraded to the point that he was forced to cease sending remittances to his family on the mainland and had to relocate his school multiple times between 1954 and 1956.[61]

In order to better understand the types of identities that were cultivated in Hong Kong's traditional martial arts community it may be worth asking exactly why the revelation of an extramarital affair had such a devastating impact on Ip Man's school. The key to this puzzle lays in Chu Shong Tin's earlier testimony that he, and many other young adults in the early 1950s, followed Ip Man because he exuded an air of Confucian glamour. They reacted strongly and positively to this traditional influence.

It is easy to read such a portrayal without giving it much thought, especially since Ip Man was a member of the new gentry and he did have a Confucian background and education. However, Chu Shong Tin's statement needs to be further unpacked. To begin with, the average Chinese citizen in this period would probably not identify traditional hand combat teachers as being particularly "Confucian." For the last thousand years real Confucian scholars had been eschewing the use of force and the cultivation of martial virtues. Force was to be used only as a last resort, and any use of power not strictly under the control of the state was subversion bordering on rebellion. Ip Man, and pretty much every other private martial arts teacher, would have been the natural enemy of a true conservative Confucian thinker during the late imperial period.

What Chu Shong Tin probably means is that Ip Man represented a way of being an adult male that was simultaneously traditional, independent, and virtuous. He was able to carve out a life for himself in the perilous "land of rivers and lakes" while at the same time maintaining an air of virtue and ethics. He succeeded in the present without forgetting the past. In short, he must have seemed like a living embodiment of the National Essence Movement.

Boretz, in his ethnography of martial arts, masculinity, and ritual violence, notes the same basic paradox in his field of study. He asks, how does one "become a man" in the world of rivers and lakes? Gender, and the range of values that go along with it, is not something that one is necessarily born with. Rather, Boretz claims that these things must be enacted by the individual. In traditional Chinese society the central masculine (or yang) values all had to do with self-restraint and transcendence. Yin (female) values were shadowy, changeable, and threatened chaos.

In a lineage-based structure, the way that an individual performed his appropriate masculine role was to submerge his personal desires and to defer to his father and elder brothers. Only by showing restraint, by waiting for tomorrow rather than seizing power by force today, could this individual show himself to be a proper Confucian patriarch. Self-restraint was the foundation of manhood.

This system begins to generate a number of problems once we bring questions of class into the picture. The prior discussion of restraint presupposed that there was a lineage and a family fortune that existed independently of the actor. In the world of working-class laborers, petty criminals, and martial artists, this is almost never the case. Lacking a family or lineage to inherit, traditional Chinese society did view these actors as being somehow less than "true" men. It became imperative that a new language of gender and resistance be created that would allow the denizens of the world of rivers and lakes to argue that, in fact, they too were capable of being "men" in the traditional Chinese cultural sphere.

Again, self-restraint and denial became the key to enacting male values and martial virtue.[62] Chinese martial artists often speak of the importance of "eating bitter" during the course of hand combat instruction. In some schools this takes the form of sadistic training regimes that have little actual physical value, offering only pain. In extreme cases, these activities can even be damaging. Yet, by cultivating self-transcendence, they are seen as the key to developing martial virtue in students.

Sexual relations are another area where self-control has become a critical marker of martial virtue. Confucian gentlemen can promise to abstain from violence in ways that professional martial artists or petty criminals simply cannot. However, these socially marginal individuals can instead abstain from sexual relations as a way of demonstrating their self-control and martial virtue.

Types of behavior that were seen as common for the wealthy (having multiple wives, engaging in affairs, or frequenting prostitutes) become strictly taboo for the hero in the mythic world of rivers and lakes. This attitude evolved into a common trope in martial arts fiction where the virtuous warrior is also sexually abstinent. Women who sleep around, and their lovers, inevitably become the antagonists in these stories who "get what is coming to them" in the end. Taking these basic principles to the extreme, some of the traditional works of Chinese martial arts fiction exhibit an almost shocking degree of misogyny. Women are seen as so polluting and so problematic that there are few female protagonists, and those who do exist usually demonstrate their virtue by reflecting the exclusively male values of the world around them. In a very real sense, the only way to be a "good" female martial artist in these stories is to cease to be a woman at all.[63]

This cultural complex, seen in so many Chinese martial arts legends and novels, is one of the things that actually makes the Wing Chun creation myth so interesting. Stories that revolve around women, and advocate the adoption of explicitly Yin values, strike at the very heart of most traditional southern kung fu mythmaking.[64] The fact that Wing Chun was originally the product of the Foshan bourgeois, and not the working class, may account for some of these symbolic and mythic differences. Yet, by the middle of the 1950s, Ip Man's economically and socially marginal students in Hong Kong were fully indoctrinated into the more romanticized elements of the Hung Mun martial identity.

An interesting asymmetry between Ip Man and his students now begins to emerge. In reality Ip Man was never fully a resident of the world of rivers and lakes. He had enjoyed a life and career under very different circumstances back in Foshan, prior to 1949. His values and his view of himself reflect these earlier circumstances. Further, Ip Man explicitly rejected the realm of popular kung fu legends and mythmaking. For him the martial arts were practical and simple. They existed as a set of principles independent from Confucianism and tales of wandering monks with amazing Qi abilities.

Yet he was never able to fully initiate his students into this worldview. Many of them came to him precisely because of the "traditional" values he seemed to represent. Even though he explicitly rejected the premise of the entire discussion, they continued to see him as the "little old Chinese man" who starred in so many kung fu stories. They used him in this way because such a mentor was a necessary figure in *their* drama of personal resistance. Throughout the Hong Kong years a tension existed between Ip Man and how he understood Wing Chun, and his students who seem to have imagined the traditional martial arts differently.

Ip Man's affair was quite understandable from his point of view. The old master was lonely without his family. Further, by the mid-1950s he must have realized that this separation would be permanent. Taking a second wife, while no longer fashionable, wasn't all that surprising given his social and geographic background.

According to his students, Ip Man had just violated the central tenant of martial virtue. Worse yet, he turned to a northern immigrant. The aura of "Confucian glamour" that Chu Shong Tin described was crushed. His students found that they had to choose between their own overly romanticized view of the martial arts and their teacher as he actually was. It seems that a great many chose the illusion.

The incident proved to be quite economically damaging to Ip Man and his school. Further, the next generation of students that he recruited was in general younger, more aggressive, and less interested in traditional Chinese culture and values than the ones who had come before. Eventually Ip Man was able to rebuild his organization, but it seemed to take on a different, more practical, character after the middle of the 1950s. These changes may have also contributed to an evolution in his teaching style as he struggled to retain old students and attract new ones.

There does seem to be some truth to the assertion that Ip Man stepped up his teaching of the wooden dummy, pole, and butterfly knives (the advanced techniques of the style) during this period. There is no more iconic piece of training equipment within the Wing Chun system than the wooden dummy. Evidently Ip Man did not feel that he had the time, space, and requisite number of advanced students to commission the construction of a wooden dummy until 1956.

Making one was a challenge because traditionally the body of a dummy is planted deep in the ground to give it a certain amount of stability. The hole around the dummy was then packed with small reeds and gravel so that the dummy would have some give when hit. The reality of apartment living made it impossible to construct a traditional style dummy, even though it is a critical aspect of the system.

In the mid-1950s Ip Man commissioned his friend Fung Shek to construct a modified dummy. After discussing the proper measurements, Fung began to work on a new mounting system. He suspended the body of the dummy on horizontal wooden slats that were supple and springy. This allowed the training device to slide to the side, or fall back, and then return to its original position when struck or kicked.

Ip Man kept Fung Shek's original dummy for the rest of his life. It can now be seen on display at the Ip Man Tong museum in Foshan. Soon afterward Fung made about ten dummies for other schools and instructors in the growing Wing Chun clan. Unfortunately, his son was killed in a tragic car accident. Fung interpreted this as retribution by the local gods for his part in the training of people who beat up and bullied others. From that point on he refused to make another one, and it would be a few years before the Wing Chun clan found a steady supply of dummies.[65]

The previous story is illuminating; it not only illustrates the sorts of innovations that were happening during the mid-1950s, but it also demonstrates the degree to which hand combat training remained a marginal and potentially tainted pursuit. These same perceptions applied to the Wing Chun clan as well. In fact, their frequent participation in challenge matches probably made them particularly suspect. Respectable citizens could expect only social, and possibly cosmic, retribution for venturing too far into the realm of rivers and lakes.

In 1957 Ip Man moved both his home and school once again, settling this time into the Li Cheng UK Estate, part of a large housing complex in Kowloon. Apparently this address did not last long, and in 1958 records indicate that his school was relocated to the Shek Kip Mei neighborhood, just a few blocks to the east.[66] This district had been the site of the 1953 fire that destroyed the refugee shanty towns. The government had since rebuilt the entire area with multistory housing units to shelter Hong Kong's growing population. Ironically, the same tragedy that contributed to the social momentum behind the reemergence of the traditional martial arts now provided Ip Man with a new neighborhood in which to spread his style.

1962–1972: Consolidating a Legacy

Throughout the mid to late 1950s Ip Man built a school that was known and respected in Hong Kong's hand combat community. In 1949, few martial artists had even heard of Wing Chun. Ip Man began to change this by teaching literally hundreds of students in classes across the territory. His younger and more energetic students also made a name for the art with their frequent challenges and street fights. By the early 1960s Wing Chun was a well-established system being taught in at least half a dozen studios by instructors trained by and loyal to Ip Man. Building such an organization with few resources and no institutional support in only a decade was a remarkable feat.

Nevertheless, the 1960s and 1970s were an era of rapid social and economic change. New opportunities and challenges were always on the horizon and martial arts schools, just like any other form of voluntary organization, were forced to adapt if they wished to survive. One of the more interesting puzzles to emerge out of the last few chapters is how Chinese hand combat schools have managed to maintain such an air of timeless tradition when they are forced to reinvent themselves, often in fundamental ways, in each generation.

It seems that Ip Man himself was consumed by many of these same thoughts and fears. During the final period of his career the old master sought to build an organization that would strengthen the Wing Chun clan while leaving it the flexibility necessary to survive in an uncertain world. Institution building was an important project in the last years of his life. As part of this effort Ip Man consciously turned away from some of the more radical and anti-social aspects of his art and worked to create a system that could appeal to middle-class professional students, including doctors, lawyers, and police officers. As Hong Kong's civil society found greater order, its culture of social rebellion and youth delinquency came under tighter surveillance and control. Adaptations were necessary to ensure the survival of the art, and these changes tended to push Wing Chun away from its older parochial identity.

Of course some things remained the same throughout this later period, including Ip Man's propensity for hunting down new real estate. In 1961 he moved his school once again, this time settling in the Hing Ip Building on Castle Peak road.[67] The venue allowed Ip Man to reach a new set of students. In the same year he also concluded a deal with the union of the Kowloon Bus Company to provide martial arts instruction to their members at a reduced rate. This relationship lasted for a number of years, and it is just one more example of the historic ties between Wing Chun and organized labor.[68]

While there are questions about how much Ip Man charged for tuition in the earlier periods, we can be relatively certain what his business practices were like from the early 1960s on. In 1961 and 1962 students were charged 15 Hong Kong dollars a month for night classes, or

10 Hong Kong dollars for the less crowded afternoon class. Members of the transportation union and bus company enjoyed a further discounted rate. To put this in perspective, the average worker in Hong Kong earned between 200 and 250 Hong Kong dollars a month in the early 1960s. Ip Man's tuition ranged from 4 percent to 8 percent of a worker's average salary.[69] This does appear to be somewhat more than what other Wing Chun instructors charged their students. Still, his tuition in this period was no more costly than what many students in North America or Europe pay today.

At this point, prospects for the future must have seemed bright. Hong Kong had successfully transitioned into a stable manufacturing-based economy and the territory as a whole was enjoying steady GDP growth. Yet, as was often the case, calamity was waiting in the wings. Events on the mainland led to a general softening of economic growth, affecting employment levels and the amount of discretionary spending workers could lavish on luxuries like martial arts instruction. This posed a serious problem for hand combat organizations across the territory.

The situation was especially difficult in Kowloon. Those areas of a city that house the most economically marginal individuals, often employed in supporting service industries, tend to feel the effects of social unrest or an economic downturn first, and most acutely. This time the neighborhood's problems were exacerbated by mainland China's 1962 decision to open Guangdong's borders and allow basically anyone to cross over to British-controlled Hong Kong. Given the hunger and social dislocation that resulted from Mao's "Great Leap Forward," and its disastrous ecological and economic policies, tens of thousands of new refugees started to stream into Kowloon.

Among the immigrants were Ip Chun and Ip Ching, the two sons that Ip Man had left behind when he fled the communist advance in 1949. When he last saw his sons they were 25 and 13 years old, respectively. Now, a decade and a half later, they were adults aged 38 and 26. Both sons had stayed behind to finish their educations. Ip Chun had excelled in the areas of traditional Chinese culture, literature, and music. He became a teacher and was actively involved in Foshan's ancient Cantonese opera tradition. While he no longer regularly practiced Wing Chun, he did develop a lifelong interest in Buddhism. His younger brother, Ip Ching, retained more of an interest in his father's art, but he had received less than a year of instruction before his father was forced to flee. In the meantime, Ip Ching had also finished both high school and college.

The late 1950s, particularly after 1958 and the advent of Mao's "Great Leap Forward," was a chaotic and destructive time on the mainland. Urban unemployment had become a substantial problem. Further, the "anti-rightist" movement picked up momentum after the premature end of the ill-conceived "Hundred Flowers Campaign." Ip Chun's work in education and the public arts put him at odds with the left-wing guardians of these establishments. He was subjected to public criticism and was sent to the countryside for "reeducation" through poverty and labor. The younger brother, Ip Ching, was also forced to take up collective farming in the countryside with the other "educated youth" of his own generation, but it does not appear that the younger university graduate was targeted to the same degree as his brother.

The exact date of the brothers' deportations to the countryside remains unclear, but Ip Chun placed it at about the same time as Mao's campaign to exterminate house sparrows (part of the "Four Pests" program).[70] That would indicate a date in the 1958–1959 time range. Given the acceleration of the anti-rightist campaigns in these years, and the state's increasing willingness to use rural labor as a reeducation tool, those dates seem likely.

Neither brother found his talents or interests well-served by a life of rural poverty and labor. Ip Chun had no cultural or artistic outlet. Ip Ching was forced to practice his martial arts forms at night, and in secret, as the party's cadres frowned on such "backwards" and "feudalistic" activities. When the government opened the frontier the brothers, like so many other individuals, decided to seek their fortunes in Hong Kong.

The ensuing wave of refugees upset Kowloon's already delicate economic balance. Ip Chun was able to find work as a newspaper reporter and an accountant. The younger Ip Ching moved in with his father. Ip Chun started to drop by the school in the evenings and eventually resumed his studies. Ip Ching, who was younger and unattached, became a live-in assistant instructor in his father's school and had a chance to closely observe how the system had changed and evolved.

Both sons noted that the material was presented to students in Hong Kong quite differently from what they were familiar with in Foshan. Rather than starting with extensive stance training and drills, chi sao had become the major focus of Ip Man's teaching system. This change accomplished two goals. It made training a much more enjoyable activity, and therefore increased student retention. The switch also forced instructors to introduce detailed discussions of punching, bridging, and evading much earlier in the training routine. It was now possible for Ip Man's Hong Kong students to develop practical self-defense skills after only a few months, rather than waiting years. These changes should probably be seen as an adaptation to Hong Kong's unique business environment where self-defense was a serious issue, and hand combat instructors needed new ways to encourage retention within their highly mobile student base.

Like Jiu Wan and Lee Shing before them, the brothers also noted that their father had substantially reformed the verbiage and metaphysical structures used to teach the art. The five elements and the eight trigrams were gone, and in their place were discussions of force and leverage. Traditional names, sayings, and poems, things that had always been part of martial arts instruction in Foshan, regardless of style, were also jettisoned. The physical structure of the wooden dummy had been adapted to apartment living, and training on the plum blossom poles was eliminated altogether. Students were also taught practical skills up front, and discussions of philosophy and principles were introduced only later when they were more likely to be personally meaningful. In short, while Ip Man was still teaching Wing Chun, the actual presentation of his system came as a surprise to his children.[71]

Being reunited with his sons (their mother having previously died of cancer in Guangdong) seems to have invigorated Ip Man.[72] He once again took a more active role in the teaching of his classes. Ip Ching helped his father to install the wooden dummy in the Castle Peak school and for a while things seemed good. However, as the economic situation further deteriorated, Ip Man was forced to once again look for a new location.

This time he received an unexpected call from an old friend. Ho Leun had known Ip Man in Foshan, but he had never studied Wing Chun. In the late 1950s he moved to Hong Kong and established the Tai Sang Restaurant on Fook Chuen Street in Tai Kok Tsui. One day, while reading the local papers, he came across a story that mentioned Ip Man and his Wing Chun school.

Ho Leun decided that it was high time that he look up his old friend. He had always wanted to study Wing Chun, and now it seemed as though he would finally have an opportunity. Ip Man told Ho of his problems with the Castle Peak location. Ho Leun in turn offered Ip Man the top floor of his restaurant as a possible school space. The area was large and it was mostly empty as it was only occasionally used as a warehouse. Ip Man gratefully accepted the offer and stayed at the restaurant location for a year and a half.

The arrangement was advantageous for another reason. Ever since the car accident that killed the son of Fung Shek, the Wing Chun clan had been without a reliable source of wooden dummies. As more schools opened and more advanced students were trained, this became a problem. Ho Leun was something of an inventor, and he helped to remedy the situation. He attempted to create a dummy with motorized arms, but when this design was found to be unsatisfactory he turned his attention instead to the way in which dummies were mounted. Rather than Fung Shek's wooden slats he used steel springs both beneath and behind the dummy. The tension on these springs could be carefully adjusted to give just the optimal amount of resistance. This style of mounting is occasionally seen today. A new dummy was waiting for Ip Man when he arrived at the school. Ho Leun made dummies for the Hong Kong Wing Chun clan until his emigration to Canada in 1973.[73]

Ip Man continued to teach secondary classes in other venues during this time period. He gave private lessons at Yee Wa's tailor shop in Tsim Sha Tsui. He also began to work privately with a number of Hong Kong police officers from the San Po Kong district.[74] Two of his initial students were quite highly placed. Tang Sang was the Chief Inspector of the district's detectives. He had already studied a little Wing Chun before being introduced to Ip Man. Lam Yin Fat was the Chief Sergeant. Both men were well connected and brought in additional students. Tang Sang even arranged for Ip Man to run a small class in the district's detectives club.[75]

While a relatively late aspect of Ip Man's career, and often mentioned only in passing, his relationships with Tang Sang and the local Kowloon police are important for a number of reasons. To begin with, his efforts at building bridges in this area demonstrated his ongoing interest in cleaning up the image of Wing Chun after the public excesses of the mid-1950s. These efforts were finally beginning to bear fruit. No longer would Wing Chun be primarily associated with street fights and juvenile delinquency. Ip Man's choice of personal students in this period illustrated the argument that independent martial arts schools could contribute to the public good. They could be part of the process of strengthening civil society. Further, the access to elite opinion and local law enforcement that he gained here would become quite important when he began to consider various ways to institutionalize his legacy in the coming years.

Ip Man appears to have retained some of his more mercurial personality traits well into his old age. His son Ip Ching relates that his father often went out to get something to eat after training in the evening. In fact, Ip Man was something of a connoisseur of café culture and quite enjoyed meeting his students and friends in the various tea houses and restaurants of the neighborhoods in which they lived. Two of his favorite restaurants were Xio Chen Huau, where he was first introduced to Bruce Lee's father, and San Pin Lau, which he frequented along with his students.[76] Given the levels of petty crime that were seen in Kowloon during the 1950s and 1960s, these late night expeditions were not always without incident, and Ip Man always managed to deal with the would-be thief or pick-pocket himself.[77]

There seemed to be something about Hong Kong's more elemental nature, where one could watch acts of both creation and destruction happening throughout the city's rapidly changing landscape, which was deeply appealing to Ip Man. Ip Ching reports that his father would often take long walks through the city, either by himself or with a few students. These expeditions might last for hours at a time. He drew elaborate philosophical lessons from the daily dramas that he saw played out around him. The smallest incident could be used to illustrate a vital hand combat theory or principle. What interested Ip Man most of all were fires. His new friends and students in the police department would call him to tell him if there was a major fire in progress, and Ip Man would race to the scene, seemingly entranced by the display of raw destructive power that had been unleashed in the city.[78]

Much of the actual execution of Wing Chun has to do with the creation and destruction of structures. While the old master may have abandoned the vocabulary of the five elements in his teaching, he could not help but see those principles played out in the world around him. Indeed, this repeated pattern of creation and destruction was the mystery that linked the microcosm of Wing Chun to the broader universe of human experience.

Given this interplay of destruction and creation, we should not be surprised to learn that Ip Man began the process of creating the institutions that would take Wing Chun into the future at the same time that the sun was setting on his own career. Having had a chance to set his business affairs in order and save up a moderate amount of money, Ip Man lived a more comfortable life in the mid to late 1960s than had been the case in the 1950s. In 1964 he bought his own apartment in the Yee Fai Building on Tung Choi Street in Kowloon. He also formally retired from daily teaching in the school, but as always, found it impossible to stay away from the art altogether and continued to teach or oversee private lessons in a number of venues. In fact, Ip Man remained quite active until the end of his life.

Upon his "retirement" in 1964, he instructed a group of senior students to begin planning an organization to promote Wing Chun. This process eventually resulted in the creation of the Hong Kong Ving Tsun Athletic Association (VTAA). The group still exists today, housed in the Cheung Ning Building, 3/F, 3 Nullah Road. The VTAA is a voluntary organization and is the closest thing that the Ip Man lineage has to an official body.

While seemingly straight forward, creating this institution turned out to be more involved than expected. Evidently different ideas were studied. It took close to four years to actually bring the entire process to a head. Riots in Hong Kong in the late 1960s caused the local government to postpone their review of the project, which further added to the delay.

His students bought an apartment that served as headquarters for the organization in 1966 and Ip Man was finally named the new association's president in 1967. The first secretary of the group was Lee Man. Ip Man's sons both participated in the group at the request of their father. Ip Chun served as the fledgling association's first treasurer; he was well suited to the post given his professional experience as an accountant.

It is unclear how much control Ip Man exercised over the creation of the institution. We know that he wrote down the Wing Chun legend, discussed in the introduction, for an early version of the proposed organization named the Ving Tsun Tong Fellowship.[79] For some unknown reason that group never came about, but false starts such as this might also have contributed to the VTAA's long incubation period.

Ip Man also found a number of other projects to occupy his time in retirement. Samuel Kwok lists no fewer than four different venues where he offered private lessons. In fact, his teaching and social schedules remained busy enough that one wonders in what respects the old master was really retired at all. Once the VTAA was up and running he frequented meetings and gatherings. He also offered personal instruction at Chan Wei Hong's home on Waterloo Road. In addition to Chan, the Siu Lung brothers, Wong Chi On, Chan Kam Ming, Chung Yau, Lau Hon Lam, and Man Yim Kwong all received instruction there. Ip Man could also be found teaching occasionally on the rooftop of Lau Lam's House on Chi Yau Road. Lastly, he taught a group of lawyers at the house of Ip Sing Cheuk in Siu Fai Toi.[80]

Again, this later teaching schedule demonstrates the increased acceptance of Wing Chun as a pro-systemic activity in the late 1960s. Ip Man also started a long-running series of classes at the Elizabeth hospital in 1967. Most of the actual classes were led by his senior students and Ip Ching formally took over teaching duties following the death of his father in 1972.

August 24, 1967, saw the final ratification of the VTAA. This group was significant for reasons other than its simple formalization of the Ip Man Wing Chun clan. It was the first private association representing a traditional martial arts society to be officially registered with, and recognized by, Hong Kong's government. In creating this society and gathering transparent and official membership data, Ip Man was essentially pledging the good behavior of his group to the government. Now the entire organization could be held responsible for the behavior of its members. The golden age of street fights and teenage challenge matches had come to an end. After a decade of building bridges with other local martial arts clans, civic groups, and even law enforcement, Ip Man decisively reoriented his art away from the narratives of personal resistance that had attracted the angry young men of the 1950s, to something much more socially acceptable and pro-systemic. In 1973 the government of Hong Kong went on to require that all private martial arts schools be licensed and registered. They were also forced to collect and turn over basic information on all of their students. This legislation followed the basic pattern pioneered by the VTAA.[81]

The VTAA remained a firmly independent organization that concentrated on the needs of the Wing Chun clan. It was not subverted by the local power structures of the day to the same extent that the Zhong Yi Athletic Association in Foshan had been. The new decade began with Ip Man striking a middle course between the extremes of the 1930s policy of accommodation and 1950s-style resistance.

His relationship with this new association was not, however, always an easy one. Early in its institutional history Tang Sang, the previously mentioned police detective and important figure in the Wing Chun clan, took a leading role in the VTAA. He attempted to alter the amount it paid its president (Ip Man) every month without first consulting him. The old master was so miffed that he simply walked out on the organization and took all of the instructors (including the assistant coaches

Ip Ching and Wong Ki Man) with him. His instructors did not return to the organization and resume teaching until Tang Sang left Hong Kong following his retirement (and just ahead of a rumored corruption investigation) in 1974.[82]

Of course, this mass exodus created a problem. It was now impossible to run a school without police and government certification, and that approval was held by the VTAA, not Ip Man. To deal with this complication a new organization, the Ip Man Martial Art Association was created in 1971. This organization briefly served as the main body of the Wing Chun clan in the early 1970s and still exists to this day. The two organizations have enjoyed cordial relations and often rotate or exchange board members.[83]

Ip Man was also involved in efforts to build broader institutions. He was a charter member of the Hong Kong Chinese Martial Arts Association (HKCMAA). Founded on August 8, 1969, this group attempted to organize traditional hand combat schools and lion dancing teams to help them navigate Hong Kong's quickly changing civic landscape. The main aim of this new association was to popularize the traditional arts, while at the same time assuring the general public that the highest ethical standards would be upheld. As we saw at the beginning of this chapter, elite and middle-class opinion was extremely distrustful of the traditional martial arts in the 1960s and 1970s. Almost all schools were viewed as fronts for criminal or anti-social behavior. Organizations like the VTAA and the HKCMAA attempted to reassure and educate a skittish public.

The VTAA and the HKCMAA maintained close ties in this period, and shared some memberships. The HKCMAA sent an official delegation to visit the VTAA offices, as well as officers to Ip Man's 71st birthday celebration.[84] The organization also sent a full delegation to the master's funeral. Tang Sang served as the first chairman of the new group. In fact, he was actually the driving force behind the inception and creation of the HKCMAA.

The Ip Man Tong Museum, built on the grounds of the Foshan Ancestral Temple, prominently displays a photo of the founding members of the HKCMAA. Over one hundred individuals are pictured. Tang Sang takes the place of honor in the center of the front row. Ip Man, also in the front, sits to his right, about a third of the way down. It is interesting to note that of the 100 or more martial artists present on that day, he was the only one still dressed in traditional Chinese clothing.

This single photograph illustrates the paradox of Ip Man's Hong Kong career. The ways in which he ran his school and reformed his system clearly mark him as an innovative thinker. He managed to take much of the Guoshu movement's reformist philosophy and put it into practice in such a way that it actually promoted, rather than stifled, one of Guangdong's unique martial arts traditions. Yet he also represented a link to China's past, to a time and place that was quickly slipping from the collective memories of Hong Kong's younger martial artists.

Conclusion

Throughout his life Ip Man had been a heavy smoker. In 1972 the aging teacher became aware that he had throat cancer. Less than two weeks before he died he recorded a series of home movies in which he demonstrated some of Wing Chun's core forms, including the wooden dummy routine. In his last days he sought to leave a visual testament of himself for those seeking to find the essence of his style. On December 1, 1972, at the age of 79, he succumbed to the cancer that was destroying his body. He died six months before his best known student, Bruce Lee (already a celebrity in Hong Kong), would explode onto the world stage as China's first true superstar. Lee's fame would make Ip Man a globally known figure within martial arts circles, and Wing Chun's popularity was set to begin its own steady ascent. What started as an obscure regional style, practiced by a few dozen individuals had, over the course of a lifetime, become one of the most popular and best known schools of the Chinese martial arts. Yet Ip Man would die without seeing the fruits of his labor.

His death did not simply represent the passing of a generation. Nor was it merely an event of political importance in Hong Kong's martial arts community. It was also a deeply felt personal tragedy for his family and students. The teacher had been loved for his skill and wisdom, as well as his perpetual humor. He had spent years cultivating close personal relationships with his students in ways that were not always seen in the traditional hand combat schools of that period.

Ip Man also refused to name a "successor" or "heir" to his system. While many have tried to claim this title for themselves, it seems that he hoped that the VTAA would collectively preserve his legacy, attract new students, and cultivate young instructors. In this loosely organized communal environment individuals were free to follow those teachers who were the most talented and successful, rather than the one who had been handpicked to lead. His refusal to name a successor is sometimes criticized, especially by those hoping to order Wing Chun within a preconceived typology labeled "traditional Chinese martial art."

Yet having the wisdom to stand back and let the best of the next generation rise to the top is an enduring aspect of this martial tradition. We have already seen this in the generations of Leung Jan and Chan Wah Shun. As the old axiom (adopted by the Wing Chun clan) clearly states, "Do not speak of who is senior or junior. The one who attains the skill first is the senior."

Epilogue

Wing Chun as a Global Art

> The world is a big place. Why limit it to "North" and "South?" It holds you back. To you this cake is the country, to me it is so much more. Break from what you know, and you will know more. The southern [martial] arts are bigger than just the North and South.
>
> —Ip Man speaking to a northern master in Wong Kar-wai's 2013 film *The Grandmaster*

The Past Is Prologue

This volume's introductory chapter began with a simple question. What significance, if any, can we attribute to the fact that, facing increased incidents of "air rage" on some flights, Hong Kong Airlines chose to train their cabin crews in Wing Chun? The decision was widely publicized, and it even became the focal point of an advertising campaign centering on the image of a female flight attendant artfully performing the system's basic movements as a way of illustrating the carrier's various destinations.[1]

Flight crews could be trained in any number of hand combat systems, so why Wing Chun? One suspects that the art was not chosen so much for its practical functionality as its larger cultural and symbolic value. When individuals nostalgically imagine the Hong Kong of the 1950s and 1960s, increasingly what they "remember" is Ip Man, the Grandmaster of Wing Chun kung fu and the teacher of Bruce Lee. On purely historical grounds this is rather odd as only a small percentage of the city's population was ever involved with traditional hand combat training in the 1950s, and only a fraction of those individuals ever had anything to do with Wing Chun.

Our volume has attempted to illustrate some of the historical, social, and even economic pathways by which Wing Chun emerged as a local and then regional art in the nineteenth and twentieth centuries. We have examined the history of the southern Chinese martial arts in the Late Imperial period, and have considered how the pressures of modernization in the Republican era set the stage for rapid evolution and change. In the final chapters of this book we presented a detailed study of the life and career of Ip Man, starting with his introduction to the art in Foshan and concluding with his efforts to create a set of institutions that would preserve his legacy in Hong Kong.

Still, our discussion remains incomplete. While we have investigated the means by which Wing Chun emerged and prospered as a regional art prior to the 1970s, we have yet to ponder its incredible growth within the global marketplace following Bruce Lee's rise to superstardom. Nor have we really considered why Wing Chun, and the media discourse that surrounds it, has come to be so closely tied to questions of identity in Hong Kong and southern China.

The present volume has been focused on questions of social history, but it has laid a foundation to address these issues. In the following epilogue we bring our discussion full circle by examining Wing Chun's success in the global arena. This requires some consideration of the media representations of the art and the impact of the "Kung Fu Craze" that Bruce Lee launched in the early 1970s. Indeed, the current resurgence of interest in Ip Man could not have happened without Lee's paradigm defining efforts in the realms of both film and martial arts theory.

Bruce Lee and Ip Man have become closely intertwined in the popular imagination. Most individuals, to the extent that they are aware of Ip Man at all, know him from the Hong Kong action films that bear his name. As Paul Bowman has argued at length, each of these stories was produced in the shadow of Bruce Lee, even if he does not assume a central role in these films.[2]

Still, we should not assume that the current representations of Ip Man are only slightly aged reflections of Lee. The symbolic dialogue between these figures has become complex. It exemplifies important tensions that have always existed within the Wing Chun clan and helps to illustrate why individuals, in both the East and West, turn to the martial arts in an attempt to deal with the challenges of globalization. While they may appear to be ageless epitomes of tradition, the Chinese martial arts (as they are experienced and practiced today) are a modern phenomenon.

To better illustrate these points we will need to consider two different approaches to the problem of globalization. The first of these focuses on the flow of goods, capital, and individuals across borders. Bruce Lee's own involvement with each of these forms of trade helped to raise the profile of all of the Asian fighting arts on the global stage. Yet, in contrast to Wing Chun, many of China's traditional hand combat systems are struggling to survive or have already slipped into obscurity.

While Lee's superstardom may have been a necessary precondition's for Wing Chun's global expansion, it is not sufficient to explain the success of this art and the simultaneous stagnation of some of its close cousins. As such, this chapter briefly considers a few of the institutional characteristics of the Wing Chun community in the middle of the 1970s to better understand how this style was able to capitalize on the openings that Lee provided.

Like the martial arts, globalization is a complex subject that must be approached from multiple perspectives. We will next reframe the question and ask what challenges it causes for cultural movements (including traditional hand combat organizations) if we instead imagine globalization as the increased flow of ideas or "modes of communication" between previously isolated states. Indeed, physical goods such as labor, capital, or specific commodities only take on social significance once that is assigned to them through a process of cultural construction.

This perspective, employed by Peter Beyer in his studies of the changing place of religion in the modern world, notes that globalization can cause a crisis to any institution which is responsible for transmitting fundamental social values.[3] Recall that the martial arts have often acted as ambassadors of "wu" or military (as opposed to "wen" or civilian) values in Chinese culture. Indeed this dialectic between wu and wen has been a defining axis of traditional Chinese social organization.[4]

More specialized types of communication in the form of increased professionalism and technological innovation threaten earlier ways of mediating meaning. Modernization theorists long suspected that identities such as ethnicity and religion would vanish in the current era. The May Fourth intellectuals, inspired by many of these same basic theories, came to similar conclusions about the likely fate of China's regional identities, dialects, and even the martial arts.

Of course, this has not actually happened. Regional identity and religion continue to exist, and more people currently study Wing Chun and the various fighting systems of southern China than at any time in the past. All of these institutions have succeeded in the modern world to the extent that they have evolved. As Beyer reminds us, while globalization may make certain modes of communication obsolete, each of the changes that it brings creates various externalities and secondary problems. These new issues present enterprising organizations with an opportunity. They can seek to maintain their social relevance either by finding some new set of difficulties to address, or they can double down on their primary mission of large scale identity formation and adopt a more fundamentalist message in the face of global challenges.

Both of these adaptive strategies can be seen in the Chinese martial arts today. Some schools focus on self-defense, stress relief, or the fitness benefits of their practices, often framing them as practical solutions to the problems of modern life. Other groups have opted to move away from this utilitarian discourse. They have redoubled their search for the "ancient" and "authentic" roots of their practice, often with an eye toward shoring up questions of social or national identity.

Nor is this discussion about the soul and future of the Chinese martial arts confined to debates between styles. Even a brief survey of the popular Wing Chun literature will show that the same disagreements shape much of the conversation within this movement today. Is Wing Chun a "modern art" focused on practical self-defense, or is it instead a key to understanding traditional southern Chinese culture? Does the art teach concrete solutions to real-world problems (many of which are endemic to modern society)? Or does the system's primary value lay in what it suggests about the true nature of the students and their relationship with the community? Beyer admits that on a certain level it is impossible to totally separate these two strategies. Still, his general approach helps to explain much of the tension within current discussions of the Chinese martial arts.

Wing Chun as a Commodity in the Global Marketplace

Ip Man did much to increase Wing Chun's profile as a regional martial art after 1949, and he set the stage for its eventual rise to prominence within the larger hand combat community. Still, one cannot understand the global growth of this system, or any of the Asian fighting arts, without appreciating the role of Bruce Lee. He is the axiomatic figure in any discussion of the late twentieth-century internationalization of the martial arts. While some individuals in both North America and Europe had been exposed to these systems during the tumultuous middle decades of the twentieth century, often as a result of military service in the Second World War, the Korean War, or Vietnam, the appeal of the traditional Asian hand combat systems had remained limited.

These limitations manifest themselves in different ways. Fewer individuals practiced these arts in the 1950s and 1960s than is the case today. In addition, they did not enjoy the almost constant exposure in the popular media to which we have become accustomed.

The few systems that had gained an international following tended to be sport oriented and of Japanese origin. Judo was popularized by veterans of WWII, many of whom were exposed to the practice in either their initial training or during periods of service in the Pacific. The first Asian martial art to gain widespread international exposure, it was initially included as an Olympic sport in 1964.

A survey of the pages of *Black Belt* magazine, then the largest American periodical dedicated to the martial arts, shows that most of the articles published in the early to middle years of the 1960s focused on Japanese hand combat systems. Karate and Aikido were probably the best known alternatives to Judo. Indeed, much ink was spilled during the decade debating the relative merits of these different systems.[5]

Bruce Lee's initial appearances on television, where he played the role of Kato on the *Green Hornet* (1966–1967) and then on the big screen (most crucially in the 1973 sensation *Enter the Dragon*), had a profound effect on the place of the Asian martial arts in Western popular culture. Given their current popularity, we often forget that prior to the 1970s very few individuals were familiar with the term "kung fu" or even knew that the Chinese had also produced hand combat systems of their own. While any child in the current era might grow up aspiring to practice the kinds of kung fu, mixed martial arts, or kickboxing that are portrayed in so many movies and television programs, prior to the emergence of Bruce Lee that sort of widespread familiarity with the global fighting arts was unthinkable.

Bruce Lee's appearance on the *Green Hornet* had an immediate impact on the North American martial arts community. A certain number of practitioners had been expressing interest in the Chinese fighting arts throughout the 1960s. Yet it was the virtuosity of Lee's performance as Kato that created a groundswell of enthusiasm for "kung fu." To the extent that it could be imagined as the root of Karate, and hence a critical factor in the ongoing debate between that style and Judo, its niche in the Western martial arts world seemed secure.

What was not evident at the time was that the boundaries of this still relatively small community were about to be fundamentally redrawn. In 1973 we saw the release of both *Enter the Dragon* and the news of Lee's death at the shockingly young age of 32. The film captivated Western audiences with its innovative fight choreography, nods to Asian philosophy (something else which had been growing in popularity since WWII), and unabashed violence.

Concerned that the public might not identify with a single leading Asian actor, the film featured a diverse cast, which gave important roles to both John Saxon and Jim Kelly.[6] These fears proved to be unfounded because audiences around the globe were drawn to Lee's charismatic performance. Still, the self-conscious decision to feature an ensemble cast of martial artists from a variety of racial, national, economic, and social backgrounds had a powerful impact on viewers. It broadcast once and for all that the potential for both self-realization and group empowerment promised by the martial arts lay within every human being regardless of his or her personal circumstances or nation of origin.

The most powerful aspect of *Enter the Dragon* was not found within its dialogue or plot (elements of which were admittedly formulaic). Rather it was Bruce Lee as a visual presence that made the film a success with audiences.[7] His physique seemed almost Olympian. It was certainly not an image of Asian masculinity, or even a type of action star, that the Western movie-going public was familiar with.

This physique became the central symbolic driver of the film. Lee's image presented audiences with an undeniable testimony of a person's ability to literally forge a new "self." A self that seemed to transcend the boundaries of what was traditional or modern; of what was "Eastern" or "Western." This was a "self" that possessed the physical and spiritual strength to pursue the most challenging goals.

It is not hard to hear echoes of the modernizing philosophies of the Jingwu and Guoshu reform movements in all of this. These schools sought to yoke the spirit of the martial arts to the advancement of the Chinese nation and state. Lee, grasping the counterculture spirit of the era, freed these means from their traditional ends and promised that they could be so much more.

The strength of symbols as a mode of visual communication resides in their multivocality. A single symbol can take on many meanings depending on the state of the viewer and the context in which it is employed. This unending series of permutations and combinations is precisely why audiences never seem to grow tired of the classic myths.

Bruce Lee proved to be the perfect symbol. Any number of desires could be read onto his visual image. In the context of the 1970s many of these were overtly political. In his films Lee always portrayed the underdog, the economically, socially, or racially disadvantaged. It is not hard to understand how his movies became powerful symbols in marginal communities around the globe.[8]

Other individuals watched his performances and saw the possibility of personal, rather than political, empowerment. Indeed, this evolution from an emphasis on radical community change to a more personal (and less political) type of struggle would go on to become the most common way in which Lee was read in the following decades. It was also critical to the successful commercialization and sale of his image within global markets.[9]

Lee's untimely death in 1973 (said to be the result of a previously unknown allergy to a commonly used medication) crystalized his image at a single moment in time.[10] He became a prophet to his followers, snatched away at the very moment of revelation. Rather than looking forward to what Lee would have done next, those who struggled to understand the promise of this message were instead forced to look back to his previous films (which had not been produced for a North American audience), television appearances, interviews, and assorted writings. All of these things could be easily commoditized.

Martial arts instruction could also be commoditized and distributed to the public. Much of this volume has been dedicated to a detailed review of how, starting in the late nineteenth century, the various Chinese martial arts were able to transform themselves from relatively small-scale structures based around traditional modes of social organization, to large public teaching institutions which catered to the needs of an increasingly modernized middle class. The wave of enthusiasm unleashed by Lee's sudden eruption into the popular consciousness filled martial arts classes of seemingly every style with new students. There simply were not enough qualified instructors in the 1970s to accommodate everyone interested in experiencing these fighting systems.

As one might expect, the previously obscure Chinese martial arts were major beneficiaries of this new attention. Wing Chun's development was forever shaped by its association with Bruce Lee. He did multiple things that helped to promote the art on the global stage.

While Lee had been involved with the film industry since his youth (when he starred in a number of movies as a child actor), he was also a dedicated martial artist. Lee had first been introduced to Wing Chun in Hong Kong in the 1950s when he became a student of Ip Man. After coming to the United States he continued to teach and promote the Chinese martial arts. His skills, personable nature, and TV roles led to appearances in *Black Belt* magazine where he mentioned his background in Wing Chun and his teacher. Multiple articles published in this period actually featured images of Ip Man sitting beside, or practicing chi sao with, his now famous student.[11]

Given how little Western media exposure the Chinese arts as a whole received, this was an unprecedented amount of publicity. Even before the advent of the "Kung Fu Craze" in 1973, Bruce Lee had assured that his Sifu was among the best known Chinese martial artists in the West. It should also be noted that throughout the 1970s and 1980s various authors tended to introduce or discuss him as the "Grandmaster" of not just his immediate clan, but of the Wing Chun system as a whole.

This does not appear to be a title that Ip Man ever attempted to claim for himself while alive. Still, its frequent repetition in popular martial arts publications tended to obscure other lineages and diminish the contributions of some of the previously discussed instructors during the Foshan period. This is a good example of how the media discourse surrounding a martial art can shape the understanding and experience of later students.

The Bruce Lee phenomenon boosted the ranks of many different Asian hand combat schools. Yet this transformation in the way that the global public perceived these fighting systems was not enough to preserve every style that had been practiced earlier in the twentieth century. At the same time that arts like Wing Chun, Taijiquan and the various schools of Karate were reaping the benefits of this unexpected windfall, other traditional Chinese systems were slipping into obscurity.

It is important to consider some of the other factors that may have facilitated Wing Chun's spread throughout the international system. The first, and possibly most critical variable, is geography. Exporting any good, whether physical or cultural, is expensive. All forms of trade are ultimately limited by the size of the "transaction costs" associated with the exchange. These costs include factors such as the expenses of adapting, translating, and shipping goods for sale in other markets.[12]

Ip Man's flight to Hong Kong late in 1949 was perhaps the single-most important factor in explaining the subsequent success of his art.

This city occupied a unique place in the post-WWII economic order. It had traditionally been a major transit port for trade between Western markets and China. While the economic character of the city changed after 1949, trade remained an important aspect of the area's economy. Residents of Hong Kong were connected to global markets in ways that most individuals on the mainland were not.

These links were manifest in many areas, all of which served to reduce Wing Chun's transaction costs as it attempted to move onto the international stage. Hong Kong itself was one of the most urban and modernized sections of southern China. It had a highly efficient educational system which actually produced more students than the local universities could absorb. Many of these individuals were fluent in English and had either family or business connections abroad.

A number of Ip Man's younger students in the 1950s and 1960s came from relatively affluent middle-class families. This combination of wealth and educational attainment allowed an unusually large number of his followers to travel to North America, Europe, or Australia to pursue additional educational opportunities. Movement across national boundaries was critical as there simply were not enough slots in Hong Kong's top university programs to accommodate all of the aspiring students that the city could produce.

Ip Ching has noted that this pattern of out-migration was one of the main ways in which the basic socioeconomic status of his father's students contributed to the spread of the Wing Chun system. Given the accelerated pace of instruction during the 1950s and 1960s, many of these younger practitioners had a fairly firm foundation in the art prior to traveling overseas. Some of them had even set up their own study groups to continue to practice skills (such as chi sao and the other sensitivity drills) that require at least two people.[13]

When the Bruce Lee phenomenon hit in the early 1970s, there were already a number of individuals studying and working in various Western cities who were able to take on students and begin to teach the Wing Chun system. Even Lee fits this general pattern. He also came to the United States as a young man seeking both educational and employment opportunities. The transnational flow of students and young adults was critical to Wing Chun's eventual success.

Other arts, even ones that had been very popular, had fewer opportunities to take advantage of this outpouring of enthusiasm if they were located in areas less connected to the global transfer of capital, ideas, and individuals. The various martial systems of Mt. Emei struggled to gain a foothold within the global market as comparatively few individuals from this region had emigrated to the West prior to the 1970s. Likewise, not all of Hong Kong's arts were blessed with a relatively affluent group of students who had access to international employment and educational opportunities.

It is also important to consider the general attitude of these students. In the current era there seems to be a push to reimagine Wing Chun as something more "traditional" than it actually was. This can be seen in a number of areas, from the reemergence of the "discipleship" system in a number of schools to the enthusiasm with which some students have greeted the rediscovery of "lost lineages," claiming direct descent from either the Shaolin Temple or late Qing revolutionary groups.[14]

Adam Frank has argued that the shifting economic opportunities presented by global expansion will not always lead to more openness within a fighting style. At times, the pressures and profits of international markets may actually lead to a renewed emphasis on secrecy and exclusion as organizations attempt to differentiate their product and control the flow of financially valuable teaching opportunities. We should not assume that the process of globalization will necessarily lead to more open or liberal styles.[15]

So how did Wing Chun, and its various students, appear to observers prior to the explosion of interest that would make it a leading Chinese art? Did it give the impression of a forward-looking system, or one that primarily sought to preserve tradition? This is a difficult question to answer as by definition most Western observers had no interest in Wing Chun, or any other Chinese martial arts, prior to Bruce Lee. Still, there are a few sources that readers may wish to consider.

In 1969 a Wing Chun student named Rolf Clausnitzer and his teacher Greco Wong published a book titled *Wing-Chun Kung-Fu: Chinese Self-Defence Methods*.[16] Clausnitzer had lived in Hong Kong as a youth and was one of the first Westerners to practice and closely observe the Wing Chun system. He had initially interviewed Ip Man in 1960 and later studied with his student Wong Shun Leung. After moving to the UK he continued his studies with Greco Wong, who was a student of Moy Yat.

While Wing Chun had previously been discussed in a few articles, this volume was the first detailed treatment of the system available to Western martial artists. Indeed, it was one of the earliest books dedicated exclusively to the art to be published anywhere.

Readers should carefully consider the timing of this publication. By 1969 Bruce Lee was well-known within martial arts circles through his television appearances. His connection to Wing Chun is mentioned approvingly by the authors.

A quick review of the sorts of articles that were being published in magazines like *Black Belt* further suggests that interest in the Chinese martial arts was growing among the modestly sized community that had coalesced around these hand combat systems during the 1960s. Much of this fascination appears to have been driven by the "Karate vs. Judo" debate and kung fu's perceived role as a precursor to the Okinawan striking arts.

It was this smaller community of individuals that Clausnitzer and Wong were attempting to reach with their publication. The general explosion of interest in the martial arts (and Wing Chun in particular) that would be unleashed with *Enter the Dragon* was still a few years off. This early work offers us a suggestion of how Ip Man's Wing Chun system might have appeared to Western martial artists prior to the launch of the "Kung Fu Craze."

> Originally from Kwangtung province he migrated to Hong Kong where he still resides. An outspoken man, Yip Man regards Wing Chun as a modern form of Kung Fu, i.e. as a style of boxing highly relevant to modern fighting conditions. Although not decrying the undoubted abilities of gifted individuals in other systems he nevertheless feels that many of their techniques are beyond the capabilities of ordinary students. Their very complexity requires years if not decades to master and hence greatly reduced their practical value in the context of our fast-moving society where time is such a vital factor. Wing Chun on the other hand is an art of which an effective working knowledge can be picked up in a much shorter time than is possible in other systems. It is highly realistic, highly logical and economical, and able to hold its own against any other style or system of unarmed combat.[17]

Obviously we must exercise caution when relying on a single account. Still, the author's assessment of Ip Man's attitudes and the way in which he was presenting Wing Chun to the public are supported by the much more detailed discussion in the previous chapter. Even more thought-provoking is Clausnitzer and Wong's description of Ip Man's students and how they compared to other groups in Hong Kong's hand combat marketplace.

> An interesting characteristic common to most practitioners of Wing Chun lies in their relatively liberal attitude to the question of teaching the art to foreigners. They are still very selective when it comes to accepting individual students, but compared with the traditional Kung Fu men they are remarkably open and frank about the art. If any one Chinese style of boxing is destined to become the first to gain popularity among foreigners, more likely than not it will be Wing Chun.[18]

Bruce Lee's rise to superstardom ushered Wing Chun, and the Chinese martial arts more generally, onto a wider stage than Clausnitzer and Wong likely envisioned in 1969. Yet the system did possess certain characteristics that allowed it to capitalize on this windfall during a time when so many other traditional Chinese styles were falling into obscurity. Perhaps the most important of these were Ip Man's decision to streamline the art and the general outlook of the students that his school attracted. Clausnitzer and Wong's early observations appear almost prophetic in light of the system's subsequent emergence as one of the most popular fighting arts within the global arena.

Nor has this success been limited only to the international market. Wing Chun is better known in Hong Kong and throughout China today than it ever was at any point in the past. Bruce Lee's fame on the mainland and the success of the recent Ip Man films have helped to resurrect and rejuvenate interest in a wide variety of Wing Chun lineages and traditions throughout southern China. Yet it was the art's global success which seems to have set the stage for its more enthusiastic embrace at home.

Two Visions of the Wing Chun Community

Some accounts suggest that Ip Man liked to play the role of the Confucian gentleman. This embodiment of traditional cultural values may even have attracted a certain type of student during the Hong Kong period.[19] Yet, as the previous quotes remind us, Wing Chun succeeded in large part because he understood it as a modern fighting system.

Likewise, while Bruce Lee's image and writings have been co-opted by various causes, it is well worth remembering that his article "Liberate Yourself from Classical Karate," one of the very few teaching statements that he put his name to while still alive, was much more concerned with conveying practical advice about training than self-realization.[20]

Even Lee's films, while examples of visual fantasy, retained a veneer of gritty social reality. His protagonists stood up to racial, social, national, and economic oppression in an era when those problems were acutely felt. Lee's fame has done much to facilitate the subsequent success of Ip Man as a media figure. The recent run of Ip Man films even contain a number of visual homages to Lee's more memorable scenes and fight choreography. As Bowman points out, it is hard not hear the echoes of Lee's 1972 "dojo fight" in *Fists of Fury* as we watch Wilson Ip's 2008 vision of Ip Man demolishing successive waves of Karate students in a very similar setting.[21]

Still, the Ip Man that seems to be the most popular with audiences today is a different sort of hero than his later student. Whereas Bruce Lee's early films appeared to carry a politically radical subtext, Ip Man has been a much more conservative figure. Portrayed as a local and national hero, he always fights to retain the values and hierarchies of the past rather than to overturn them.

There are a number of ways to approach this disjoint of structure. When reimagining Ip Man for the big screen it is no longer enough to see him only as a southern style kung fu teacher. For these movies to be a commercial success they had to be embraced by wide audiences in both Hong Kong and on the mainland. As such, a dual discourse was adopted where Ip Man found expression as both a local and a national figure. Wilson Ip's 2008 effort succeeded precisely because it managed to strike a masterful balance between these two audiences.[22] This attempted construction of Ip Man as a unifying symbol could certainly help to explain the lack of a critique of social (as opposed to national) injustice in these films.

Still, Peter Beyer might remind us that there is more than one way to think about the process of globalization. While ultimately a continuation of the drive toward modernity that was launched in nineteenth-century Europe, we can also understand it as a transformation of the ways in which meaning is communicated between society and individuals. That, in turn, may shed some light on the sorts of roles that the martial arts, and Wing Chun in particular, are being called on to perform in the current era.

According to Beyer, the process of globalization has resulted in traditional means of value creation being displaced by schools of thought that privilege efficiency and professionalism. Religious modes of communication have been one of the great losers in this process. Indeed, Beyer's work is centrally concerned with the fate of organized religion in an increasingly global world.

To create systems of meaning (which can then be used to support a variety of administrative and political functions), Beyer argues that religions, and other "generalized" modes of communication, begin by positing the existence of two realms: a "transcendent" and an "imminent." Given that the imminent defines the totality of our daily existence, we actually have trouble talking about it as we have no exterior points of reference from which to define abstract values and concepts. This problem is overcome by postulating the existence of a "transcendent" state in which none of the basic conditions that define daily life are said to exist. Through their monopoly on socially meaningful communication, religions (and other ritual systems) were traditionally able to make themselves essential in all sorts of social spheres.[23]

This balance was upset by the rise of more professionalized modes of action during the modern era. Highly focused types of communication are more efficient than those based on general cultural ideas. Modern societies value this increase in efficiency. As a result, the priests and nuns that had overseen so many elements of Western life were replaced with doctors, nurses, teachers, counselors, lawyers, and bureaucrats.[24]

This same process of increased specialization and professionalization has now found expression all over the globe. Religious institutions are not the only ones to be challenged by these fundamental shifts in social values. Any "generalist" mode of communication can potentially find its social influence threatened by the rise of professionalism and increased rationalization.

This is a very brief summary of Beyer's complex argument, yet it brings us back to the fundamental transformation of the Chinese martial arts which we have followed throughout this volume. Obviously Beyer composed his own study of the role of religion in an increasingly globalized world precisely because (contrary to the expectations of the early modernization and secularization theorists) it did not simply vanish. Instead, the disruptions created by globalization presented new opportunities for these institutions to retain some degree of social relevance.

On the one hand, they could focus on new aspects of "public performance" by addressing the secondary problems caused by this massive economic and social transformation. This more liberal strategy proved to be popular and can be seen in places as diverse as the rise of "liberation theology" in Latin American or the increased concern with environmental protection by a number of different types of churches in the more affluent West. Yet on the other hand, some organizations have instead adopted a more conservative approach by refocusing their energies on the question of "fundamental communication" about the transcendent.[25]

This second strategy is especially useful if one wishes to address questions of identity, and hence the definition and boundaries of the community, in the face of global pressures. Such approaches have proved to be popular and their influence can be seen in the rise of fundamentalist communities in many world religions.

Nor is there any reason to think that these two adaptive strategies are restricted to discussions of religion. Chinese society has traditionally drawn a distinction between the realms of "wu" and "wen," or "military" and "civil" values. The martial arts have been one way in which core military values found their social expression. Douglas Wile has noted that the disruptions, which imperiled the empire in the middle of the nineteenth century (including the Taiping Rebellion and the Opium Wars), badly shook China's self-confidence. This, in turn, became a critical moment in the formation of modern Taijiquan.

He argues that the Wu brothers' subsequent research and development of the *Taiji Classics* can be understood as an attempt to find, reevaluate, and reassemble what was valuable in Chinese culture in the face of an existential challenge.[26] While the art clearly has technical roots which stretch back for centuries, it is this late nineteenth-century agenda, expanded and reimagined in explicitly nationalist terms during the twentieth century, which defines how many people experience the system today.

Still, there are debates as to what Taiji should become. There are groups who see in the art a cultural repository of what is essentially "Chinese." While foreign students might learn the techniques, it is doubtful that they could even gain the deep cultural knowledge necessary to correlate and perfect this mass of material. For some teachers what lies at the root of the system is an essentialist ideal of racial or national identity.[27]

Other reformers have claimed that for Taiji to survive in the modern world it must adapt. Specifically, it must evolve to meet the needs of its changing student.[28] An aging population can benefit from the increased feelings of health, balance, and well-being that come with daily forms practice. Busy corporate executives can turn to simplified versions of the art for stress relief and lifestyle advice. Other sorts of students might decide to establish a reputation in large push-hands tournaments and open a school for themselves.

Here we see the two adaptive strategies that Beyer suggested were open to traditional modes of communication threatened by the globalization. The first camp has focused on the question of primary communication, which in the modern era so often finds its expression in the exploration of national identity. The second group has instead sought to adapt the art to deal with the ancillary problems created by life in an increasingly fast-paced and interconnected modern society.

This same process can also be seen in the Wing Chun community. Certain schools continue to focus on the "solutions" (be they self-defense, health, or psychological well-being) that Wing Chun can provide. Yet not every discussion of the art trends in this direction. The endless debates of the deep (and basically unknowable) historical origins of this style signal an ongoing interest in the idea that a hidden and somehow more "real" identity is out there. It is interesting to note how often that search leads back to nationally motivated myths of resistance grounded in either the Shaolin Temple or legendary rebel groups.[29]

Indeed, the impulse to see Ip Man as something more than a martial arts teacher is not confined to recent films. It also reflects a fundamental current within the Wing Chun community. What defines the heart of this system, and what should it become in the future? Is this a style built around the solutions to pressing technical and social problems? Or is it, instead, one that attempts to imagine a space in which its members have a better, and more empowered, understanding of who they are?

This epilogue began with a few lines of dialogue from Wong Kar-wai's 2013 film *The Grandmaster*. This scene is fascinating as it seems to contemplate the rise of Ip Man as a cultural icon and then goes on to address this debate in almost explicit terms. What is the value of the Southern Chinese martial arts? Are they an expression of local identity? Are they subservient to the nation? Or do they somehow transcend this? Can they become more?

Of course, this is not the first time that these questions have been asked. We have seen nearly identical debates arise throughout this study as various martial artists confronted the challenges and opportunities of creating new institutions in a rapidly evolving world. Nor, if Beyer is correct, should we expect to see this debate resolved in the near future.

The dialectic tension between these two competing visions generates much of the emotional power that drives the Chinese martial arts today. While these fighting systems may appear to be "traditional," in their present form they are inescapably the product of a modern global world. Ip Man's genius lay in his perception and embrace of this fundamental truth.

Notes

Introduction

1. Ip Man, "The Origin of Ving Tsun: Written by the Late Grand Master Ip Man," <http://www.vingtsun.org.hk/>. This document was originally written for the opening of a planned organization called the "Ving Tsun Tong Fellowship." This group never came together and instead the "Ving Tsun Athletic Association" was created a few years later.

2. Emily Lodish, "Hong Kong's Kung Fu Flight Attendants," *Global Post*, April 29, 2011. <http://www.globalpost.com/dispatches/globalpost-blogs/the-rice-bowl/hong-kong-airlines-kung-fu-bruce-lee>.

3. Hong Kong Airlines produced one advertisement in which a flight attendant used assorted Wing Chun motions to elegantly map out the carrier's various routes in Asia. An English-language version of this advertisement was subsequently uploaded to YouTube. Also uploaded were videos of dozens of female flight attendants, all wearing their uniforms, attempting to learn the basics of the art at a gym in Hong Kong. Ironically, one of their primary instructors was an American.

4. Anthony Fung, "Postcolonial Hong Kong Identity: Hybridising the Local and the National," *Social Identities: Journal for the Study of Race, Nation and Culture* 10, no. 3 (2004): 399–414.

5. Zhao Shiqing, "Imagining Martial Arts in Hong Kong: Understanding Local Identity through Ip Man," *Journal of Chinese Martial Studies* 1, no. 3 (2010): 86.

6. For a discussion of popular ideas about physical culture and the martial arts in late imperial China see Andrew D. Morris, *Marrow of the Nation: A History of Sport and Physical Culture in Republican China* (Berkeley: University of California Press, 2004), especially chapter 7.

7. Zhao, "Martial Arts in Hong Kong," 88.

8. This account of the Wing Chun creation myth is a summary of the following sources: Ip Man, "The Origins of Ving Tsun: Written by the Late

Grand Master Ip Man," <http://www.vingtsun.org.hk/>; Ip Ching, "History of Wing Chun" (Ip Ching Ving Tsun Association, 1998), DVD; Ip Chun, *Wing Chun Kung Fu* (New York: St. Martin's Press, 1998), 17–20.

9. Leung Jan is the first individual within this account whose existence can be independently verified. As such he represents the transition point between myth and history. While it is certainly plausible that he learned the art from the two opera singers referenced in the story, their existence cannot be confirmed.

10. Wing Chun researchers will already know that the identity of Leung Jan's students is a point of major disagreement between the various lineages and factions. We are currently reviewing the history as it is conveyed in the Ip Man lineage for reasons that will be discussed shortly.

11. The first martial arts novel that featured the exploits of the Shaolin monks was the anonymously published 1890's work *Shengchao Ding Sheng Wannian Qing*, whose simplified title in English is usually rendered the *Everlasting Qing*, or just *Everlasting*. This work was published in Guangdong and it had an impact on the subsequent development of the region's martial arts stories and mythology. John Christopher Hamm, *Paper Swordsman: Jin Yong and the Modern Chinese Martial Arts Novel* (Honolulu: University of Hawai'i Press, 2006), 34.

12. Female figures are also cited in the creation narratives of Fujianese White Crane and Chuka Shaolin. Wing Chun shares certain core characteristics with both of these arts.

13. For an overview of the historical Shaolin tradition see Meir Shahar, *The Shaolin Monastery: History, Religion and the Chinese Martial Arts* (Honolulu: University of Hawai'i Press, 2008).

14. Hamm, *Paper Swordsmen*, 35–36. See especially the evolution of Ng Mui's character between *Everlasting* (1893) and *Shaolin Xiao Yingxiong* (*Young Heroes from Shaolin*), published in the 1930s.

15. Stanley Henning, "China: Martial Arts," In *Martial Arts of the World*, ed. Thomas A. Green and Joseph R. Svinth (Santa Barbra, CA: ABC-CLIO, 2010), 173.

16. Benjamin Judkins, "Inventing Kung Fu," *JOMEC Journal* 5 (2014), 1–26.

17. An extended discussion of the issues surrounding the etymology of the martial arts is provided in Stanley Henning, "What is in a Name: The Etymology of Chinese Boxing," *Journal of Asian Martial Arts* 10, no. 4 (2001): 8–19.

18. A detailed critique of the "martial arts" concept and a discussion of the term's definition in an academic setting are provided in Joseph Svinth, "What are Martial Arts?" *InYo: The Journal of Alternative Perspectives on the Martial Arts and Sciences* 11, no 1. (2011), 7–12. Much of the conflict in the later chapters of this book can be conceptualized as a meta-debate on what the definition of the Chinese martial arts should be in the modern era. Must the martial artists of Guangdong and Hong Kong bow to the demands of northern reformers, reimagining their systems as what Svinth termed a "regulated recreational activity?" Or should outside attempts at standardization and rationalization be rejected

allowing the hand combat traditions of southern China to remain a "vernacular system," tailored to the needs of local groups, though not necessarily the nation as a whole? This is the crux of the issue.

19. For a good example see Robert W. Smith, *The Secrets of Shaolin Temple Boxing* (North Clarendon, VT: Tuttle Publishing, 1964). At the time Smith was considered to be the gold standard for western authors writing about the Chinese martial arts. Much of his information came from interviews with various teachers and informants in Taiwan, rather than actual historical or document based research. As a result he often passed on folklore instead of verifiable facts. Smith's strongest book is probably *Chinese Boxing: Masters and Methods*, published by Kodansha International in 1974. This book should be required reading for all students of the development and spread of the Chinese martial arts. Yet even this invaluable work is really a snapshot of events at a given place and time. When it comes to evaluating the arts of southern China, or historical questions generally, Smith tends to reflect the biases of his informants.

20. Brian Kennedy and Elizabeth Guo, *Chinese Martial Arts Training Manuals: A Historical Survey* (Berkeley, CA: Blue Snake, 2005), 38–60. Two of his essential contributions are Tang Hao, "Jiu Zhongguo Tiyushi Shang Fuhui De Damo," (The Unfounded Association of Bodhidharma with the Ancient History of Chinese Physical Education,) Parts 1, 2 in vol. 4 and vol. 6 of *ZhongguoTiyushi Cankao Ziliao* (*Research Materials on the History of Chinese Physical Education*) (Beijing: Renmin Tiyu, 1958); Tang Hao, *Shaolin Wudang Kao* (*Shaolin and Wudang Research*) 1930, Photographic Reprint, (Hong Kong: Qilin Tushu, 1958).

21. For a discussion of Xu Zhen see Kennedy and Guo, *Training Manuals*, 60–61. Like Tang Hao, Xu Zhen is remembered for his contributions to the modern understanding of the Shaolin and Taiji traditions. His work on a body of historical literature known as the "Taiji Classics" has proved to be particularly important. Xu was also an avid martial artist. Perhaps his most important work was Xu Zhen, *Guoji Lunlue* (Summery of the Chinese Martial Arts), 1929 edition, Photographic reprint in Series 1, Vol. 50 of *Minguo Congushu* (*Collected Works from the Republic Period*) (Shanghai: Shanghai Shudian, 1989).

22. See for instance Kuang Wennam, *Zhongguo Wushu Wenhua Gailun* (*A General Discussion of Chinese Martial Arts and Culture*) (Chengdu: Sichuan Jiayu Chubanshe, 1990); Cheng Dali, *Zhongguo Wushu—Lishi yu Wenhua* (*Chinese Martial Arts—History and Culture*) (Chengdu: Sichuan University Press, 1995); Lin Boyan, *Zhongguo Wushushi* (*Chinese Martial Arts History*) (Taipei: Wuzhou Chuban Youxian Gongsi, 1996).

23. Guojia Tiwei Wushu Yanjiuyan, bianzuan (National Physical Culture and Sports Commission Martial Arts Research Institute, editors and compilers), *Zhongguo Wushushi* (*Chinese Martial Arts History*) (Beijing: Peoples Physical Culture Publishers, 1997); Ma Mingda, *Wuxue Tanzhen* (Seeking Facts in Martial Studies), two volumes (Taipei: Yiwen Chuban Youxian Gongsi, 2003); Zhou Weiliang, *Zhongguo Wushushi* (*Chinese Martial Arts History*) (Beijing: Gaodeng Jiaoyu Chubanshe, 2003).

24. Stanley E. Henning, "China's New Wave of Martial Studies Scholars," *Journal of Asian Martial Arts* 15, no. 2 (2006) 8–21.

25. For an example of the problems inherent in deeply historical national level studies see Kang Gewu, *Spring and Autumn: The Spring and Autumn of Chinese Martial Arts—5000 Years* (Santa Cruz, CA: Plum Publishing, 1995). This volume, authored by a Chinese professor and Wushu expert, is structured around an extensive timeline that notes any important development anywhere in the Chinese cultural area. The end result is the creation of an illusion that a unified field of "Chinese martial arts" has always existed, and that it was inevitably moving toward its current (state-dominated) configuration. A more finely grained historical study, such as the one presented here, demonstrates that this view is simply false. It would be better to speak of the evolution of China's "martial cultures" in the plural rather than the singular tense. Some have survived to the present day, but many have not.

26. Zeng Zhaosheng, *Nan Quan (Southern Chinese Boxing)* (Guangdong: Guangdong Renmin Chubanshe, 1983); Zeng Zhaosheng, *Guangdong Wushu Shi. (A History of Guangdong Martial Arts)* (Guangzhou: Guangdong ren min chu ban she, 1989); Ma Zineng, *Foshan Wushu Wen Hua (Foshan Martial Arts Culture)* (*Foshan*: Foshanshi Chanchengqu Feiyinglixing Chubanwu, 2001).

27. Zhang Xue Lian, *Foshan Jingwu Tiyu Hui (The Foshan Pure Martial Athletic Association)* (Guangzhou: Guangdong Renmín Chuban She, 2009).

28. See for instance Ip Chun, Lu De'an and Peng Yaojun, *Ye Wen, Yong Chun 2* (Ip Man, Wing Chun, 2 volumes, Revised Edition) (Xianggang: Hui zhi chu ban you xian gong si, 2010). These Chinese language volumes co-authored with Ip Chun provide both biographical and philosophical insights into Ip Man's life and career. While a collection of family history and lore rather than an academic biography, they do provide important details that when combined with information from other sources helps to paint a more comprehensive picture of how modern Wing Chun emerged.

29. Zhou Weiliang, "Research on the Southern Shaolin in Fujian Province in the Context of Wushu Culture and the Culture of Societies and Parties," *Journal of Capital Institute of Physical Education* 18, no. 6 (2006): 1–10, 14. Readers should note that while the journal publishes its titles and abstracts in English, the body of the articles are in Chinese. Also see: Yimin He, "Prosperity and Decline: A Comparison of the Fate of Jingdezhen, Zhuxianzhen, Foshan and Hankou in Modern Times," *Frontiers of History in China* 5, no. 1 (2010): 52–85. Translated by Weiwei Zhou from *Xueshu Yuekan* (Academic Monthly) 12 (2008): 122–133.

30. Daniel Miles Amos, "A Hong Kong Southern Praying Mantis Cult," *Journal of Asian Martial Arts* 6, no. 4 (1997): 30–61; Adam D. Frank, *Taijiquan and the Search for the Little Old Chinese Man: Understanding Identity through Martial Arts* (New York: Palgrave Macmillan, 2006); Avron Boretz, *Gods, Ghosts and Gangsters: Ritual Violence, Martial Arts, and Masculinity on the Margins of Chinese Society* (Honolulu: University of Hawai'i Press, 2011).

31. D. S. Farrer, *Shadows of the Prophet: Martial Arts and Sufi Mysticism* (Dordrecht: Springer, 2009).

32. Douglas Wile, *Lost Tai-Chi Classics from the Late Ching Dynasty* (Albany: State University of New York Press, 1996).

33. Kennedy and Guo, *Training Manuals*, 2005; Brian L. Kennedy and Elizabeth Guo, *Jingwu: the School that Transformed Kung Fu* (Berkeley, CA: Blue Snake Books, 2010).

34. Morris, *Marrow of the Nation*, 2004.

35. Shahar, *Shaolin Monastery*, 2008.

36. See for instance: Wile, *Lost T'ai-Chi Classics*, 1996; Waysun Liao, *The T'ai Chi Classics* (Boston: Shambhala, 2000); Marnix Wells, *Scholar Boxer: Chang Naizhou's Theory of the Internal Martial Arts and the Evolution of Taijiquan* (Berkeley, CA: North Atlantic Books, 2005); Dennis Rovere, *The Xingyi Quan of the Chinese Army: Huang Bo Nien's Xingyi Fist and Weapon Instruction* (Berkeley, CA: Blue Snake Books, 2008).

37. Sun Lutang, Dan Miller, and Albert Liu, *Xing Yi Quan Xue: The Study of Form/Mind Boxing* (Burbank: Unique Books, 2001); Sun Lutang and Tim Cartmell, *A Study in Taijiquan* (Berkeley, CA: North Atlantic Books, 2003).

38. Stephen Selby, *Chinese Archery* (Hong Kong: Hong Kong University Press, 2000).

39. Patrick McCarthy, *Bubishi: The Classic Manual of Combat* (North Clarendon, VT: Tuttle Publishing, 2008). It should also be noted that the great Hung Gar master Lam Sai-wing (1861–1942) wrote three texts that might be considered "classic" statements on the southern martial arts. Unfortunately, his work has not received the same attention as Sun Lutang's.

40. Cheng Zongyou, *Ancient Art of Chinese Long Saber*, trans., Jack Chen (Singapore: Historical Combat Association, 2010); Yu Dayou, *Sword Treatise*, trans., Jack Chen (Singapore: Historical Combat Association, 2011). A number of other translations by the same group are available in electronic format on their webpage. Also see Meir Shahar, "Cheng Zongyou, Exposition of the Original Shaolin Staff Method" in *Hawaii Reader in Traditional Chinese Culture*, eds. Victor H. Mair, Nancy S. Steinhardt, and Paul R. Goldin (Honolulu: Hawai'i University Press, 2005), 514–517.

41. Thomas A. Green and Joseph R. Svinth, eds., *Martial Arts in the Modern World* (London: Praeger, 2003). See especially "The Martial Arts in Chinese Physical Culture, 1865–1965" by Stanley Henning (13–36) and "Sense in Nonsense: the Role of Folk History in the Martial Arts" by Thomas A. Green (1–13); S. R. Gilbert, "Mengzi's Art of War: The Kangxi Emperor Reforms the Qing Military Examinations," In *Military Culture in Imperial China*, ed. Nicola Di Cosmo (Cambridge, MA: Harvard University Press, 2009), 243–256.

42. D. S. Farrer and John Whalen-Bridge, *Martial Arts as Embodied Knowledge: Asian Traditions in a Transnational World* (Albany: State University of New York Press, 2011).

43. Peter Lorge, *Chinese Martial Arts: From Antiquity to the Twenty First Century* (New York: Cambridge University Press, 2011).

44. Stephen Teo, *Chinese Martial Arts Cinema: The Wuxia Tradition* (Edinburgh: Edinburgh University Press, 2007).

45. T. M. Kato, *From Kung Fu to Hip Hop: Revolution, Globalization and Popular Culture* (Albany: State University of New York Press, 2007).

46. Paul Bowman, *Theorizing Bruce Lee: Film—Fantasy—Fighting—Philosophy* (New York: Rodopi, 2010); Paul Bowman, *Beyond Bruce Lee: Chasing the Dragon through Film, Philosophy and Popular Culture* (New York: Wallflower, 2013).

47. Sasha Vojkovic, *Yuen Woo Ping's Wing Chun* (Hong Kong: Hong Kong University Press, 2009).

48. Petrus Liu, *Stateless Subjects: Chinese Martial Arts Literature & Postcolonial History* (Ithaca, NY: Cornell University East Asia Program, 2011).

Chapter 1

1. Translation cited in Robert J. Antony, *Like Froth Floating on the Seas: The World of Pirates and Seafarers in Late Imperial South China* (Berkeley: Institute of East Asian Studies, 2003), 84.

2. For a discussion of the evolution of civilian hand combat at the end of the Ming dynasty see Meir Shahar, *The Shaolin Monastery* (Honolulu: University of Hawai'i Press, 2008), especially chapter 5.

3. Ma Zineng, *Foshan Wushu Wenhua* (*Foshan Martial Arts Culture*) (Foshan: Foshanshi Chanchengqu Feiyinglixing Chubanwu, 2001), 15–16.

4. Patricia Buckley Ebrey, *Cambridge Illustrated History: China* (Cambridge: Cambridge University Press, 2007), 220–224.

5. See Jonathan Manthorpe, *Forbidden Nation: a History of Taiwan* (New York: Palgrave MacMillan, 2002) and Jonathan Clements, *Coxinga and the fall of the Ming Dynasty* (Stroud, UK: Sutton Publishing, 2004).

6. James Hayes, "The Hong Kong Region: Its Place in Traditional Chinese Historiography and Principal Events since the Establishment of Hsin-an County in 1573," *Journal of the Royal Asiatic Society Hong Kong Branch* 14 (1974): 108–135.

7. Patrick Hase, "Alliance of Ten" in *Down to Earth: The Territorial Bond in South China*, eds. David Faure and Helen Siu (Stanford: Stanford University Press, 1995), 123–160.

8. Barend J. ter Haar, *Ritual & Mythology of the Chinese Triads: Creating an Identity* (Boston: Brill Academic Publishers, 2000), 263.

9. Ebrey, *Illustrated History*, 224–225.

10. Meir Shahar, *The Shaolin Monastery: History, Religion and the Chinese Martial Arts* (Honolulu: Hawai'i University Press, 2008), 190–191.

11. Ebrey, *Illustrated History*, 225–226.

12. Shahar, *Shaolin*, 192.
13. Benjamin Judkins, "Does Religiously Generated Social Capital Intensify or Mediate Violent Conflict? Lessons from the Boxer Uprising" (paper presented at the 67th MPSA National Meetings in Chicago, IL, April 2–5, 2009).
14. Ebrey, *Illustrated History*, 229–231.
15. See for instance Joanna Waley-Cohen, "Militarization of Culture in Eighteenth-Century China," in *Military Culture in Imperial China*, ed. Nicola Di Cosmo (Cambridge, MA: Harvard University Press, 2009), 278–296.
16. John King Fairbank and Merle Goldman, *China: A New History*, 2nd ed., (Cambridge, MA: Harvard University Press), 168.
17. For a classic treatment of farm wages in relation to land-labor ratio and expanding trade see: Ronald Rogowski, *Commerce and Coalitions: How Trade Affects Domestic Political Alignments* (Princeton, NJ: Princeton University Press, 1990), chapter 1.
18. The best detailed discussion of land usage and rural standards of living within the Foshan region is provided by Alfred H. Y. Lin, *The Rural Economy of Guangdong, 1870–1937* (New York: St. Martin's Press, 1997).
19. Ebrey, *Illustrated History*, 240.
20. Joseph W. Esherick, *The Origins of the Boxer Uprising* (Berkeley, CA: University of California Press, 1988), 44.
21. Shahar, *Shaolin*, 34–35.
22. Esherick, *Boxer Uprising*, 97.
23. Ibid., 45–54.
24. Ebrey, *Illustrated History*, 240.
25. Ibid., 242.
26. ter Haar, *Chinese Triads*, 77–78; 280–281.
27. Ebrey, *Illustrated History*, 242.
28. Fairbank and Goldman, *China*, 207.
29. For a classic discussion of the structure and details of militia movements during the Qing dynasty see Philip A. Kuhn, *Rebellion and its Enemies in Late Imperial China: Militarization and Social Structure, 1796–1864* (Cambridge, MA: Harvard University Press, 1970).
30. For perhaps the best discussion of the local militia system, and its subsequent impact on both national and international politics, see Fredrick Wakeman Jr., *Strangers at the Gate: Social Disorder in Southern China, 1839–1861* (Los Angeles: University of California Press, 1997).
31. Fairbank and Goldman, *China*, 134–137; 196–197.
32. Ebrey, *Illustrated History*, 242, 235–236.
33. Ebrey, *Illustrated History*, 236–240; Fairbank and Goldman, *China*, 198–201.
34. David Faure, *Empire and Ancestor: State and Lineage in Southern China* (Stanford, CA: Stanford University Press, 2007).
35. Wakeman, *Strangers at the Gate*, 13–14.
36. Ibid., 18–19.

37. John Walter, *Guns of the Gurkhas* (Gladstone Institute: Tharston Press, 2005), 30–31; 41–42.

38. Wakeman, *Strangers at the Gate*, 16–21.

39. Esherick, *Boxer Uprising*, 271–315.

40. Faure, *Empire and Ancestor*, 17–27.

41. Lin, *Rural Economy*, 19.

42. Lin, *Rural Economy*, 70.

43. Lin, *Rural Economy*, 68; Wakeman, *Strangers at the Gate*, 99.

44. David Pong, *A Critical Guide to the Kwangtung Provincial Archives Deposited at the Public Records Office of London* (Cambridge, MA: Harvard University Press, 1975), 81–133.

45. Faure, *Emperor and Ancestor*, 9–10, 126; Wakeman, *Strangers at the Gate*, 109–111.

46. Lin, *Rural Economy*, 121–125.

47. Wakeman, *Strangers at the Gate*, 109–111.

48. Ibid., 109.

49. Ibid., 116.

50. For an excellent introduction to the basic history of the Triads see Dian Murray and Qin Baoqi, *The Origins of the Tiandihui: The Chinese Triads in Legend and History* (Stanford, CA: Stanford University Press, 1994) and David Ownby, *Brotherhoods and Secret Societies in Early and Mid-Qing China* (Stanford, CA: Stanford University Press, 1996). For a treatment of secret societies as popular religious movements (as well as a partial chronology of society uprisings in Southern China) see Robert J. Antony, "Demons, Gangsters, and Secret Societies in Early Modern China," *East Asian History* 27 (2004): 71–98. For the most comprehensive discussion of the ritual and mythology of individual secret societies, including their appropriation of the Shaolin mythos see Barend J. ter Haar, *Ritual & Mythology of the Chinese Triads: Creating an Identity* (Boston: Brill, 2000), especially 402–419.

51. Antony, *Secret Societies*, 77–86; ter Haar, *Chinese Triads*, 263–301.

52. Note for instance that the actual phrase that Li Wen Mao, one of the leaders of the Red Turban Uprising, adopted and subsequently had printed on his "kingdom's" coinage was "restoring the Han and destroying the Manchu." Daphne P. Lei, *Operatic China: Staging Chinese Identity across the Pacific* (New York: Palgrave, 2006), 165.

53. Wakeman, *Strangers at the Gate*, 118–119; ter Haar, *Chinese Triads*, 368–390.

54. ter Haar, *Chinese Triads*, 432–433.

55. Ibid., 402–418.

56. Wakeman, *Strangers at the Gate*, 137–138.

57. David Faure, "What Made Foshan a Town? The Evolution of Rural-Urban Identities in Ming-Qing China," *Late Imperial China* 11, no. 2 (1990): 13.

58. Wakeman, *Strangers at the Gate*, 139.

59. Faure, "What Made Foshan," 2–7.
60. Yimin He, "Prosperity and Decline: A Comparison of the Fate of Jingdezhen, Zhuxianzhen, Foshan and Hankou in Modern Times," *Frontiers of History in China* 5, no. 1 (2010): 52–85. Translated by Weiwei Zhou from *Xueshu Yuekan* (Academic Monthly) 12 (2008): 122–133.
61. Faure, "What Made Foshan," 2–7.
62. Ibid., 15.
63. It is also interesting to note that Foshan had a powerful "Ginseng and Medicine" guild. One wonders whether either of the famous martial artists were members of that body (Ibid.).
64. Cited in Ma Zineng, *Foshan Wushu Wenhua* (*Foshan Martial Arts Culture*). (Foshan: Foshanshi Chanchengqu Feiyinglixing Chubanwu, 2001), 23.
65. Lei, *Operatic China*, 139.
66. Ma, *Foshan Martial Arts Culture*, 28.
67. Cited in Ma, *Foshan Martial Arts Culture*, 22.
68. Like Mt. Song (central), Mt. Heng (southern) is one of the five sacred mountains of China. The location is revered in both Buddhist and Daoist traditions and has been the site of many temples.
69. This list of arts should be treated with caution. For instance, Taiji and Eagle Claw were only introduced to Guangdong in the 1920s as part of the Jingwu Association's expansion into the south. It is extremely unlikely that Cheung Ng (Zhang Wu) had mastered these arts while in the north and independently introduced them 200 years earlier.
70. Ibid., 23. Note that the personal names have been translated from Cantonese first, with the Mandarin Romanization being provided in parentheses. Also see Ip Chun and Michael Tse, *Wing Chun Kung Fu: Traditional Chinese Kung Fu for Self-Defense and Health* (New York, St. Martin's Griffin, 1998), 20–21. The tradition tracing Wing Chun's origins back to Cheung Ng (Zhang Wu) is also favored by Pan Nam's school in Foshan. See Robert Chu, Rene Ritchie and Y. Wu, *Complete Wing Chun: the Definitive Guide to Wing Chun's History and Traditions: The Definitive Guide to Wing Chun's History and Traditions* (North Clarendon, VT: Tuttle Publishing, 1998), 69–70. For more on Zhang Wu see Marjorie K. M. Chan, "Cantonese Opera and the Growth and Spread of Vernacular Written Cantonese in the Twentieth Century" In *Proceedings of the Seventeenth North American Conference on Chinese Linguistics*, ed. Qian Gao (Los Angeles: GSIL Publications, 2005), 8. Note that Chan, and most opera historians, date Zhang Wu departure from the capital to the Yongzheng's reign (1723–1736), which seems to be a few generations earlier that what Ma implies in the previous quote.
71. http://www.foshanmuseum.com. Webpage of the Foshan Cantonese Opera Museum.
72. J. Y. Wong, *Yeh Ming-ch'en: Viceroy of Liang Kuang (1852–8)* (Cambridge, MA: Cambridge University Press, 1976), 95–97.
73. Lei, *Operatic China*, 160–161.

74. ter Haar, *Chinese Triads*, 142.
75. Wakeman, *Strangers at the Gate*, 139.
76. ter Haar, *Chinese Triads*, 116–117.
77. Wong, *Yeh Ming-ch'en*, 104.
78. Wakeman, *Strangers at the Gate*, 141–144.
79. Ibid., 145.
80. Ibid., 148.
81. Lei, *Operatic China*, 166–167.
82. Wakeman, *Strangers at the Gate*, 149–150.

Chapter 2

1. This couplet is seen written vertically on the left and right side of the altars in many Choy Li Fut schools. It is said to have been composed by Chan Heung, the founder of the style, when his disciples were dispersing to open their own public schools in 1848. The couplet is actually a clever word puzzle. If one writes the two lines in traditional Chinese characters and places them (vertically) next to each other, each of the seven characters in one line combines with its opposite number in the other column to form a variation of the word "hero."

2. Frederic Wakeman Jr., *Strangers at the Gate: Social Disorder in South China 1839–1861* (Los Angeles: University of California Press, 1997), 22–42. For more on militias in nineteenth-century China, see Philip A. Kuhn, *Rebellion and its Enemies in Late Imperial China: Militarization and Social Structure, 1796–1864* (Cambridge, MA: Harvard University Press, 1970).

3. Joseph W. Esherick, *The Origins of the Boxer Uprising* (Los Angeles: University of California Press, 1987), 65–66.

4. Edward J. M. Rhodes, *China's Republican Revolution: The Case of Kwangtung, 1895–1913* (Cambridge, MA: Harvard University Press, 1975). For a particularly relevant discussion of the link between decommissioning military units and banditry in the early republican period see pages 238–240.

5. Wing Lam, *Hung Gar: Southern Shaolin Kung Fu Ling Nam* (Sunnyvale, CA: Wing Lam Enterprises, 2003), 104–105.

6. L. C. P. "The Noble Art of Self Defense in China," *The China Review* 3, no. 2 (1874): 92.

7. For a discussion of the role of pawnshops in the economy of the Pearl River Delta see Alfred H. Y. Lin, *The Rural Economy of Guangdong, 1870–1937* (New York: St. Martin's Press, 1997), 140–145.

8. Ma Zineng, *Foshan Wushu Wenhua* (*Foshan Martial Arts Culture*) (Foshan: Foshanshi Chanchengqu Feiyinglixing Chubanwu, 2001), 44

9. Rene Ritchie, *Yuen Kay-San Wing Chun Kuen: History and Foundation* (Los Angeles: Multimedia Books, 1998), 16.

10. Brian Kennedy and Elizabeth Guo, *Chinese Martial Arts Training Manuals: A Historical Survey* (Berkeley, CA: Blue Snake Books, 2005), 137–141.

11. Li Jinlong and Liu Yinghai, *Qingdai Biaoju yu Shanxi Wushu* (*Qing Period Armed Escort Agencies and Shanxi Martial Arts*) (Beijing: Beijing Tiyu Daxue Chubanshe, 2007); CCTV9, "Masters and Armed Escorts," *New Frontiers*, First aired August 28, 2009.

12. Ma, *Foshan Martial Arts Culture*, 44–46.

13. Ip Chun, "Fifteen Years—Traveling the World to Sell my Skills," *Qi Magazine* 48 (2000): 26–28.

14. Ma, *Foshan Martial Arts Culture*, 45.

15. Wing Lam, *Hung Gar*, 104–105.

16. Robert Chu, Rene Ritchie, and Y. Wu, *Complete Wing Chun: The Definitive Guide to Wing Chun's History and Traditions* (North Clarendon, VT: Tuttle Publishing, 1998), 6.

17. Leung Ting, *Roots and Branches of Wing Chun*, 2nd ed. (Hong Kong: Leung's Publications, 2003), 60.

18. Ip Man, "The Origins of Ving Tsun: Written by the Late Grand Master Ip Man," Hong Kong: Ving Tsun Athletic Association, 1967. <http://www.vingtsun.org.hk/>.

19. Esherick, *Boxer Uprising*, 43–52.

20. The six boxers were Chen Kai, Di Huagu, Huang Zhenshan, Zhang Jiaxiang, and Yao Xinchang. Period records also indicate that Di Huagu was a female martial artists and rebel leader. Jaeyoon Kim, "The Heaven and Earth Society and the Red Turban Rebellion in Late Qing China," *Journal of Humanities & Social Sciences* 3, no. 1 (2009): 13–14.

21. Lin Boyan, "Zhongguo jindai qiaqi wushujia xiang chengshi de yidong yiji dui wushu liupai fenshua de yingxiang," (*The early modern Chinese martial artists' migration towards cities and its influence on the diversion of the martial arts clans*) *Tiyu Wenshi* 79, May (1996): 14–16.

22. Lin, *Rural Economy*, 22, 69–70.

23. Ma, *Foshan Martial Arts Culture*, 5. For a more detailed discussion of the rise and fall of Foshan as a regional economic power see Yimin He, "Prosperity and Decline: A Comparison of the Fate of Jingdezhen, Zhuxianzhen, Foshan and Hankou in Modern Times," *Frontiers of History in China* 5, no. 1 (2010): 52–85. Translated by Weiwei Zhou from *Xueshu Yuekan* (Academic Monthly) 12 (2008): 122–133.

24. Rhoads, *China's Republican Revolution*, 12–13.

25. Not many academic sources deal directly with this conflict though it had a critical impact on the development of the Hakka community and its spread overseas. For a Chinese language discussion of these events see Zheng De Lua, *A Study of Armed Conflicts between the Punti and the Hakka in Central Kwangtung, 1856–1867*, Thesis, University of Hong Kong, 1989.

26. It should immediately be noted that these labels apply to an idealized past that may or may not have ever really existed. In practice one can find examples of all ethnic groups within all of the major arts in the region. However, there do seem to be some historical and demographic trends upon which this classification scheme is based.

27. For a discussion of these classifications from the perspective of a modern martial artist see S. L. Fung, *Pak Mei Kung Fu: The Myth & the Martial Art* (New York City: TNP Multimedia, 2008), 35–36.

28. Ibid., 54–62. It is interesting to note that some White Eyebrow lineages do claim to have a "superior" version of the art as their school was originally headed by a Hakka disciple in the 1920s. Yet given that none of these organizations were recruiting exclusively Hakka students by the 1930s or 1940s, it is hard to see this as anything other than typical inter-lineage bickering of the type that Tang Hao has warned us against.

29. Cheong Cheng Leong and Donn F. Draeger, *Phoenix-Eye Fist: A Shaolin Fighting Art of Southern China* (New York City: Weatherhill, 1977), 11–13.

30. Ma, *Foshan Martial Arts Culture*, 5–6.

31. Ma Lianzhen, "From Ape Worship in Ancient China to Monkey Imitation in Modern Competition Wu Shu," *Journal of Chinese Martial Studies* 2 (2010): 20–25.

32. See Faure (2007) for a detailed discussion of the evolution of the lineage structures in the Pearl River Delta region.

33. *Salvatore Canzonieri*, "The story of traditional Chinese martial arts: History of Hakka Martial Art and its relationship to Southern Chinese and Shaolin martial arts." <http://www.bgtent.com/naturalcma/CMAarticle31-hakka.htm>.

34. Fung, *Pak Mei Kung Fu*, 37.

35. B. J. ter Haar, *Ritual and Mythology of the Chinese Triads: Creating an Identity* (Brill Academic Publishers, 2000), 402–419.

36. Wing Lam, *Hung Gar*, 16–17.

37. Taiping Institute, "Hung Kuen," <http://taipinginstitute.com/>.

38. Zeng Zhaosheng, *Guangdong Wushu Shi (A History of Guangdong Martial Arts)*. (Guangzhou: Guangdong ren min chu ban she, 1989). See Chapter 2 for an overview of the history of the province's formal martial arts institutions and associations between 1800 and 1949.

39. Shi Naian, *The Water Margin: Outlaws of the Marsh*, trans. J. H. Jackson (Rutland, VT: Tuttle Publishing, 2010).

40. For a discussion of the militia movement in nineteenth-century Guangdong see Wakeman, *Strangers at the Gate*, 11–61; Zeng, *Guangdong Wushu Shi*, chapter 2 section 1, and Kuhn, *Rebellion and its Enemies*, 64–105.

41. Rhoads, *China's Republican Revolution*, 23–24.

42. There is some debate as to when Chan Heung was born. Oral tradition handed down by Wong Doc Fai places his birth in 1806 (see Wong, *Choy Li Fut*, 2). Tradition in the Foshan Hung Sing lineage places his birth later in 1815 (Ma, *Foshan Martial Arts Culture*, "History of the Hung Sing School").

43. Wong, *Choy Li Fut*, 4–5.

44. Ma, *Foshan Martial Arts Culture*, 63.

45. J. Elliot Bingham, *Narrative of the Expedition to China, from the Commencement of the Present Period*, vol. 1 (London: Henry Colburn Publisher, 1842), 177–178.

46. Wong, *Choy Li Fut*, 5.
47. Ibid., 7.
48. Kim, "Red Turban Rebellion," 13–14.
49. Zeng, *Guangdong Martial Arts*, 68.
50. Ma, *Foshan Martial Arts Culture*, 62–63.
51. These are conservative estimates. If one counts all of the lion dance teams and the other peripheral associations, Hung Sing may have had up to 10,000 members in Foshan. When Chan died in 1926 it is estimated that 5,000 Hung Sing members attended his funeral. See Zeng, *Guangdong Martial Arts*, 68–72.
52. Ma, *Foshan Martial Arts Culture*, 62–63; Zeng, *Guangdong Martial Arts*, 68–72.
53. Ma, *Foshan Martial Arts Culture*, 69.
54. See for instance Garrett Gee, Benny Meng and Richard Loewenhagen, *Mastering Kung Fu: Featuring Shaolin Wing Chun* (Champaign, IL: Human Kinetics Publishers, 2003).
55. ter Haar, *Chinese Triads*, 420–425.
56. Jeff Takacs, "A Case of Contagious Legitimacy: Kinship, Ritual and Manipulation in Chinese Martial Arts Societies," *Modern Asian Studies* 37, no. 4 (2003): 885–917.
57. Christine Moll-Murata, "Chinese Guilds from the Seventeenth to the Twentieth Centuries: An Overview," *International Review of Social History* 53 (2008): 213–247.
58. In Western literature Holcombe has argued the most forcefully in favor of the religious origins of the Chinese martial arts. Charles Holcombe, "Theater of Combat: A Critical Look at the Chinese Martial Arts," *Historian* 52, no. 3 (1990): 411–431; Charles Holcombe, "The Daoist Origins of the Chinese Martial Arts," *Journal of Asian Martial Arts* 2, no. 1 (1993): 10–25. For responses to this position see Stanley Henning, "Academia Encounters the Chinese Martial Arts," *China Review International* 6, no. 2 (1999): 319–332; Kennedy and Guo, *Martial Arts Training Manuals*, 84–87.
59. For an ethnographic investigation of Southern Mantis that discusses the modern practice of spirit possession and the esoteric aspects of unicorn dancing, see Daniel Miles Amos, "Marginality and the Heroes Art: Martial Artists in Hong Kong and Guangzhou (Canton)" (PhD diss., University of California, Los Angeles, 1983), 159–256.
60. Stanley Henning, "Martial Arts in Chinese Physical Culture, 1865–1965," In *Martial Arts in the Modern World*, ed. Thomas A. Green and Joseph R. Svinth (London: Praeger, 2003), 13–35.
61. Douglas Wile, *Lost Tai-Chi Classics from the Late Ch'ing Dynasty* (Albany: State University of New York Press, 1996), 27–30.
62. John Christopher Hamm, "Local Heroes: Guangdong School *Wuxia* Fiction and Hong Kong's Imagining of China," *Twentieth-Century China* 27, no. 1 (2001): 71–96.

63. Ip Ching, and Ron Heimberger, *Ip Man: Portrait of a Kung Fu Master* (Springville, UT: King Dragon Press, 2003), 3–4.

64. Ma, *Foshan Martial Arts Culture*, 68–70.

65. It should be noted that Lin Jia Quan (Mandarin) might be better known to southern martial artists as Lam Gar Kuen, or "Lam Family Style."

66. Zeng, *Guangdong Martial Arts*, 72.

67. In Cantonese the name "Tin Hua" means "Heavenly Queen." This is one of the many titles of Mazu, the sea goddess, who is responsible for the safety of sailors and fishermen. Mazu's cult was first popularized in the Ming dynasty, but by the Qing era she was ubiquitous. Her temples can still be seen all along the coastal areas of Guangdong, Fujian, Taiwan and Hong Kong. If one was really about to fight pirates using only martial arts, her assistance certainly could not hurt. Unfortunately the goddess's loyalties were somewhat complicated as the local pirates also took Tin Hua as their patron deity. For more discussion of religion in coastal southern China at the end of the Qing dynasty see Robert J. Antony, *Like Froth Floating on the Sea: The World of Pirates and Seafarers in Late Imperial China* (Berkeley, CA: Institute of East Asian Studies, 2003), 152–161.

68. Zeng, *Guangdong Martial Arts*, 73.

69. For an overview of the history of Lin Jia Martial Arts Institute, the Ying Wu Tong, and the Xu Wen Dongguan Martial Arts Institute see Zeng, *Guangdong Martial Arts*, chapter 2 section 2.

Chapter 3

1. Quoted in Andrew D. Morris, *Marrow of the Nation: A History of Sport and Physical Culture in Republican China* (Los Angeles: University of California Press, 2004), 195–196.

2. Edward J. M. Rhoads, *China's Republican Revolution: The Case of Kwangtung, 1895–1913* (Cambridge, MA: Harvard University Press, 1975).

3. Ma Zineng, *Foshan Wushu Wenhua* (*Foshan Martial Arts Culture*) (Foshan: Foshanshi Chanchengqu Feiyinglixing Chubanwu, 2001), 66–70.

4. Patricia Buckley Ebrey, *China: Cambridge Illustrated History* (Cambridge: Cambridge University Press, 2007), 273–275.

5. Daniel Y. K. Kwan, *Marxist Intellectuals and the Chinese Labor Movement: A Study of Deng Zhongxia 1894–1933* (Seattle: University of Washington Press, 1997).

6. "Yellow trade unions" refer to collective labor arrangements that are vertically integrated within a single firm, but not across an industrial sector. Because these unions include both labor and management in a single organization they tend to promote the success of the firm, rather than the interests of the workers. As such they are often viewed as a threat to labor's collective bargaining power. The yellow trade unions in southern China might include both workers and management across an entire sector and were sometimes closely

aligned with the GMD. This further decreased the worker's bargaining power. See Kwan, *Marxist Intellectuals*, 73.

7. For a more detailed discussion of the labor violence that involved these groups see Kwan, *Marxist Intellectuals*, 180–183.

8. Ebrey, *Illustrated History*, 276–277.

9. Doc Fai Wong and Jane Hallander, *Choy Li Fut Kung Fu: The Dynamic Fighting Art Descended from the Monks of the Shaolin Temple* (Burbank, CA: Unique Publications, 1985), 11–13.

10. John Christopher Hamm, *Paper Swordsmen: Jin Yong and the Modern Chinese Martial Arts Novel* (Honolulu: University of Hawaii Press, 2006), 37.

11. Ma, *Foshan Martial Arts Culture*, 70.

12. Ibid., 66.

13. The Chinese term "Zhong Yi" has no direct translation in English. It indicates both the concepts of loyalty and "martial virtue."

14. Ma, *Foshan Martial Arts Culture*, 120. Note that when read in Mandarin Jiu Chao's name translates as Zhao Jiu.

15. Rene Ritchie, *Yuen Kay-San Wing Chun Kuen: History and Foundation* (New York: Multi-Media Books, 1999), 20.

16. Ma, *Foshan Martial Arts Culture*, 120–121.

17. The group adopted the term "Guoshu" (national art) for their title. This name was coined by the GMD for use by its newly created "Central Guoshu Institute" and party-sponsored martial arts programs. The word seems to have implied a belief in a rectified and modernized art, truly national in scope, placed at the disposal of the state. See the more extensive discussion below.

18. Reconciling the names and locations of all of the known branches of the Zhong Yi Association is difficult. Ma provides a partial list of nine schools where at least some information on their specific location is known: The Tai Ping branch was on Tai Guan Street; the Fu Min branch was located within the Hua Guang Great Emperor Temple; the Tai Xu branch had its headquarters on Lian Hua Road; the exact location of the Tai Ji Mei branch is still unknown; the Shi Jiao branch met in the Wen Yi building; the Feng Ning branch was situated at the Jian Xin road water plant; the Fu De branch was located at the Tai Shang Temple on She Ren Street; lastly, the Lu Feng group met at the Yue Fei Temple. Ma, *Foshan Martial Arts Culture*, 70–72.

19. Ibid.

20. Samuel Kwok, "A Chronicle of the Life of Ip Man," *WT Danmark* 3 (2006): 8.

21. Leung Ting, *Roots and Branches of Wing Tsun* (Hong Kong: Leung's Publications, 2000), 304. Leung also lists a number of Hung Gar teachers who instructed Pan Nam in Foshan, and he states that he got a job working as a martial arts instructor for the Union of Cake Industry Workers of Foshan (303). It seems at least possible that this was one of the yellow trade unions associated with the Zhong Yi schools.

22. Kwan, *Marxist Intellectuals*, 73.

23. Ibid., 67.

24. Ma, *Foshan Martial Arts Culture*, 70–72.

25. S. L. Fung, *Pak Mei Kung Fu: The Myth & the Martial Art* (New York: TNP Multimedia LLC, 2008), 16–17.

26. For a review of the oral histories surrounding the origins of Dragon and White Eyebrow see the database maintained by the Taiping Institute, <http://taipinginstitute.com/>.

27. Ibid.

28. William Acevedo and Mei Cheung, in their survey of Republican-era Guoshu periodicals, find that both Guangdong and Fujian are conspicuously underrepresented. The only local publications that they report during this time period were produced by the Jingwu Association. The Guoshu movement never managed to launch a successful journal in the south, though they note that it is likely that at least some of their periodicals, published in Shanghai and other areas, circulated in the region. Their findings confirm Andrew Morris's earlier observation that the Guoshu movement seems to have been the most successful in the eastern coastal zone and in those places where the regional government was loyal to the GMD's ruling clique. William Acevedo and Mei Cheung, "Republican Period Guoshu Periodicals," *Classical Fighting Arts* 2, no. 26 (2014): 56–68.

29. Fung, *Pak Mei Kung Fu*, 57–58.

30. The Chinese characters used to represent Fat San, the organization, are different from Foshan (sometimes transliterated as Fatsan) the town. However, the characters behind the Cheung Yee Wui are identical to those used by the Zhong Yi Association. Given that both groups were heavily influenced by the GMD, it seems likely that the connection is intentional. In light of the Zhong Yi Association's long history of fighting communism in the region, it was most likely incorporated into General Kot's new umbrella organization. One wonders if perhaps a better functional translation of either Zhong Yi, or Cheung Yee, in the context of late 1940s would be "anti-communist league."

31. Kingsley Bolton and Christopher Hutton, *Triad Societies: Western Accounts of the History, Sociology and Linguistics of Chinese Secret Societies* (London, Routledge, 2000): 80–82.

32. It should be remembered that Ng Mui also conspires to destroy the Shaolin Temple in the original text of *Everlasting*, yet she has been rehabilitated by later generations of martial arts fans.

33. Fung, *Pak Mei Kung Fu*, 58–59.

34. Stanley E. Henning, "Martial Arts in Chinese Physical Culture, 1865–1965," in *Martial Arts in the Modern World*, ed. Thomas A. Green and Joseph R. Svinth, 13–36, (London: Praeger, 2003), provides a good overview of national trends in Chinese martial arts from the 1920s through the 1940s. The most detailed discussion of the national debate regarding the worth of indigenous martial arts in the English language literature is provided by Morris, *Marrow of the Nation*, 185–230. Kennedy and Gao also make a substantial contribution to

this discussion in their review of martial arts training manuals (2005) and their monograph on the history of the "Pure Martial" movement is very valuable. See Brian Kennedy and Elizabeth Guo, *Jingwu: the School that Transformed Kung Fu* (Berkeley, CA: Blue Snake Books, 2010). Ma and Zeng both provide a more detailed discussion of how these movements manifest themselves in Foshan and Guangzhou respectively.

35. Hamm's discussion of the early "Guangdong school" of martial arts novels clearly demonstrated the degree to which these cultural traditions were in fact aggressively parochial in their identity and goals. Hamm, *Paper Swordsmen*, 34–48.

36. Morris, *Marrow of the Nation*, 185–195.

37. Ibid., 187.

38. Kennedy and Guo, *Jingwu*, 23–25.

39. Morris, *Marrow of the Nation*, 198–199.

40. Ibid., 192–193.

41. Ibid., 197–198.

42. Henning, "Martial Arts in Physical Culture," 32–34, provides a brief review of the Cultural Revolution and its effect on traditional Chinese martial arts.

43. Morris, *Marrow of the Nation*, 204.

44. These sets included such northern classics as "Twelve Rows of Springing Legs," "Big Battle Fist," "Power Fist," "Connecting Fist," "Eight Diagram (Bagua) Fist," "Shepard Staff," "Five Tiger Spear'" "Tan Tui Sparring," "Tao Quan (Fist Set)," and a broadsword versus spear form.

45. Zeng Zhaosheng, *Guangdong Wushu Shi* (*A History of Guangdong Martial Arts*) (Guangzhou: Guangdong ren min chu ban she, 1989), 74–76.

46. Morris, *Marrow of the Nation*, 199–200.

47. Zeng, *Guangdong Martial Arts*, 75–76.

48. Ibid., 74–86.

49. Ma, *Foshan Martial Arts Culture*, 47–49.

50. Zeng, *Guangdong Martial Arts*, 76–77.

51. Leung, *Roots and Branches*, 239–240, and Rene Ritchie, *Yuen Kay-San Wing Chun Kuen: History and Foundations* (Los Angeles: Multimedia Books, 1997), 19, suggest that the dual was fought by Yuen Kay San. However, it is clear that both of these accounts are fairly distant from the original events and Leung's dramatic retelling of the fight is actually disturbingly close to the version published in the later pulp novel. A secondhand account of the fight was published by Ip Ching in 2003 (21–22). Here he states that it was his father, Ip Man, and not his close friend, Yuen Kay San, who actually accepted the challenge. The accounts given by both Leung and Ritchie begin with Yu appearing, demanding to see Ip Man, and (not finding him) taking on a surprised Yuen Kay San instead.

52. Ching and Heimberger, *Ip Man*, 21–22.

53. Zeng, *Guangdong Martial Arts*, 75.

54. Ma, *Foshan Martial Arts Culture*, 54.
55. Ibid., 56.
56. Ibid., 57–60.
57. Ibid., 55.
58. Ibid., 56–57.
59. A "Zhongshan Park" is basically a monument dedicated to the memory of Sun Yat-sen and the creation of the modern Chinese State. Such parks are located throughout China, and can even be found in other places with large Chinese populations.
60. Ma, *Foshan Martial Arts Culture*, 50.
61. Ibid., 50–51.
62. Morris, *Marrow of the Nation*, 206–207.
63. Henning, "Martial Arts in Physical Culture," 22–23.
64. Morris, *Marrow of the Nation*, 214.
65. Ibid., 205.
66. Ibid., 213–214.
67. Henning, "Martial Arts in Physical Culture," 22.
68. Morris, *Marrow of the Nation*, 213.
69. Ibid., 205.
70. Ibid.
71. Henning, "Martial Arts in Physical Culture," 24–25; Morris, *Marrow of the Nation*, 205.
72. Morris, *Marrow of the Nation*, 207–209.
73. Henning, "Martial Arts in Physical Culture," 23–24.
74. Morris, *Marrow of the Nation*, 210.
75. Henning, "Martial Arts in Physical Culture," 22; Morris, *Marrow of the Nation*, 210–211.
76. Morris, *Marrow of the Nation*, 214.
77. A discussion of the basic facts regarding the Liangguang Guoshu Institute is provided in Zeng's overview of the martial arts associations of Guangdong province prior to WWII. See Zeng, *Guangdong Martial Arts*, 78–80.
78. Ibid.
79. Ibid.
80. Kennedy and Guo, *Training Manuals*, 291–292.
81. Zeng, *Guangdong Martial Arts*, 83.
82. Ma, *Foshan Martial Arts Culture*, 70.
83. Morris, *Marrow of the Nation*, 207.
84. Ma, *Foshan Martial Arts Culture*, 71.
85. Hamm, *Paper Swordsmen*, 36–38. Readers may recall that it was during the 1930s that both Wong Fei Hung and Leung Jan, two of Foshan's most enduring martial heroes, achieved a certain fame and immortality that had escaped both men in life.
86. Petrus Liu, *Stateless Subjects: Chinese Martial Arts Literature & Postcolonial History* (Ithaca, NY: East Asia Program Cornell University, 2011), 6.

87. Morris, *Marrow of the Nation*, 215–229.
88. Henning, "Martial Arts in Physical Culture," 24–25.
89. Xu Zhen, "Fakan Ci," *Qiushi Jikan* 1, no. 1 (1934): 1. Translation cited in Morris, *Marrow of the Nation*, 217.
90. Morris, *Marrow of the Nation*, 218–220.
91. Ching and Heimberger, *Ip Man*, 27–30.
92. It is no exaggeration to say that more has been written on the life and thoughts of Bruce Lee than any other single Chinese martial artist. For a brief overview of his life and critique of traditional martial arts see Bruce Thomas, *Bruce Lee: Fighting Spirit* (Berkeley, CA: Blue Snake Books, 1994) and James Bishop, *Bruce Lee: Dynamic Becoming* (Carrollton, TX: Promethean Press, 2004).

Chapter 4

1. Ma Zineng, *Foshan Wushu Wenhua* (*Foshan Martial Arts Culture*) (Foshan: Foshanshi Chanchengqu Feiyinglixing Chubanwu, 2001), 112.
2. This widely discussed find is called the "Xishuipo Site" and it is located in Puyang, *Henan Province*. It was first studied in 1987. In tomb M45 the shell mosaic dragon (left) and tiger (right) were laid out on either side of the body of a tall male. Three additional bodies (all young children) were deposited in the grave and some archeologists believe that the tomb was constructed for a shaman. Sarah Allen, ed., *The Formation of Chinese Civilization: An Archeological Perspective* (New Haven, CT: Yale University Press, 2005), 77–78.
3. See the introductory quote to Chapter 2 in the present volume.
4. For a discussion of Painted Face Kam and his alleged relationship with modern Wing Chun see Rene Ritchie, *Yuen Kay-San Wing Chun Kuen: History and Foundation* (New York: Multi-Media Books, 1997), 13–14; Robert Chu, Rene Ritchie, and Y. Wu, *Complete Wing Chun* (North Clarendon, VT: Tuttle Publishing, 1998), 92–94; Leung Ting, *Roots and Branches of Wing Tsun*, 2nd edition (Hong Kong: Leung's Publications, 2003), 241.
5. See Ip Chun and Michael Tse, *Wing Chun Kung Fu: Traditional Chinese Kung Fu for Self-Defense and Health* (New York: St. Martin's Griffin, 1998), 19; Chu, Ritchie, and Wu, *Complete Wing Chun*, 5–6; Ma, *Foshan Martial Arts Culture*, 112.
6. For one of the best accounts of the social causes and implications of the Red Turban Rebellion see Frederick Wakeman, Jr., *Strangers at the Gate: Social Disorder in South China, 1839–1861* (Los Angeles: University of California Press, 1997), chapters 13–15.
7. It should be remembered that while the wealthy merchants and gentry were distinct classes in other parts of China; in Guangdong these two groups came to be substantially overlapped. Alfred H. Y. Lin, *The Rural Economy of Guangdong, 1870–1937* (New York: St. Martin's Press, 1997). The story of Leung

Caixin, reviewed previously in some detail, demonstrates how a single clan could come to monopolize both roles in the south.

8. Leung, *Roots and Branches*, 60.
9. Ibid., 60–64.
10. Ma, *Foshan Martial Arts Culture*, 117.
11. Ip and Tse, *Wing Chun Kung Fu*, 20.
12. Leung, *Roots and Branches*, 61.
13. Ma, *Foshan Martial Arts Culture*, 117.
14. Chu, Ritchie, and Wu, *Complete Wing Chun*, 45–52; Leung, *Roots and Branches*, 289–291.
15. Ma, *Foshan Martial Arts Culture*, 117.
16. Ip Man, "The Origin of Ving Tsun: Written by the Late Grand Master Ip Man," (Hong Kong: Ving Tsun Athletic Association, 1967). <http://www.vingtsun.org.hk/1967>.
17. Ma, *Foshan Martial Arts Culture*, 68–70.
18. Leung, *Roots and Branches*, 64; Ma, *Foshan Martial Arts Culture*, 117.
19. Ma, *Foshan Martial Arts Culture*, 117.
20. Lin, *Rural Economy*, 1997.
21. Ma, *Foshan Martial Arts Culture*, 63.
22. Ibid., 117.
23. Ip and Tse, *Wing Chun Kung Fu*, 20.
24. Ma, *Foshan Martial Arts Culture*, 117.
25. Leung, *Roots and Branches*, 64; Ma, *Foshan Martial Arts Culture*, 117.
26. For an extensive discussion of these debates see Andrew Morris, *Marrow of the Nation: A History of Sport and Physical Culture in Republican China* (Los Angeles: University of California Press, 2004), 185–230.
27. Leung, *Roots and Branches*, 111.
28. Ma, *Foshan Martial Arts Culture*, 117–121.
29. Ibid., 118.
30. Ip and Tse, *Wing Chun Kung Fu*, 22.
31. Ip Ching and Ron Heimberger, *Ip Man: Portrait of a Kung Fu Master* (Springville, UT: King Dragon Press, 2003), 3.
32. Ip and Tse, *Wing Chun Kung Fu*, 28.
33. For an extensive discussion of the evolution of ancestral temples see David Faure, *Empire and Ancestor: State and Lineage in Southern China* (Stanford, CA: Stanford University Press, 2007). Much of Faure's historical research was conducted on families in the Foshan area.
34. Ip and Heimberger, *Ip Man*, 4. It should be noted that Ip Chun states that his father was eleven when he initially petitioned Chan Wah Shun for instruction (Ip and Tse, *Wing Chun Kung Fu*, 22).
35. Ma, *Foshan Martial Arts Culture*, 115.
36. Ip and Tse, *Wing Chun Kung Fu*, 24; Leung, *Roots and Branches*, 111. Ip Ching places the same figure at 500 Tai Yeung (silver dollar) coins.
37. Ip and Tse, *Wing Chun Kung Fu*, 22–25, 42; Ip and Heimberger, *Ip Man*, 4–5, 11.

38. See, for instance, Frederic Wakeman's treatment of the famous San Yuan Li incident during the Opium Wars. Wakeman, *Strangers at the Gate*, 11–22.

39. Ip and Tse, *Wing Chun Kung Fu*, 25; Ip and Heimberger, *Ip Man*, 11–13. We should also note that in an interview granted to *New Martial Hero* magazine in 1972 Ip Man related a slightly different version of how he met Leung Bik which did not include an altercation with a police officer. Instead, it was his frequent fights with classmates at school that brought him to the master's attention. It is hard to judge which account is more reliable. The version with the police officer (favored by Ip Man's sons) has an undeniably nationalist element which might signal an exaggeration. Nevertheless, there are very understandable reasons why a martial arts master in Hong Kong in the early 1970s would want to play down past violent conflicts with law enforcement in his public statements. In terms of understanding Wing Chun as a social system, what is probably most important is to consider why some versions of this story seem to be favored in certain situations rather than others. For the alternate account see "Interview with Wing Chun Grandmaster Ip Man," *New Martial Hero*, no. 56, February, 30–33.

40. Ip and Tse, *Wing Chun Kung Fu*, 26–27.

41. This speculation seems to be reinforced by Ip family lore. When asked by Leung Bik to demonstrate the three unarmed forms at their first meeting Ip Man refused to perform the final set. He claimed that he could not demonstrate it publicly because of its supposedly confidential nature. His son Ip Ching instead asserts that his father did not perform it because he did not yet know it. Ip and Heimberger, *Ip Man*, 13–14.

42. Leung, *Roots and Branches*, 117.

43. Ip and Heimberger, *Ip Man*, 15–17.

44. Ibid., 15. Ip Man's role in presiding at Leung Bik's funeral was outlined in the author's personal correspondence with Ip Ching. Ip Chun has published accounts claiming that the two actually studied together for approximately two years (Ip and Tse, *Wing Chun Kung Fu*, 27). Whichever figure is more accurate, it is clear that the actual relationship between the teacher and student was brief.

45. Leung, *Roots and Branches*, 68.

46. See the extensive discussion of these events in Chapter 3. Also see Ip and Heimberger, *Ip Man*, 21. Note the date that he provides (1918) is most likely incorrect as there was not yet a Jingwu branch in Foshan; 1921–1922 seems a much more likely time frame.

47. Ip and Tse, *Wing Chun Kung Fu*, 28.

48. For the best economic history of the area see Lin, *Rural Economy of Guangdong*, 1997.

49. Ip Chun, Lu De'an, and Peng Yaojun, *Ye Wen, Yong Chun 2* (Ip Man, Wing Chun, 2 volumes, revised edition) (Xianggang: Hui zhi chu ban you xian gong si, 2010), 207–210.

50. In a personal interview Ip Ching related that his parents had in total eight children. Four of these were boys and four were girls. Only half of the siblings survived to adulthood.

51. This incident was related by Michael Tse in the introduction to his book coauthored with Ip Chun. Ip and Tse, *Wing Chun Kung Fu*, 10.

52. Ma, *Foshan Martial Arts Culture*, 118; Leung, *Roots and Branches*, 64.

53. Ma, *Foshan Martial Arts Culture*, 118.

54. Leung, *Roots and Branches*, 69.

55. For a discussion of the role of anti-opium sentiments during the national revolution in Guangdong see Edward J. M. Rhodes, *China's Republican Revolution: The Case of Kwangtung, 1895–1913* (Cambridge, MA: Harvard University Press, 1975). For a more recent discussion that explores popular and sometimes socially permissive attitudes towards the use of opium see Virgil K. Y. Ho, *Understanding Canton: Rethinking Popular Culture in the Republican Period* (Oxford: Oxford University Press, 2005), 95–156.

56. Duncan Leung, another student of Ip Man's from the 1950s goes even further. In a sensationalistic account of his own martial arts career he states that his teacher became an opium addict as a young man. He speculates that this is why he later found it necessary to charge such high tuition and to sell the true applications of his techniques only to his wealthiest students and disciples. Not surprisingly, other students, including Ip Man's children, deny these charges. See Ken Ing, *Wing Chun Warrior: The True Tales of Wing Chun Kung Fu Master Duncan Leung, Bruce Lee's Fighting Companion* (Hong Kong: Blacksmith Books, 2009), 110; Ip and Heimberger, *Ip Man*, 37–38.

57. Ma, *Foshan Martial Arts Culture*, 118.

58. Leung, *Roots and Branches*, 296.

59. Ma, *Foshan Martial Arts Culture*, 118.

60. A description of various long fighting poles, including those made of iron, is provided in Meir Shahar, *The Shaolin Monastery: History, Religion and the Chinese Martial Arts* (Honolulu: Hawai'i University Press, 2008), 59.

61. Ma, *Foshan Martial Arts Culture*, 120.

62. Many accounts claim that Lai Yip Chi actually began as a disciple of Chan Wah Shun and later transitioned to Lui Yu Chai when the older teacher became incapacitated. In that sense his situation was actually very similar to Ip Man. This detail may affect which generation Lai claims, but either way, it is clear that the bulk of his Wing Chun came from Lui Yu Chai.

63. Ma, *Foshan Martial Arts Culture*, 119.

64. Chu, Ritchie and Wu, *Complete Wing Chun*, 72.

65. Ma, *Foshan Martial Arts Culture*, 119.

66. Ibid., 120.

67. Leung, *Roots and Branches*, 341.

68. Ritchie, *Yuen Kay-San*, 20; Ma, *Foshan Martial Arts Culture*, 120.

69. Ma, *Foshan Martial Arts Culture*, 120–121.

70. Ma, *Foshan Martial Arts Culture*, 119–120; Ritchie, *Yuen Kay-San*. 15–20.

71. Yiu Kay, the son of Yiu Choi relates that Yuen Chai Wan taught his father something that he called Sheh Ying Wing Chun, or "Snake Pattern Wing

Chun." The style was simple, consisting only of a single unarmed form called Siu Lin Tao (similar to, but not the same as, the name shared by the first boxing form in most Wing Chun schools today), a double broadsword form, and a set of hand techniques that were practices on a "bamboo dummy" quite distinct from the wooden dummy used today (Leung, *Roots and Branches*, 246). This information is a valuable reminder that a style like Wing Chun is a "social construction" just as much as it is a compilation of individual forms or techniques.

72. Ma, *Foshan Martial Arts Culture*, 121.
73. Leung, *Roots and Branches*, 246–247.
74. See, for instance, Ip and Tse, *Wing Chun Kung Fu*, 36.
75. Patricia Buckley Ebrey, *China: Cambridge Illustrated History* (Cambridge: Cambridge University Press, 2007), 275.
76. For a detailed discussion of these events see Chapter 3.
77. Personal Correspondence with Ip Ching.
78. Lo Man Kam, "Wing Chun & My Uncle, Yip Man: a Lo Man Kam Narrative," *Wing Chun Teahouse* 1 (2006): 10–11.
79. Leung, *Roots and Branches*, 69–70.
80. Ip and Tse, *Wing Chun Kung Fu*, 35–36.
81. Leung, *Roots and Branches*, 70.
82. Samuel Kwok and Tony Massengill, *Mastering Wing Chun: The Keys to Ip Man's Kung Fu* (Los Angeles: E. B. Empire Books, 2007), 287.
83. Ip and Heimberger, *Ip Man*, 28.
84. Ibid., 107.
85. Kwok and Massengill, *Mastering Wing Chun*, 287; Leung, *Roots and Branches*, 70.
86. Ip and Heimberger, *Ip Man*, 33.
87. Leung, *Roots and Branches*, 68.
88. Ip and Heimberger, *Ip Man*, 107, 79.
89. Kwok and Massengill, *Mastering Wing Chun*, 287.
90. Chu, Ritchie, and Wu, *Complete Wing Chun*, 7.

Chapter 5

1. Hawkins Cheung and Robert Chu, "Bruce Lee's Mother Art: Wing Chun," *Inside Kung Fu*, January, 1992.
2. Adam D. Frank, *Taijiquan and the Search for the Little Old Chinese Man: Understanding Identity through Martial Arts* (New York: Palgrave Macmillan, 2006).
3. For a discussion of Foshan's economic decline see Yimin He, "Prosperity and Decline: A Comparison of the Fate of Jingdezhen, Zhuxianzhen, Foshan and Hankou in Modern Times," *Frontiers of History in China* 5, no. 1 (2010): 52–85. Translated by Weiwei Zhou from *Xueshu Yuekan* (*Academic Monthly*) 12 (2008): 122–133.

4. 1997 launched another period of change for Hong Kong's economy. Political reintegration with the mainland allowed the city to reclaim its traditional position as a transit port. Most of the manufacturing that happened in Hong Kong was transferred to lower wage areas in Guangdong and the city began to invest heavily in knowledge, service, and financial industries. Nevertheless, this period of economic transformation takes us far beyond the time frame of the current chapter.

5. For a detailed examination of Hong Kong's economic history and development see Catherine Schenk, "Economic History of Hong Kong," *EH.Net Encyclopedia*, edited by Robert Whaples, March 16, 2008. Also see D. R. Meyer, *Hong Kong as a Global Metropolis* (Cambridge: Cambridge University Press, 2000); C. R. Schenk, *Hong Kong as an International Financial Centre: Emergence and Development, 1945–65* (London: Routledge, 2001).

6. Daniel M. Amos, "Spirit Boxing in Hong Kong: Two Observers, Native and Foreign," *Journal of Asian Martial Arts* 8, no. 4. (1999): 10. It should be noted that Amos originally presented this research in his doctoral dissertation titled "Marginality and the Heroes Art: Martial Artists in Hong Kong and Guangzhou (Canton)" (PhD Diss., University of California, 1983). This dissertation has since become an important source in the ethnographic literature on Chinese martial arts based communities. Much of what Amos writes in his articles is an updated version of discussions that he originally laid down, in much greater detail, twenty years before. Researchers may find it useful to compare the original and updated versions of these accounts when trying to gain the fullest picture of the author's arguments.

7. Amos, "Spirit Boxing," 12.

8. Ibid., 10.

9. Daniel M. Amos, "A Hong Kong Southern Praying Mantis Cult," *Journal of Asian Martial Arts* 6, No. 4 (1997): 39.

10. Avron Boretz, *Gods, Ghosts and Gangsters: Ritual Violence, Martial Arts, and Masculinity on the Margins of Chinese Society* (Honolulu: University of Hawai'i Press, 2011): 10.

11. Amos, "Southern Praying Mantis Cult," 42.

12. Amos, "Marginality and the Heroes Art," 216–219.

13. Ibid., 210–211. For a discussion of the myth of Shaolin Temple in Triad initiation rituals and its relationship to the myth told in martial arts schools see Barend J. ter Haar, *Ritual and Mythology of the Chinese Triads: Creating an Identity* (Boston: Brill Academic Publishers, 2000), 402–418.

14. Sek Kai and Rolanda Chu, "A Brief Historical Tour of Hong Kong Martial Arts Film," *Bright Lights Film Journal* 13 (1994).

15. John Christopher Hamm, *Paper Swordsmen: Jin Yong and the Modern Chinese Martial Arts Novel* (Honolulu: University of Hawai'i Press, 2005), 42–43 and 49–79. For an English translation of an important early novel see Louis Cha, *The Book and the Sword* (Hong Kong: Oxford University Press, 2004).

16. Ip Man was issued a Hong Kong government identity card (#1353297) in December of 1950, roughly a year after he first arrived, and about six months after he started teaching. However, the Immigration Department did not issue him a passport until March 15, 1963. These documents are on display at the Ip Man Tong museum on the grounds of the Ancestral Temple in Foshan. His passport photo is said to be the only picture of Ip Man wearing Western-style clothing (in this case a dark suit and silver or grey tie).
17. Ip Ching and Ron Heimberger, *Ip Man: Portrait of a Kung Fu Master* (Springville, UT: King Dragon Press, 2003), 82.
18. Ving Tsun Athletic Association, "Development of Ving Tsun Kung Fu in Hong Kong: 1950–1953, 1954–1960, 1961–1970," <http://www.vingtsun.org.hk/>.
19. Chu Shong Tin, *The Book of Wing Chun* (Revised Edition) (Hong Kong: Hong Kong Social Science Press, 2011), 46.
20. Ving Tsun Athletic Association, "Development of Ving Tsun Kung Fu in Hong Kong," <http://www.vingtsun.org.hk/>.
21. Ip and Heimberger, *Ip Man*, 68.
22. Chu, *The Book of Wing Chun*, 46.
23. Samuel Kwok and Tony Massengill, *Mastering Wing Chun: The Keys to Ip Man's Kung Fu* (Los Angeles: EB Empire Books, 2007), 288.
24. See Chapter 4.
25. Little has been published on Lee Shing, and most of the biographical information available on this individual is provided by students in his lineage in the United Kingdom (where he eventually taught).
26. Interestingly the students and grand students of Lee Shing seem increasingly drawn to their teacher's earlier Gulao training, which does not seem to have been his major focus during this period.
27. Ip Chun and Michael Tse, *Wing Chun Kung Fu: Traditional Chinese Kung Fu for Self-Defence and Health* (New York: St. Martin's Press, 1998), 41–42.
28. Yip Chun and Danny Connor, *Wing Chun Martial Arts: Principles & Techniques* (San Francisco: Weiser Books, 1992), 26. Note that "Yip" is a spelling variant of "Ip." "Yip Chun" is Ip Man's oldest son, Ip Chun.
29. Given this move toward a formal curriculum and teaching structure in the Hong Kong period, one might expect that there would be a great deal of agreement among Ip Man's students as to what he actually taught. In practice this turns out not to be the case. Some of these disagreements can be attributed to simple gamesmanship, prominent students attempting to justify their own innovations by claiming that this was how the Master did things. In other cases it appears that Ip Man's geographic instability undermined his attempts at standardization. As this case study makes clear, he was constantly moving the location of his school and every time he did he gained some students and lost others. In some places there was no room to teach the wooden dummy or the pole; in other places there was. While Ip Man had a coherent teaching

curriculum, only his most persistent followers managed to see the entire thing. It seems that the majority of his students followed him to one or two locations and then drifted away.

30. Leung Ting, *Roots and Branches of Wing Chun* (Hong Kong: Leung's Publications, 2003), 120.

31. Chu, *The Book of Wing Chun*, 43–45.

32. Ip Chun, Lu De'an, and Peng Yaojun, *Ye Wen, Yong Chun 2* (Ip Man, Wing Chun. 2 Volumes, Revised Edition) (Xianggang: Hui zhi chu ban you xian gong si, 2010), 209–210.

33. Chu, *The Book of Wing Chun*, 48.

34. Ibid., 47.

35. Interview with Ip Ching, Hong Kong, December 2012.

36. Ip, Lu, and Peng, *Ye Wen*, 210. In interviews Ip Ching has stated that his mother died slightly earlier in 1957.

37. Hamm, *Paper Swordsmen*, 4.

38. For a comprehensive discussion of the Wu style of Taiji and its history see Frank, *Search for the Little Old Chinese Man*, chapter 2.

39. Chen Kefu studied Tibetan White Crane, a style which claims western China and Tibet as its ancestral home. It is distinct from the White Crane schools found in Fujian Province, previously discussed elsewhere in this volume. The antecedents of this western White Crane first appeared in Guangdong Province during the 1860s.

40. Hamm, *Paper Swordsmen*, 4–5.

41. Some of the English language biographical information of Wu Zhaozhong has been gathered from auction house catalogues discussing his poetry and calligraphy. See Christie's "Fine Chinese Modern Paintings" November 30, 2010, Lot 2520; Sale 2822.

42. Hamm, *Paper Swordsmen*, 7–10.

43. "The Development of Ving Tsun Kung Fu in Hong Kong, 1954–1960," Ving Tsun Athletic Association, accessed June 15, 2014, <http://www.vingtsun.org.hk/>.

44. Interview with Chan Chee Man in Darrell Jordan, *The Sound of Ving Tsun: The Grandmasters and Masters* (Winter Park: Florida Ving Tsun Athletic Association, 2004), 5–6.

45. Ibid., 7.

46. Hawkins Cheung and Robert Chu, "Bruce's Classical Mess: Cleaning up the Mess the 'Little Dragon' Left Behind," *Inside Kung Fu*, February, 1992.

47. Ip and Heimberger, *Ip Man*, 53

48. Cheung, "Bruce Lee's Mother Art."

49. "Sifu Peng" is a pseudonym. Following the professional guidelines established within his field Amos does not publish the names of his informants within his ethnographic accounts.

50. Amos, "Southern Praying Mantis Cult," 38.

51. Ving Tsun Athletic Association, "Development of Ving Tsun Kung Fu in Hong Kong, 1954–1960," <http://www.vingtsun.org.hk/>.
52. Bruce Thomas, *Bruce Lee: Fighting Spirit* (Berkeley, CA: Blue Snake Books, 1994), 29–30.
53. Ving Tsun Athletic Association, "Development of Ving Tsun Kung Fu in Hong Kong, 1954–1960," <http://www.vingtsun.org.hk/>.
54. Thomas, *Fighting Spirit*, 26–27.
55. Ken Ing, *Wing Chun Warrior: The True Tales of Wing Chun Kung Fu Master Duncan Leung, Bruce Lee's Fighting Companion* (Hong Kong: Blacksmith Books, 2009), 83–88, 105, 110.
56. Leung, *Roots and Branches*, 122–124.
57. Hawkins Cheung and Robert Chu, "Bruce Lee's Hong Kong Years: A couple of 'juvenile delinquents' named Bruce Lee and Hawkins Cheung roamed the streets of Hong Kong, picking fights, having fun and refining their martial arts techniques," *Inside Kung Fu*, November, 1991. Also see Hawkins and Chu in December 1991 and January 1992.
58. Jordan, *Sound of Ving Tsun*, 2004.
59. The Cantonese expression "Shanghai Lady," used by both Ip Man and his students, was a common term applied to immigrant women from that area of China in Hong Kong at the time. It should be noted that it was not a particularly polite term.
60. Ip, Lu, and Peng, *Ye Wen*, 209–213.
61. Ibid., 209.
62. For a more general discussion of martial values and the construction of Chinese manhood see Kam Louie, *Theorizing Chinese Masculinity* (Cambridge: Cambridge University Press, 2002). In chapter 8 Kam explicitly addresses the public perception of martial arts masters and how they relate to the evolving question of gender in China today. However, Kam's entire approach is quite relevant to the discussion in Boretz and the current chapter.
63. Boretz, *Gods, Ghosts and Gangsters*, 21–58. For an early literary example of a female martial character who makes her virtue known by adopting explicitly male traits and behaviors see Hu Sanniang who makes her first appearance in chapter 47 of *Heroes of the Water Margin*.
64. They also invert the logic of "demonic exorcism" which Boretz sees as structuring the entire field of ritualized violence and Chinese popular religion. Almost all of the Hung Mun creation myths focus on a male hero who exhibits yang traits and overcomes the shadowy (yin based) forces of disorder and chaos. It is the ultimate triumph of these yang values that allows the resumption of normal life. This is the same basic logic that is seen in temple "military processions" (where a local god and his warriors are escorted around the neighborhood) and other forms of ritually enacted Daoist exorcism. Yet in the Wing Chun myth a shadowy old woman teaches a young girl a martial art based on softness and evasion (explicitly yin values) so that she may overcome

a yang-filled local gangster/hero who wishes to control her sexual destiny. While some elements of the Wing Chun creation myth are quite typical of the Hung Mun movement, other elements pose a challenge for those thinking in ritual or gendered terms. Readers may also recall that when the character of Ng Mui was first introduced in the late nineteenth century she was explicitly viewed as a shadowy, scheming, and untrustworthy villain who was responsible for the destruction of the Shaolin Temple. It was only later in the twentieth century that she was reimagined as a protagonist.

65. Ip Ching, Ron Heimberger, Eric Li, and Garner Train, *Ip Man's Wing Chun: Mook Yan Jong Sum Fat* (Springville, UT: King Dragon Press, 2004), 27.

66. Ving Tsun Athletic Association, "Development of Ving Tsun Kung Fu in Hong Kong," <http://www.vingtsun.org.hk/>; Ip et al., *Mook Yan Jong*, 32.

67. The VTAA timeline places the move in 1961. Samuel Kwok, in his timeline of the period, claims that the year was 1962.

68. Ip and Heimberger, *Ip Man*, 32.

69. Ibid., 38.

70. Ip and Tse, *Wing Chun Kung Fu*, 39–40.

71. Ibid. Also see Michael Tse, "Master Ip Ching," *Qi Magazine* 24 (1996): 16–20.

72. Interview with Ip Ching, Hong Kong, December 2012.

73. Ip et al., *Mook Yan Jong*, 27–28.

74. Kwok and Massengill, *Mastering Wing Chun*, 289.

75. Leung, *Roots and Branches*, 123.

76. Ip Man Tong, *Ip Man Tong: Special Memorial Issue for Opening* (Hong Kong: Ving Tsun Athletic Association, 2002), 19–20; Ip and Heimberger, *Ip Man*, 61–63.

77. Ip and Heimberger, *Ip Man*, 77–78.

78. Ibid., 71–72.

79. Ip Man, "The Origins of Ving Tsun in Hong Kong," <http://www.vingtsun.org.hk/>.

80. Kwok and Massengill, *Mastering Wing Chun*, 289–290.

81. Amos, *Southern Praying Mantis Cult*, 42.

82. Ip and Heimberger, *Ip Man*, 60.

83. Ip Chun et al., "Stories of Grandmaster Ip Man," In *Ip Man Ving Tsun 50th Anniversary*, ed. Donald Mak (Hong Kong: Ving Tsun Athletic Association, 2005), 90.

84. Ip Man Tong, Special Memorial Issue, 34.

Epilogue

1. Emily Lodish, "Hong Kong's Kung Fu Flight Attendants," *Global Post*, April 29, 2011. <http://www.globalpost.com/dispatches/globalpost-blogs/the-rice-bowl/hong-kong-airlines-kung-fu-bruce-lee>.

2. Paul Bowman, *Beyond Bruce Lee: Chasing the Dragon through Film, Philosophy and Popular Culture* (New York: Wallflower Press, 2013), 171.

3. Peter Beyer, *Religion and Globalization* (Thousand Oaks, CA: Sage Publications, 2000), 81–93.

4. For a discussion of these categories as they apply to Chinese martial culture see Avron Boretz, *Gods, Ghosts and Gangsters: Ritual Violence, Martial Arts and Masculinity on the Margins of Chinese Society* (Honolulu: University of Hawaii Press, 2011), 40–43.

5. See the September 1966 issue of *Black Belt* for a representative sample of the sorts of discussions that dominated the period. This edition of the magazine featured six articles. Three of these covered recent events in the Judo world, and the rest were dedicated to various discussions of Karate. The October 1967 issue is also informative as it ran a number of articles that spoke directly to Karate's rising prominence in the western martial arts community.

6. Even Lee worried that audiences might not be ready for an Asian action hero. At the same time he was aware that by playing a more sophisticated intelligence agent who cooperated with the British he risked alienating his Chinese viewers who preferred to see him as an "everyman" turned national hero. Bruce Thomas, *Bruce Lee: A Biography* (Berkeley, CA: Blue Snake Books, 1994), 174.

7. Bowman, *Beyond Bruce Lee*, 22–25.

8. Ibid., 25–26, 44–46.

9. Ibid., 55.

10. Thomas, *Fighting Spirit*, 208–209.

11. Lee received his first extensive profiles in the 1967 October and November issues of *Black Belt*. These discussions focused on his television role as Kato but he did mention his background in Wing Chun and provided a picture of him practicing chi sao with his teacher. Soon after the magazine's February edition (1968) dedicated extensive coverage to the traditional Chinese martial arts. Wing Chun was one of a handful of systems that was profiled and both Bruce Lee and Ip Man were prominently featured in that article. In September of 1972, *Black Belt* featured Wing Chun on the cover and ran an article promoting James Yimm Lee's recent book, *Wing Chun Kung Fu: The Chinese Art of Self Defense* (Santa Clarita, CA: Ohara Publications, 1972). A number of photographs of Ip Man and his younger student were used to illustrate this piece.

12. For a classic discussion of transaction costs as an economic concept see Oliver E. Williamson, "The Economics of Organization: The Transaction Cost Approach," *The American Journal of Sociology* 87, no. 3 (1981): 548–577.

13. Ip Ching, "History of Wing Chun" (Ip Ching Ving Tsun Association, 1998), DVD.

14. For an introduction to some of the more popular non-Ip Man lineages of Wing Chun see Robert Chu, René Ritchie, and Y. Wu, *Complete Wing Chun: The Definitive Guide to Wing Chun's History and Traditions* (Boston: Tuttle Publishing, 1998). Readers should also note that a number of additional groups have

emerged since the initial publication of this work. See for instance Garrett Gee, Benny Meng, and Richard Loewenhagen, *Mastering Kung Fu: Featuring Shaolin Wing Chun* (Champaign, IL: Human Kinetics Publishers, 2003).

15. Adam D. Frank, "Unstructuring Structure and Communicating Secrets inside/outside a Chinese Martial Arts Association," *JOMEC Journal* 5 (2014): 18 pages. <http://www.cardiff.ac.uk/jomec/jomecjournal/5-june2014/Frank_Structure.pdf>.

16. R. Clausnitzer and Greco Wong, *Wing Chun Kung Fu: Chinese Self-Defence Methods* (London: Paul H. Crompton LTD, 1969).

17. Clausnitzer and Wong, *Kung Fu*, 10.

18. Ibid., 12.

19. Chu Shong Tin, *The Book of Wing Chun* (Revised Edition) trans., Eddie Chan (Hong Kong: Hong Kong Social Science Press, 2011), 46.

20. Bruce Lee, "Liberate Yourself From Classical Karate," *Black Belt* 9, no. 9 (1971): 27; Bowman, *Beyond Bruce Lee*, 65–75.

21. Bowman, *Beyond Bruce Lee*, 171.

22. Zhao Shiqing, "Imagining Martial Arts in Hong Kong: Understanding Local Identity through 'Ip Man,'" *Journal of Chinese Martial Studies* 1, no. 3 (2010): 85–89.

23. Beyer, *Religion and Globalization*, 5–6.

24. Ibid., 77–78; 81–86.

25. Ibid., 86–93.

26. Douglas Wile, *Lost T'ai-Chi Classics from the late Ch'ing Dynasty* (Albany: State University of New York Press, 1996), 5, 20–26.

27. Adam D. Frank, *Taijiquan and the Search for the Little Old Chinese Man: Understanding Identity through the Martial Arts* (New York: Palgrave, 2006), 78–79, 272. The internal debate in one Shanghai based Taiji organization as to whether and under what conditions foreign students could be taught "secret family techniques" was the central theme of Frank's 2014 article.

28. Far from being a recent phenomenon, such discussions have been going on for decades. For an important example dating to the "Guoshu era" see Andrew Morris's discussion of Chu Minyi's "Taijicao" (or Taiji Calisthenics). Introduced in the early 1930s, this modified version of the art was aimed at the increasingly influential urban middle class demographic. Andrew D. Morris, *Marrow of the Nation: A History of Sport and Physical Culture in Republican China* (Berkeley: University of California Press, 2004), 223–227.

29. Such theories are a common topic of conversation on internet discussion forums. These approaches to understanding Wing Chun's history and nature are also a staple of the popular literature. See for instance Gee, Meng, and Loewenhagen, *Mastering Kung Fu*, 2003; Order of Shaolin Ch'an, *The Shaolin Grandmasters' Text: History, Philosophy, and the Gung Fu of Shaolin Ch'an* (Beaverton, OR: Order of Shaolin Chan, 2006), 215–218. Note that the early chapters of this work are dedicated to the task of reimagining the modern Chinese martial arts within an explicitly sectarian framework.

Selected Glossary of Names and Terms

Personal names, geographic places, and common terms that are readily available in standard reference works have been omitted.

Agnes Ng 吳夢珍
Au Si 區士
Bagua Quan 八卦拳
Bai Ling 百齡
Bak Mei 白眉
Bak Siu Lam 北少林
Bawang Fist 霸王拳
Beidi Temple 北帝廟
Beimo 比武
Biu Jee 標指
Bruce Lee 李小龍
Cai Mian Qing 蔡勉卿
Cha Quan 查拳
Chan Chee Man 陳志文
Chan Dao 陳斗
Chan Din Fune 陳典桓
Chan Din Yao 陳典尤
Chan Gee Sun 陳志新
Chan Heung 陳享
Chan Kam Ming 陳錦銘
Chan Kau 陳球
Chan Ngau Sing 陳吽盛
Chan Sum 陳森
Chan Wah Shun (Moneychanger Wah) 陳華順 (找錢華)
Chan Wei Hong 陳衛匡

Chan Yiu Min 陳汝棉
Chan Yuet Fat 陳月法
Chang Xing Street 長興街
Chao Guan Lane 朝觀里
Chaoyang Street 朝陽街
Chen Gong Zhe 陳公哲
Chen Hung Shu 陳鴻書
Chen Jitang 陳濟棠
Chen Ji Xiu 沈季修
Chen Kai 陳開
Chen Kefu 陳克夫
Chen Lian Bo 陳廉伯
Chen Shi Chao 陳士超
Chen Tie Sheng 陳鐵笙
Chen Village 陳家溝
Chen Wei Xian 陳維賢
Chen Zhen Dai 陳振代
Chen Zi Zheng 陳子正
Cheng Dali 程大利
Cheung Bo 張保
Cheung Lai Chuen 張禮泉
Cheung Ng 張五
Cheung Ning Building 長寧大廈
Cheung Wing Sing 張永成
Cheung Yee Wui 忠義會
Chi Kung 氣功
Chi Yau Road 自由道
Chin Opera 秦腔
Cho Doi Street 草堆街
Chow Kwong Yiu 周光耀
Chow Sai Keung 周世強
Chow Wing Yiu 周榮耀
Chow Chang Yiu 周燦耀
Choy Fok 蔡福
Choy Gar 蔡家
Choy Li Fut 蔡李佛
Chu Family 朱家
Chu Shong Tin 徐尚田
Chu Southern Mantis 朱家南螳螂
Chukah Shaolin 朱家少林

Chum (Tsum) Kiu 尋橋
Chung Yau 鍾佑
Chung Yee Wui 忠義會
Dadao 大刀
Dajiwei 大基尾
Den Yugong 鄧羽公
Dianshizhai Huabao 點石齋畫報
Do Pai 道派
Doc Fai Wong 黃德輝
Dongguan Martial Arts Institute 東關武術館
Duncan Leung 梁紹鴻
Fai Jee Street 筷子街
Fan Yong Zhen 范永鎮
Feng Keshan 馮克善
Feng Yuxiang 馮玉祥
Fenghuangyi Troupe 鳳凰儀班
Fengning Road 豐寧路
Fok Bo-Chuen 霍保全
Foling 佛嶺
Fong Wing Chun 方詠春
Fong Yee Ming 方宜明
Fook Chuen Street 福全街
Foshan Hung Sing Kwoon 佛山鴻勝館
Fu Xian Road 福賢路
Fu Zhensong 傅振嵩
Fung Shek 馮石
Fung Siu Ching 馮少青
Fut Gar 佛家
Gao Dao 高道
Gao Jian Fu 高奇峰
Gao Zhendong 高振東
Gong Fu (gongfu) 功夫
Gu Ru Zhang 顧汝章
Guan Chao 關超
Gui Hua 桂花
Gulao 古勞
Guoshi 國士
Guoshu 國術
Guoshu Yanjiuguan 國術研究館
Haizu Theater 海珠戲院

Hakka Quan 客家拳
Han Pei Kee 韓沛記
Hang Chai Tong 杏濟堂
Hap Gar 俠家
Hawkins Cheung 張學健
He Zhao Chu 何兆初
Hexing Photo Studio 和興攝影
Hing Ip Building 興業大廈
Ho Leun 何聯
Ho Liu 何六
Hoi Tan Street 海壇街
Hong Kong Jianquan Taiji Association 香港太極拳研究室
Hong Kong Ving Tsun Athletic Association 香港詠春體育會
Hong Xi Guan 洪熙官
Hongde 洪德
Hongmen 洪門
Hooligan Qi 流氓奇
Hu De Wen 胡德文
Huan Jin Biao 黃金標
Huang Hong 黃虹
Huang Renhua 黃任華
Huang Shao Bo 黃少波
Huang Shao Qiang 黃少強
Huang Xiao Hui 黃曉蕙
Huang Xing 鴻勝
Huang Xiaoyang 黃蕭養
Hui Fu East Road 惠福東路
Hui Yee 會議
Hui Yi Martial Arts School 會義館
Huicho 惠州
Hung Fat San 洪發山
Hung Gar 洪家
Hung Kuen 洪拳
Hung Mun 洪門
Hung Sing 鴻勝
Huo Dong Ge 霍東閣
Huo Yong Min 霍雍民
Huo Yuan Jia 霍元甲
Ip Ar Sum 葉雅心
Ip Ar Woon 葉雅媛

Ip Ching 葉正
Ip Chun 葉準
Ip Kai Gak 葉繼格
Ip Man (Ip Kai Man) 葉問 (葉繼問)
Ip Oi Dor 葉靄多
Ip Sing Cheuk 葉承芍
Ip Wan Hum 葉允堪
Ip Wan Mei 葉允媚
Jan Sang Tong 贊生堂
Jee Shim 至善
Jeong Yim 張炎
Jian Zhao Nan 簡照南
Jianan Hall 嘉南堂
Jianglan Road 槳欄路
Jiaochang 較場
Jin Xian Street 金錢街
Jin Yong 金庸
Jingdezhen 景德鎮
Jingwu 精武
Jiu Chao 招就
Jiu Tong 招棠
Jiu Wan 招允
Jiuneihong Fist 九內紅大下等破法
Ju Hao 居浩
Ju Yi 聚義
Juen Ma 轉馬
Kar Wai Wong 王家衛
King Mui Village 京梅村
Kong Chang 孔昌
Kot Siu Wong 葛肇煌
Ku Yu Cheong 顧汝章
Kuai Zi Lane 筷子里
Kung Fu 功夫
Kung On 公安
Kunshan Opera 昆山腔
Kwan Tak Hing 關德興
Kwok Fu 郭富
Lai Yip Chi 黎協箎
Lam Gar 林家
Lam Sek 林石

Lam Yin Fat 藍賢發
Lam Yiu Kwai 林耀桂
Lang Bian Village 朗邊鄉
Lau Gar 劉家
Lau Hon Lam 劉漢琳
Lau Ming 劉明
Lee Chi Ho 李家
Lee Gar 李家
Lee Kong Hoi 李廣海
Lee Man 李民
Lee Shing 李勝
Lee Tat Street 利達街
Lei Dat Ng 李達伍
Leung Bik 梁璧
Leung Bok Chau 梁博濤
Leung Caixin 梁財信
Leung Chun 梁春
Leung Gee 梁知
Leung Jan 梁贊
Leung Ko 梁高
Leung Lan Kwai 梁蘭桂
Leung Mengzhan 梁夢占
Leung Sheung 梁相
Leung Tak Nam 梁德南
Leung Tak Wing 梁德榮
Leung Ting 梁挺
Leung Yee Tai 梁二娣
Leung Yuen 梁元
Li Bao Ying 李寶英
Li Bin 李彬
Li Cheng Uk Estate 李鄭屋邨
Li Chi Ho 李賜豪
Li Chung Shing Tong 李衆勝堂
Li Ci Hao 李賜豪
Li Fu Lin 李福林
Li Gar 李家
Li Hua (Wooden Man Hua) 李華 (木人華)
Li Hui Ting 李滙亭
Li Jinglin 李景林
Li Jishen 李濟深

Li Ming 黎銘
Li Ming Kai 黎鳴楷
Li Mung 李蒙
Li Pei Xian 李佩弦
Li Shou Peng 李壽鵬
Li Su 李蘇
Li Wen Mao 李文茂
Li Xian Wu 李先五
Li Yau San 李友山
Li Zhan Feng 李占風
Lian Feng Paper Guild Hall 蓮峰紙行會館
Liang Du Yuan 梁敦遠
Liang Fu Chu 梁福初
Liang Gui Hua 梁桂華
Liang Lane 梁巷
Liang Ming San 梁銘三
Liangguang Guoshu Institute 兩廣國術館
Liangguang Martial Arts Institute 兩廣武館
Lianghua Xu 梁化墟
Lie Wing-Fok 劉永福
Lin Boyan 林伯原
Lin He 林合
Lin Jia Martial Arts Institute 林家武館
Lin Qingyuan 林慶元
Lin Shuangwen Rebellion 林爽文起義
Lin Xiao Ya 林小亞
Lin Yin Tang 林堂蔭
Lin Yu 林榆
Liu Chun Fan 廖俊笵
Liu Fa Meng 劉法孟
Liu Jing Chun 劉景春
Liu Qin Gui 劉清桂
Liu Yinhu 劉印虎
Lo Kuang Yu 羅光玉
Lo Man Kam 盧文錦
Lok Yiu 駱耀
Long Feng Shuang Dao 龍鳳雙刀
Long Xi Quan 龍形拳
Lu Wei Chang 盧煒昌
Lui Pak Ying 呂柏應

Lui Yu Chai 雷汝濟
Luk Ah Choi 陸阿采
Lun Kai 倫佳
Lung Ji Choi 龍子才
Luo Da Qing 羅達卿
Luo Guang Yu 羅光玉
Luo Huo Fu 羅厚甫
Luo Shan Fist 羅山拳
Luo Yong 螺涌
Ma Chaojun 馬超俊
Ma Liang 馬良
Ma Mingda 馬明達
Ma Yufu 馬裕甫
Ma Zineng 馬梓能
Mainzhang Defensive Fist 眠張短打破法
Man Yim Kwong 文彥光
Mao Dun 茅盾
Meihua Quan 梅花拳
Mizongyi 迷踪拳
Mo Cai Zhang 莫采章
Mok Gar 莫家
Nan Quan 南拳
Ng Chung So 吳仲素
Ng Kam Chuen 吳鑑泉
Ng Mui (Wu Me) 五枚
Ng Shui 吳瑞
Ng Siu Lo 吳小魯
Nianfo Sharen 念佛山人
Nie Yuntai 聶雲台
Nullah Road 水渠道
Painted Face Kam 大花面錦
Pak Mai 白眉
Pan Nam 彭南
Pin Sun Wing Chun 偏身咏春拳
Ping Xin Restaurant 平心茶樓
Po Chi Lam Clinic 寶芝林醫館
Po Wa Road 寶華路
Pork Gui 猪肉桂
Qi Mei Staff 齊眉棍
Qian Wei Fang 錢維方

Qionghua (Guild) Hall 瓊花會館
Qionghua Ford 瓊花水埗
Quanbang 拳棒
Qun Yi 群義
Ren Sheng Kui 任生魁
Ren Xiao An 任孝安
Renan Street 仁安里
Sam Tai Tze Temple 三太子宮
Samuel Kwok 郭思牧
San Pin Lau 三品樓
San Yuan Li Incident 三元里民眾抗英事件
Sanshou 散手
Sha Shou Jian 殺手鐧
Shanghai Po 上海婆
Shangtang 上塘
Shaohua 少華
Shaolin 少林
Shaolin Quan 少林拳
She 勝
Shek Kien 石堅
Shi Ken Village 石肯鄉
Shi Lu Tou Street 石路头街
Shi Pan Village Boxing 石盤村 拳法
Shi Zai Xian 石再賢
Sifu 師傅
Siu Fai Toi 肇輝臺
Siu Lim Tao 小念頭
Siu Lung Brothers 陳兆龍兄弟
Sum Num 岑能
Sun Lu Tang 孫祿堂
Sun Shou Qing 孫守慶
Sun Wen Long 孫文勇
Sun Yu Feng 孫玉峰
Taijiquan (Tai Chi Chuan) 太極拳
Tai Sang Restaurant 大生茶樓
Tan Sao 攤手
Tan Sao Ng 攤手五
Tang Hao 唐豪
Tang Sang 鄧生
Tao Jie Girl's School 陶潔女子學校

Tiandihui 天地會
Tien Hoi Restaurant 天海酒家
Tieqiufen 鐵丘墳
Tin Hua Temple 天后廟
Todai 徒弟
Tong Jong 唐裝衫褲
Tsang So 曾蘇
Tung Choi Street 通菜街
Ving Tsun (Wing Chun) 詠春
Ving Tsun Athletic Association 詠春体育會
Ving Tsun Tong Fellowship 詠春堂聯誼會
Wah Ying 華英
Wah Ying Restaurant 華英茶樓
Wai Yuk Sang 韋玉笙
Wan Lai Sheng 萬籟聲
Wan Laimin 萬籟鳴
Wang Shaozhou 王少周
Wang Ziping 王子平
Wei Bang Ping 魏邦平
Wen Fist 温家鉤卦拳
Weng Chun 永春
William Cheung 張卓慶
Wilson Ip 葉偉信
Wing Chun 詠春
Wong Chi On 王子安
Wong Fei Hung 黃飛鴻
Wong Kei Ying 黃麒英
Wong Ki Man 黃紀民
Wong Shun Leung 黃淳樑
Wong Wah Bo 黃華寶
Wu Gong Zu 吳公祖
Wu Gongyi 吳公儀
Wu Jianquan 吳鑑泉
Wu Qin 吳勤
Wu Quanyou 吳全佑
Wu Style Taiji 吳式太極拳
Wu Tai Xie 吳大燮
Wu Zhaozhong 吳肇鍾
Wudang 武當
Wulin Magazine 台灣武林

Wushi 武士
Wushu 武術
Xi Bian Lane 西便巷
Xi Fist 西拳
Xian Feng Gu Road 先鋒古道
Xiang-Kun Opera Troupe 京劇戲班
Xiao Hai Ming 肖海明
Xiao Jian Nong 蕭劍農
Xiaozhi Lu 小知錄
Xie Lian Group 協聯
Xingyi Quan 形意拳
Xinhu 新會
Xio Chen Huau 笑塵寰茶樓
Xiong Chang Qing 熊長興
Xiong Yi 雄義
Xu Cai Dong 許才棟
Xu Kairu 許凱如
Xu Zhen 徐震
Ya Bang Street 衙旁街
Yan Xishan 閻錫山
Yang Chen Lun 楊琛倫
Yang Luchan 楊露禪
Yang Mei Bin 楊梅賓
Yang Shou Zhang 楊守中
Yang Style Taiji 楊氏太極拳
Yang Ting Xia 楊英俠
Yangtze River Fist 長江派
Yao Chan Bo 姚蟾伯
Yao Dian Xia 姚電俠
Yat Chan Um Chu 一塵庵主
Yee Fai Building 怡輝大樓
Yee Wa 式華
Yi Chen 一塵
Yi Schools 義字系統武館
Yim Wing Chun 嚴咏春
Yim Yee 嚴二
Yimin He 何一民
Yin Tong Law Enforcement 燕堂
Ying Wu Tong 英武堂
Ying Yi 英義

Yip (Ip) Man 葉問
Yiu Choi 姚才
Yiu Lam 姚霖
Yiyang Opera 弋陽腔
Yong Yi 勇義
Yu Chau Street 汝州街
Yu Dayou 俞大猷
Yu Le Jiang 于樂江
Yuan Jia Schools 元甲國民學校
Yuan Style Opera 元曲
Yue An 悅安
Yuen Chai Wan 阮濟雲
Yuen Kay San 阮奇山
Yuen Woo 遠護
Yufan 裕繁
Zeng Guofan 曾國藩
Zeng Zhaosheng 曾昭勝
Zhang Fei 張飛
Zhang Fist 張飛神拳
Zhang Liquan 張禮泉
Zhang Qi Duan 張啟端
Zhang Sheng Ruo 張升若
Zhang Shusheng 張樹聲
Zhang Wu 張五
Zhang Zhijiang 張之江
Zhangcha Village 張槎朗邊鄉
Zhao Fist 趙家拳
Zhao Gui Lin 趙桂林
Zhao Jing Group 昭敬
Zhao Lian He 趙連和
Zhao Xi 招錫
Zhen Xi Street 汾水西街
Zheng Chenggong 鄭成功
Zheng Jing 鄭經
Zheng Village 鄭村
Zheng Zhilong 鄭芝龍
Zheng Zhou Chen 鄭灼臣
Zhong Miao Zhen 鍾妙真
Zhong Yi (Guang) 忠義(館)
Zhou Weiliang 周煒良

Zhu Yu Ping 朱玉平
Zhu Ziyao 朱子堯
Zou Wen Ping 鄒文平

Works Cited

Acevedo, William, and Mei Cheung. "Republican Period Guoshu Periodicals." *Classical Fighting Arts* 2, no. 26 (2014): 56–68.
Allen, Sarah. *The Formation of Chinese Civilization: An Archeological Perspective.* New Haven, CT: Yale University Press, 2005.
Amos, Daniel Miles. "Marginality and the Heroes Art: Martial Artists in Hong Kong and Guangzhou (Canton)." PhD Diss., University of California, 1983.
———. "A Hong Kong Southern Praying Mantis Cult." *Journal of Asian Martial Arts* 6, no. 4 (1997): 30–61.
———. "Spirit Boxing in Hong Kong: Two Observers, Native and Foreign." *Journal of Asian Martial Arts* 8, no. 4 (1999): 8–27.
Antony, Robert J. *Like Froth Floating on the Sea: The World of Pirates and Seafarers in Late Imperial South China.* Berkeley, CA: Institute of Asian Studies, 2003.
———. "Demons, Gangsters, and Secret Societies in Early Modern China." *East Asian History* 27 (2004): 71–98.
Beyer, Peter. *Religion and Globalization.* Thousand Oaks, CA: Sage Publications, 2000.
Bingham, J. Elliot. *Narrative of the Expedition to China, from the Commencement of the Present Period.* London: Henry Colburn Publisher, 1842.
Bishop, James. *Bruce Lee: Dynamic Becoming.* Carrollton, TX: Promethean Press, 2004.
Bolton, Kingsley, and Christopher Hutton. *Triad Societies: Western Accounts of the History, Sociology and Linguistics of Chinese Secret Societies.* London: Routledge, 2000.
Boretz, Avron. *Gods, Ghosts and Gangsters: Ritual Violence, Martial Arts, and Masculinity on the Margins of Chinese Society.* Honolulu: University of Hawai'i Press, 2011.
Bowman, Paul. *Theorizing Bruce Lee: Film—Fantasy—Fighting—Philosophy.* New York: Rodopi, 2010.

———. *Beyond Bruce Lee: Chasing the Dragon through Film, Philosophy and Popular Culture*. New York: Wallflower, 2013.

Canzonieri, Salvatore. "The story of traditional Chinese martial arts: History of Hakka Martial Art and its relationship to Southern Chinese and Shaolin martial arts."

CCTV9. "Kung Fu Masters and Armed Escorts." *New Frontiers*. August 28, 2009.

Cha, Louis. *The Book and the Sword*. Translated by John Minford. Oxford: Oxford University Press, 2004.

Chan, Marjorie K. M. "Cantonese Opera and the Growth and Spread of Vernacular Written Cantonese in the Twentieth Century." In *Proceedings of the Seventeenth North American Conference on Chinese Linguistics*, edited by Qian Gao, 1–18. Los Angeles: GSIL Publications, 2005.

Cheng Dali. *Zhongguo Wushu—Lishi Yu Wenhua (Chinese Martial Arts—History and Culture)*. Chengdu: Sichuan University Press, 1995.

Cheng Zongyou. *Ancient Art of the Chinese Long Saber*. Translated by Jack Chen. Singapore: Historical Combat Association, 2010.

Cheong Cheng Leong, and Donn F. Draeger. *Phoenix-Eye Fist: A Shaolin Fighting Art of Southern China*. New York City: Weatherhill, 1977.

Cheung, Hawkins, and Robert Chu. "Bruce Lee's Hong Kong Years: A couple of 'juvenile delinquents' named Bruce Lee and Hawkins Cheung roamed the streets of Hong Kong, picking fights, having fun and refining their martial arts techniques." *Inside Kung Fu*, November, 1991.

———, and Robert Chu. "Bruce Lee's Mother Art: Wing Chun." *Inside Kung Fu*, January, 1992.

———. "Bruce's Classical Mess: Cleaning up the Mess the 'Little Dragon' Left Behind." *Inside Kung Fu*, February, 1992.

Christie's. "Fine Chinese Modern Paintings." *Christie's Fine Art Catalogue*, November 30, 2010. Lot 2520, Sale 2822.

Chu Shong Tin. *The Book of Wing Chun*. Rev. ed. Translated by Eddie Chan. Hong Kong: Hong Kong Social Science Press, 2011.

Chu, Robert, Rene Ritchie, and Y. Wu. *Complete Wing Chun: The Definitive Guide to Wing Chun's History and Traditions*. North Clarendon, VT: Tuttle Publishing, 1998.

Clausnitzer, R., and Greco Wong. *Wing Chun Kung Fu: Chinese Self-Defence Methods*. London: Paul H. Crompton Ltd., 1969.

Clements, Jonathan. *Coxinga and the Fall of the Ming Dynasty*. Stroud, UK: Sutton Publishing, 2004.

Di Cosmo, Nicola, ed. *Military Culture in Imperial China*. Cambridge, MA: Harvard University Press, 2009.

Durkheim, Emile. *The Elementary Forms of Religious Life*. Oxford: Oxford University Press, 2001.

Ebrey, Patricia Buckley. *China: Cambridge Illustrated History*. Cambridge: Cambridge University Press, 2007.

Esherick, Joseph W. *Origins of the Boxer Uprising.* Berkeley: University of California Press, 1988.
Fairbank, John King, and Merle Goldman. *China: A New History.* Cambridge, MA: Harvard University Press, 2006.
Farrer, D. S. *Shadows of the Prophet: Martial Arts and Sufi Mysticism.* Dordrecht, Germany: Springer Publishing, 2009.
Farrer, D. S., and John Whalen-Bridge. *Martial Arts as Embodied Knowledge: Asian Traditions in a Transnational World.* Albany: State University of New York Press, 2011.
Faure, David. "What Made Foshan a Town? The Evolution of Urban-Rural Identities in Ming-Ching China." *Late Imperial China* 11, no. 2 (1990): 1-31.
———. *Empire and Ancestor: State and Lineage in Southern China.* Stanford, CA: Stanford University Press, 2007.
Frank, Adam D. *Taijiquan and the Search for the Little Old Chinese Man: Understanding Identity through Martial Arts.* New York: Palgrave Macmillan, 2006.
———. "Unstructuring Structure and Communicating Secrets inside/outside a Chinese Martial Arts Association." *JOMEC Journal* 5 (2014): 18 pages.
Fung, Anthony. "Postcolonial Hong Kong Identity: Hybridising the Local and the National." *Social Identities: Journal for the Study of Race, Nation and Culture* 10, no. 3 (2004): 399-414.
Fung, S. L. *Pak Mei Kung Fu: The Myth & the Martial Art.* New York City: TNP Multimedia, 2008.
Gee, Garrett, Benny Meng, and Richard Loewenhagen. *Mastering Kung Fu: Featuring Shaolin Wing Chun.* Champaign, IL: Human Kinetics Publishers, 2003.
Gilbert, S. R. "Mengzi's Art of War: The Kangxi Emperor Reforms the Qing Military Examinations." In *Military Culture in Imperial China*, edited by Nicola Di Cosmo, 243-256. Cambridge, MA: Harvard University Press, 2009.
Green, Thomas A., and Joseph R. Svinth, eds. *Martial Arts of the World: An Encyclopedia of History and Innovation.* 2 volumes. Santa Barbra, CA: ABC-CLIO, 2010.
Green, Thomas A. "Sense in Nonsense: the Role of Folk History in the Martial Arts." In *Martial Arts in the Modern World*, edited by Thomas A. Green and Joseph R. Svinth, 1-13. London: Praeger, 2003.
Guojia Tiwei Wushu Yanjiuyan, bianzuan (National Physical Culture and Sports Commission Martial Arts Research Institute, editors and compilers). *Zhongguo Wushushi (Chinese Martial Arts History).* Beijing: Peoples Physical Culture Publishers, 1997.
Hamm, John Christopher. *Paper Swordsmen: Jin Yong and the Modern Chinese Martial Arts Novel.* University of Hawaii Press, 2006.

———. "Local Heroes: Guangdong School *Wuxia* Fiction and Hong Kong's Imagining of China." *Twentieth-Century China* 27, no. 1 (2001): 71–96.
Harpers Weekly. "Chinese Highbinders." *Harpers Weekly*, February 13, 1886, 103–106.
Hase, Patrick. "Alliance of Ten" in *Down to Earth: The Territorial Bond in South China*, edited by David Faure and Helen Siu, 123–160. Stanford, CA: Stanford University Press, 1995.
Hayes, James. "The Hong Kong Region: Its Place in Traditional Chinese Historiography and Principal Events Since the Establishment of Hsin-an County in 1573." *Journal of the Royal Asiatic Society Hong Kong Branch* 14 (1974): 108–135.
Heine-Geldern, Robert. "Conceptions of State and Kingship in Southeast Asia." *The Far Eastern Quarterly* 2 (1942): 15–30.
Henning, Stanley. "Academia Encounters the Chinese Martial Arts." *China Review International* 6, no. 2 (1999): 319–332.
———. "What is in a Name: The Etymology of Chinese Boxing." *Journal of Asian Martial Arts* 10, no. 4 (2001): 8–19.
———. "Martial Arts in Chinese Physical Culture, 1865–1965." In *Martial Arts in the Modern World*, edited by Thomas A. Green and Joseph R. Svinth, 13–35. London: Praeger, 2003.
———. "China's New Wave of Martial Studies Scholars." *Journal of Asian Martial Arts* Vol. 15, No. 2 (2006): 8–21.
———. "Thoughts on the Origins and Transmission to Okinawa of Yongchun Boxing." *Classical Fighting Arts* 2, no. 15 (2009): 42–47.
———. "China: Martial Arts." in *Martial Arts of the World*, edited by Thomas A. Green and Joseph R. Svinth, 92–98. Santa Barbra, CA: ABC-CLIO, 2010.
Ho, Virgil K. Y. *Understanding Canton: Rethinking Popular Culture in the Republican Period.* Oxford: Oxford University Press, 2005.
Holcombe, Charles. "Theater of Combat: A Critical Look at the Chinese Martial Arts." *Historian* 52, no. 3 (1990): 411–431.
———. "The Daoist Origins of the Chinese Martial Arts." *Journal of Asian Martial Arts* Vol. 2, No. 1 (1993): 10–25.
Ing, Ken. *Wing Chun Warrior: The true tales of Wing Chun kung fu master Duncan Leung, Bruce Lee's fighting companion*. Hong Kong: Blacksmith Books, 2009.
Ip Ching. "History of Wing Chun." DVD. Ip Ching Wing Chun Athletic Association, 1998.
Ip Ching, and Ron Heimberger. *Ip Man: Portrait of a Kung Fu Master*. Springville, UT: King Dragon Press, 2003.
Ip Ching, Ron Heimberger, Eric Li, and Garner Train. *Ip Man's Wing Chun: Mook Yan Jong Sum Fat*. Springville, UT: King Dragon Press, 2004.
Ip Chun. "Fifteen Years—Traveling the World to Sell my Skills." *Qi Magazine* 48 (2000): 26–28.
Ip Chun, Ip Ching, Chu Shong Tin, Siu Yuk Men, Wong Ki Man, and Pang Yiu Kwan. "Stories of Grandmaster Ip Man." In *Ip Man Ving Tsun 50th*

Anniversary, edited by Donald Mak, 89–91. Hong Kong: Ving Tsun Athletic Association, 2005.
Ip Chun, Lu De'an, and Peng Yaojun. *Ye Wen, Yong Chun 2* (Ip Man, Wing Chun. 2 volumes). Rev. ed. Xianggang: Hui zhi chu ban you xian gong si, 2010.
Ip Chun, and Michael Tse. *Wing Chun Kung Fu: Traditional Chinese Kung Fu for Self-Defense and Health*. New York: St. Martin's Press, 1998.
Ip Man. "The Origins of Ving Tsun: Written by the Late Grand Master Ip Man." Hong Kong: Ving Tsun Athletic Association, 1967.
Ip Man Tong. *Ip Man Tong: Special Memorial Issue for Opening*. Hong Kong: Ving Tsun Athletic Association, 2002.
Jordan, Darrell. *The Sound of Ving Tsun: The Grandmasters and Masters*. Winter Park: Florida Ving Tsun Athletic Association, 2004.
Judkins, Benjamin. "Does Religiously Generated Social Capital Intensify or Mediate Violent Conflict? Lessons from the Boxer Uprising." Presentation at the 67th MPSA National Meetings in Chicago, IL, April 2–5, 2009.
———. "Inventing Kung Fu." *JOMEC Journal* 5 (2014): 26 pages.
Kai, Sek, and Rolanda Chu. "A Brief Historical Tour of Hong Kong Martial Arts Film." *Bright Lights Film Journal* 13 (1994).
Kang Gewu. *The Spring and Autumn of Chinese Martial Arts: 5000 Years*. Santa Cruz, CA: Plum Publishing, 1995.
Kato, T. M. *From Kung Fu to Hip Hop: Revolution, Globalization and Popular Culture*. Albany: State University of New York Press, 2007.
Kennedy, Brian L., and Elizabeth Guo. *Chinese Martial Arts Training Manuals: A Historical Survey*. Berkeley, CA: Blue Snake Books, 2005.
———. *Jingwu: the School that Transformed Kung Fu*. Berkeley, CA: Blue Snake Books, 2010.
Kim, Jaeyoon. "The Heaven and Earth Society and the Red Turban Rebellion in Late Qing China." *Journal of Humanities & Social Sciences* 3, no 1 (2009): 1–35.
Kuang Wennam. *Zhongguo Wushu Wenhua Gailun* (A General Discussion of Chinese Martial Arts and Culture). Chengdu: Sichuan Jiayu Chubanshe, 1990.
Kuhn, Philip A. *Rebellion and its Enemies in Late Imperial China: Militarization and Social Structure, 1796–1864*. Cambridge, MA: Harvard University Press, 1970.
Kwan, Daniel Y. K. *Marxist Intellectuals and the Chinese Labor Movement: A Study of Deng Zhongxia 1894–1933*. Seattle: University of Washington Press, 1997.
Kwok, Samuel. "A Chronicle of the Life of Ip Man." *WT Danmark* 3 (2006): 8.
Kwok, Samuel, and Tony Massengill. *Mastering Wing Chun: the keys to Ip Man's Kung Fu*. Los Angeles: E. B. Empire Books, 2007.
Lam, Wing. *Hung Gar: Southern Shaolin Kung Fu Ling Nam*. Sunnyvale, CA: Wing Lam Enterprises, 2003.

Lee, Bruce. *The Tao of Gung Fu: A Study in the Way of Chinese Martial Art*, edited by John Little. Rutland, VT: Tuttle, 1997.

———. "Liberate Yourself From Classical Karate." *Black Belt* 9, no. 9 (1971): 25–27.

Lei, Daphne P. *Operatic China: Staging Chinese Identity across the Pacific*. New York: Palgrave, 2006.

Leung Ting. *Roots and Branches of Wing Chun*. 2nd ed. Hong Kong: Leung's Publications, 2003.

Li Jinlong, and Liu Yinghai. *Qingdai Biaoju yu Shanxi Wushu* (*Qing Period Armed Escort Agencies and Shanxi Martial Arts*). Beijing: Beijing Tiyu Daxue Chubanshe, 2007.

Liao, Waysun. *The T'ai Chi Classics*. Boston: Shambhala, 2000.

Lin, Alfred H. Y. *The Rural Economy of Guangdong, 1870–1937*. New York: St. Martin's Press, 1997.

Lin Boyan. *Zhongguo Wushushi* (*Chinese Martial Arts History*). Taipei: Wuzhou Chuban Youxian Gongsi, 1996.

———. "Zhongguo jindai qiaqi wushujia xiang chengshi de yidong yiji dui wushu liupai fenshua de yingxiang." (The early modern Chinese martial artists' migration towards cities and its influence on the diversion of the martial arts clans.) *Tiyu Wenshi* 79 May (1996): 14–16.

Liu, Petrus. *Stateless Subjects: Chinese Martial Arts Literature & Postcolonial History*. Ithaca, NY: East Asia Program Cornell University, 2011.

Lo Man Kam. "Wing Chun & My Uncle, Yip Man: a Lo Man Kam Narrative." *Wing Chun Teahouse* 1 (2006): 10–11.

Lorge, Peter. *Chinese Martial Arts: From Antiquity to the Twenty First Century*. New York: Cambridge University Press, 2011.

Louie, Kam. *Theorizing Chinese Masculinity*. Cambridge: Cambridge University Press, 2002.

Ma Lianzhen. "From Ape Worship in Ancient China to Monkey Imitation in Modern Competition Wu Shu." *Journal of Chinese Martial Studies* 2 (2010): 20–25.

Ma Mingda. *Wuxue Tanzhen* (Seeking Facts in Martial Studies), 2 volumes. Taipei: Yiwen Chuban Youxian Gongsi, 2003.

Ma Zineng. *Foshan Wushu Wenhua*. (*Foshan Martial Arts Culture*). Foshan: Foshanshi Chanchengqu Feiyinglixing Chubanwu, 2001.

Manthorpe, Jonathan. *Forbidden Nation: a History of Taiwan*. New York: Palgrave MacMillan, 2002.

McCarthy, Patrick. *Bubishi: The Classic Manual of Combat*. North Clarendon, VT: Tuttle Publishing, 2008.

Meyer, D. R. *Hong Kong as a Global Metropolis*. Cambridge: Cambridge University Press, 2000.

Moll-Murata, Christine. "Chinese Guilds from the Seventeenth to the Twentieth Centuries: An Overview." *International Review of Social History* 53 (2008): 213–247.

Morris, Andrew D. *Marrow of the Nation: A History of Sport and Physical Culture in Republican China*. Berkeley: University of California Press, 2004.
Murray, Dian, and Qin Baoqi. *The Origins of the Tiandihui: The Chinese Triads in Legend and History*. Stanford, CA: Stanford University Press, 1994.
Order of Shaolin Ch'an. *The Shaolin Grandmasters' Text: History, Philosophy, and Gung Fu of Shaolin Ch'an*. Rev ed. Beaverton: Order of Shaolin Ch'an, 2006.
Ownby, David. *Brotherhoods and Secret Societies in Early and Mid-Qing China*. Stanford, CA: Stanford University Press, 1996.
Perry, Elizabeth J. *Rebels and Revolutionaries in North China 1845–1945*. Stanford, CA: Stanford University Press, 1980.
Pong, David. *A Critical Guide to the Kwangtung Provincial Archives Deposited at the Public Records Office of London*. Cambridge, MA: Harvard University Press, 1975.
Rhodes, Edward J. M. *China's Republican Revolution: The Case of Kwangtung, 1895–1913*. Cambridge, MA: Harvard University Press, 1975.
Ritchie, Rene. *Yuen Kay-San Wing Chun Kuen: History and Foundation*. Los Angeles: Multimedia Books, 1998.
Rogowski, Ronald. *Commerce and Coalitions: How Trade Affects Domestic Political Alignments*. Princeton, NJ: Princeton University Press, 1990.
Rovere, Dennis. *The Xingyi Quan of the Chinese Army: Huang Bo Nien's Xingyi Fist and Weapon Instruction*. Berkeley, CA: Blue Snake Books, 2008.
Schenk, Catherine. *Hong Kong as an International Financial Centre: Emergence and Development, 1945–65*. London: Routledge, 2001.
———. "Economic History of Hong Kong." *EH.Net Encyclopedia*, edited by Robert Whaples. March 16, 2008.
Selby, Stephen. *Chinese Archery*. Hong Kong: Hong Kong University Press, 2000.
Shahar, Meir. "Chen Zongyou, Exposition of the Original Shaolin Staff Method" in *Hawaii Reader in Traditional Chinese Culture*, edited by Victor H. Mair, Nancy S. Steinhardt and Paul R. Goldin, 514–517. Honolulu: Hawai'i University Press, 2005.
———. *The Shaolin Monastery: History, Religion and Chinese Martial Arts*. University of Hawaii Press, 2008.
Shi Naian. *The Water Margin: Outlaws of the Marsh*. Translated by J. H. Jackson. Rutland, VT: Tuttle Publishing, 2010.
Smith, Robert W. *Secrets of Shaolin Temple Boxing*. North Clarendon: Tuttle Publishing, 1964.
———. *Chinese Boxing: Master's and Methods*. New York: Kodansha International, 1974.
Sun Lutang, and Tim Cartmell. *A Study in Taijiquan*. Berkeley, CA: North Atlantic Books, 2003.
Sun Lutang, Dan Miller, and Albert Liu. *Xing Yi Quan Xue: The Study of Form/ Mind Boxing*. Burbank, CA: Unique Books, 2001.
Svinth, Joseph. "What are Martial Arts?" *InYo: The Journal of Alternative Perspectives on the Martial Arts and Sciences* 11, no. 1 (2011): 7–12.

Takacs, Jeff. "A Case of Contagious Legitimacy: Kinship, Ritual and Manipulation in Chinese Martial Arts Societies." *Modern Asian Studies* 37, no. 4 (2003): 885–917.
Tang Hao. "Jiu Zhongguo Tiyushi Shang Fuhui De Damo." (*The Unfounded Association of Bodhidharma with the Ancient History of Chinese Physical Education.*) Parts 1, 2 in vol. 4 and vol. 6 of *Zhongguo Tiyushi Cankao Ziliao* (*Research Materials on the History of Chinese Physical Education.*) Beijing: Renmin Tiyu, 1958.
Tang Hao. *Shaolin Wudang Kao* (Shaolin and Wudang Research). 1930. Reprint ed. Hong Kong: Qilin Tushu, 1968.
Teo, Stephen. *Chinese Martial Arts Cinema: The Wuxia Tradition*. Edinburgh: Edinburgh University Press, 2007.
ter Haar, Barend J. *Ritual and Mythology of the Chinese Triads: Creating an Identity*. Boston: Brill Academic Publishers, 2000.
Thomas, Bruce. *Bruce Lee: Fighting Spirit*. Berkeley, CA: Blue Snake Books, 1994.
Tse, Michael. "Master Ip Ching." *Qi Magazine* 25 (1996): 16–20.
Ving Tsun Athletic Association. "Development of Ving Tsun Kung Fu in Hong Kong: 1950–1953, 1954–1960, 1961–1970."
Vojkovic, Sasha. *Yuen Woo Ping's Wing Chun*. Hong Kong: Hong Kong University Press, 2009.
Wakeman, Fredrick, Jr. *Strangers at the Gate: Social Disorder in Southern China, 1839–1861*. Berkeley: University of California Press, 1997.
Waley-Cohen, Joanna. "Militarization of Culture in Eighteenth-Century China." In *Military Culture in Imperial China*, edited by Nicola Di Cosmo, 278–295. Cambridge, MA: Harvard University Press, 2009.
Walter, John. *Guns of the Gurkhas*. Gladstone Institute, Norfolk, UK: Tharston Press, 2005.
Wells, Marnix. *Scholar Boxer: Chang Naizhou's Theory of the Internal Martial Arts and the Evolution of Taijiquan*. Berkeley, CA: North Atlantic Books, 2005.
Wile, Douglas. *Lost T'ai-Chi Classics from the late Ch'ing Dynasty*. Albany: State University of New York Press, 1996.
Williamson, Oliver E. "The Economics of Organization: The Transaction Cost Approach." *The American Journal of Sociology* 87, no. 3 (1981): 548–577.
Wong, J. Y. *Yeh Ming-ch'en: Viceroy of Lian Kuan (1852–8)*. Cambridge: Cambridge University Press, 1976.
Xu Zhen (style: Zhedong). *Guoji Lunlue* (Summary of the Chinese Martial Arts). 1929 ed. Photographic reprint in Series 1, Vol. 50 of *Minguo Congushu* (*Collected Works from the Republic Period.*) Shanghai: Shanghai Shudian, 1989.
Yimin He. "Prosperity and Decline: A Comparison of the Fate of Jingdezhen, Zhuxianzhen, Foshan and Hankou in Modern Times." *Frontiers of History in China* 5, no. 1 (2010): 52–85. Translated by Weiwei Zhou from *Xueshu Yuekan* (Academic Monthly) 12 (2008): 122–133.

Yip Chun, and Danny Connor. *Wing Chun Martial Arts: Principles & Techniques*. San Francisco: Weiser Books, 1992.
Yu Dayou. *Sword Treatise*. Translated by Jack Chen. Singapore: Historical Combat Association, 2011.
Zeng Zhaosheng. *Nan Quan* (Southern Chinese Boxing). Guangzhou: Guangdong Renmin Chubanshe, 1983.
———. *Guangdong Wushu Shi* (A History of Guangdong Martial Arts). Guangzhou: Guangdong Renmin Chubanshe, 1989.
Zhang Xue Lian. *Foshan Jingwu Tiyu Hui* (*The Foshan Pure Martial Athletic Association*). Guangzhou: Guangdong Renmín Chuban She, 2009.
Zhao Shiqing. "Imagining Martial Arts in Hong Kong: Understanding Local Identity Through 'Ip Man.'" *Journal of Chinese Martial Studies* 1, no. 3 (2010): 85–89.
Zheng De Lua. *A Study of Armed Conflicts between the Punti and the Hakka in Central Kwangtung, 1856–1867*. Thesis, University of Hong Kong, 1989.
Zhou Weiliang. *Zhongguo Wushushi* (*Chinese Martial Arts History*). Beijing: Gaodeng Jiaoyu Chubanshe, 2003.
———. "Research on the Southern Shaolin in Fujian Province in the Context of Wushu Culture and the Culture of Societies and Parties." *Journal of Capital Institute of Physical Education* 18, no. 6 (2006): 1–10, 14.

Index

14k, 128–129
1920s, 5, 15, 74, 78, 82, 91, 102, 107, 112, 116, 119, 120, 125, 126, 129, 130, 132, 135, 146, 160, 165, 189, 190, 193, 195, 197, 199, 244
1930s, 5, 14, 78, 82, 86, 91, 107, 112, 113, 116, 118, 120, 121, 126, 129, 135, 146, 154, 160, 163, 164, 165, 197, 199, 209, 213, 239, 244, 260, 300n85
1940s, 116, 188, 120, 129, 163, 191, 195, 197, 213, 239
1950s, 1, 3, 6, 113, 118, 128, 164, 165, 187, 196, 213, 219, 222, 223, 231, 232, 233, 240, 241, 242, 244, 247, 248, 250, 251, 252, 255, 257, 260, 265, 266, 273
1960s, 215, 218, 222, 223, 242, 248, 253, 258, 259, 260, 261, 265, 273
1970s, 215, 218, 219, 242, 253, 261, 266, 273, 303n.38

Acevedo, William, 298n.28
Agriculture, 33, 48, 50, 80, 202, 289n.17; poor harvests and banditry, 69; sericulture, 48, 80
Amos, Daniel Miles, 17, 217, 218–219, 220, 221, 242, 295n.59, 306n.6
Antony, Robert J., 52, 290n.50, 296n.67

April 12 Incident (Shanghai Massacre of 1927), 68, 117, 128, 159, 201
Archery, 18, 25, 71

Bak Mei (White Eyebrow Boxing), 5, 27, 30, 82, 106, 110, 124, 125–126, 128–129, 155, 162, 227, 294n.28, 298n.26
Bak Siu Lam (Northern Shaolin Boxing), 155, 157, 158
Black Belt (Magazine), 269, 272, 275, 311nn.5, 11
Baguazhang (Eight Trigrams Palm), 18, 157
Banditry, 27, 44, 49, 52, 55, 57, 67, 68, 69–70, 72, 86, 78, 94, 105, 292n.4
Beyer, Peter, 267, 268, 277–278, 280
Bingham, J. Elliot, 94
Bishop, James, 301n.92
Bodhidharma, 285n.20
Boretz, Avron, 17, 219, 220, 221, 249–250, 309n.64, 311n.4
Bowman, Paul, 20, 266, 277
Boxer Uprising, 12, 46, 78, 105, 108, 114, 131, 175, 177, 178, 187, 198, 208
Braves (Hired Mercenaries), 69, 71, 93–94
Bruce Lee. *See* Lee, Bruce

337

Bubishi, 18, 287n.39
Buddhism, 13, 32, 34, 36, 95, 106, 164, 254
Butterfly Swords. *See* Hudiedao

Cantonese Opera, 8, 58–61, 65, 171, 243, 254; opera ban, 66, 96, 173, 175; opera costumes and rebellion, 62–63; origins of wing chun, 61, 66, 73, 170, 171, 208, 291nn.69, 70; red boats, 60, 87
Challenge Fights and Beimo, 8, 77, 97, 126, 131, 140–141, 203–204, 228, 234–236, 237–239, 242–243, 252, 253, 260
Chan Chee Man, 237–238, 239
Chan Dao, 227, 233
Chan Heung, 67, 92–96, 101, 169, 176, 292n.1, 294n.42, 295n.51
Chan, Marjorie, 291n.70
Chan Ngau Sing, 96–99, 102, 104, 105
Chan Wah Shun, 9, 10, 77, 97, 108, 120, 164, 174, 175–179, 180, 182, 183, 186, 187, 188, 190, 191, 192, 193, 194, 196, 206, 208, 209, 263, 304n.62
Chan Yiu Min, 120, 178, 190, 206, 229
Chen, Jack, 287n.40
Chen Kai, 62–65, 78, 93, 293n.20
Chen Kefu, 234–237, 308n.39
Cheng Dali, 14
Cheng Zongyou, 19, 287n.40
Cheung Bo, 120, 194–195, 198, 199
Cheung Lai Chuen, 125–129
Cheung, Hawkins, 211, 239, 240, 241, 243, 244, 246
Cheung Ng, 61, 291nn.69, 70
Cheung, William, 237–239, 241, 244, 245
Choy Li Fut, 5, 6, 27, 81, 83, 84, 92–99, 104, 105, 110, 117–118, 169, 175, 176, 203–204, 227, 238–239, 292n.1. *See also* Hung Sing Association
Chu Minyi, 312n.28
Chu, Robert, 291n.70, 301n.4, 311n.14
Chu Shong Tin, 228, 232, 233, 248, 251
Chuka Shaolin Boxing, 82, 83, 284n.12
Chiang Kai-shek, 113, 117, 127, 128, 134, 148, 154, 156, 157, 161
Chin Woo Athletic Association. *See* Jingwu Athletic Association
Chinese Martial Studies: academic literature, 14–21; local and regional history, 15, 83
Cinema, 3–4, 6, 7, 20, 110, 152, 160, 185, 189, 211, 212, 221, 222–223, 224, 225, 237, 265, 266, 270–271, 272, 276, 277, 280
Class (Social and Economic), 6, 50–51, 68, 79, 98, 110, 112, 113, 116, 117, 122–123, 133, 135, 137, 141, 142–143, 148, 150, 153, 173, 178, 179, 188, 193, 196, 208, 209, 213, 216, 217–219, 221, 222, 225, 227, 235, 241, 249–250, 253, 261, 271, 273; Confucian class structure, 40, 42, 60, 66
Clausnitzer, R., 274–276
Communist Party, 4, 11, 102, 115–116, 117, 119, 157, 159, 172, 197, 201, 202, 204, 208, 209; 1949 Liberation and aftermath, 6, 108, 111, 124, 127, 128, 134, 170, 191, 200, 205, 207, 223, 225, 229
Confucianism, 28, 31–32, 34, 40, 42, 60, 66, 75, 91, 100, 103, 130, 164, 179, 180, 185, 228, 235, 248–249, 250, 251, 276
Cultural Revolution, 14, 134, 145, 170, 194, 215, 254–255

Daoism, 13, 32, 36, 63, 95, 164, 291n.68, 295n.58, 296n.67; in the work of Avron Boretz, 17, 220, 309n.64; invulnerability magic, 35, 63, 131
Delinquency, 6, 212, 218–220, 239, 241–244, 253
Den Yugong, 118
Di Cosmo, Nicola, 19
Do Pai, 227
Dongguan (Guangdong Province), 57
Dongguan Martial Arts Institute, 108, 296n.69
Dragon Shaped Rubbing Bridges, 30, 82, 85, 106, 124, 125–126, 227, 298n.26

East River Fist, 85
Ebrey, Patricia Buckley, 32
Eight Trigrams Rebellion, 34–35
Emei, Mountain, 273–274
Empowerment and the Martial Arts, 99, 102, 196, 211–212, 270–271
Enter the Dragon, 1, 269, 270, 274
Esherick, Joseph W., 35, 69, 78
Ethnicity, 67, 82, 267
Examination System: civil service, 29, 65; military, 71, 76

Fairbank, John King, 33, 38
Farrer, D. S., 17, 19
Faure, David, 57, 294n.32, 302n.33
Feng Keshan, 34–35
Feng Yuxiang, 111, 149
Firearms, 35, 39, 40, 43, 44, 45–46, 70, 72, 74, 90, 110, 125, 217; and the Red Turban Revolt, 58, 63, 64
First World War, 115
Folklore, 7–10, 15, 18, 21, 59, 72, 77, 93, 169, 171, 185, 188, 190, 198; of the San Yuan Li Incident, 44–46
Fong Wing Chun, 87
Fung Siu Ching, 72–73, 195, 197

Fung, S. L., 294n.27
Frank, Adam, 17, 274, 312n.27
Fujian Province, 8, 29, 30, 48, 52, 58, 80, 105, 125, 149, 154, 223; development of the martial arts, 18, 27, 81, 84, 86–88, 89, 99, 106, 107, 108, 109, 126, 149, 284n.12
Foshan, 163, 174, 176, 179, 200, 202–203, 205, 226, 232, 250, 261, 266; Cantonese Opera, 58–61, 66, 171, 254, 291nn.69, 70; class/labor conflict, 6, 99, 113, 116–117, 120–121, 122–124, 178, 188, 193, 201, 209, 250; economic role and decline, 2, 5, 16, 47, 57–58, 71–72, 80, 97, 101–102, 181, 184, 214, 289n.18, 293n.23, 305n.3; lineage associations, 51, 294n.32; martial arts community, 3, 4, 5, 6, 9, 16, 68, 79, 81, 83, 86, 88, 95–99, 105, 109, 110, 114, 115, 118, 119–121, 129, 130, 133–135, 138–146, 158–159, 165, 169, 173, 175, 178, 182–183, 186–187, 189, 191–192, 194–196, 197–199, 201, 204, 206, 208–209, 214, 230, 239, 244–245, 255–256, 260; medical industry, 70, 75, 76–77; popularity of the martial arts, 79, 97, 187, 160, 195–196, 204, 222; population, 57, 80; Red Turban Revolt, 28, 57–58, 62–63, 64–65, 78, 95–96, 172; Sericulture, 48, 80

Gender, 9, 17, 104, 137–138, 142, 165, 220, 231, 249–250, 265, 283n.3, 284n.12, 309nn.62, 63; female participation in the Guoshu movement, 150, 151, 153, 155, 158; Jingwu's promotion of women in the martial arts, 112, 132, 137–138, 141; participation in Wing Chun, 228

Gentry, 37, 51, 60, 73, 89, 91, 173, 184, 200, 248; Guangdong Province, 38, 50, 51, 65, 172, 176, 196, 301n.7; militia involvement, 28, 37, 43–44, 46, 51, 64, 68–69, 88, 90, 91, 93; new gentry, 91, 181, 183, 198, 207, 216, 248

Globalization, 15, 19, 266, 267–268, 274, 277–280; North American martial arts, 20, 269–276

Goldman, Merle, 33, 38

Green, Thomas A., 19

Gu Ru Zhang, 155, 157–158, 234

Guangdong Province, 29, 56, 104–105, 127, 157, 161, 172, 201, 205, 213, 225, 227, 230, 294n.40, 304n.55; banditry and piracy, 69, 70, 86, 95, 107, 110, 296n.67; border with Hong Kong, 2, 128, 232–233, 254; civil society, 8, 89, 91, 170, 172, 196, 301n.7; development of local martial arts, 5, 6, 10, 16, 17, 21, 27, 66, 67–68, 79, 81, 82, 83–84, 85, 87, 88, 89, 92, 95, 99, 101, 104–110, 111, 114, 117, 126, 130, 134, 135–138, 138–146, 149, 154–160, 162, 165, 177, 208, 209, 216, 262, 284n.18, 291n.69, 294n.38, 298n.28, 308n39; Guangdong Opera, 58, 60; immigration, 12, 58, 61, 86, 88, 223; imperialism, 28, 38, 66, 86, 70, 90, 97, 110; lineage associations, 44, 47, 49–51, 54, 70, 85, 100–101; martial arts novels, 118–119, 160, 284n.11, 299n.35; population, 48, 79–80; Qing era coastal evacuation, 30, 80; secret societies, 52, 55–57, 62–65, 72, 86–87, 95, 100, 170; trade, 48–49, 69, 72, 80, 106, 132, 303n.48

Guangzhou, 2, 59, 113, 115, 117, 122, 127–128, 157, 188, 201, 205, 207, 228; economics and trade, 5, 33, 41–42, 47–49, 78–79, 80, 88, 106, 131, 181, 184, 214; martial arts community, 28, 30, 70, 71, 73, 76, 79, 82, 83, 86, 87, 88, 96, 105, 109, 113, 118, 124–126, 130, 133, 135, 137, 138, 144, 146, 155–156, 157, 158, 160, 183, 222, 250, 299n.34, 306n.6; Opium Wars, 43, 44–45, 46, 49, 90, 93; Red Turban Revolt, 56, 57, 62, 63–64, 65, 66, 78, 93

Guangzhou Guoshu Institute, 157–158

Guangzhou Martial Arts Association, 144

Guilds: development of martial arts institutions, 101, 103, 109, 139; criminal, 56; hometown, 58, 101, 102, 103; merchant, 41, 80, 90, 91, 101, 102, 103, 104, 109, 139, 291n.63; opera guild (Guangdong), 61, 66

Gulao Village, 173, 175; Gulao Wing Chu, 175, 195, 230, 307n.26

Guo, Elizabeth, 17, 295n.58, 298n.34

Guomindang (National Party), 6, 11, 113, 115, 117, 119, 120, 122–123, 126, 127–128, 129, 135, 148, 149, 151, 152, 153–154, 157, 158–159, 160, 161, 162, 188, 200–201, 204, 205, 206, 207, 208, 213, 217, 297nn.6, 17, 298nn.28, 30

Guoshu (National Arts) Movement, 11, 112–113, 114, 148, 149, 151, 154, 158, 160, 162, 164, 235, 262, 270, 297n.17, 298n.28, 312n.28; Central Guoshu Institute, 6, 14, 15, 126, 141–142, 148–163, 151–153, 165, 222, 230; Foshan, 158–159, 163–165; Guangzhou, 155–156, 157–158; literature, 161–163, 165, 217; national examinations, 150–151, 165

Hakka, 30, 35, 37, 80, 106, 219, 293n.25; Hakka martial arts, 30, 67, 81–83, 85, 88, 89, 92, 106, 124–129, 143, 145, 293n.26, 294n.28, 296n.69
Hamm, John Christopher, 21, 105, 118, 160, 224, 233, 235, 284n.11, 299n.35, 300n85
Handicraft Industries, 33, 88, 78, 97, 120, 122, 172, 187, 193, 214
Heimberger, Ron, 303n.46, 304n.56
Henning, Stanley, 14, 152, 284n.17, 295n.58, 298n.34, 299n.42
Ho, Virgil K. Y., 304n.55
Holcombe, Charles, 295n.58
Hong Kong, 4, 6, 9, 17, 43, 47, 105, 119, 128, 158, 170, 177, 179, 180, 181, 183–184, 206, 207, 254, 258, 272–273; airline, 1, 3, 4, 7, 265, 283n.3; civil society, 213, 223, 237, 253, 261; economic development, 2, 116, 122–123, 181, 184, 212, 213–216, 241, 254, 272–273, 306nn.4, 5; elite and public opinion regarding the martial arts, 6, 213, 216–225, 235, 236–237, 242, 252, 257, 261; film industry, 4, 6, 211, 221, 222–223, 224, 266, 272, 276, 277; Hong Kong Strike (1925), 123, 184, 201; identity, 2, 5, 21, 212, 223, 232–233, 237, 248, 250, 265, 266; martial arts literature, 20, 118, 160, 224, 236–237, 248, 256; martial arts practice and community, 1, 3, 4–5, 6, 86, 113–114, 117, 118, 129, 165, 171, 189, 191, 199, 200, 212, 213, 222, 225, 227, 228, 229, 234–236, 238–240, 242–243, 260, 261, 262, 273–276, 284n.18, 295n.59, 303n.39, 306n.6; population, 223, 255; World War Two, 202

Hong Kong Chinese Martial Arts Association, 261
Hong Kong Ving Tsun Athletic Association, 212, 259–261, 262, 283n.1, 310n.67
Hong Xi Guan, 86–87
Hong Xiuquan, 35–37
Hudiedao, 94, 182, 191, 245, 251
Hung Gar, 27, 58, 70, 76, 81, 83, 94, 97, 105, 121, 171, 191, 227, 287n.39, 297n.21; origin, 86–87, 92; Zhong Yi Association 120, 159, 183
Hung Mun Style Martial Arts, 81–82, 83–84, 85, 86, 89, 100, 114, 122, 141, 250, 294n.27, 309n.64
Hung Sing Association, 81, 96–99, 107, 108, 120, 134, 162, 175, 294n.42; closure by the government, 105, 117, 119, 159, 201; conflict with the Zhong Yi Association, 116, 120–121, 123–124, 159, 201; Communist Party, 116–117, 119, 159; creation, 95–97, 99, 102; novels, 118; size, 97, 183, 295n.51; socio-economic profile, 98–99, 102, 114–115, 122, 123, 137, 178; three exclusions; 98
Huo Yuan Jia, 131–132, 135

Identity, 140, 151, 196, 212, 220, 250–251; construction through the martial arts, 5, 8, 17, 68, 101, 104, 105, 110, 112, 131, 160, 177, 196, 208; globalization, 267–268, 279, 280; Hong Kong, 2–3, 222, 223–224, 266; lineage, 50, 101; national, 15, 31, 68, 104, 111, 112, 148, 160, 183, 208, 214, 217, 224, 237, 268, 279, 280; novels, 224–225, 250, 299n.35; ritual, 103; southern Chinese, 2–3, 8, 11, 105, 113, 118, 160, 165, 266

Imperialism, 27–28, 32–33, 39, 40–47, 49, 69, 90, 97, 105, 112, 114, 130; martial arts as a response, 44–46, 68, 70, 104, 110, 113, 132
Internal vs. External Martial Arts, 81, 104, 164
Invulnerability Magic, 35, 131
Ip Ching, 4, 121, 183, 184, 202, 206, 225, 227, 231, 240, 254–256, 258, 260, 261, 273, 299n.51, 303nn.41, 44, 303n.50
Ip Chun, 75, 121, 183, 200, 202, 206, 225, 227, 231, 232, 247, 254–256, 259, 303nn.41, 44, 50, 308n.36
Ip Man, 1, 5–6, 75, 91, 105, 129, 175, 179–186, 189, 191–192, 194, 195, 197–199, 200–207, 211–212, 218, 225–263, 266, 268, 274, 281, 311n.11; as a cultural symbol, 7, 21, 211, 250–251, 265, 266, 277, 280; challenge fights, 4, 140–141, 183, 203–204, 299n.51, 303n.46; Confucian education and bearing, 180, 209, 228–229, 248–249, 251, 276; death, 262–263; drug use, 244–247, 304n.56; economic situation, 6, 9, 120, 183–184, 200–201, 202, 205, 206, 214, 215, 226–227, 245, 248, 251, 253–254, 256, 258–259; education, 164, 179, 180–181, 186; family life, 178, 179, 184–185, 188, 198, 202–203, 207, 231–233, 256, 303n.50, 308n.36; flight to Hong Kong, 4, 6, 21, 128, 170, 200, 207, 225, 272, 307n.16; in film, 3–4, 5, 189, 265, 266, 276, 277, 280; infidelity, 247–251, 309n.59; institution building, 212, 231, 253, 257, 258–260, 261, 266, 283n.1; introduction to Wing Chun, 3, 179–182, 185, 303nn.39, 41, 44; Ip Man lineage, 8, 10, 77, 284n.10; teaching career (Foshan), 121, 183, 199, 203–205, 206; teaching career (Hong Kong), 225, 226–262; personality, 238, 240–241, 258, 275; reform of Wing Chun, 113–114, 164, 170, 180, 187, 192–193, 199, 209, 212–213, 230–231, 233, 251–252, 253, 255–256, 257, 260, 261–262, 275–276, 281, 307n.29; response to Guoshu and other movements, 158, 163–165; student of Chan Wah Shun, 9, 77, 120, 178, 179–180, 186, 208, 302nn.34, 36; students of Ip Man, 10, 191, 203, 212, 213, 216, 227–229, 237, 239, 241–242, 248–251, 257, 259–260, 272, 273, 275–276, 307n.29
Ip Man Ving Tsun Tong, 5, 252, 261, 307n.16
Ip, Wilson, 3–4, 5, 277

Japan, 29, 101, 127, 132, 161, 181, 183, 215; imperialism, 44, 90, 115, 234; Japanese martial arts, 5, 12–13, 14, 18, 101, 112, 235, 269, 270, 275, 311n.5; occupation of southern China, 4, 107, 108, 119, 135, 141, 144, 146, 158, 193, 200, 202, 204, 234
Jee Shim, 9, 84, 86–87, 171, 172
Jeong Yim, 96–97, 118, 175
Jiu Chao, 120, 121, 190–191, 199, 206, 229
Jiu Wan, 191–192, 229–230, 244, 256
Jin Yong, 6, 21, 224, 236, 306n.15
Jingwu (Pure Martial) Athletic Association, 6, 15, 17, 107, 112, 130–147, 148, 154, 200, 204, 222, 270, 298n.34; comparison with the Guoshu movement, 114, 141–142, 148, 149, 155, 156, 160, 162, 298n.28; creation, 131–132,

183; decline, 134–135; female students, 112, 132,137–138, 150; Foshan branch, 16, 138–148, 165, 183, 191, 204, 229, 303n.46; Guangdong branch, 135–138; institutional organization, 133, 135, 137, 139, 140, 141; mission, 112, 133, 208; student profile, 133–134, 135, 143, 145
Jordan, Darrell, 246
Judo, 13, 235, 269, 270, 272, 275, 277, 311n.5

Kang Gewu, 286n.25
Kangxi, 31
Karate, 13, 269, 270, 272, 275, 277, 311n.5
Kato, T. M., 20
Kennedy, Brian, 17, 18, 103, 157, 295n.58, 298n.34
Kim, Jaeyoon, 78, 95, 293n.20
Kot Siu Wong, 127–128, 205, 206
Kuhn, Philip A., 69, 289n.29, 292n.2, 294n.40
Kung Fu, 11–12, 13
Kwan, Daniel Y. K., 297n.6
Kwok, Samuel, 121–122, 259, 310n.67

Labor Movement, 68, 99, 102, 113, 116, 119, 122, 123, 159, 195, 197, 253, 291n.63; Foshan Federation of Trade Unions, 116; Guangdong Machinery Trade Union, 122–123; Guangdong Provincial Trade Union, 122; journeymen's guilds, 102; Kowloon Bus Company Union, 253–254; Restaurant Workers Union (Hong Kong), 9, 207, 226, 227, 228, 229, 233, 237; violence against labor, 110, 117, 120–121, 122, 159; Workers Congress, 116, 117, 122, 123; Yellow Trade Unions, 116, 120, 159, 193–194, 208, 296n.6, 297n.21
Lai Yip Chi, 192–194, 195, 199, 200, 304n.62
Lam Sai-wing, 287n.39
Lam Yiu Kwai, 125–126
Law Enforcement, 70, 105, 126, 127, 152, 191, 181, 203, 214, 229, 257, 260; attitude towards martial artists, 216, 217, 219, 220–221, 242–244, 253, 257, 261, 303n.39; Ip Man's employment with, 6, 113, 129, 158, 163, 191, 200, 205–206, 207, 226, 229
Lee, Bruce, 1, 189, 243–244, 246, 258, 268–272, 273, 274, 276, 301n.92; acting career, 7, 20, 132, 262, 266, 269–270, 277; Death, 271; *Enter the Dragon*, 1, 269, 270–271, 275, 311n.6; Ip Man, 3, 9, 192, 199, 211, 212, 216, 245, 262, 265, 266, 272; philosophy of the martial arts, 164–165, 277; use of the term kung fu (gong fu), 12; Wing Chun, 3, 7, 10, 20, 21, 239, 241, 242, 243, 244, 266–267, 271–272, 275, 276, 311n.11
Lee, James Yim, 311n.11
Lee Man, 207, 226, 227, 228, 233, 259
Lee Shing, 230, 244, 256, 307nn.25, 26
Lei, Daphne, 290n.52
Leung Bik, 174, 180, 181–182, 186, 303nn.39, 41, 44
Leung Bok Chau, 8, 172
Leung Caixin, 72, 75–76
Leung, Duncan, 239, 241, 245, 246, 247, 304n.56
Leung Lan Kwai, 8, 172
Leung Jan, 21, 96, 118, 171–175, 176, 182, 263, 284nn.9, 10, 300n85; birth and childhood, 173–174; medicine, 58, 77, 176,

Leung Jan (*continued*)
  retirement and death, 77, 175, 187, 190, 195, 230; Wing Chun, 9, 61, 66, 88, 171, 172, 174, 176–177, 208
Leung Ting, 121, 173, 174, 175–177, 182, 183, 188, 190, 194, 203, 205, 230, 245–246, 247, 297n.21, 299n.51, 301n.4
Leung Sheung, 227, 228, 229, 231, 233, 237, 244
Leung Yee Tai, 8, 9, 66, 73, 169, 170, 171–173, 175, 197
Li Jishen, 154–157
Li Pei Xian, 143–144, 145, 146
Li Wen Mao, 61–62, 65, 78, 93, 170, 172, 290n.52
Liangguang Guoshu Institute, 154–157, 159, 300n.77
Lin, Alfred H. Y., 289n.18, 292n.7, 301n.7, 303n.48
Lin, Boyan, 78
Lin Jia Martial Arts Institute, 106
Lin He, 106
Lineage Associations, 47, 49–51, 53, 55, 84, 91, 99, 100–101; feuding, 44, 69, 70; temples, 49–50, 302n.33
Lion Dance, 123, 141, 220, 295n.51
Liu, Petrus, 21, 161
Lo Man Kam, 202–203
Lorge, Peter A., 19–20
Louie, Kam, 309n.62
Luk Ah Choi, 76
Luofu, Mount, 82, 92, 106, 125

Ma Mingda, 14
Ma Zineng, 16, 178, 291n.70, 294n.42, 297n.18, 299n.34
Manchu, 26, 29, 31, 70; anti-Manchu sentiment, 117, 290n.52
Marginality, 6, 61, 212, 213, 218, 219, 220, 241, 250, 252, 254, 271, 295n.59, 306n.6

Martial Arts (Chinese): between the Ming and Qing dynasty, 26, 27, 47, 59, 83–84, 89, 288n.2; definitions of, 11–13, 148, 284nn.17, 18; development during the Qing, 32–33, 38, 66, 67–110, 294n.38; development during the Republic, 79, 104, 111–165, 294n.38, 298n.34; evolution of modern organizational structures, 87–89, 99–104, 108–109; folklore and legends, 3, 7–10, 18, 21, 59, 72, 77, 84, 86, 100, 112, 114, 169, 185, 198, 211, 284n.11, 290n.50, 306n.13; globalization, 7, 10, 15, 17, 20, 123, 192, 209, 216, 266, 267, 277–281; identity formation, 3, 5, 8, 15, 17, 68, 101, 103, 104, 105, 110, 111, 112, 118, 131, 148, 160, 165, 177, 183, 196, 208, 214, 217, 237, 250, 266, 267–268, 279–280, 299n.35; kinship structures, 85, 100–101, 109, 221; "National Salvation," 105, 112, 133, 138, 141, 143, 163, 208; social resistance, 5, 6, 21, 213, 218, 249, 251, 260; social control, 101, 148, 196–197, 208; social status, 5, 72, 212, 220, 222; strengthening the state, 6, 68, 104, 112, 113, 130–131, 213
Martial Arts Literature, 104, 112, 118, 199, 222, 250; advertising, 125, 132, 138; female heroes, 9, 104; Guoshu, 161–163, 165; newspapers, 4, 76, 96, 143, 144, 160, 224, 236, 237, 256; novels, 9, 20–21, 104–105, 110, 118–119, 140, 160, 161, 196, 224–225, 236, 284n.11, 299n.35, 300n85; *Romance of the Three Kingdoms*, 62, 63; *Water Margin*, 89, 309n.63
Martial Arts Studies, 13, 16–17, 81, 110; academic literature, 13–21,

26; local and regional history, 15, 19–20
Medicine, 75–78, 144–145, 235; Leung Caixin, 72, 75, 302n.7; patent medicine sellers, 75; traditional medicine and Wing Chun, 77–78, 173, 176, 178, 190, 192–193, 291n.63
Mei Cheung, 298n.28
Meihuaquan (Plum Blossom Boxing), 34–35
Meir, Shahar, 12, 18, 35, 284n.13, 287n.35, 287n.40, 288n.2
Merchants, 41, 73, 91, 101, 208, 301n.7
Militias, 34, 43, 56, 64, 68–70, 93–94, 101, 289n.29, 292n.2, 294n.40; arms, 45, 64, 70, 94; banditry, 69–70, 138; San Yuan Li Incident, 44–46, 63; social stability, 27–28, 37, 38, 50, 51, 69, 90–91, 289n.30, 292n.4; martial arts instruction, 67, 70, 88, 94, 126–127, 176; WWII era, 119, 127, 144; martial artists as military trainers, 69, 70, 76, 93, 101, 127, 153, 176

Ming Dynasty, 50, 52, 89, 112; criticism of Ming culture by Qing scholars, 32; Huang Xiaoyang's siege of Foshan, 59; martial arts, 26, 27, 47, 73, 83–84, 288n.2; resistance to the Qing, 29–30, 53
Mok Gar, 81, 84, 108
Mook Yan Jong (Wooden Dummy), 182, 245, 251–252, 256, 257, 262, 305n.71, 307n.29
Morris, Andrew, 18, 151, 154, 159, 283n.6, 298n.28, 298n.34, 312n.28
Murray, Diane, 52, 290n.50
Mythology, 7–10, 19, 25, 52, 53, 82, 85–86, 100, 104, 112, 114, 211, 250, 309n.64, 312n.29

Nationalism, 21, 97, 111, 165, 181; and the martial arts, 6, 11, 68, 110, 112, 130, 148, 208, 213–214, 217, 279
National Essence Movement, 130, 142, 249
New Culture Movement, 112; and the martial arts, 130–131, 141; May Fourth reformers, 20, 130, 148–149, 162
Ng Chung So, 178, 180, 182, 183, 184, 187–190, 198, 199, 206, 230, 244
Ng Mui, 8–9, 10, 284n.14, 298n.32, 310n.64
Northern Expedition, 117, 134, 149, 201

Opera Rebellion. *See* Red Turban Revolt
Opium, 36, 40, 42–43, 49, 69, 188, 206, 245, 304nn.55, 56
Opium Wars, 28, 35, 37, 42–46, 47, 49, 51, 69, 90, 93, 94, 172, 213, 279, 303n.38
Ownby, David, 52, 290n.50

Painted Face Kam, 73, 169, 170, 171, 197, 301n.4
Pawnshops, 72, 193, 292n.7
Pan Nam, 120, 121–122, 191, 193, 206, 291n.70, 297n.21
Pearl River: conflict, 43, 47, 56, 65, 69, 105, 124, 177; geography and social geography, 47, 48, 57, 80, 82, 84, 92, 234, 294n.32; Pearl River Delta region, 2, 3, 5, 67, 90, 107, 147, 172, 205, 224; piracy, 44, 49; trade, 34–35, 41, 42, 47–49, 73, 78, 80, 172, 181, 214, 215
Physical Culture: Chinese, 16, 112, 130–131, 145, 283n.6, 298n.34; Western, 112, 130, 148–149
Pin Sun Wing Chun, 175

Piracy, 25, 29–30, 33, 44, 49, 60, 69, 86, 106–107, 296n.67
Popular Culture, 7, 20, 52, 211, 233, 269, 304n.55
Population: China, 26–27, 31, 33, 34; Foshan, 57, 58, 62, 78, 97; Guangdong Province, 48, 79–80, 89; Hong Kong, 223, 252

Qi, 113, 162, 164, 224, 250
Qi Jiguang, 19
Qianlong, 31–32, 41
Qigong, 75, 145
Qing Dynasty, 26–27, 32, 37, 38, 90; economic growth and decline, 31, 33, 48; founding, 28–29; martial arts, 11, 26, 70–71, 94, 105; "Overthrow the Qing, Restore the Ming," 30–31, 52–53, 65, 218, 222; rebellions, 27, 28, 34–40, 52, 55, 57, 62–66, 78, 84, 90, 94, 172, 279, 293n.20, 301n.6; Shaolin Temple, 8, 9, 53, 81; western imperialism, 28, 39, 40–46, 49, 70, 90, 91, 104, 114

Rebellion: late Qing, 27, 28, 34–40, 90, 94; Eight Trigrams, 34–35; heterodox religion, 34–35, 91; Lin Shuangwen (Taiwan), 55; secret society, 52, 84; Small Sword Uprising (Shanghai), 62; Taiping, 35–40, 47, 55–56, 94, 172, 279; White Lotus, 34. *See also* Red Turban Revolt, Boxer Uprising
Red Turban Revolt, 28, 55–58, 61–66, 93, 95, 170, 172, 290n.52, 301n.6; ensuing pacification campaign, 65–66, 95–96, 172; martial arts background of leadership, 78, 95, 293n.20; opera costumes, 62–63; symbolic value of the color red, 63

Red Boats, 8, 59–61, 87, 173. *See also* Cantonese Opera
Restaurant Workers Union (Hong Kong), 9, 207, 226, 227, 228, 229, 232, 237
Revolution of 1911 (Xinhai Revolution), 115, 181, 196
Rhodes, Edward, 292n.4, 304n.55
Ritchie, Rene, 120, 194, 195, 198, 291n.70, 299n.51, 301n.4, 311n.14
Rogowski, Ronald, 289n.17

San Yuan Li Incident, 44–46, 63, 303n.38
Security Guards, 38, 39, 72–74, 75, 77, 110; armed escort company, 73–74, 79, 107, 293n.11; crop watchers, 69
Selby, Stephen, 18
Self-cultivation, 26, 133, 249, 270
Self-defense, 1, 28, 256, 268, 280
Second World War, 14, 107, 108, 127, 135, 146, 158, 193, 196, 226, 269, 270
Secrecy, 133, 162, 164, 193, 230, 245, 255, 274, 312n.27
Secret Societies, 51, 52–55, 78, 81, 84, 86, 94, 98, 99, 100, 114, 290n.50; and the GMD, 117, 127–128, 205; Red Turban Revolt, 55–57, 62–65
Shaolin, 14, 25, 31, 32, 35, 105, 106, 113, 118, 125, 126, 151, 152, 164, 274, 280, 284nn.11, 12, 289nn.11, 13; academic literature, 16, 18, 19, 26, 55, 169, 284n.13, 285n.21, 290n.50; in secret society folklore, 53–55, 114, 222, 306n.13; legendary destruction of, 7–10, 21, 82, 84, 86, 92, 104–105, 222, 298n.32, 310n.64
Shek Kip Mei Fire (1953), 233–234, 252

Shi Pan Village Boxing, 83, 106
Shunde County, 93, 115, 176, 178, 184, 190
Sima Qian, 26
Smith, Robert W., 285n.19
Social Capital, 142
Social History, 10, 15, 110, 266
Southern Praying Mantis, 30, 82, 83, 85, 103, 219, 220, 242, 243, 295n.59
Soviet Union/Russia, 31, 115–116, 117, 126
St Stephen's College (Hong Kong), 180, 202
Staff (Pole), 70, 85, 94, 191, 304n.60; six and a half point pole form, 9, 60, 172, 182, 245, 251, 307n.29
Sticky Hands (Chi Sao), 182, 184, 189, 198, 240–241, 246, 255, 272, 273, 311n.11
Sum Num, 72, 120, 194, 198–199
Sun Lutang, 18, 287n.39
Sun Yat-sen, 114, 115, 122, 134, 201, 300n.59
Svinth, Joseph R., 19, 284n.18

Tang Hao, 13–14, 103, 152, 161, 163, 216, 285nn.20, 21
Tang Sang, 257, 260, 261
Taiping Rebellion, 35–40, 47, 55–56, 62, 65, 94–95, 172, 279
Taijiquan, 11, 14, 17, 18, 61, 104, 136, 139, 144, 145, 155, 157, 158, 161, 234, 272, 279–280, 285n.21, 291n.69, 308n.38, 312nn.27, 28
Teo, Stephen, 20
ter Haar, B. J., 36, 52, 55, 62, 290n.50, 306n.13
"Three Heroes of Wing Chun," 189, 197–199, 203
Tibetan White Crane Boxing, 308n.39

Triads, 29, 52–56, 63, 127, 214, 217, 218, 220–221, 222, 243, 290n.50, 306n.13
Thomas, Bruce, 301n.92
Trade, 27–28, 33, 35, 40–43, 47, 48–49, 78, 80, 86, 97, 106, 123, 172, 181, 202, 267, 272, 273, 289n.17; armed escort companies, 73–74; economic sanctions, 214–215; "most favored nation" trade status, 44

United Kingdom, 38, 41, 42–46, 90, 105, 132, 216, 274, 307n.25
United States of America, 13, 38–39, 41, 90, 130, 202, 214, 216, 234, 243, 244, 246, 269, 271, 272, 273
Urbanization, 33, 49, 57, 78, 80, 88, 89, 111–112, 216; of the Chinese martial arts, 27–28, 67–68, 70–71, 78–79, 88–89, 98, 109, 112, 113, 133, 135, 137, 138, 145, 148, 160, 177, 209, 225, 312n.28

Ving Tsun. See Wing Chun
Vojkovic, Sasha, 20

Wakeman, Fredric Jr., 57, 69, 91, 289n.30, 294n.40, 301n.6, 303n.38
Waley-Cohen, Joanna, 289n.15
Water Margin (Outlaws of the Marsh), 89, 309n.63
Whalen-Bridge, John, 19
White Crane Boxing, 18, 27, 87, 192, 234, 243, 284n.12, 308n.39
White Eyebrow. See Bak Mei
White Lotus Rebellion, 34
Wile, Douglas, 17, 104, 279
Wing Chun, 5, 16, 27, 30, 58, 88, 94, 95, 100, 105, 110, 114, 118, 120, 121, 140, 159, 200, 274–276, 277; creation myths, 8–10, 25, 61, 72–73, 81, 82, 84, 85, 86, 104,

Wing Chun (continued)
169, 170–172, 250, 280, 284n.12, 289n.12, 291n.70, 309n.64, 312n.29; development and public emergence, 6, 16, 21, 27, 28, 61, 66, 68, 77, 79, 92, 113, 158, 163–165, 169, 170, 171–179, 183, 186–196, 204, 208–209; film, 3–4, 5, 20, 265, 277, 280; forms, 164, 172, 182, 185, 191, 230, 251–252, 262, 305n.71, 307n.29; global art, 7, 20, 209, 211, 216, 262, 266–267, 271–273, 276, 311n.11; Hong Kong period, 113–114, 165, 180, 200, 206, 225–263, 275; identity, 1–3, 5, 11, 21, 197, 212, 241, 265–266, 268, 280–281; medicine, 58, 77, 88, 120, 173, 176, 178, 190, 192–193; militia training, 94; multiple lineages, 10, 171, 175, 193, 194–195, 197–199, 274, 276, 284n.10, 301n.4, 304n.71, 311n.14; organized labor, 193–195, 197–198, 227–228, 253; social and economic class, 6, 91, 170, 173, 178, 188, 189, 190, 192, 193, 208, 227, 241, 245, 250, 253–254, 257, 273; social/personal conflict, 140–141, 159, 172, 183, 203–204, 215, 228, 238–242, 252, 299n.51, 303n.39

Wong Fei Hung, 21, 58, 70, 71, 76, 77, 86, 101, 118, 222, 224, 300n85

Wong, Greco, 274–276

Wong Kar-wai, 4–5, 265, 280

Wong Kei Ying, 76

Wong Shun Leung, 212, 237, 239, 241, 242, 243, 244, 245, 274

Wong Wah Bo, 8, 9, 61, 66, 73, 169, 170, 171–173, 175, 197

Wu Gongyi, 234–237

Wu Zhaozhong, 234–235

Wude (Martial Virtue), 26, 118, 196, 212, 224, 248–251

Wushu, 11–12, 16

Xingyi Quan (Form-Intent Fist), 18, 153, 192

Xu Kairu, 118

Xu Zhen, 14, 285n.21

Xuwen Martial Arts Association, 106–107, 108

Yau, Herman, 4

Yim Wing Chun, 8, 172

Yimin He, 16, 293n.23, 305n.3

Yin/Yang (Feminine/Masculine), 170, 220, 249, 250, 309n.64

Ying Wu Tong, 106–107, 108

Yiu Choi, 188, 189, 196, 197, 198–199, 304n.71

Yongzheng, 31, 291n.70

Yu Dayou, 19

Yuen Kay San, 72, 91, 120, 121, 170, 171, 186, 189, 193, 194, 195, 196, 197–199, 299n.51

Zhang Xue Lian, 16

Zhang Zhijiang, 149

Zeng Guofan, 37–38

Zeng Zhaosheng, 15, 16, 89, 96, 294nn.38, 40, 296n.69, 299n.34

Zheng Chenggong (Koxinga), 29–30, 31

Zhong Yi Martial Arts Athletic Association, 119–122, 123, 124, 134, 137, 159, 162, 183, 187, 191, 193–194, 195, 201, 204, 206, 208, 260, 297nn.13, 17, 18, 21, 298n.30; student profile, 121; "Yi" schools, 116, 117, 120, 121, 122, 123, 159, 183, 195, 201

Zhou Weiliang, 14, 16, 286n.29

www.ingramcontent.com/pod-product-compliance
Lightning Source LLC
Chambersburg PA
CBHW020240240426
43672CB00006B/589